DIRECTORS ON DIRECTING

Directors
on Directing

A Source Book of the Modern Theatre

Edited by
Toby Cole *and* **Helen Krich Chinoy**

With an Illustrated History of Directing by
Helen Krich Chinoy

Bobbs-Merrill Educational Publishing
Indianapolis

Acknowledgments

The editors thank the following persons who contributed information on directors and directing: Nora Beeson, Eric Bentley, Robert Corrigan, Marie-Hélène Dasté, Tamara Daykarhanova, Alexander M. Drummond, John Gassner, Andre van Gyseghem, William W. Melnitz, Donald Oenslager, Kurt Pinthus, Michel St. Denis, Robert Sencer, Lee Simonson, Lee Strasberg, and Samuel M. Waxman.

We are especially grateful to Tyrone Guthrie, Elia Kazan, and Harold Clurman, who allowed us to use unpublished material, and to those other contemporary directors, noted in the text, who permitted us to reprint articles originally published elsewhere.

We want to acknowledge the assistance of the translators cited individually in the text for helping us to make available the material published here for the first time.

We thank Alfred A. Knopf for the use of quotations from *The Fervent Years* by Harold Clurman, and Harcourt, Brace & World for passages from *Moscow Rehearsals* by Norris Houghton and *The Stage is Set* by Lee Simonson, as well as the many publishers who gave their permission, as noted in the text, to reprint from their publications.

Particular acknowledgment is made of the kindness of Lee Strasberg, who put his extraordinary private theater collection at our disposal, and Else Pinthus, of the Brander Matthews Dramatic Museum at Columbia University, whose cooperation facilitated our work immeasurably.

Finally, we owe a great debt to those of our mutual family circle who, without being named, must know how much they helped to make this book.

TOBY COLE KRICH

HELEN KRICH CHINOY

Preface to the Revised Edition

In the preface to the first edition this book was offered as a guide to what has been called the "unknown theater" of the director. Now almost a decade later, despite the authority and acclaim won by the director in the interim, the theater exemplified by the artists in this volume remains substantially "unknown" as an influence or ideal to emulate. In the United States particularly, where the director has become a star—interviewed, publicized, and paradoxically lionized and unionized at the same time—his work, for all its technical brilliance, suffers from the absence of any consistent point of view, any strong conviction of what modern theater can be and do.

This collection, brought up to date and enlarged, sets forth the original vision out of which the current prestige and often abused power of the director have come. The pioneer directors dedicated themselves to forging the instrument of modern stagecraft. By transforming a theater ridden by Victorian convention into a dynamic modern medium, they aimed at nothing less than the reinstatement of a meaningful institution in which they could give creative form to their image of contemporary life. Their voice needs to be heard in the theater today.

"The Emergence of the Director," Part 1, provides the historical context for the selections that follow. In this illustrated survey an attempt has been made to trace the rise of the director from his shadowy origins, to interpret the search for consummate theatrical form which culminated at the turn of the century in the preeminence of a single artist, and to suggest some of the varied images of modern life projected on the stage by the director.

"Vision and Method," Part 2, consists of twenty essays in which the animators of the modern theater state their credo and explore their craft. To the numerous selections that originally made their first appearance in English here have now been added important contributions, some newly translated, by Konstantin Stanislavsky, Vsevolod Meyerhold, Nikolai Okhlopkov, Jean Vilar, and the playwright-director whose theory and practice have already begun to exert a great influence in the international theater—Bertolt Brecht. Vladimir Nemirovich-Danchenko and Harley Granville-Barker, important innovators slighted earlier because of lack of space, now are added to the indispensable classics of the director's art that appeared in the first edition.

"The Director at Work," Part 3, provides, by means of pages from promptbooks and personal notebooks as well as verbatim transcripts of rehearsals, perhaps the closest possible approximation in words to observing the director in action. Stanislavsky's Production Plan for a scene from Gorky's *The Lower Depths* and Brecht's Notes from the *Courage-Modell,* followed by his comments on the use of an Epic Model, are made available here for the first time in English. Joan Littlewood's work, perhaps the most original now on the English-speaking stage, is fondly described by several members of her company.

This revised edition has given us the opportunity to add the wholly new Part 4: "Staging Shakespeare: A Survey of Current Problems and Opinions." In the last decade the Shakespeare "boom" at numerous festivals in England and America has presented the contemporary director with one of his most challenging tasks—the translation of the classics into living theater. The practical value of including this sampling of opinions in a comprehensive book on directing is obvious, but here the editors see more than the immediate enrichment of their anthology. How Shakespeare is staged has provided an important index to theatrical values from the Restoration on. His plays are the raw material used by successive generations to define and redefine what theater means to them. We hope this brief survey will serve to suggest how a modern idea of theater is being evolved.

This four-part organization, juxtaposing history, theory, and practice, discloses the aesthetics as well as the techniques of those who have written their creative signature on the modern theater. It highlights the spirit of a small group of visionary craftsmen who wanted to bring about a total renovation of theatrical life. Their heritage is more than history; it is the animating spirit which keeps the theater alive.

A note on terminology:

The person we in the United States call the director is called in England the producer, in Germany and Russia the *régisseur*. In France, however, *régisseur* refers to the stage manager, while the director is known as the *metteur en scène*. The term *mise en scène* is used interchangeably for staging and production as a whole.

Contents

3 THE DIRECTOR AT WORK

4 STAGING SHAKESPEARE: A SURVEY OF CURRENT PROBLEMS AND OPINIONS 403

Illustrations

ACKNOWLEDGMENTS FOR ILLUSTRATIONS:

The Living Stage, by Kenneth Macgowan and William Melnitz, © 1955, by permission of Prentice-Hall, Inc.; *New Theatres for Old,* by Mordecai Gorelik, by permission of the author; *From Stage to Screen,* by Nicholas Vardac, by permission of the Harvard Theatre Collection; *Twentieth Century Stage Decoration,* by W. R. Fuerst and S. J. Hume, by permission of Alfred A. Knopf, Inc.; *Continental Stagecraft,* by Kenneth Macgowan and Robert Edmond Jones, by permission of Harcourt, Brace & Co.

1

The Emergence
of the Director

The Swan Theatre (1596). Drawing after contemporary description by Johann de Witt.

Helen Krich Chinoy

Less than a hundred years ago the director was only an ideal projected by disgruntled critics of the chaotic Victorian theater. He did
not even have a name, for the terms "director," "*régisseur*," and
"*metteur en scène*" had barely begun to acquire their present theatrical meaning. He was imaged as a "disciplinarian" who would
superintend the "whole conduct of a piece and exact a rigid but a
just decorum." He was conceived as a super stage manager who
would be "at one and the same time a poet, an antiquarian and a
costumier." When the director did finally appear toward the end
of the nineteenth century, he filled so pressing a need that he quickly
pre-empted the hegemony that had rested for centuries with playwrights and actors. Working behind the scenes, the director stamped
his individuality on a rich and varied international stage. By blending diverse arts into a single organic image he gave form to the complex modern theater, just as the poet had given shape to the Elizabethan stage by words and the actor had crystallized the theatrical
idea of the eighteenth century by his personal magnetism. The appearance of the director ushered in a new and original theatrical
epoch. His experiments, his failures, and his triumphs set and sustained the stage.

When the animators of modern theater—Antoine, Stanislavsky,
Appia, Craig, Reinhardt, Meyerhold, Copeau—examined the *fin de
siècle* theaters, they saw only an appalling absence of homogeneous
values in the production itself and in its appeal to the audience.
They insisted that if theater was to retrieve its unique, primitive,
communal power, a director would have to impose a point of view

that would integrate play, production, and spectators. By his interpretation a director would weld a harmonious art and a cohesive
audience out of the disturbing diversity increasingly apparent in
our urban, industrial, mass society. By his multifarious activities
the director would restore the artistic and social unity that has always been the central demand of the collective art of theater.

The pristine epochs when writing and staging a play were a single
creative process inspired these pioneer directors. Dramatic conception and theatrical performance had gone hand in hand in ancient
Greece, medieval Europe, Tudor England, and the France of Louis
the Fourteenth. The titans of these eras—Aeschylus, Shakespeare,
Molière—had done more than envision a fictive world; they had
made that world live on the stage.

Chorus-teacher at work.

The Greek poet symbolized the ideal toward which Gordon Craig's
"artist of the theater" aspired. Emergent directors could see that the
Greek poet had been *didaskalos,* or teacher, because he had in-
structed his performers in the intricate movements of their dance,
had rehearsed his poetic strophes with them, had originated cos-

A medieval mystery play. Detail after the miniature by
Jean Fouquet.

tumes and scenic conventions for them. Aeschylus, for example, stood out as the triumphant man of the theater whom even ancient critics had distinguished for "the brilliant mounting of his plays."

The new director felt himself a lineal descendant of the medieval *maître de jeu.* Baton and book of the play in hand (the image is preserved, for example, in the miniature painted by Jean Fouquet), the *maître de jeu* realized Jacques Copeau's injunction that the director should be able to handle a text "as a musician reads notes and sings them right at the first sight." The superintendents appointed by the *compagnons* at Valenciennes to stage the Passion in 1547 seemed a primitive version of Max Reinhardt's corps of *Regisseurs* and Meyerhold's battery of stage managers. One superintendent was in charge of sets, one prepared the music, one handled the stage effects (the *secrets*), and three arranged the text. Firmin Gémier contemplated with deep emotion the staging of the Mons Passion Play discovered by Professor Gustave Cohen. Sensing in the many pages of this 1501 promptbook the labors of a predecessor, Gémier suggested that these old records be called *Le Livre de conduite du régisseur.*

In the Elizabethan dramatist the director found a more recent and more familiar progenitor. Shakespeare seemed the first modern artist of the theater. Directors could hear his voice in Hamlet's advice to the players. He was one of them, coaching and coaxing his actors to conform to his standards. Dissatisfied with the physical limitations of their own stages, they could sympathize with Shakespeare's complaint about his "unworthy scaffold." In each of his great plays they found a director's *Regiebuch,* a producer's plan.

Molière spoke directly to the modern craftsman from the pages of his *Impromptu at Versailles.* They could hear him convincing a reluctant actress of the correctness of his casting, follow him as he analyzed roles or explained fine points of acting technique. They recalled that his co-worker, the invaluable record keeper La Grange, had said that Molière's special perfection lay in his handling of *le jeu des acteurs:* "A glance of the eye, a step, a gesture, these things were observed with an exactitude that was unknown until then in the theaters of Paris."

In seeking historical precedents for their role, however, the originators of the director's art tended to romanticize the past. Often
they forgot, for example, that none of their predecessors had been
quite the unfettered superman pictured in Craig's dreams. Like the
modern director, the Greek poet had been dependent upon his "producers": the archon, who regulated dramatic performances at the
Festival of Dionysus, and the choregus, the wealthy citizen who paid
the bill. The *maître de jeu* had struggled with a host of amateur
players, keeping them in line by imposing heavy fines. The Elizabethan dramatist had often found his job exasperating. Ben Jonson
described the poet-director in the "tiring house," prompting the
actors aloud, stamping at the book holder, swearing for the properties, cursing the poor tireman, railing that the music was out of tune
and swearing over every venial trespass the actors committed. Molière, so devoted to the *jeu* of the actors, found himself composing
plays to exploit the spectacular potentialities of Mazarin's *Salle des
Machines*.

As the new director sought to become an artist of the theater like
his great exemplars, he discovered that the comprehensive harmony
of the theater that he took as his ideal could not have been the
simple consequence of autocratic domination. He came to realize
that the clue to the unity he admired did not lie in any specific theatrical expedients—the poet-director, the size of the arena, the shape
of the platform, the absence of realistic scenery—nostrums that directors frequently offered for the moribund contemporary theater. The
unity existed prior to theatrical creation. The concord sprang from
a cohesive society whose common thoughts and emotions found in
an "idea of a theater" a basic vision of human life.

The practices of the Greek theater, for example, were based, as
Francis Fergusson has pointed out, upon "the perspectives of the
myth, of the rituals, and of the traditional *hodos,* the way of life of
the city." These perspectives provided patterns of response that
embraced the audience and the diverse arts of the theater. To their
contemporaries the plays of the Greek poets had significance only as
performances. "Antique drama was the event, the act itself, not a

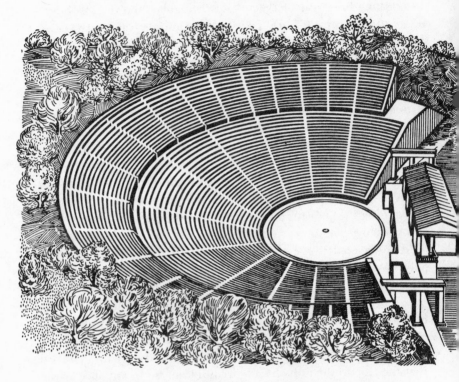

*Hellenistic theater reconstructed from ruins of playhouse
built in the fourth century B.C. at Epidaurus in Greece.
Drawing by Gerda Becker With. (From **The Living Stage**,
by Kenneth Macgowan and William Melnitz.)*

spectacle," Adolphe Appia concluded. Religious observance and
civic pride brought the whole community together yearly to honor
the god Dionysus with dramatic presentations. Artists and audiences
alike were caught up in the ritual emotion of the occasion. Their
collective social experience found its natural expression in the collective art of the theater.

These perspectives basically distinguish the directorial activities
of the antique poet from those of his modern counterpart. They
took the place of the integrating interpretation to which the creative

director today devotes his energies. The existence of accepted values and conventional modes of action in and out of the theater made the director as a distinct craftsman unnecessary. His basic function is to supply these now-absent values for a segmented society by means of the unifying principles of synthesis and interpretation.

Thus, for example, the *maître de jeu* who seems so like the modern director is in terms of this definition of the director's task essentially a stage manager only. The medieval drama, which originated in Christian ritual, became an elaborate and complex civic production of the Biblical epic from Creation to the Judgment Day. Someone had to organize the host of amateur players, the profusion of visual and aural displays, and the multitude of scenes of performances that could last for many days. A man who could do this effectively would be in great demand. Jean Bouchet, for example, staged the Passion so successfully at Poitiers in 1508 that his advice was sought throughout France and Belgium. The *Livre de conduite du régisseur* of the Mons Passion Play embodied the work of two specialists, Guillaume and Jehan Delechiere. It is significant that these men were called *conducteurs des secrets*, manipulators of machines for staging such scenic effects as the Deluge or Thunder in Hell with extraordinary literal realism.

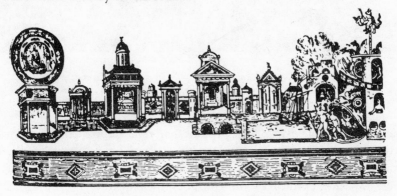

Staging of Valenciennes Passion Play (1547).

The work of these *conducteurs des secrets* was an organizational

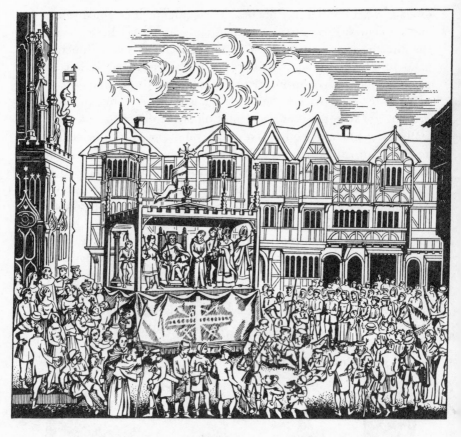

An English pageant wagon in a town square. Drawing by Gerda Becker With. (From **The Living Stage**, *by Kenneth Macgowan and William Melnitz.)*

task of a complexity and magnitude that would appall the modern director. At Mons some six months of preparation preceded the single eight-day performance. Yet the task of the *conducteur des secrets* was simplified by the conventional nature of the materials with which he dealt and by the ritual preparedness of his audience. The script, despite variations, was always basically the same: the Biblical story, familiar to performers and audience alike. The point of view was always basically the same: the performance was an expression and a reinforcement of the values of the medieval world. The stage setting contained the same essential elements, whether the technique used was the English pageant wagon or the simultaneous display of mansions, in the Continental manner. There were Paradise and Hell and between them all the necessary terrestrial stations for the oft-repeated Christian saga. Like the Greek stage before it, this medieval scene pictured a comprehensive view of life that could embrace all the contradictions of human experience. What seem to us destructive antinomies between a lofty symbolism and a naïve realism in their productions were integrated not by the individual interpretation of a director, but by the act of faith that motivated these communal performances.

*Sketch of a scene from Shakespeare's **Titus Andronicus**, made by a playgoer, Henry Peacham, in 1595. (By permission of the Marquess of Bath.)*

The Elizabethan theater, although no longer a religious or a communal enterprise, encompassed the aggregate values of its society. The dramatist used a conventional stage to image an accepted view of life; he used it as a mirror to "show virtue her own feature, scorn her own image, and the very age and body of the time his form and pressure." Groundlings and noblemen surrounded the theatrical microcosm, with its Heavens above and its trap-door Hell, as they

The Globe Theatre, from Visscher's "View of London,"
engraved in 1616.

gathered at the perhaps symbolically named Globe, which had as its
motto *"Totus mundus agit histrionem."*

Molière too had a cohesive, if limited, public. With the protection
of the king, he could project a subtle, urbane comedy whose implications satisfied yet went beyond the extravagant and complacent audience for which it was performed. Like his great peers, he worked
within a popular theatrical tradition, the ensemble art of the old
Italian comedians. For him, therefore, as for the other prototypes
of the director, "staging did not pose distinct aesthetic problems. For
him," as a French theater historian noted, "it was concomitant with
literary creation. It was an integral part of it."

The director as an artist who, in Lee Strasberg's words, must provide "that angle of viewing the play from which the actions of the

Molière as Sganarelle.

characters will appear most plausible, most meaningful . . . most truthful and most exciting" cannot be found in these great theaters to which the modern director has turned for inspiration. These theaters did not need an integrating specialist, for they had an *innere Regie*—to adapt a phrase used often by German writers on directing —a unity and control intrinsic to the theater arts and to the social conception of theater. Modern theater tends more and more toward an *äussere Regie,* a unity imposed by historically accurate sets and costumes, by realistic imitation, and ultimately by the external hand of the director charged with finding a collective focus for theater in an atomized society.

The decay of a universal system of values and a traditional way of life at the beginning of our modern era deprived theater of its homogeneous and representative public and of its accepted conventions for mirroring a shared human experience. As the audience lost its collective emotion, the diverse arts of theater lost their internal cohesiveness. The play yielded its focal position to scenic display and to virtuoso acting. Theater became as fragmented as the society around it.

In the midst of these revolutionary social changes, however, theater still sought its ideal condition. If intrinsic unity was no longer possible, then perhaps some substitute amalgam could bring together the diverse arts of a heterogeneous community. In rough historical succession four ideas of theater emerged as possible restoratives. Out of Renaissance experimentation came the idea of the pictorial stage; out of eighteenth-century rationalism and nineteenth-century determinism came the facsimile stage; out of twentieth-century subjectivism and relativism came the expressionistic stage and the theatrical stage. The emergence of the director followed these formulas for unity. His genesis lay in the pictorial stage; his first successes in the facsimile stage; and his triumphs in the expressionistic and theatrical stages.

The Renaissance discovery of painted perspective suggested a direct, palpable organizing principle for theater in an increasingly complex, diversified, rationalistic era. Having lost the communal agreement to accept the stage as a metaphorical, symbolic microcosm, audiences could yet find a replica of the world in the *trompe-l'œil* painted stage. The completely integrated stage picture could be achieved, however, only by replacing the popular periwigged tragedian displaying the "points" of his histrionic art on a green baize carpet with groups of actors appropriately garbed moving in front of accurately limned backdrops.

The time-honored arts of acting and playwriting did not possess

Proscenium and scenery for **The Empress of Morocco,**
produced in London, 1673. (From the first printed text.)

Perspective stage setting for **Il Granchio** *(1566).*

the capacity for creating the essentially external, visual unity of the pictorial stage. A special art of production was, therefore, developed to organize all the theatrical elements into a relatively harmonious illusory world, and with the art of production came the embryonic director.

The beginnings of this new art may be seen as early as the mid-sixteenth century. In his preoccupation with production, Leone de Sommi, theatrical adviser to the Mantuan court, sounds like a true forerunner of the modern director. In his *Dialogues on Stage Affairs,* De Sommi suggested that "it is far more essential to get good actors than a good play." He went on to insist that his actors must be ready "to follow [his] instructions." An incipient realistic bias is apparent in his remarks. In instructions on acting he stressed verisimilitude; in costuming he emphasized historical accuracy, splendidly and exotically embellished; in lighting he introduced primitive hints of psychological atmosphere.

But it was only during the century roughly from 1750 to 1850 that leading theater artists in various countries gradually prepared the kind of theater over which the director would eventually have absolute control. As production more and more usurped the power once held by the play itself, they perfected the implements with which the director would work—the rehearsal, the co-ordinated acting group, and the scenic paraphernalia of accurate backdrops and authentic costumes and props. Their activities revealed little by little the creative contribution to be made by a single autocrat in charge of production.

David Garrick, for example, as artistic manager at Drury Lane,

Spectators seated on the stage during an eighteenth-century
production. Engraving by Gravelot.

turned the platform for declamation into a rudimentary picture stage by dispossessing the gallants from their stage seats. He devoted more attention than was usual in the period to rehearsals and casting of minor roles. He encouraged the designer, P. J. de Loutherbourg, who invented more picturesque and more realistic scenic and lighting effects.

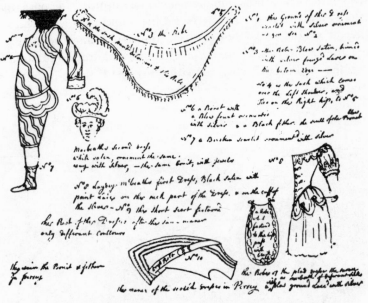

David Garrick's notes and drawings for a production of
Macbeth in 1777. (Courtesy of Sir Laurence Olivier.)

In Germany Konrad Ekhof pointed the way with his concept of the *Konzertierung des Spiels.* In plans prepared for his short-lived Academy for Actors in 1753, he declared that no play was to be produced before it had had an initial reading, that all roles were to be thoroughly analyzed beforehand, and that the objective needs of the production were to take precedence over the prejudices and special desires of members of the company.

Friedrich Schroeder, like Garrick primarily remembered as a portrayer of Shakespearean roles, was a stern taskmaster who showed his company exactly how he wanted them to perform their parts. In his own work he provided the model for them. "It does not occur to me to stand out and be dazzling," he observed, "but to fill out and be the character." Seeking a blending of stage effects, he made use of Ekhof's valuable idea of the initial reading to establish some image of the whole play. Like other nascent producers, he invested each major production with punctiliously planned sets and costumes.

A sketch by Goethe for the setting of his **Iphigenia,** *drawn in 1787-1788. (From* **The Living Stage,** *by Kenneth Macgowan and William Melnitz.)*

At the turn of the century Johann Wolfgang von Goethe, as supervisor of the Weimar Court Theater, perfected many techniques of the new art of production. He utilized readings and rigorous rehearsals, stipulating: "One should not permit himself to do anything in rehearsal that he cannot do in the play." In choosing actors he revealed a growing concern for the group as opposed to the starring performer. When he hired a new member of his company, he would let the new actor show his talents and see "how he suited the others; whether his style and manner disturbed [the] ensemble, or whether he would supply a deficiency." Once chosen, the actor had to submit himself to Goethe's absolute control. P. A. Wolff, the best actor to come from his troupe, reported that "on the stage marked out in squares every single position and movement was determined beforehand with the aim of producing a harmonious and pleasing spectacle." Tradition has it that Goethe even used a baton at rehearsals.

Since plays remained largely untouched by the concept of the pictorial stage, acting, settings, and costumes were the primary components of the art of production. As always the strictly theatrical arts, directly responsive to vicissitudes in audience taste, anticipated changes in the more private creations of the dramatists. "Truth in plays was unobtainable," cried the great French actor Talma at the beginning of the nineteenth century; "I had to be content with putting it into the costumes."

In England, too, "truth" was found in costumes and staging, not in new plays. Shakespeare's works were often made the vehicle for working out new pictorial values. In "producing" Shakespeare the famous actor-managers of the period took upon themselves tasks that were neither simply those of an actor nor of a manager. John Philip Kemble, for example, had as his objective "a more stately and perfect representation of his plays . . . to attend to all details as well as the grand features, and by aid of scenery and dress to perfect the dramatic illusion."

Kemble's attention to details was an early attempt to efface the usual careless disorder of the London theaters. His disciplined rehearsals must be contrasted with the normal preparation of a play, as described by William Charles Macready in his *Reminiscences:* "It was the custom of London actors, especially the leading ones, to do little more at rehearsals than read or repeat the words of their parts, marking on them their entrances and exits, as settled by the stage manager, and their respective places on stage. To make any display of passion or energy would be to expose oneself to the ridicule or sneers of the green room."

Macready as Macbeth.

When Macready himself became a manager he too tried to elevate production standards. For him the rehearsal became an artistic proving ground, not a run-through. He tried to harmonize settings, lighting, and stage groupings. After analyzing Macready's promptbook for *Macbeth* Alan Downer concluded: "In his constant emphasis on the necessity for unity in production, Macready foreshadowed the modern *régisseur*."

By the mid-point of the century the tentative beginnings of the Kembles and the Macreadys began to show results. Samuel Phelps transformed the Sadler's Wells Theatre from an out-of-the-way melodrama house into the equivalent of a national theater with an unparalleled series of Shakespearean revivals. Here his productions were marked by an evident concern for total integration. In the vivid critical notes of his contemporary Henry Morley we read, for example, that in *A Midsummer Night's Dream* "Mr. Phelps has never for a minute lost sight of the main idea which governs the whole play, and this is the great secret of his success in the presentation of it. . . . Everything has been subdued as far as possible at Sadler's Wells to this ruling idea."

Charles Kean earned his fame as the "Prince of Managers" because he, like Phelps, was perfecting the unified pictorial illusion. His splendid and archaeologically exact sets and costumes were supplemented by the orderly movement of supernumeraries as well as leading players. His productions were unexcelled because, as one critic pointed out, every aspect "came under the immediate superintendence of Mr. Charles Kean."

Although the progress from Garrick to Kean established the art of production and the primacy of the stage picture, none of these precursors of the director was able to achieve consistently the total integration that had emerged as the ideal. Their contributions were the necessary spadework. The consummation of their efforts was left to an artistic nobleman of an obscure German duchy, George II, Duke of Saxe-Meiningen.

May 1, 1874, has come to have a special place in the history of the director, for on that date the Duke of Saxe-Meiningen brought his unknown troupe to Berlin to display the unique accomplishments of a director's theater. The Duke of Saxe-Meiningen utilized all the innovations we have been chronicling—intensive rehearsals, disciplined, integrated acting, and historically accurate sets and costumes—to create realistic stage pictures. But the Duke went significantly beyond his predecessors in that he attempted a reconciliation between the usually competing illusions of the painted set and the moving actor. In the words of his ardent admirer Lee Simonson, "the human figure in movement was made the pictorial unit." For the occasional moments of pictorial plasticity that one glimpses in the productions of men like Kean, whose work directly influenced him, the Duke perfected a sequence of continuous and integrated movement. The Duke not only sought the reconciliation of actor and set, but also molded the text into his plastic picture by extensive use of business. He interpreted the text through the medium of all the theatrical arts.

The authority of the Duke as *Regisseur,* director, made possible this complex integration. Although he was assisted by his wife and by his stage manager, Ludwig Chronegk, he alone was the artistic creator of each production. He designed the sets and costumes, but

*Banquet scene from **Macbeth**. Design by
the Duke of Saxe-Meiningen.*

he went further and designed every movement and every position on
stage. He dictated the very folds of each actor's costume. Everyone
in his small theater had to be subservient to the production, whose
form he determined and sustained through an iron discipline. The
mob scenes, for which the Meininger were greatly admired, were
made possible by this discipline. Each actor had to take his turn
as a supernumerary; those who refused were dismissed from the
company. The Duke's ensemble was the product of his skill in using
actors as theatrical material, rather than the natural result of individual acting talent at his disposal.

Nowhere were the Duke's powers more in evidence than at rehearsals. Here he blended the theatrical arts into a symphony of
visual and aural minutiae. No detail could be allowed to destroy the
total effect, since these details, rather than the play itself, transformed the stage picture into a successful image of the world. The
very first rehearsal was conducted with the actual sets, costumes, and
properties to be used in performance. With plenty of time to spend

on his work, the Duke spared no effort in achieving the exact nuance he envisioned. Aloys Prasch in his "Reminiscences of the Meininger" describes an amusing illustration of this in rehearsals of Ibsen's *The Pretenders*. The Duke wanted the voices of the besiegers to sound muffled. After several unsuccessful attempts to get the right tone from his actors, he finally had some mattresses brought in and

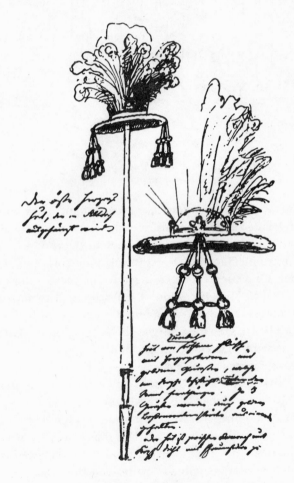

*A staff and hat designed by the Duke of Saxe-Meiningen
for Wilhelm Tell.*

forced the whole cast to lie on their stomachs and cry into the mattresses. "In this way," says Prasch, "was the intended effect obtained, and it speaks well for the discipline of the Meininger that on this occasion not one single performer laughed at the comical situation."

With the Duke of Saxe-Meiningen the art of production found its master. His work, which inspired Antoine and Stanislavsky among others, revealed, in the words of Lee Simonson, "the necessity for a commanding director who could visualize an entire performance and give it unity as an interpretation by complete control of every moment of it; the interpretive value of the smallest details of lighting, costuming, make-up, stage setting; the immense discipline and the degree of organization needed before the performance was capable of expressing the 'soul of a play.'"

Until the advent of the art of production the "soul of a play" had usually resided in the words of the playwright. Now the playwright could be relegated to a secondary position. A shifting panorama of framed pictures provided visual, rather than dramatic, proof that the stage was still a world in miniature. This scenic documentation of reality sustained theater in an era whose "form and pressure" were becoming more and more difficult to assess.

While production did shape the stage arts into a complex and flexible medium, the attitude of the producer was potentially dangerous. He could claim, as did Henry Irving, exponent of lavish graphic stagings, that "the theater is bigger than the playwright, that its destiny is a higher one than that of the mouthpiece for an author's theses, and finally that plays are made for the theater and not theater for plays." Without the imaginative values of the playwright, however, theater could be only a show, such as Irving offered, a spectacle, not the social act it had once been.

But the new scenic realism could be made to serve the playwright if it became the milieu, the "experimental situation," in which the writer placed his fictional creatures in order to observe, with scientific detachment, how environment determined character. The doctrine of naturalism, promulgated by Emile Zola, offered this scientific attitude as a new, uniquely modern point of view uniting play-writing, production, and audience.

In his manifestoes Zola confessed somewhat uneasily that the spirit of the nineteenth century did not supply the kind of communal focus that had made the theater of Molière, for example, "an exact reproduction of contemporaneous society." Yet he insisted that the "experimental and scientific spirit of the century" would enter the domain of the drama, and that in it lay "its only possible salvation." He outlined the advances in production that were preparing theater for "science" and "truth." The next step, as he saw it, was for the appearance of plays so written that they would control the external scenic decoration by making it the environment for the presentation of "life itself."

"Either the theater will become naturalistic or it will not be at all," Zola declared with desperate finality. But when plays written in the new mode began to appear, the public responded to them with shock rather than with sympathy or with "scientific objectivity." It was only when a director, imbued with the naturalistic ideals, gathered a special audience for these plays and performed them on a new facsimile stage that a satisfying theatrical experience became possible.

Despite its emphasis on the playwright, therefore, the facsimile stage, like the pictorial one, found the director an indispensable figure. In the "free theaters" devoted to naturalism the director had his first sustained successes. Here he interpreted new plays in a new style for an organized public. In a world that no longer had a total unity which theater could reflect, the director created for audiences selected from the mass a limited approximation of the ancient ideal.

André Antoine, first significant French director, put Zola's "man of flesh and bones on the stage, taken from reality, scientifically analyzed, without one lie." The facsimile stage was born when this lowly clerk from a Parisian gas company and his amateur actors performed an adaptation of Zola's *Jacques Damour* in a setting whose furnishings the director himself had carted from his home.

At the Théâtre Libre, model of all "free theaters," Antoine trans-

*Contemporary sketch of a scene from **The Wild Duck**
at Antoine's Théâtre Libre (1891).*

lated Zola's theory of environment into living theater. In a now-famous letter to the influential critic Sarcey, Antoine raised the central question of the new stage: "In modern works written in a vein of realism and naturalism, where the theory of environment and the influence of exterior things have become so important, is not the setting the indispensable complement of the work?" In this new "theater of situations" the *metteur en scène,* the director, was essential, Antoine insisted, for unless the naturalistic plays were staged and acted the right way, they would fail, as had Becque's *La Parisienne* at the classic Comédie Française.

As a director Antoine took his cue from the accomplishments of the Duke of Saxe-Meiningen, learning from him the manipulation of the disciplined corps of actors. But he went significantly beyond the plastic picture stage of the Meininger to create the facsimile stage of naturalism. For Antoine the setting had to be more than a harmonious functional background. It had to be the environment that shaped the life and actions of the characters. In describing his directorial procedures, Antoine explained: "First of all, I found it useful, in fact, indispensable, carefully to create the setting and the environment, without worrying at all about the events that were to occur on the stage. For it is the environment that determines the movements of the characters, not the movement of the characters

Poster of the Théâtre Antoine.

that determines the environment." After fashioning the total milieu Antoine would then decide where to remove the "famous fourth wall," which would expose a "slice of life" for the audience.

Antoine pursued the new métier of the director rather than accept the plaudits that might easily have come to him as an actor, because to a large extent his mission included more than production; it included literary discovery and defense of new authors. The naturalist's desire for complete theatrical unity tied the director's work to the craft of the playwright to such an extent that Antoine could say, after the failure of his production of Curel's *Les Fossiles*, "I am far happier to have discovered *Les Fossiles* in a pile of manuscripts and to have brought Curel to your attention, than vexed at having played the piece badly." To his contemporaries it seemed that Antoine had "introduced a factor unknown till now in the theater: the director, defender of the author, of the play, of the ensemble interpretation." Antoine "was an apostle teaching new doctrines," said Curel, "and a master in indicating the way to apply them."

As an "apostle of new doctrines" Antoine was confined not only to one type of play but also to one type of audience. He could not understand why, for example, his real butcher shops and real water fountains fascinated audiences. To him these effects were part of a philosophy; the audience, not always sharing his point of view, simply enjoyed the stage trick. Antoine realized that his theater had to be directed toward a select public. It was, in his words, "reserved for an elite."

Yet this "amusing and droll director" with his "foreman's whistle" and his *"noms du Dieu"* was not content to remain leader of a partisan theater. Feeling that naturalism was the only possible point of view for modern theater, Antoine wanted to impose it on all plays given *au grand public.* He explained his desire to become director of the Odéon, second state theater, in these terms: "I felt the need to encounter the great plays, the classical and foreign works of art, to try to create for the classics the same movement of progress that I had the good fortune to release for the contemporary repertory." In the years from 1906 to 1916 at the Odéon, Antoine with varying degrees of success stamped his theatrical ideal on *les grands ouvrages* of Shakespeare and Molière, trying to bring them within the confines of the "slice of life."

Antoine's Théâtre Libre was the model for Otto Brahm, director of the Freie Buehne, Germany's naturalist experiment. Devotion to new plays was even more marked in Brahm than it had been in Antoine, since Brahm had been a scholar and critic before he became a director. In one of his critical essays Brahm had observed:

"Two capacities are required of the producer in a repertory theater: he must be capable of both directing and literary discovery." Like Antoine, too, Brahm moved from directing naturalistic plays to doing all plays in the naturalistic manner. When he undertook the supervision of the Deutsches Theater in 1894, Brahm's motives were like those Antoine expressed when he sought his position at the Odéon. Brahm "wanted to produce the classics but not in the traditional and conventional way; his intention was to make them come to life by utilizing the new methods and direction."

Brahm saw his directorial task in terms of work with the actors and playwrights. He tried to tread a path between the weakness of a *"wort Regisseur"* like his predecessor Heinrich Laube, who, Brahm felt, had concentrated "one-sidedly on the listening not the seeing audience," and the limitations of the Meininger, who, he wrote, "unfortunately forgot one thing: to project onto the true-to-life sets of their stage human beings who acted naturally." Although Brahm did insist that the milieu of a play be faithfully represented, he let his aides, Carl Hachmann and Emil Lessing, handle the external facets of production. It is interesting to note that Hachmann and Lessing were listed as "directors" on the programs. Brahm's name did not appear in that capacity, but what became known in Germany as the "Brahm style," the German naturalist style, was nevertheless his creation.

For Brahm the director is a man who must be "sensitive to the inner spirit of a work" and project "in its representation the individual tone and mood born of that certain work and none other. He who wishes to bring a dramatist's creation to stage-life must be capable of perceiving those basic mood-creating tones and of making them resound in the audience through the medium of his performers."

One of Brahm's major tasks in the Freie Buehne was to find actors to accomplish this goal. Unlike Antoine and his troupe of amateurs, Brahm did not have his own company, but used professional stars who would spare time for his productions. It was in part his desire for an acting group that led him to seek the position of producer at the Deutsches Theater. The ensemble was his ideal, as it had been

Antoine's and Saxe-Meiningen's. But unlike the last, who achieved co-ordinated effects at the expense of the individual actor, Brahm tried to create the ensemble through individual talents.

Neither Brahm nor Antoine used a *Regiebuch,* or production plan, for their performances. Since Brahm preferred to allow the play to take shape during rehearsals, he had no use for detailed, advance preparation. Professor Samuel Waxman, who had access to Antoine's complete files for his study of Antoine and the Théâtre Libre, indicated in answer to a query that he could not find any production plans. It would seem that intense respect for the playwright's text prevented both Brahm and Antoine from using it merely as a stimulus to their directorial imagination. Even the production books of Brahm's stage managers, still extant, indicate that they did not feel free to deviate from the dramatist's instructions.

Konstantin Stanislavsky, perhaps the greatest naturalistic director, differed from Brahm and Antoine in that his initial concern was with new theatrical form rather than with new dramatic content. His three published production plans for *The Sea Gull, The Lower Depths,* and *Othello,* although they reveal great changes in technique, suggest that the play itself was never Stanislavsky's full source of inspiration. In his early work, particularly, the play was only the starting point for directorial elaboration. An assistant once said of him that "a stage direction or a single phrase in a play called forth all sorts of images in his mind and these very often played havoc with the author's text." Stanislavsky, in reminiscing about his production of *The Bells* in 1896, said that he produced the play "not as it was written but as [his] imagination prompted [him]." Indeed he chose this melodrama because it offered great scope for the director's manipulation of stage effects.

In his long career Stanislavsky seemed to recapitulate in striking fashion the history of the director. He began as a disciple of the Meininger's pictorial stage, became a facsimile realist devoting his theater to new authors, and went beyond realism to rediscover the basic sources of theatrical art.

Stanislavsky started out with an ideal of what he called the "producer-autocrat," which he derived from his careful observation of Ludwig Chronegk directing the Meininger on tour in Moscow in 1890. "I began to imitate Chronegk," he wrote, "and with time I became a producer-autocrat myself and many Russian producers began imitating me as I had imitated Chronegk. A whole generation of producer-autocrats arose, but alas, as they did not possess Chronegk's talent, the producers of this new type merely became theatrical managers who treated actors as if they were props, as mere pawns to be moved about as they liked in their *mises en scène.*"

The talent of Chronegk that Stanislavsky so admired was the creative directorial imagination which, he felt, made possible excel-

*Stanislavsky as Rakitin in Turgenev's **A Month in the Country** (1910). Drawing by Mstislav Dobujinsky.*

lent performances with unskilled actors. "It seemed to me at that time that we amateur producers were in the same position as Chronegk and the Duke of Saxe-Meiningen. We, too, wanted to put on great plays and to reveal the thoughts and feelings of the great playwrights, but as we had no trained actors we had to relegate all the power to the producer, who alone had to create the performance of the play with the help of scenery, props, interesting *mises en scène* and his own imagination. That is why the despotism of the Meiningen producer seemed justified to me."

Like the Meininger, Stanislavsky was intrigued by the perfection of external realism. In preparing Alexei Tolstoy's *Czar Fyodor*, for example, he insisted on visiting the actual historical locales and purchasing authentic accessories. Looking back at this early period in his career, he decided: "This artistic truth was at the time merely external; it was the truth of objects, furniture, costumes, stage properties, light and sound effects, the reproduction of the typical features of a stage character and his external, physical life, but the very fact that we succeeded in bringing real, though only external artistic truth on the stage, which at that time knew only artistic falsehood, opened up some new perspectives for the future."

In order to create this external truth, Stanislavsky began his preparations by working out enormously detailed production notes. Then in innumerable rehearsals these plans were translated into stage life. Increasingly the production plan and the rehearsal were becoming the basic implements of the director's craft, because through them the director could most effectively impose his interpretation of a play.

The procedures of external realism were particularly useful to Stanislavsky in preparing the initial production of Chekhov's *The Sea Gull* for the Moscow Art Theater since, as he himself admitted, he did not perceive the theatrical values in Chekhov. "I shut myself up in my study," he explained, "and wrote a detailed *mise en scène* as I felt it and as I saw and heard it with my inner eye and ear. At those moments I did not care for the feelings of the actor! I sincerely believed it was possible to tell people to live and feel as I liked them to; I wrote down directions for everybody and those directions had to be carried out. I put down everything in those production notes; how and where, in what way a part had to be interpreted and the playwright's stage directions were carried out, what kind of inflections the actor had to use, how he had to move about and act, and when and how he had to cross the stage. I added all sorts of sketches for every *mise en scène*—exits, entries, crossings from one place to another, and so on and so forth. I described the scenery, costumes, make-up, deportment, gaits, and habits of the characters, etc." Any line taken at random from the published production score of the play reveals this scrupulous detail; for example, "Konstantin delivers the whole of his speech while smoking, taking the cigarette out of his mouth, replacing it, inhaling the smoke, and so on."

Although Stanislavsky's *mise en scène* for the play brought the Art Theater great success, Chekhov was not completely satisfied. By interpreting the play through his production art Stanislavsky had created values that the author felt were not in his play. Despite Chekhov's criticisms the challenge of his plays stimulated Stanislavsky's creative efforts.

*Trigorin and Nina. Sketch by Stanislavsky from his production plan for **The Sea Gull** (1898).*

Through his search for a proper style for Chekhov's plays, and through his growing concern with the art of the actor, Stanislavsky moved from the purely external realism of his early work to an inner verity, to psychological realism. This subtle refinement did not involve a break with external realism, but rather made it the key to the inner reality of the play. In his work on Gorky's *The Lower Depths* Stanislavsky felt his methods were changing. He undertook an expedition to the Khitrov market to find the real-life equivalent of Gorky's locale in accordance with his usual initial step in preparing a production. This time he observed the people more than the place. This expedition made him "aware of the inner meaning of the play."

Stanislavsky's own growing dissatisfaction with the limitations of external realism coincided with the attempt in Russia as elsewhere to do away with what a Russian symbolist magazine called "unnecessary truth." Meyerhold and others were turning from realism to symbolism, and Stanislavsky, by establishing the Studio on Povarskaya Street where Meyerhold had a chance to experiment, aided the new movement. He himself struck out in new paths, producing plays by men like Andreyev. As part of the general ferment, Stanislavsky invited Gordon Craig, leader of the antinaturalist movement, to visit and work with the Moscow Art Theater. In 1908 he wrote: "Of course we have returned to realism, to a deeper, more refined and more psychological realism. Let us get a little stronger in it and we shall once more continue our quest. That is why we have invited Gordon Craig. After wandering about in search of new ways, we shall again return to realism for more strength. I do not doubt that every abstraction on the stage, such as impressionism, for instance, could be attained by way of a more refined and deeper realism. All other ways are false and dead."

This path of refined realism led Stanislavsky deeper and deeper into work with the actor, whose human form, he felt after seeing some of Meyerhold's experiments, could not be twisted to comply with abstract ideas. From the producer-autocrat, devoted to the facsimile stage, he became, through his work on acting, the producer-instructor, who located the heart of theater in the actor. This development led him to a new appreciation of the playwright, whom he no longer relegated to a mere stimulus for his imagination. Thus in the last years of his active career, from 1927 on, his whole conception of the director underwent a profound change. "No producer," he wrote, "can produce a play unless he first finds its ruling idea. At present the producer of a play in our theaters and even in the Moscow Art Theater does not care about the ruling idea at all, but builds up his production entirely on all sorts of clever tricks. This is the very negation of the art of the stage. It is true that such clever tricks are usually rewarded by a thunder of applause, which is what the actors want, but it was not for this that Pushkin and Shakespeare wrote."

His change in attitude meant a change in directing technique, illustrated in the following statement in David Magarshack's biography, which discusses in some detail changes in Stanislavsky's methods: "Before, a producer planned his *mises en scène* and the nature of the inner feelings of the *dramatis personae* in his own study. He then went to the rehearsal and told the actor to carry them out. The actor was quite naturally expected to copy his producer. But when I arrive at a rehearsal now, I am no more prepared than the actor and I go through all the phases of his work with him. The producer must approach the play with a mind as fresh and clear as the actor's and then grow together with him." Stanislavsky even discarded his use of elaborate historical study, which had absorbed much of his time in earlier years. "The best analysis of a play," he now said, "is to act it in the given circumstances. For in the process of action the actor gradually obtains mastery over the inner incentives of the actions of the character he is representing, evoking in himself emotions and thoughts which resulted in those actions."

While Stanislavsky remained essentially within the framework of the naturalistic tradition, he found a new and profound basis for it in his work with the actor. His quest for the primal source of theater art, for the simple physical action, linked him with those very artists who ultimately turned against naturalism.

What could result when naturalism was used as mere technique unrelated to new content in plays or to new concepts in acting was evident in the work of David Belasco. In the history of American theater, David Belasco was the first significant directorial figure. Unlike his European colleagues, who had all begun in revolt against the commercial theater, Belasco, bred in the commercial theater, became its leading exponent. His tradition stemmed largely from craftsmen like Dion Boucicault, whose sensational realistic stage effects anticipated cinematic movement, or Tom Robertson, whom Allardyce Nicoll credits with being "the first man in England to conceive of stage realism as a complete whole."

Belasco transformed the lowly position of stage manager into the major role of director through know-how accumulated in years as actor, playwright, and play-doctor. Early in his career, in his western days, his directorial activities were lauded by his co-workers: "Your quick apprehension and remarkable analytical ability in discovering and describing the mental intentions of an author are so superior to anything we have heretofore experienced that we feel sure that the position of master dramatic director of the American stage must finally fall on you."

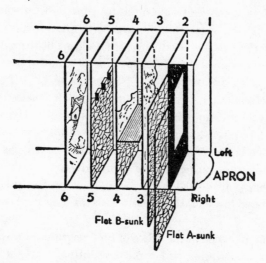

*Multiple flats for escape scene of Boucicault's **Arrah-na-Pogue** (1865). (From **Stage to Screen**, by Nicholas A. Vardac.)*

Belasco did become "master dramatic director of the American stage" by bringing to it carefully organized, unified productions. Even so vitriolic an opponent of all that Belasco stood for as George Jean Nathan had to concede: "Mr. Belasco has contributed one—and only one—thing for judicious praise to the American theater. He has brought to that theater a standard of tidiness in production and maturation of manuscript, a standard that has discouraged to no little extent that theater's erstwhile not-uncommon frowzy hustle and slipshod manner of presentation."

Belasco made his mark primarily as master of the mechanics, the externals of theater. Montrose Moses aptly labeled him "the psychologist of the switchboard," suggesting with this pregnant phrase Belasco's special contribution. The subtle use of lights which transformed fourteen minutes into Cho-Cho-San's night-long vigil for the return of Pinkerton attested, in the words of Belasco's adulatory biographer William Winter, to his "resource and skill in stage management and stage mechanics." While on occasion Belasco paid lip service to the importance of the play and the actors, his description of his directorial practices suggests how basic was his concern with what he himself called "the material things"—the perfect California sunset for *The Girl of the Golden West*, the actual cheap boardinghouse furniture for *The Easiest Way*, the interior of Child's Restaurant in *The Governor's Lady*.

An inventive master of stage techniques, Belasco deserves credit for his many innovations in making stage life real. His major significance as a pioneer director lies in his use of his materials to form a unified production. But his type of facsimile realism was a manner of stage production rather than a thoroughgoing vision. For that reason, perhaps, it satisfied the popular taste for photographic effects, but it had lost its rationale as a basis for theatrical integration.

As men like Belasco cut the "slice of life" terribly thin, voices cried out in alarm that drama had a purpose loftier than the technical reproduction of physical reality. Even the richer naturalism of the European masters had been rejected quickly as a narrow, partial view of human experience. Thus, despite its essentially modern scientific and objective qualities, the facsimile stage, like the antiquated pictorial one, did not generate an organic theater. Its failure raised pressing questions about the very nature of the theatrical impulse.

The newly emerged director, whom the realistic-naturalistic movement had elevated to a dominant position, became the prime mover in the re-examination of theater art. The men whom we may call the visionaries of the director's art—Appia, Craig, Meyerhold, Copeau—were those who consciously assigned the director this task of rediscovering the wellsprings of theater. To them we owe the flamboyant image of the "artist of the theater." The realists had stumbled on the director out of necessity. The rebels proclaimed the director the messiah of a new theatrical synthesis.

Just as Zola stands behind the naturalistic movement, so Richard Wagner stands behind what Sheldon Cheney has called the "synthetic movement." During the mid-years of the nineteenth century Wagner had attacked a decaying theater because it could not house the "deepest and noblest of man's consciousness." He looked back to the Greeks, whose theater he saw as the profound expression of the whole people gathered "within the ample boundaries of the Greek amphitheater." He asserted that the inherent characteristics of modern society—its degradation of religion, its emphasis on "industrial gain," its denial of art—robbed audience and artist alike of an ennobling idea of theater. He schematized the cause as the "Art-Antagonistic Shape of Present Life, under the Sway of Abstract Thought and Fashion." Damning the whole social structure, Wagner looked forward to a revolutionary new "art work of the future."

This "art work of the future" would be a *Gesamtkunstwerk*, a composite art work, which would fuse all theatrical elements. He offered the word-tone-drama, the music drama, as the magic formula not only for uniting the disparate arts of the theater but also for spanning the gap between art and the folk. He explained the unique advantages of a musical orientation. "A subject," he wrote, "which is comprehended merely by the intelligence can also be expressed merely through the language of words; but the more it expands into an emotional concept, the more does it call for an expression which in its final and essential fullness can alone be obtained through the language of sounds. Hereby the essence of that which the Word-Tone-Poet has to express results quite by itself: it is the Purely Human, freed from all conventions."

Expression of the universal, elemental, inner man was thus disclosed as the theatrical motive in opposition to the naturalist's rational exposure of selected segments of reality. In shifting the theatrical objective from the reproduction of external reality to the externalization of hidden emotional life, the expressionists increased the demands made on the director. In the absence of a social definition of what was universal or elemental, he alone could define these qualities in the theatrical experience.

Adolphe Appia, Swiss designer and theoretician, made the Wagnerian ideal the touchstone for a comprehensive scrutiny of theater art. He suggested that "to derive a play from music does not mean that musical sounds must themselves be the source of the dramatic idea, but merely that the object of music should also be the object of that idea. It is an *interiorization* of the dramatic emotion, prompted by the assurance that music will furnish the means of expressing all that hidden life unhampered." The "hidden life" was too complex to be revealed by the realistic theater of conversation. Appia's *art vivant* demanded emotional participation such as he admired in the antique theater. His basic question was: "How can we once more live art instead of merely contemplating works of art?"

In translating this philosophical concern into technical exposition, Appia laid the groundwork for modern stage practice. Although it is impossible here to outline all the theatrical issues with which he was concerned, we can suggest his chief preoccupation. How, he asked, can theater be turned into a "supreme union of all art" when the various theatrical elements are irreconcilably divided into time and space arts? In the actor's movement, controlled by the discipline of music, he found the connection between time and space. In light Appia saw the living medium which could bring into a single emotional plane the perpendicular scenery, the horizontal floor, and the moving actor. "Only light and music," he wrote, "can express 'the inner nature of all appearance!' "

Basic to Appia's complex theoretical and technical explorations was the concept of a single artist controlling the interaction of light, music, and movement. Ideally, he pointed out in *L'Oeuvre d'art vivant,* the author-director is this artist. "It is a sacrilege," he wrote, "to specialize these two functions." In modern theater, however, the traditional "artist of the theater" did not seem able to exercise both functions. "There is only one way to emerge from this blind alley," Appia asserted in his *Staging Wagnerian Drama,* "and that is to entrust the entire interpretation of the drama to a single person."

In *Die Musik und die Inscenierung* (1895) Appia assigned that interpretation to the director. "The man we call director today," he wrote, "whose job consists in merely arranging completed stage sets, will, in poetic drama, play the role of a despotic drillmaster who will have to understand how much preliminary study stage setting requires, utilize every element of scenic production in order to create an artistic synthesis, reanimate everything under his control at the expense of the actor, who must eventually be dominated. Whatever he does will to a great extent depend upon his individual taste; he must work both as an experimenter and as a poet, play with his scenic materials but at the same time be careful not to create a purely personal formula. . . . He will be very like the leader of an orchestra; his effect will be a similarly magnetic one."

Appia was not the first to insist on the need for a director, but he was the first to bind him to the aesthetic program for a living theater. Yet it was not his fortune to be the recognized herald of a new era. The synthetic ideal and the new synthesizing artist were popularized by a less rigorous thinker but more effective propagandist.

Gordon Craig was the evangelist of the "new movement." In 1905 he sounded the clarion call in *The Art of the Theater.* Here Craig declared: "The art of the theater is neither acting nor the play, it is not scene nor dance, but it consists of all the elements of which these things are composed: action, which is the very spirit of acting;

words, which are the body of the play; line and color, which are the
very heart of the scenes; rhythm, which is the very essence of dance."
Only an "artist of the theater" could master "actions, words, lines,
color, and rhythm." By his mastery this artist "would restore the art
of the theater to its home by means of his own creative genius." In
Craig's manifesto the director became the alchemist of theater.

In his magical laboratory the artist of the theater would unite performance and audience by rhythmic incantation. Craig said: "The
theater was for the people, and always for the people. The poets
would make theater for the select dilettanti. They would put difficult psychological thoughts before the public expressed in difficult
words, and would make for this public something which was impossible for them to understand, and unnecessary for them to know;
whereas the theater must show them sights, show them life, show
them beauty, and not speak in difficult sentences." In place of sentences made difficult by the absence of common values, Craig offered
patterns of light, color, and movement. "The theater of the future
will be a theater of visions, not a theater of sermons nor a theater
of epigrams . . . an art which says less yet shows more than all; an
art which is simple for all to understand it feelingly; an art which
springs from movement, movement which is the very symbol of life."

Because his cry voiced the malaise of all theater workers, Craig's
manifestoes, though intensely personal, became the common language of an international movement. His own productions were
few and never completely successful. His romantic nocturnal
sketches were basically impractical as scenic designs. Even the manifestoes were contradictory and often illogical. Craig himself was not
oblivious to the pitfalls of his neurotic perfectionism. A caption to
a design called "Wapping Old Stairs" reads: "Quite an impossible
scene; that is to say, impossible to realize on a stage. But I wanted
to know for once what it felt like to be mounting up impossible ladders and beckoning to people to come up after me." Few were able
or wanted to climb "impossible ladders," but the challenge to make
the climb had to be taken up. Stanislavsky invited Craig to the
Moscow Art Theater; Brahm let him work at the Lessing Theater;

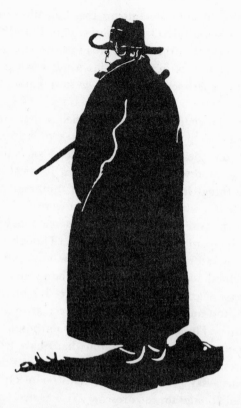

Self-portrait (1919). Woodcut by Gordon Craig. (From
***Edward Gordon Craig,** by Janet Leeper.)*

Reinhardt learned from him; Copeau drew sustenance from him.
The theatrical world was shaken by an ineffectual dreamer.

Craig more than anyone else insisted that the rediscovery of the
art of theater must grow out of research and experimentation, unhampered by the limitations of the commercial stage. He propa-
gandized for a school, for "new lives—new habits—a new order of
work." In 1913 he himself founded a school at the Arena Goldoni
in Florence. For one fateful year the master and some thirty students lived in an atmosphere of "new sights and sounds . . . to breed
. . . new feelings, new thoughts . . . and open eyes." "After that,"

Craig exclaimed, "it only remains for the dramatic spirit to honor us by appearing in our midst." The outbreak of World War I closed Craig's school. But the fruitful impetus rather than the actual accomplishment, in this as in most of his work, was what mattered. Research, study, experimentation in a new fresh atmosphere became the ideal.

In directorial procedure Craig exemplified a new emotional approach. In 1926 when he went to Denmark to stage Ibsen's *The Pretenders* for Johannes Poulsen, he explained his working methods: "In preparing a production I proceed in an illogical manner and try to perceive things feelingly, rather than thinkingly. . . . I reach out and touch a play with my left hand, as it were, and try to receive the thing through my senses, and then make some note with my right hand which will record what it is I have felt. Though I have found that I have often had to revise the first impression . . . I continue to employ this method because I have so often found that this sensitive way of touching a piece—when it is a real piece—is more illuminating to me than to stop and begin thinking it over at once. Thinking comes afterwards. Thinking is for practical purposes. I think out a method of making clear to the spectator what I have felt and seen."

Craig's subjective method is evident, for example, in his conversations with Stanislavsky concerning the character of Ophelia in his interpretation of *Hamlet* for the Moscow Art Theater. Craig insisted that Ophelia was "an insignificant creature." To Stanislavsky's question "Why then was Hamlet in love with her?" Craig replied: "He was in love with his own imagination, with an imaginary woman." "I'm afraid then," Stanislavsky countered, "we shall have to explain it to the audience during one of the intervals." Otto Brahm, in examining one of Craig's designs for *Venice Preserved,* asked: "Where is the door?" He received the characteristic reply: "There is no door; there is a way in and out."

Although both Craig and Appia sought to bring together in an effective whole all the theater arts, their primary impact was on scenery. The designs of both men, rather than their theoretical justifications, set a generation dreaming. Scenic illusion has always

*Hamlet: "Lights, lights, lights." Woodcut by Gordon Craig (1927). (From **Edward Gordon Craig**, by Janet Leeper.)*

been the easiest theatrical component to shape to new purposes. The synthetic movement, which produced no new plays and no new actors, reduced itself to a scenic reform in which suggestive simplicity covered with a "veil of light or darkness" the clumsy literalism of the naturalist's "tasteless parlor." Expressionism, like naturalism, became a technique of staging. It could be used, as Sheldon Cheney once complained, by an astute commercial manager who was unaware of and indifferent to the aesthetic values of which the staging was to be the mere outer form.

Neither naturalism nor expressionism succeeded in the perhaps impossible task of imposing a single point of view—either objective or subjective—on the theater of an age whose distinguishing quality was its multiplicity of views. The failure of these partial perspectives led to an eclectic theater in which the director was the sole creator of significant form. In the "theatrical" theaters of Jacques Copeau, Max Reinhardt, and Vsevolod Meyerhold the director reached the acme of his powers.

Both as practicing director and as theorist, the ascetic Jacques Copeau revealed in their finest and most dedicated form all the preoccupations of the artist of the theater. In founding the Vieux Colombier in 1913 Copeau wanted to bring together "under the direction of one man, a troupe of young, disinterested, and enthusiastic players" whose ambition was to *serve* the art to which they had devoted themselves. The creative director was essential for the unity of which Copeau so frequently spoke. In a letter to Louis Jouvet, his co-worker and *régisseur* (stage manager), Copeau wrote: "I would put all the books under lock and key, to forbid you to use them (that bothers you, eh?). . . . The science of the past, it is I who will absorb it, who will direct it, who will clarify it and who will transmit it to you little by little, all fresh, all new, pell-mell with the personal god-send of my unpublished science. No substitution. A creation. Life."

Copeau's unpublished science involved more than the synthesis of theatrical arts. "Nothing is easier," he wrote, "than to relate artistically the dimension, the decoration, the lighting, etc., of the stage to the character and requirements of each play we produce." But he declared: "That is not my ambition. . . . It will never bring about a renovation or transformation of the scenic *life*."

What Copeau sought was "a certain emancipation" which involved first of all a clear understanding of the director-author relationship in modern theater. "It is true," he wrote, "that creating a dramatic work in words and actually mounting it on the stage with live actors are but two phases of one and the same intellectual operation." Aeschylus, Shakespeare, and Molière illustrate this single artistic creativity. But Copeau revealed that "in our day the playwright is usually a master who has let slip the instrument of his mastery." He must therefore turn to the director, who is a specialist in methods of interpretation.

Since Copeau saw the poet alone as "the true origin and life of all drama as Aeschylus was of Greek drama," he insisted that "the director must capture the spirit of the primitive unity of drama and incorporate its rhythm in his work." He described the virtues of the director as "sincerity and modesty, maturity, reflection, eclecticism; he does not invent ideas, he recovers them. His role is to translate the author, to read the text, to feel the inspiration of it, to possess it as a musician reads notes and sings them at the first sight."

Unlike some of his peers, Copeau did not deny the playwright's text, substituting for it pure stage technique. Although this led to the accusation that he was excessively literary, Copeau's attachment to the play was not at all literary. He saw the play itself in a new theatrical light. What Appia found in the precise definitions of musical notation, Copeau found in plays themselves, which, he said, contained "time-spans—movements and rhythms—comparable to those in music, and as in music, capable of engendering space." He

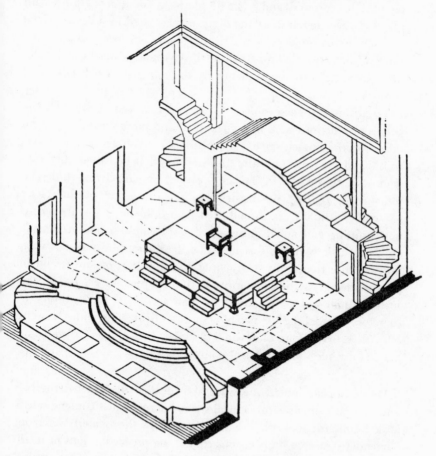

Copeau's stage at the Vieux Colombier. Drawing by Louis Jouvet. (From **Twentieth Century Stage Decoration,** *by W. R. Fuerst and S. J. Hume.)*

discovered a "stage economy that corresponds to dramatic economy; a performing style engendered by a literary style."

Copeau believed that the physical structure of the theater could "heighten and enhance the intellectual structure of a play." This led him to evolve a stage which has been called the first presentational playhouse in the modern world. By using a permanent architectural background and a small platform—*un tréteau nu*—as his playing space, he felt that "the *décor* was replaced by a device which by itself, by its presence, was already action, which materialized the form of the action." This functional playing area was brought into direct contact with the audience by the removal of footlights and proscenium.

To achieve all these objectives was no easy task. Although Copeau's productions were more beautiful and more meaningful than others on the French stage, Copeau himself never felt satisfied. He considered his work only the first step in what he called "our conscientious researches." "Theater cannot remain living unless it remains an *atelier*," he insisted. In the prospectus of the Vieux Colombier school Copeau endorsed Craig's belief that only out of new training and new conditions of work would a new scenic life appear. In the syllabus for the school he offered unity of doctrine, unity of direction, unity of teaching, based in part on music and in part on the old rhythms and forms of the antique theater. To Copeau such research was more important than successful production. He therefore allowed the Vieux Colombier to disintegrate while he went off with a small group of devoted disciples, *les Copiaux*, to continue his lifelong quest for theatrical renovation.

While Copeau sought the "idea of a theater" in dramatic rhythm and in a permanent architectural stage, his renowned contemporary Max Reinhardt took the other path open to the modern director. Surrendering to the multifarious conflicting preoccupations of modern man, Reinhardt never regarded the form of theater as set. In his long years of productivity he used techniques which, culled from all stages of history, ran the gamut of theatrical invention.

No characteristic of Reinhardt more astounded the theatrical world than the rich diversity of his productions. No one style, no one method of decoration or interpretation, no one point of view animated his many theaters. In one of his few published utterances Reinhardt defended his catholicity: "It would be a theory as barbaric as it is incompatible with the principles of theatrical art, to measure with the same yardstick, to press into the same mold, the wonderful wealth of the world's literature. The mere suggestion of such an attempt is an example of pedantic scholasticism. There is no one form of theater which is the only true artistic form." For Reinhardt "all depends on realizing the specific atmosphere of the play, and on making the play live." How did Reinhardt make his plays live in the absence of some accepted idea of what the theater is and does, in the absence of a point of view shared by dramatist, director, and audience?

The slogan "The theater belongs to the theater" epitomizes Reinhardt's accomplishment. He offered audiences theater for theater's sake. Like modern poets and painters, Reinhardt wanted to exploit the intrinsic qualities of his medium. He was able to achieve any and every theatrical effect by carefully organizing and arranging his materials—play, actors, mass movement, music, light, stage space, and auditorium.

The great Reinhardt *Regiebuch* contains his dexterous use of the theatrical medium. In it, wrote Arthur Kahane, his literary adviser and spokesman, Reinhardt gives "physical form to the text, describing in the most minute detail and in a continuous series all situations, positions, and expressions. Thus by the very reality of his technical means, he remodels and reworks the entire drama, provides lyric paraphrases, scenic directions, and hints for the actor. When this book is finished, the first picture of the entire work stands ready before his eyes; also the entire plan for the ensuing preparations, for the dramaturgy, for the music, for the distribution and studying of the parts." Reinhardt's *Regiebuch* represents "a complete, detailed paraphrase of the play in the stage manager's language."

Rehearsals, Reinhardt told Morton Eustis, were a "period of ad-

Notation from first page of Reinhardt's **Regiebuch** *for*
Danton's Death. *(By courtesy of William W. Melnitz.)*

justment" in which all participants in the production were, "in some
manner, adapted to his own conception of the play," a conception
recorded in the *Regiebuch*. Reinhardt came to rehearsals with his
corps of *Regisseurs* "all laden with books," as R. Ben Ari described
it on the basis of his experience as a Reinhardt actor, and he molded
the performance in the light of the detailed notes of his master plan.

In the elaborate Reinhardt workshop the dramatist's text was no longer the primary material. It had become merely one of many theatrical ingredients. In *Sumurun* and *The Miracle* he dispensed with words completely. Reinhardt's influence on most writers was bad, observed Richard Beer-Hofmann, for they depended on Reinhardt to fill in what their meager imaginations could not supply. Reinhardt rather liked incomplete, imperfect plays, said Beer-Hofmann, "for he found therein the opportunity to do what he wished in the depth of his heart to do, and did: Be a poet or at least collaborate in the creation of poetry."

For the actor the Reinhardt touch was a hypnotic one. "He tortures us, he drives us forward, he resolves every doubt," said Gertrude Eysoldt. According to Morton Eustis, at early rehearsals Reinhardt treated his actors "almost as if they were puppets, controlling every movement and gesture, the slightest change in intonation, impressing the stamp of his personality on them collectively and individually until they [were] molded into his own conception of the roles."

Lacking a sanctioned image of what theater is and does, Reinhardt made the theater his world and the world his theater. In Berlin, London, and New York, theaters were turned into Gothic cathedrals for *The Miracle,* and at Salzburg he turned the cathedral into a theater for *Jedermann.* To him, Kahane wrote, the theater was not "the willing servant of literature, satisfied with producing preconceived scenes in as correct and intelligible a manner as possible." It was "a thing in itself, following its own laws, its own path, a *theatrum mundi.*" To him every new production was a new world which he created with "its own lights and shadows, its own beauty and ugliness, its heaven and its hell."

Nothing suggests so forcibly the relationship of the modern director to his antique predecessors as this panegyric to Reinhardt's theater. Here was the rediscovery of theater, but revolutionary changes in society had robbed the rediscovery of significant meaning. In the past, theater had been a world with its Heaven and its Hell, but it was a microcosm, a mirror of the real world, not a purely theatrical con-

Interior view of the Grosses Schauspielhaus.

coction whose references to the larger world were tenuous and vapid.

Reinhardt actually tried to reproduce the antique theater in his Grosses Schauspielhaus, hoping that this "Theater of the Five Thousand" could contain modern life as once the great arena had contained the Greek community. "Under the influence of these mighty spaces, these big, severe lines," Kahane explained, "all that is small and petty disappears, and it becomes a matter of course to appeal to the hearts of great audiences with the strongest and deepest elements. The petty and unimportant—elements that are not eternal in us—cease to have effect. The theater can only express the great eternal elemental passions and the problems of humanity. In it spectators cease to be mere spectators; they become the people; their emotions are simple and primitive, but great and powerful, as becomes the eternal human race."

Without a traditional way of life, a myth, a ritual attitude, or an ideology to sustain it, this theater was doomed to failure. What successes it did have in its brief existence under Reinhardt were the successes of a director who played on very generalized emotions through the theatrical devices of light, color, mass movement, and music. Huntly Carter asked of Reinhardt's production of *Oedipus*: "If Reinhardt is not giving us Greek drama, what is he giving us? The reply is Reinhardtism—an essence of drama of his own distilling."

The personal distillation of the director was the modern substitute for the whole complex of social and theatrical factors that had once made theater the great collective art. Reinhardt illustrates this process in its baroque, Wagnerian aspect. Vsevolod Meyerhold illustrates it in its constructivist, Marxian aspect.

Different as their theaters were, Reinhardt and Meyerhold have much in common. Both, for example, began as actors under great naturalist directors—Reinhardt under Brahm, Meyerhold under Stanislavsky. Both experimented with expressionist drama; both went on to attempt a new social integration—Reinhardt in the Theater of the Five Thousand, Meyerhold in the Theater of the Revolution.

Meyerhold's revolt early in the century against the naturalism of Stanislavsky inevitably led him to follow the director's métier. In place of naturalism's "morbid human curiosity," Meyerhold wanted symbolic expression of life. Since there were no conventional or traditional symbols available, Meyerhold, as *régisseur,* had to invent them. In place of naturalism's attempt to reproduce reality of detail Meyerhold wanted to "point the irony of a situation." Since there was no accepted framework in which to place theatrical situations, Meyerhold had to impose his own point of view. Instead of naturalism's "intelligent reader" Meyerhold wanted actors who could convey ideas technically. Since there was no frankly *theatrical* technique, Meyerhold had to invent it and teach it to his actors. For well over a quarter of a century—through the Revolution and the first decades of the Soviets—Meyerhold tried to create a modern equivalent of the vital, symbolic, *theatrical* theaters of the past.

Meyerhold's directorial art, like the acting of the old Italian comedians he admired, was an improvised one. He prepared no *Regiebuch*. He told Harold Clurman: "I am able to keep everything quite clearly in my head. Anyhow, I am likely to stage a scene one way and days later come to rehearsal and change the staging completely. For me every rehearsal is a sketch." Each improvised effect, however, was dictated·by an exacting sense of form. Meyerhold conceived production in terms of musical analogies. *The Inspector General,* for example, was planned along the lines of a sonata. Each new improvisation was then a variation on a theme. Norris Houghton, in *Moscow Rehearsals,* remarks: "One line may become the motivation for five minutes of cadenzas which the virtuosity of Meyerhold will have invented, before the theme—that is, the text of the play—is continued."

Here is Meyerhold talking to the actors at the first rehearsal of a proposed program of three Chekhov one-acters—*The Proposal, The Bear,* and *The Jubilee*—as recorded by Houghton: "Two things are

Drawing by Gogol for **The Inspector General** *(1836). (From* **New Theatres for Old,** *by Mordecai Gorelik.)*

essential for a play's production, as I have often told you. First, we must find the thought of the author; then we must reveal that thought in a theatrical form. This form I call á *jeu de théâtre* and around it I shall build the performance. Molière was a master of *jeux de théâtre:* a central idea and the use of incidents, comments, mockery, jokes—anything to put it over. In this production I am going to use the technique of the traditional vaudeville as the *jeu.* Let me explain what it is to be. In these three plays of Chekhov I have found that there are thirty-eight times when characters either faint, say they are going to faint, turn pale, clutch their hearts, or call for a glass of water; so I am going to take this idea of fainting and use it as a sort of leitmotif for the performance. Everything will contribute to this *jeu.*"

Both the play and the actors were raw material for Meyerhold's art. The text took a position subordinate to his *jeu,* his creative business. One Russian commentator suggested that Meyerhold's production of *The Inspector General* "should be called Meyerhold's mental associations apropos *The Inspector General.*" In rehearsing scenes from this most famous of his productions Meyerhold kept his brigade of *régisseurs* busy recording business for a character who had no lines at all in Gogol's text. On the programs of his theater Meyerhold's name appeared as "author of the spectacle."

To realize his conception of a play Meyerhold used his actors as a sculptor uses clay. The actor's objective was to be pliable in order to become the living embodiment of Meyerhold's ideas. In his school they were prepared for this task. There each day's work began with practice in "bio-mechanics," stage movement, that gave Meyerhold's actors "the trained body, the well-functioning nervous system, correct reflexes, vivacity and exactness of reaction, the control of one's body." In addition to this training all that Meyerhold wanted of actors was "a certain talent for music and a certain amount of intelligence." In the 1930's he defended his training procedure against misinterpretation by "socialist realists" in these illuminating words (translated by Nora Beeson in *Meyerhold on Theater*): "We speak of the fact that an actor should have dexterity in performance, precision, and athleticism. He has to know acrobatics. He has to understand that he is a human being operating in space. He should be familiar with spatial art. All this has been interpreted erroneously. For example, acrobatics, eccentricity, and grotesque devices have been mistakenly spotlighted and the devil only knows what the result is. It is thought that the monologue 'To be or not to be' should be read as follows:

On entering the stage do a somersault, recite a few lines, then lie down stage center, walk on all fours like a bear, get up and continue reading. Or when we say that an actor should be a good juggler it is understood as follows: On stage, in some contemporary play, a man starts juggling; he takes some balls out of his pocket and delivers a monologue, juggling. We suggest a whole series of things as a training process, for perfecting techniques. To develop the wrists, we make an actor juggle; but we are misunderstood and the opposite is done."

Vsevolod Meyerhold. Caricature by Kukriniksi.

Since Meyerhold was the sole creative figure in his theater, the work of art was often the rehearsal, not the performance. At rehearsals one could see "a full production as well as a fascinating performance," observed a young Russian director, Yuri Zavadsky. The actual performance, Zavadsky suggested, was like "great music wheezed out on a barrel-organ. . . . Each repeated presentation of a production more and more 'forgets' its creator, Meyerhold."

What makes Meyerhold so fascinating a figure in the history of directing is the fact that out of his own creative research he had rediscovered the use of symbols and the vigorous theatricality that once had made theater the great public art. As early as 1908 he had written: "The new theater gravitates toward the dynamic beginning, for the latest theatrical experiments approach the theater of antiquity. . . . The directors of our new experimental stages are working to create a Symbolic Theater in order to reintroduce a more unified theater." Then unique social circumstances gave him unrestricted opportunity to experiment. Liberated by the Russian Revolution from the demands of established taste, Meyerhold was authorized to evolve a significant dramatic form for a new audience in a "new" society. He was the logical choice to inaugurate a "theatrical October" in emulation of the "political October." In the early days of the Soviets, theater again became an art at the center of the life of its time, and Meyerhold, as the artist of the Revolution, rallied actor and audience around collective sentiments. Messages from the fighting front interrupted the performance that prefigured in theatrical symbols the new social life.

Despite seemingly propitious circumstances, Meyerhold's continued search for vital theatrical conventions never culminated in a persisting idea of theater. The "Picasso of theater," as Louis Lozowick calls him, Meyerhold experimented with endless inventiveness. "His whole career," Norris Houghton suggests, "seems to have been a search for a style which would completely satisfy him. He has never found the perfect form." Meyerhold was seemingly in a race with his own brilliant eclecticism, and the audience could not keep up the pace. As Soviet society became more stabilized it self-consciously turned away from revolutionary innovation. When "socialist realism" emerged in the thirties as the official style, Meyerhold's productions were violently criticized and his personal integrity attacked. After twenty years of brilliant theatrical *jeux* he was stripped of his theater and charged with the sin of "formalism." Instead of renouncing his past, it is reported, he fearlessly defended his point of view. "This pitiful and sterile something which aspires to the title of socialist realism has nothing in common with art. Go to the Moscow theaters and look at the colorless and boring productions which are all alike and which only differ in their degree of worthlessness. No longer can we identify the creative signatures of the Maly Theater, of the Vakhtangov Theater, of the Kamerny Theater, of the Moscow Art Theater.... In your effort to eradicate formalism you have destroyed art."

Meyerhold paid heavily for his integrity. He was arrested for this speech. All trace of his name and his work was eradicated from Soviet theater. With the death of Stalin, however, and the subsequent "thaw," Meyerhold's ideas and teachings began to be felt as a liberating force. Although he died in internment in 1942, he was officially reinstated in July 1956. Among the most exciting Soviet productions since then have been revivals of his stagings of Mayakovsky's *The Bedbug, The Bathhouse,* and *Mystery Bouffe,* and new works by his disciple Nikolai Okhlopkov. Soviet theater is once again being enriched by this brilliant exponent of the director's art.

The great directors stand pre-eminent because of the grandeur of their vision or the magnitude of their accomplishment, but many others contributed significant ideas and practices to make the modern theater the theater of the director. In Russia, for example, Vladimir Nemirovich-Danchenko, co-founder with Stanislavsky of the Moscow Art Theater, was more than the partner with the "literary veto" who brought the plays of Chekhov to the theater. He was a practicing director who, for example, handled more rehearsals of the initial Art Theater production of *The Sea Gull* than Stanislavsky himself. He and Stanislavsky were listed jointly as *régisseurs* on the playbills of the Art Theater. The division of labor they decided upon initially, however, brought greater notice to Stanislavsky, for he provided the *mise en scène,* with all the dazzling effects of which he was master. Nemirovich-Danchenko gave the basic interpretation of the play: profound, essential, but not spectacular work. In his autobiography, Nemirovich-Danchenko wrote: "In approaching a new production, Stanislavsky sooner or later would say to me: 'Now fill me up with what you think I ought to have especially in mind making up my *régisseur's* copy.' . . . I spoke while he listened and made notes."

It was Nemirovich-Danchenko who brought the writers and the plays to the theater—Chekhov, Gorky, and even Tolstoy—and saw to it that words, content, and histrionic interpretation were not overwhelmed by his partner's devotion to sets, costumes, and sound effects. He outlived his famous collaborator by several years, and the Moscow Art Theater as it exists today and many of its outstanding productions are largely his creation.

Alexander Tairov stood outside the Art Theater company, although his actress-wife, Alice Koonen, came from its ranks. At his Kamerny Theater, Tairov experimented with projects for a "theater unbound" in which heroic gesture and formalized rhythm would replace the facsimile naturalism of Stanislavsky He focused upon the ballet as the model for modern theater. "As there is a *corps de*

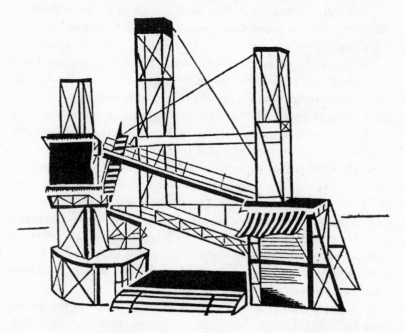

Constructivist setting for Tairov's production of **The Man Who Was Thursday** *(1923). (From* **New Theatres for Old,** *by Mordecai Gorelik.)*

ballet," he wrote, "so there should be a *corps de théâtre"* led by a *régisseur* whose "first task is to find the form of the production." In the twenties Tairov gave striking form to many plays, including constructivist presentations of Eugene O'Neill's *The Hairy Ape, Desire Under the Elms,* and *All God's Chillun Got Wings.* Like Meyerhold, he lost control of his theater during the struggle between socialist realism and formalism.

Several young Russian directors tried to mediate between the theatricality of Meyerhold and Tairov and Stanislavsky's "truth of inner experience." Eugene Vakhtangov, one of Stanislavsky's best pupils, sought a robust theatricality capable of expressing the harsh but vibrant life of the revolutionary period. The rich mingling of fantasy and reality in his staging of Gozzi's *Turandot,* for example, was based on acute perception of both theatrical needs and audience interests. "What do our spectators want today?" he asked. "Something they see around them all the time? The inspiring fight to rebuild the country after the devastation of the Civil War? Someone has yet to write about it. Today, the audience wants to see their future, too. They're dreaming about it. But the playwrights haven't written anything about it either. We have fairy-tales, however—dreams of what people will be when they purify themselves, when they overcome the evil forces. Let's dream about that in *Turandot.* Let's show in our fairy-tale what people experience in their struggle against evil, for their future." His free-wheeling, dynamic fantasy gave unique form to this play as it did to Ansky's *The Dybbuk.* He never lectured his casts or his students, but rather participated actively and imaginatively in the creative life being nurtured at rehearsals. He projected a theater suited to the needs of the new socialist society when he suggested a theatrical collective in which a modest, efficient craftsman would replace the autocratic director.

After Vakhtangov's untimely death in 1922 his disciples, among them Boris E. Zakhava, who is still director of the Vakhtangov Theater and a leading Soviet producer, translated his ideals into a theatrical structure. At the Vakhtangov Theater they practice a directorial procedure designed for a socialist society, but one which could well be used by groups with other political views. The theatrical collective decides what plays are to be produced, and then assigns to one of its directors the play most suited to his special talents. Before actual production work begins, the director submits a formal, standardized report of his plans. Actor and author, if possible, discuss with the director his ideas. If accepted or acceptably revised, the plans are then put into operation. Yet even at this point the director's control does not become absolute, for rehearsals begin with round-table discussions by the actors on interpretation of roles. They contribute their ideas to those outlined by the director. Only then, scene by scene, section by section, does the play assume its theatrical form under the supervision of the director, who has cooperated and consulted with the whole company.

Nikolai Okhlopkov, one of Meyerhold's epigones, also tried to synthesize the Meyerhold and Stanislavsky approaches in the light of new social needs. In the arena of his Realistic Theater he sought an emotional union in which "actor and spectator must clasp hands in fraternity." Okhlopkov stated his aims in the following words: "Thus we assert the realism of the theater through theatrical means, appealing to the imagination of the spectator and at the same time providing it with a powerful stimulus. Thus the audience cooperates with the actors in every performance, so that the actor applauds the audience as well as the audience the actor."

As a result of his experimental use of space, Okhlopkov, like Meyerhold and Tairov, had to defend himself against charges of formalism and withdrew from the theater to cinema acting. With the "thaw" of the fifties he reappeared as a director still devoted to theatrical explorations. In 1962 his production of Euripides' *Medea* was "the event of Moscow's artistic year." Staged in Tchaikovsky Hall, the huge theater built according to plans made by Meyerhold but completed only after his internment, the classical tragedy was turned into a monumental "mass spectacle" by Okhlopkov. He utilized a Greek chorus of forty women and a symphony orchestra and choir of nearly one hundred men and women placed in the center of the auditorium and surrounded by spectators. It was Okhlopkov's hope that in his

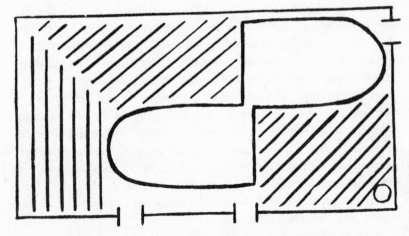

*Playing area of Okhlopkov's arena staging of **Aristocrats**.*

unique staging would be heard "the angry and proud voice of the greatest of the ancient poets, raised in defense of man, his rights and dignity."

In Germany it was not only Brahm and Reinhardt who prepared the way for later directors, but also early innovators like Georg Fuchs. At his Kuenstler Theater in Munich, Fuchs, like Appia and Craig, invoked rhythm as the primal element capable of reviving the ritualistic theater of communal exaltation. Taking as his inspiration the slogan *"Rethéâtraliser le théâtre,"* he constructed a "relief stage," a shallow platform that thrust the actors forward to the audience, as his solution to the international quest for closer union between stage and auditorium.

During the twenties Leopold Jessner seemed a successor to Reinhardt in his forceful theatricality. But Jessner distinguished his art from what he called the "impressionism" of Reinhardt as well as from the realism of the Meininger-Brahm tradition. Jessner offered a concentrated, intense theater of symbols in place of the detailed, formless verisimilitude of the realists or the subtle illusion of Reinhardt. He felt that theater, the unique amalgam of many arts, expressed with special urgency the whole modern search for fresh means of artistic expression. He insisted that new forms in the theater could be created only by the will of the *Regisseur,* who had the right to rearrange each text in accordance with his theatrical interpretation.

The actual practice of the theater of symbols is suggested in Jessner's commentary on his most famous production, *Richard III,* in which all the major action was played on an enormous stairway (the *Jessnertreppen*) that occupied the whole center of the stage: "Glou-

Jessner's steps in scene from Grabbe's Napoleon, or the Hundred Days (1922).

cester's coronation takes place on this staircase, which is entirely covered in red, the color of blood. On the highest step the newly crowned King stands. At his feet the courtiers gather, not any more the historical presentation of the courtiers of that time, but symbols of a uniform society, numbed by nepotism, all in blood-red gowns.

The following battle scenes are also enacted on this staircase, symbolized by the rhythm of countless drums behind the stage. This is not to give the illusion of an actual battle, but to show its dynamic tension. Even the costumes are symbolic. The party of Richmond, the army which fights for truth, is clothed in white. The warriors of Richard, who shed blood for blood's sake, are dressed in red. This significant performance found the strongest expression of its inner laws in the scene of the breakdown. Richard III sways down the same red stairs on which he stood in the zenith of his glory, a king, now half undressed, torn, confused, already insane, and at the bottom he is killed by the white warriors."

Erwin Piscator joined Reinhardt and Jessner as the dominant figures of the German stage during the twenties. In place of Reinhardt's eclecticism and Jessner's expressionism, although strongly influenced by both, Piscator evolved the "agitprop," documentary, living newspaper style of staging, which he called "Epic Drama." He challenged audiences with his daring exploitation of unusual stage devices—conveyor belt, slides, charts, maps—in the cause of a political idea. He turned the stage of the Volksbuehne, built to house "Art for the People," into a tribunal for judging current issues. The Volksbuehne, whose artistic roots went back to Brahm's Freie Buehne, had already witnessed the revolutionary staging of Ernst Toller's *Masse Mensch* by Juergen Fehling, but from 1924 to 1927 Piscator used this theater for relentless and striking experimentation, which ultimately resulted in his dismissal. At his own Theater am Nollendorfplatz he made an outstanding popular success of his Epic staging of *The Good Soldier Schweik* against the backdrops of George Grosz, a production that greatly influenced Bertolt Brecht, who had worked with Piscator on the adaptation of the Czech novel. In the United States, where he lived during the Nazi period, Piscator continued to seek ways to achieve a "new reality" and a "new objectivity." When he returned to West Berlin in the 1950's, he was still considered a most controversial director. His striking productions—Tolstoy's *War and Peace* in his own adaptation, Schiller's *Don Carlos* and *The Robbers*,

Drawing by George Grosz for animated film used with
The Good Soldier Schweik, *staged by Piscator (1928).*
(From **New Theatres for Old,** *by Mordecai Gorelik.)*

Brecht's *Mother Courage*—are making a deep impression on contemporary German theater.

Bertolt Brecht, playwright-poet-director, transformed his radical political ideology into a new theater aesthetic. The Epic Theater, whose theories he based in large part on unusual stagings by Piscator and himself in the twenties, is one of the few distinctively modern theatrical conceptions. Brecht posed the basic question: "What is the productive attitude toward nature and society which we children of a scientific age can accept with pleasure in our theater?" He recognized the great social changes that had made the old theatrical unity impossible. He insisted that "society has no common mouthpiece as long as it is split into struggling classes. For art to be unpartisan means only that it belongs to the ruling party." Brecht called for a point of view that is chosen "outside the theater." He invoked alienation in place of empathy since his objective was to "astonish" the audience into a realization that "society is susceptible of change."

Brecht used all the varied theatrical arts to achieve his purpose: to stimulate a critical attitude in the spectator. "The story is set out," he wrote, "brought forward, and shown by the theater as a whole, by actors, stage designers, mask-makers, costumers, composers, and choreographers. They unite their various arts for the joint operation, without, of course, sacrificing their independence in the process." Brecht's call to "all the sister arts" was not for the Wagnerian purpose of producing a "composite art work (*Gesamtkunstwerk*) in which they all surrender and lose themselves. They should, together with the art of acting, promote the common task each in his own way. Their intercourse with each other consists in reciprocal alienation." Thus Brecht used music, dance, and light not with the Wagnerian end of creating "an atmosphere which allows the audience to lose itself unreservedly in the events on the stage," or to express the

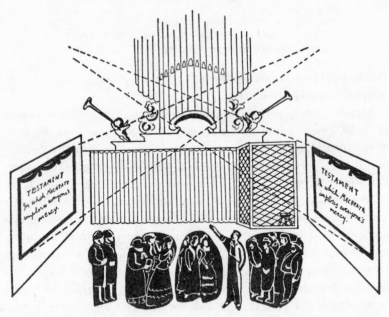

Bertolt Brecht's **Threepenny Opera.** *Design by Caspar Neher (sketch by Mordecai Gorelik, after a photograph). (By permission of Mordecai Gorelik.)*

hidden emotional life of the characters, but to emphasize the basic *"Gestus"* of each play, that is, the "clear and stylized expression of the social behavior of human beings toward each other" in all its objective complexity.

Much that went into Brecht's theories grew out of his actual practice as director of his own plays and later as head of his own theater. In the twenties his *Threepenny Opera* was staged with such fresh virtuosity that it had the greatest success of any modern play of serious import produced in Berlin. His knowledge of audiences and of performers was enriched by experience with his revolutionary *Lehrstuecke,* learning pieces. During his years of exile he was without a theater in which to work, but he composed his masterpieces, *Galileo, The Good Woman of Setzuan,* and *Mother Courage.* On his return to East Berlin in 1948 he gathered together the nucleus of his own company; by 1954 the Berliner Ensemble was established in the Theater am Schiffbauerdamm that Brecht had made famous in the twenties. With a company and theater Brecht as a director came into his own; his productions of his late plays—*Mother Courage, The Caucasian Chalk Circle,* and others—revealed a dynamic, modern style unmatched in the theaters of Europe and America.

As a working director Brecht was patient and pragmatic, not at all given to explaining or invoking his theories. During long months of rehearsal he tested many alternatives for each scene; when he found what he considered the most expressive presentation, he recorded it in his own version of a *Regiebuch,* the *"Modellbuch."* In these records the form of a particular play was crystallized by interpretative comment, detailed blocking and timing, and a minute photographic record of each action. The *Modell* was not simply Brecht's record of how he understood and staged the play; it was intended as a guide for all further productions of the same play by Brecht himself or by other directors. To the charge that the *Modell* limited the director's artistic freedom, Brecht retorted: "Surprisingly little is lost by renouncing the complete freedom of 'artistic creativity.' No matter what, one must start somewhere, and with something: why should it not be something that had been thought through before? One regains one's freedom, no doubt, by the spirit of contradiction that stirs here and there inside one."

Brecht's theories, with their typically high-sounding, abstract, and often confusing German terms—*Verfremdungseffect* (alienation), *Gestus*, non-Aristotelian, Epic, have been so eagerly pondered and debated in Europe and America that Brecht felt called upon to say: "My theories are altogether far more naïve than one might think— more naïve than any way of expressing them might allow one to suspect." The attraction of Brecht's ideas stems in part from their intriguing and suggestive character and the absence of any comprehensive alternative. But they have also gained their wide interest because of Brecht's accomplishments as a rare "artist of the theater," whose plays and new techniques of staging and acting have provided a personal instrument attuned to the peculiar temper of our time.

In France, Antoine and Copeau provided the basic training for succeeding theatrical generations. Firmin Gémier, a director who sought inspiration in antiquity and the Middle Ages, was one of Antoine's early co-workers. He attacked the purely literary view of drama, seeking "to create an atmosphere where each assisting celebrant communes with his neighbors and the author in a sort of social religion." The phrases of the great playwrights, he asserted, "are like caskets which one must open so that their soul is liberated and displays itself in action. That is why the text does not entirely contain them. They absolutely demand the stage and *mise en scène.*"

Gaston Baty, who worked with Gémier and had studied with Reinhardt, also revolted against *Sire le Mot*. Often attacked as a rare example in France of the dictator-director, he countered the criticism that he treated great dramatic works only as "pretexts" for his imagination by saying: "A text cannot say everything. It can go only as far as all words can go. Beyond them begins another zone, a zone of mystery, of silence, which one calls the atmosphere, the *ambiance,* the climate, as you wish. It is that which it is the work of the director to express."

Georges Pitoëff, who worked with Baty, Louis Jouvet, and Charles

Dullin as a theatrical *Cartel des Quatre,* wanted to project on his stage what he called *"une autre vérité,"* the impalpable essence of things. "With realism," as he notes, "it was sufficient to copy life exactly. With what can the new *mise en scène* be compared? With imaginary truth? That is not easy. It is necessary to have confidence, to believe and not to know. It is almost in the domain of religion." His productions were therefore schematized and abstract rather than detailed and realistic. Yet his spare scenic devices could richly underscore a dramatist's meaning. In his staging of Pirandello's *Henry IV*, Henry madly tried to prop up the flimsy cardboard sets which were about to collapse on him, a striking visualization of the theme endorsed by Pirandello himself.

Dullin, Jouvet, Jean-Louis Barrault, and Jean Vilar owe their inspiration directly or indirectly to Copeau, as does Michel Saint-Denis, Copeau's nephew, who has brought his disciplined devotion to art to theater schools in England and America. Dullin tried to achieve at his Atelier what Copeau had sought at the Vieux Colombier, to create "a living organism having its function in modern society, responsive to the preoccupations, the enthusiasms of everyone." Music, color, and improvised mime marked his productions. His theater was a school in which playwrights and actors learned, in the words of his pupil Barrault, a "method" rather than a "métier."

Jouvet, who had been Copeau's stage manager, preserved in his own Théâtre Athénée the artistic taste and poetic distinction of his mentor. But Jouvet came to feel that the search for laws of theater and of directing, to which Copeau had devoted his efforts, was of little avail. On the publication of Copeau's *mise en scène* for *Les Fourberies de Scapin* Jouvet declared: "The art of the director is an art of adjusting to contingencies. It isn't a profession, it is a state. One is a director as one is a lover. The varieties are infinite." Exceedingly modest about his contribution as a director, he put himself totally at the service of the playwright. His pragmatic, careful, well-disciplined, almost hesitant approach, coupled with his talent and imagination, enabled him to breathe theatrical life into the tradition-worn stagings of Molière and the plays of Giraudoux. His production of

Molière's *L'Ecole des Femmes* was heralded as a "return to classic art," while his collaboration with Giraudoux is testimony to the positive role a director can play in rescuing a literary and dramatic imagination for the stage.

Jean-Louis Barrault in **Baptiste** *(drawing by Mayo).*

Jean-Louis Barrault's masters were Dullin, Etienne Decroux, teacher of mime, and Antonin Artaud, prophet of a primitive, physical "theater of cruelty." Barrault's eclectic art has revived the French classical tradition in his productions of Molière, Racine, and Marivaux and has projected the ideas of new writers like Gide, Kafka, and Claudel. Barrault has stated the aims of his company in these words: ". . . from the classics we seek nourishment, through the study of gesture and speech we hope to perfect our technique, by periodic excursions into the unknown we hope to enrich ourselves, and all *in the service of modern authors*." The spirit of Copeau's quest still echoes in the pages of Barrault's "reflections," even if one sometimes feels, as Harold Clurman observed, that Copeau's "comprehensive feeling for theater as a craft and cultural instrument" has given place to the more immediate challenge of tasteful staging of individual plays.

Although often caught up in practical and technical problems (he now heads the government-subsidized Théâtre de France at the Odéon), he has continued to pursue the ideal of a "total drama" in which theatrical resources are used to the full.

Jean Vilar has brought to the tradition of Copeau a desire to make his "theater without pretensions accessible to all." Instead of appealing to an elite, he has dedicated his stage to a vast, popular, working-class audience with whom he performs the "collective ceremony of theater." At the Théâtre National Populaire, also government-supported, Vilar and his company offer a repertory ranging from Molière to Strindberg and Brecht, staged with a simplicity, concentration, beauty, and understanding calculated to appeal to an unsophisticated but enthusiastic audience. Despite his use of a huge stage in a huge theater both in Paris and in Avignon, Vilar does not produce elaborate visual spectacles. Scenery is kept to a minimum, while lighting serves to define playing areas and to illuminate the actors, who are the heart of his theater. "Performance = text + interpreters," he has stated. In view of the texts he has chosen and the members of his troupe—Marie Casares, George Wilson, the late Gerard Phillipe, and Vilar himself—one can understand why many feel that Vilar's theater "for the greatest number" is the most vital in France.

New talents have been stimulated by the avant-garde theaters, where Roger Blin has staged with striking impact the plays of Samuel Beckett and Jean Genet, and by the creation of provincial "Centres Dramatiques" in which Roger Planchon and Jean Dasté, among others, have had an opportunity to work out their ideas.

In England the director has never assumed the dominant position of his continental counterpart. The actor-producer tradition has lived on nobly from Henry Irving to John Gielgud and Laurence Olivier, who have enriched it by the social and artistic spirit that informed their early years at the Old Vic. Apart from Gordon Craig, who popularized the modern conception of the director but who actually staged very few productions in England or elsewhere, only Harley Granville-Barker stands with the innovators. Early in the century at the Court Theatre he perfected an acting and scenic style for realistic dramas—his own, Shaw's, Galsworthy's, and those of other contemporaries. But Granville-Barker was not a naturalist in the manner of Antoine or Stanislavsky, although he confessed he learned much about acting from the Russian master. His profound sense of different dramatic methods also enabled him to produce successfully classics like Euripides and to revolutionize the staging of Shakespeare along lines suggested by his mentor, William Poel. His *Prefaces to Shakespeare* offer a rare combination of scholarship and theatrical insight. In addition he proposed an "exemplary theater" to spur a reorientation of theatrical life.

Directing in England has meant in large measure directing Shakespeare, for his plays provide not only the touchstone of the director's craft, but also the basis for institutions in which the director can do more than package a saleable commercial play. At the Stratford Memorial Theatre and the Old Vic, directors from Ben Greet and Sir Barry Jackson to Tyrone Guthrie and, more recently, Michael Benthall, Peter Brook, and Peter Hall, have tried to find meaningful modern forms for Shakespeare.

Guthrie has been second only to Granville-Barker in his influence on Shakespearean production and in the variety of his activity. A flamboyant theatricalist, he has experimented with new stages and theaters. In recent years England has been less and less his laboratory as he has been called upon to work in other countries. Instead of committing himself to a continuing theatrical enterprise he has staged individual plays wherever he has found himself. Yet his impulse to start theaters—in Stratford, Ontario, and Minneapolis, Minnesota, for example—is the impulse of all the outstanding directors to do more than just stage plays skillfully. In assessing his motives for rejoining the Old Vic in 1936 Guthrie wrote: "But I think the dominant reason was to attach myself to something more significant than my own career; to feel part of something more permanent, and rooted in more serious intentions, than the short-term, superficial professional alliances of the commercial theater."

The same impulse lies behind two vital new English theaters. The

Theatre Workshop, originated by Joan Littlewood and sustained by her passionate theatricality, is committed to theater "in the present tense" for the "people." George Devine and Tony Richardson have rededicated the Royal Court Theatre, once the stage of Granville-Barker and Shaw, as the proving ground for new dramatists—John Osborne, Arnold Wesker, John Arden, Ann Jellicoe, and others.

American directors, in typical American fashion, have been essentially pragmatic. They have elaborated the "know-how" absorbed from indigenous craftsmen such as Augustin Daly, Steele MacKaye, and David Belasco and from the European innovators to give Broadway a very high technical standard of production. Their local brand of theatrical synthesis, however, has all too often turned out purely synthetic concoctions, especially in that popular native product, the musical play. Missing in the usual Broadway entertainment, with or without music, has been any consistent solicitude for the artistic expression of meaningful, contemporary ideas and experiences. The little theater movement of the twenties first introduced some concern for the "craft and the cultural instrument" in opposition to the conventions of "show business." The seminal theories and practices of Craig, Reinhardt, and others were felt in the artistry of Robert Edmond Jones and Norman Bel Geddes and in the staging and essays of Maurice Browne, who offered a new artistic and social perspective, as did other advocates of the "new movement" in the Provincetown Playhouse, the Washington Square Players, and the Neighborhood Playhouse.

On Broadway a few directors took up the challenge of the new ideas. Arthur Hopkins, who used Jones as his collaborator, sought to "make the stage speak with one voice." He diagnosed the basic problem of modern theater as the difficulty of eliciting a "unanimous reaction" from an audience composed of diverse spectators. He offered as his cure the theory of "unconscious projection" in which the director "stills the conscious mind of the spectator" by his skillful technique and makes him accessible to an "unconscious ideal common to all." Philip Moeller, working as part of the Theatre Guild

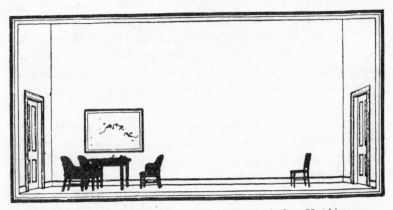

*Robert Edmond Jones's first setting for an Arthur Hopkins
production,* **The Devil's Garden.**

directorate, staged many of the new American plays of the twenties—
those of Elmer Rice, Sidney Howard, S. N. Behrman, and Eugene
O'Neill. He placed his urbane, sophisticated theatrical imagination
and literary skill at the service of the group expression which he felt
to be the major contribution of the Guild's methods of production
in the early days.

The ferment of the thirties added a striking social and political
dimension to the primarily artistic revival of the twenties. The
Federal Theatre, for example, administered by Hallie Flannagan,
revitalized in its manifold activities the whole theatrical community.
Among its many notable deeds was the opportunity it gave to one
of America's most dynamic and original directors, Orson Welles, who
with John Houseman offered brilliant, modern reinterpretations of
the classics and pointed contemporary experiments. Their Mercury
Theatre was an unfortunately shortlived attempt to continue the
fresh, vigorous theatricalism fostered by the Federal Theatre.

Early in the great depression the directors of the Group Theatre—
Harold Clurman, Lee Strasberg, Cheryl Crawford—wanted to "say
something" with their plays and wanted their productions to be informed by a consistent theatrical technique. They achieved a com-

Operating room in the Group Theatre production of **Men in White**. *Design by Mordecai Gorelik.*

mon artistic point of view with a permanent company trained in the use of the Stanislavsky method. They nurtured new playwrights such as Clifford Odets who shared their values and utilized their technique. The success of their efforts cannot be measured only by their impressive accomplishments during a decade of production on Broadway. The value of their orientation can be seen further in the subsequent creative role of the founders and their followers. Lee Strasberg, as head of the Actors' Studio, organized by Elia Kazan and Cheryl Crawford, has given American actors—and more recently directors and playwrights—a "method" and a home in the midst of the chaotic, rootless commercial theater. The decision taken by the Studio in 1962 to form a production unit may turn what has sometimes unfortunately become a mysterious, personal cult into a dynamic new theater. Harold Clurman, as critic, has most articulately championed in his comments on the contemporary scene the idea that "A Theater is a body of dramatic craftsmen dedicated as a unit to a continuous effort to achieve its character or style so that it may make a statement. . . . The quest is impelled by an aesthetic and/or moral ideology, a faith of some kind that integrates and gives meaning (thus an identity) to the group's work as a whole. . . ."

Elia Kazan, who started as a Group Theatre actor, has written his strong personal signature on the most important plays of the post-World War II period. His intense, almost violent style, in which realistic "method" acting is combined with theatricalist staging, has practically become the American idiom. After many successes in which his virtuosity gave powerful form to compassionate plays, or sometimes only displayed itself, he has decided to leave the commercial theater, whose limited rehearsal schedules and repertory he deplores. As artistic head of the Repertory Theatre at the Lincoln Center of Performing Arts, where he is associated with Robert Lewis, another distinguished Group Theatre alumnus, he hopes to recreate the kind of theater he had known with the Group, a permanent company dedicated to staging plays in a way that would, in his words, "energize" the commercial theater, develop new talents, and make American theater "interesting, exciting, vital to us in contemporary terms."

A significant development of the past decade has been the emergence of the off-Broadway theaters. In their modest way, several of these, recalling the notable groups of the twenties, have tried to keep alive a notion of theater as more than a seasonal, personal display. Up to 1962 the only off-Broadway group that has created a repertory company is the persevering Living Theatre of Judith Malina and Julian Beck. Dedicated to the undiscovered territory of the modern sensibility, they have maintained a point of view and style without regard for commercial success. During the same period the Circle-in-the-Square has tried to offer some sense of continuity, experiment, and personal growth to Jose Quintero and other promising directors. The Phoenix Theatre, now in its tenth year, experimented for one season with a permanent director, Stuart Vaughan, and a permanent company made possible by Ford Foundation grants. The Phoenix has attained a high degree of professional production, chalking up several artistic successes despite many set-backs. Most of the fleeting off-Broadway ventures lack the stability that can come only from a kind of personal commitment and social awareness rarely found either off or on Broadway.

The total involvement demanded by the theater of the director was voiced in one of the early manifestoes of the Group Theatre: "In the end, however, the development of playwrights, actors, repertory and the rest are important only as they lead to the creation of a tradition of common values, an active consciousness of a common way of looking at and dealing with life. A theater in our country today should aim to create an audience. When an audience feels that it is really at one with a theater; when audience and theater-people feel that they are both the answer to one another, and that both may act as leader to one another, there we have the Theater in its truest form. To create such a Theater is our real purpose."

It was out of the impulse to create such a theater that the director originally came into being. The absence of shared values and a casual rather than a consecrated audience meant that integrated theater could not spontaneously emerge. Missing from our depersonalized society were the collective experiences basic to the theaters that we take as our ideal. The director as a single creative force tried to organize the conditions necessary for "theater in its truest form." Within the proscenium frame or in the reconstructed arena, he forced the varied arts to blend harmoniously. By his artistic vitality and omnipotence he often made it possible for the stage to reflect the kaleidoscopic images of modern life. The great directors, who were not content simply to sell their skill on a play-to-play basis, organized their own companies or committed their talent to institutions dedicated to something larger than their own vanity. Even when they achieved their aspirations on the microcosm of the stage, they were frustrated by the realm beyond the footlights in their basic intention of restoring the communal idea of theater. To make these two worlds one remains the challenge of the theater of tomorrow.

2
Vision and Method

GEORGE II, DUKE OF SAXE-MEININGEN
(1826-1914)

Pictorial Motion

In composing a stage effect, it is important to keep the middle of the picture from being congruent with the middle of the stage. If one follows the geometric principle of the golden mean, the stage divides into two even parts, which is likely to lead to monotony in the distribution and grouping. Assimilation in the total picture becomes more or less symmetrical, creating a wooden, stiff and boring impression.

(The charm of Japanese art can be largely attributed to their avoidance of symmetry. *"L'ennui naquit un jour de l'uniformité,"* Boileau remarked about art in general. In the graphic arts, the uniformity the French esthetes call "the mother of boredom" is symmetry.)

The exception proves the rule; the grouping of the principal figure —or the principal mass of figures—in the center can work out if the neighboring figures or groups are placed on the side at more or less regular intervals. It can create a happy artistic effect, particularly if a powerfully exalted mood is desired. (One is reminded of the Sistine Chapel. There the picture is one of leisurely rest.) But the stage must always depict movement, the continuous unfolding of a story. That is why this method is to be generally avoided, as it creates a lifeless effect and holds up the action.

It rarely works to have a figure dead center. Scenery and other

Quoted by Max Grube: *Geschichte der Meininger*. Stuttgart: Deutsche Verlags-Anstalt, 1926, 51-58.

objects are to be placed whenever possible on the sides, of course at a certain distance from the wings, and so as to be visible to the audience.

The actor must never stand dead center directly in front of the prompter, but always slightly to the left or right of his box.

The middle foreground of the stage, about the width of the prompter's box, from the footlights to the background, should be considered by the actor merely as a passageway from right to left or vice versa; otherwise he has no business there.

Likewise, two actors should avoid standing in similar relation to the prompter's box.

One should give special attention, also, to the relative position of the actor and the scenery. That relation must be correct.

Directors are frequently remiss in not paying enough attention to the actor's relation to the scenery—the trees, buildings, etc., which are painted in perspective. It is of course impossible to be free of all error, since every time a live actor—whose physical proportions are unchanging—takes a step backward, he appears proportionately bigger with respect to the painted sets. But such errors can be kept down to a minimum, and flagrant violations can be avoided.

Thus, when going toward a set depicting a receding street or any other background perspective, the actor should not walk so close that the physical disproportion becomes conspicuous. He should not—as so often is the case—stand directly in front of a painted house, where the door reaches as high as his hips, where without extending himself he can look into the second-story windows, and where, when he raises his arm, he can touch the chimney.

Set pieces toward which the actor must walk should always have at least approximately the correct dimensions relative to the human beings on stage. That is why, for example, the temple in Goethe's *Iphigenie auf Tauris* should be placed 'way downstage so that the pillars, which can extend almost to the top of the flies, tower over the human figures. It is not a question of allowing the audience to get a full view of the temple from top to bottom. It is enough if they can see a part of the colonnade, the end of a joist, and a section of the roof, whereas the rest—the crown of the pediment—can be concealed in the foliage of the trees in the flies.

Similarly, the balcony in *Romeo and Juliet* is usually situated much too low. The fact that Juliet may be a little too high up if the balcony is built at about the proper height is less of a drawback than the conventional way of setting the scene. Usually, when the balcony is rather low, the audience is disturbed at the thought that Romeo, even if he is not an especially good athlete, has only to make one leap to reach his "unattainable" beloved and hold her in his arms.

Actors should never lean against painted pieces of scenery (pillars and the like). If they move about freely, they cannot help touching the painted piece, thus causing it to shake and destroying the stage illusion; if they move about very carefully so as not to disturb the canvas flat, their stage business conveys a feeling of constraint and they perform in an obviously self-conscious manner.

Set pieces on which the actor can lean or sit (such as doorposts, tree trunks, and the like) must be made of resistant materials, and they must be plastic objects. As a matter of fact, this is usually the case in all our better modern theaters today.

When both painted and sculptured pieces are used on the stage, the director should see to it that the different materials employed do not achieve two different effects which are disturbing to the audience. Transitions from natural or artificial flowers to painted ones, for example, must be made with unusual smoothness, so that the one can hardly be distinguished from the other.

It is completely unartistic, even absurd, when, for example, the one rose that has to be plucked from a rosebush is a palpable flower (whether real or artificial) whereas all the rest are painted roses; or when, in the workshop of the *Violin-Maker of Cremona,* one sees a half-dozen violins painted on the back flat together with their shadows and there, right in the midst of them, is the real violin with its real shadow. In addition to everything else, this honest-to-goodness violin seems out of proportion alongside the painted violins and appears to be too large, more like a viola than a violin.

It is a mistake to try to harmonize walk-ons with what is painted in perspective on the flats at the rear of the stage. In the scene of the building of Zwing-Uri in Schiller's *Wilhelm Tell,* for example, young-sters made up and dressed like building workers will not give the impression of adults simply because they are 'way upstage. All the motions and gestures of children are quite different from those of grownups. Moreover, the blurring of contours and the softening of colors, which nature achieves by means of distance and which painting can reproduce, cannot be achieved by live persons moving about on the stage. Living beings are much more sharply defined than painted objects. Hence what the audience sees are not adults reduced in size by the perspective of distance but tiny gnomelike creatures, children made up to look like old men.

Strips of canvas, carefully cut, painted blue, and running diagonally above the stage—in stage parlance, "ozones"—should never be used. In landscape sets, you should always use trees with a broad expanse of branches that arch above the stage picture and set it in relief. Usually, these arched effects can also be used for city, street, or market scenes. Often too the action permits one to string garlands of flowers or flags, pennants, and streamers above streets and squares. If that is not feasible and the sky must appear above the stage, painted clouds in the flies are always preferable to blue strips. Monotonous-looking, ugly blue "ozones" should not be found in any reputable scene designer's storeroom.

Generally, the first rehearsals of a new play with crowd scenes and a large cast make the director's hair stand on end. He almost doubts the possibility of bringing to life and molding this rigid, inflexible mass. It helps him a great deal in this task to have the scenery unchanged from the beginning. Changing the sets, rehanging certain parts of the scenery, moving the furniture during the rehearsals slows up everything, gets on the director's nerves, bores his co-workers and puts them to sleep.

In costume plays, weapons, helmets, arms, swords, etc., must be used as soon as possible, so that the actor is not encumbered by the unusual handling of heavy armor during the performance.

With these plays it is obligatory that the actors rehearse in costume even before the dress rehearsal, which only differs from the opening night by the exclusion of the public. He should wear either his own costume, or if it is not yet ready, or has to be saved, one distinctly similar in cut. The actors must have, for many rehearsals before the dress rehearsal, the same headgear, coats, trains, etc., or at least costumes like the ones they will wear at the performance. The performance should not present the actor with any unforeseen or surprising situation. The spectator must be given the opportunity of becoming accustomed to the unusual apparel of the past. The actor should not, by his appearance or gestures, give the impression of wearing some costume the wardrobe mistress has just handed him; one must not be reminded of a costume ball or a carnival.

Carriage and gestures are influenced by changing from modern clothes to those of the past. Our perfectly familiar way of standing with heels together, which is the accepted one for the military at a halt, and which civilians also use in greeting superior and notable people, looks out of place in older costumes—from the ancient Greek period to the Renaissance—and is completely wrong. This position, heel to heel, seems to have been introduced along with the step of the minuet. A peasant leader cannot stand like an *Abbé galant* from the time of wigs, or with clicked heels, like a lieutenant in a modern drawing room.

The natural, correct and visually satisfying posture in costume from the days of pigtails on, is feet apart and placed one in front of the other.

The general rule is: all parallels on the stage are to be avoided as much as possible. This applies to costume plays in certain ways as well.

Spears, halberds, lances, javelins, etc., should never be carried pointing in the same direction as the modern guns and bayonets of our infantry and cavalry. There should be a certain freedom in the holding of old weapons; they should not be held at even intervals or point in the same direction. Here, they should be made to crowd each other, there be further apart, not perpendicular but at an angle and intersecting.

Any helmet, not antique, worn by an actor must be pulled down over the forehead until only the muscle above the eyebrows is visible. The popular way of wearing it on the back of the head and neck is tenor-style and does not belong in the theater. Our costumed heroes and lovers are undoubtedly afraid of disturbing their ringlets by pulling a helmet on correctly. But we can't be affected by that!

The use of parallels is particularly bad in relating the position of one actor with another. Since the parallel position of a single person, facing the footlights squarely, is bad; so two or three actors of approximately the same height doing likewise will give a most disagreeable impression.

Nor should an actor move in a parallel line. For example, an actor moving from forward right to left forward should, by imperceptible and subtle means, break the straight line, not the best on the stage, by moving on a diagonal.

If three or more actors play a scene together, they should never be placed in a straight line. They must stand at angles to each other. The space between the individual actors must always be uneven. Regular intervals create a sense of boredom and lifelessness like figures on a chessboard.

It is always an advantage to have an actor touch a piece of furniture or some other near-by object naturally. That enhances the impression of reality.

Should the stage have different levels—steps, an uneven floor strewn with rocks, and the like—the actor must remember to give his posture a rhythmical, living line. He must never stand with both feet on the same step. He should, if there is a stone close by, stand with one foot on it. Should he be walking down stairs and for some reason—such as having to speak a line or notice some object—be obliged to stop, one foot should always be placed lower than the other. By this device, his entire appearance takes on freedom and ease. "One foot off the ground," should be the director's theme song in such cases.

The handling of crowds on the stage requires a special preparation.

Hardly any theater exists that can afford to use its own personnel as walk-ons. With the exception of the chorus and the so-called supers, among whom there frequently exist some well-trained actors who feel at home on the stage and can act, a considerable crowd has to be used, for whom these rehearsals and performances are only a side line, and who must be paid each time. Among this fluctuating crowd whom the director does not know, occasionally are found a few usable people who can take direction, understand what is said to them and are not too clumsy in rehearsals. Naturally, one also finds a completely un-usable element, with whom nothing can be done, who are awkward and ridiculous and who sometimes even follow their own inspiration, want to act their way and cause great disruption. It is the first job of the director to sort out of this crowd, and as soon as possible, the talented from the untalented, separating the goats from the sheep. The doubtful and naïve ones must only serve as padding.

The walk-ons should then be divided into small groups and trained separately.

Each group is then led by an experienced actor or member of the chorus, who acts as "cover" and stands in front of them on the stage. It is in a way the responsibility of this leader to see to it that the group entrusted to him follows orders. He is responsible to the director in seeing that the positions, gestures, etc., are taken at the right moment.

The leader is given cues and certain general directions from the script such as "noise, tumult, murmurs, cries, etc." These are then translated into words by the director and must be learned by heart. These interpolations should naturally be dealt with in various ways and should never be handled in unison.

The job of these leaders is not an easy one. It is a pity and some-times an artistic error that these "actors" of the group consider their responsibility inferior and unworthy of a real artist. They rid them-selves of the job wherever possible, or brush it off and at the per-formance make obvious their lack of enthusiasm.

At Meiningen, various artists without exception are used as lead-ers of walk-ons. The amazing effectiveness of first-night performances at Meiningen can be largely attributed to the lively participation of the crowds. This is in contrast to the awkward, wooden apathy of the supers to which we had accustomed ourselves and which makes such a disastrous impression.

The ugly and erroneous positions of individual actors in relation to each other are particularly disturbing in crowd scenes. The chief charm of groups is in the line of the heads. Just as a similarity of posture is to be avoided, so a regularity of height in actors standing near each other is, wherever possible, to be shunned. When it can be done, individuals should stand on different levels. Some can kneel, some stand near by, some bending, some upright. It is effective to have those looking at one person or situation form an uneven semicircle whenever it can be done.

Care must be taken that the actors nearest to the public and seen most by the spectators stand so that their shoulders are in various relations to the footlights. One should remind a walk-on to change his position as soon as he notices himself standing like his neighbor. In a good picture, one finds few figures in the same position or facing the same way. One has to repeat this order to the actors and supers at nearly every rehearsal, as it is continuously forgotten.

Special reminders must be given the supers not to stare at the audience. They do this naturally, since for many of them acting is a new and unusual experience, and their aroused curiosity makes them look around the dark auditorium.

Disturbing events like the removal of dead or wounded people should be "covered," meaning kept as much as possible from the audience's sight. This must not be done by means of a thick impenetrable wall of people, which looks self-conscious and ridiculous. The "cover" must be rather flexible so that one sees enough and not too much of what is taking place and can understand what it is all about.

When the impression of a great crowd is desired, one should place the groups so that the people on the sides are lost in the shadows of the wings. No one in the audience can be permitted to see where the grouping stops. The grouping must give the illusion that other crowds are also forming behind the scene.

Translated by Helen Burlin

ANDRÉ ANTOINE
(1858-1943)

Behind the Fourth Wall

First of all, what is directing? One of the most authoritative men of our time, Monsieur Porel, speaking at the International Theater Congress of 1900, has defined our art in terms that are so precise and well chosen that I feel it a duty and a pleasure to quote his comments:

Without directing, without this respectful and precise science, this powerful and subtle art, many plays would not have come down to us; many comedies would not be understood; many plays would not enjoy success.

To grasp clearly the author's idea in a manuscript, to explain it patiently and accurately to the hesitant actors, to see the play develop and take shape from minute to minute. To watch over the production down to its slightest details, its stage business, even its silences, which are sometimes as eloquent as the written script. To place the bewildered or awkward supernumeraries where they belong and to train them, to bring together in one cast obscure actors and stars. To harmonize all these voices, all these gestures, all these various movements, all these dissimilar things—in order to achieve the right interpretation of the work entrusted to you.

Then, having accomplished this and having methodically done all your preliminary studying in the calm of your library, to take charge of the material side of production. To supervise patiently and accurately the carpenters, scene-painters, costumers, upholsterers, and electricians.

Then when this second part of the job is finished, to fuse it with the first by making the cast perform with real furniture and props. Finally, to view the finished production at arm's length, as a whole. To take into account

André Antoine: "Causerie sur la mise en scène," *La Revue de Paris*, Vol. X, April 1, 1903, 596-612.

the tastes and habits of the audience in just the right proportions, to omit anything that may be needlessly dangerous, to cut anything that is too long, to eliminate errors of details that are inevitable in any work that is done quickly.

To listen to advice from interested parties, to weigh it in the mind, to decide when to follow and when to reject their advice. Finally, with a quickening of the heart, to open one's hand, give the signal, let the work appear before so many assembled people! It is an admirable profession, is it not? One of the most curious, one of the most fascinating, one of the most subtle in the world!

I shall certainly not make any effort to find a clearer or more artistic formula. In my opinion, modern directing must perform the same function in the theater as descriptions in a novel. Directing should—as, in fact, is generally the case today—not only fit the action in its proper framework but also determine its true character and create its atmosphere.

This is an important task—and one that is completely new—for which our classical French theater has done little to prepare us. The result is that, despite the wealth of effort expended these past twenty years, we have not yet formulated any principles, laid down any foundations, established any teaching methods, trained any personnel.

A few independent-minded innovators in the theater—Montigny, Perrin, and Porel—have shown initiative, under the stress of the growing needs of contemporary stage production. They have begun to break the old molds; but the results have been slow to appear. These results have been paralyzed by throwbacks to classicism in the individuals themselves as well as in the people under them.

Taught by them and under their direct influence, we have been able, for other reasons, to continue the work that was initiated. In my own case, I was influenced by the new needs and new conditions in the freer and more living works submitted to me by my associates in the Théâtre Libre.

I entered the theater quite late—when I was close to thirty. I was rejected by the Conservatoire to which I had instinctively applied in order to draw inspiration from such masters as Got and Coquelin, whose genius dazzled me. To compensate for my lack of experience, I was fortunate enough not to be weighed down by old traditions or hampered by routine methods. I learned about the theater by following logic and common sense—as must have been the case in bygone days, when the theater first developed.

For a long time—some fifteen years—during my spare time as a white-collar employee with a passionate curiosity about things of the theater, I realized that the actor's "profession" and the complacency of audiences had stifled all simplicity, life, and naturalness—in the matter of directing as well as acting.

Experience is the best teacher. Since everyone around me—playwrights and actors—was new, without preconceived notions or falsified traditions, we did our best in what we felt was the truest, clearest manner. Thus experience and practice preceded theory.

Here I must reiterate: directing is an art that has just been born. Nothing—absolutely nothing—prior to the past century with its theater of intrigue and situation, led to its flowering.

Without going back to the earliest examples of our dramatic literature—ceremonies that arose from the church and remained solemn events held in the open air—we may say that the classical French theater did not, for several centuries, need "staging," in the sense in which we use the term.

A simple backdrop was enough to denote a palace, a public square, or a drawing room.

As far as the actor was concerned, often he received a court costume from the king or one of the high nobility (thus, Richelieu gave Bellecoeur a knight's costume in which to create the role of the Cid); and the actor's sole ambition was to appear in a splendid costume before a chosen audience and to recite his part rather than to play it or live it. . . .

Nevertheless, drama continued to evolve. A theater of intrigue and material situations appeared, a theater which took into account the social status and daily life of its characters. Unity of place was violated. Figaro leaped through windows and Count Almaviva broke down doors. Hugo published his preface to *Cromwell* and the great

Alexander Dumas joined with him. The Middle Ages replaced antiquity. Tragic episodes and heroic combats were no longer the themes of the stage: Hernani fenced, Saint-Mégrin looked up at the stars before going to see the Duchesse de Guise, and Ruy Blas pushed pieces of furniture in front of the doors of his low-ceilinged room before dying in peace. Géronte, Célimène, and Sganarelle gave way to Marguerite Gautier, Giboyer, and Poirier. Actors ate on the stage, slept there, sat down on their bed to dream—as did Chatterton. Directing was born and thenceforth became a faithful servant of dramatic production.

Acting itself, always lagging, began to change. Frédéric no longer acted in the style of Talma, although he was just as great; and the romantic "white plume"—in reality, a striving for truth, for life—made audiences forget rhetorical declamation of tragedy.

But if you bear in mind Porel's outline of the work that is necessary in producing a play, you can just imagine what ceaseless efforts and what tireless patience are needed in order to achieve truth and life!

Apparently, the audience has no idea of the labor that goes into a play it has just applauded. In the theater, after the fifth or sixth performance, many persons imagine that the physical arrangement of the scenes and the movements of the characters are left to chance or to the initiative of the actors.

The better the play is acted and the more lifelike it seems, the more convinced is the naïve spectator of this supposition. He has no idea of the slow and complicated work of rehearsals. . . .

Let us begin now at the beginning. The producer, after assigning the actors their parts, gives the script to the director. From that point on, the latter is in charge.

I have purposely made a sharp distinction between these two: the producer and the director. Generally speaking, our producers assume these two functions. But they are quite distinct and require talents that are almost always incompatible.

To be a producer, first of all, is a profession. To be a director—or *metteur en scène*—is an art.

In our time, the profession of producer demands above all the qualities of a manager, a businessman; if, in addition, our producer has a little boldness and, by chance, the desire to hunt for interesting works, if through experience he acquires that special flair for "hits," then he will not find the day long enough for his many tasks.

On the other hand, the director or *metteur en scène* must remain free of any financial worries or calculations. Many producers, taken up with the problems I have just mentioned, have a director on their pay roll—almost always a veteran actor or one who has not had much success. They use him to sketch out the staging, to do the preliminary work which they probably consider of little interest. They are wrong. They fail to realize that these first hours are crucial: later, when they step into the picture, it is too late. The play has already taken shape and is in a definite mold. Would a painter give someone else the job of drawing the sketch for a picture he wanted to paint?

In other theaters—at the Comédie Française, for example—one of the actors in the cast, the most "talented" or the most famous, is given the task of conducting rehearsals. This is likewise a bad method: a talented actor is not necessarily endowed with the qualities that make him a good director. Many great artists are often unfit for that job; their personal temperament and the creative instinct which is their forte deprive them of one of the essential faculties of a true director: a view of the whole. No matter how hard he tries, an actor sees only his own part; and if he is the director, unconsciously but nonetheless surely he will increase the scope and importance of that part—to the detriment of all the others. A mediocre actor who is not in the cast is always superior, on the other side of the footlights, to the noted artist playing on the stage.

The difficulty lies in finding artistic men of the theater who are willing to confine themselves to this exciting but obscure work. In some countries, where the value of this teamwork has been more quickly recognized than here in France, the director's name appears on the playbill.

Remember that such a man must have the actors in the palm of his hand and that actors, in Molière's words, are "strange animals to drive." To obtain the maximum from them—not only in effort but also in results—one must know them and live with them. Methods of work and ways of acting differ with each artist, according to his temperament or character. It is a little world all its own, a nervous and impressionable world, which has to be now coaxed and now scolded.

Many actors, through negligence or especially because of shyness, use every possible excuse to try to get out of working, as a thoroughbred sometimes refuses to jump over a hurdle. It is quite an art and also a pleasure to persuade them—for they are almost always the most gifted and the most interesting actors.

Others, touchy and vain, must be guided, advised, and convinced without their being aware of it.

In short, directing is a career by itself—an amusing but subtle kind of diplomacy. Then too, when you realize that the director must also understand the author, feel his work, transcribe it, transpose it, and interpret to every one of the actors the part assigned to him, you will understand why I am so keen to see this special kind of career develop in our country, why I am so desirous of developing this personnel which we do not now have. Great producers are not those who have made millions but those I have mentioned above. I prefer to call them great directors, for they have molded artists, developed talents, and created new modes of expression.

The first time I had to direct a play, I saw clearly that the work was divided into two distinct parts: one was quite tangible, that is, finding the right *décor* for the action and the proper way of grouping the characters; the other was impalpable, that is, the interpretation and flow of the dialogue.

First of all, therefore, I found it useful, in fact, indispensable, carefully to create the setting and the environment, without worrying at all about the events that were to occur on the stage. For it is the environment that determines the movements of the characters, not the movements of the characters that determine the environment.

This simple sentence does not seem to express anything very new; yet that is the whole secret of the impression of newness which came from the initial efforts of the Théâtre Libre.

Since our theater has the bad habit of assigning the actors to their first places in an empty theater on a bare stage, before the sets are built, we are constantly thrown back on the four or five classic "positions," more or less elaborated according to the director's taste or the scene designer's talent, but always identically the same.

For a stage set to be original, striking, and authentic, it should first be built in accordance with something seen—whether a landscape or an interior. If it is an interior, it should be built with its four sides, its four walls, without worrying about the fourth wall, which will later disappear so as to enable the audience to see what is going on.

Next, the logical exits should be taken care of, with due regard for architectural accuracy; and, outside the set proper, the halls and rooms connecting with these exits should be plainly indicated and sketched. Those rooms that will only be partly seen, when a door opens slightly, should be furnished on paper. In short, the whole house—and not just the part in which the action takes place—should be sketched.

Once this work is done, can you see how easy and interesting it is, after examining the landscape or an interior from every one of its angles, to choose the exact point at which we shall have to cut in order to remove the famous fourth wall, while retaining a set that is most authentic in character and best suited to the action?

It is very simple, is it not? Well, we do not always proceed in that manner—either through negligence, or lack of time, or because we press into service old sets that have been used in other plays. Yet it is only too true that you can never stage a play well in an old set.

Once we have sketched the four-sided plan, according to the method outlined above, it may be that the whole apartment is not absolutely necessary for the action. In modern life, in our living rooms, bedrooms, and studies, the floor plan as well as the nature of our occupations causes us unconsciously to live and work in certain places rather than in others. In winter, we are more apt to gather around a fireplace or a stove; in summer, on the contrary, we are drawn toward the sunlit windows, and we instinctively go there to read or breathe.

You will understand how important these considerations gradually become when you have to build your set. The Germans and the English do not hesitate: they combine, cut, and ingeniously break up space, so as to present in the central portion of the stage picture nothing but the fireplace, window, desk, or corner they need.

These settings—so picturesque, so alive, with such novel and intimate charm—are sadly neglected in France because our scene designers are still influenced, in spite of everything, by the traditional heritage of our classical theater. They feel that the eye will not tolerate a lack of symmetry.

Their hidebound timidity is all the more inexcusable in that our architects, within the small land areas at their disposal, have built modern houses with unusual designs and broken lines; and to the scene designer these can be an inexhaustible source of picturesqueness and variety.

I shall deliberately pass over the actual building of our set. A detailed study of the various questions involved would lead us too far afield: the use of different woods, of iron, of cloth or paper, and of woodwork in relief, which the English frequently utilize.

Yet I must confess that several experiments I have made have failed to give any appreciable results. Thus, genuine wallpaper, upholstered fabrics, leather, woodwork paneling, expensive and perishable cardboards do not alter the general look of the set much; and frequently, since they light up badly, they simply look as though they were painted.

Nevertheless, ceilings in relief and visible beams give a sense of solidity and weight which was unknown in the make-believe painting of the old stage sets. It is also of considerable practical value, both for the actor's ease of mind and the authenticity of the set, to fashion complete doorframes and window frames. . . .

Now our set is built, with its four walls. Before rehearsing his actors on the stage, our director must walk across it many times and conjure up all the action which is to take place on it. He must also furnish it sensibly and logically, decorating it with all the familiar objects which the inhabitants of the place use, even outside the action of the play itself, in the time-lapses between acts.

This operation, conducted painstakingly and lovingly, gives life to the set. The pieces of furniture are placed where they belong, still without any attention being paid to the audience; and later, when the fourth wall disappears, they will give the most picturesque effects.

Much progress, however, remains to be made. For a long time our scene designers painted beds, tables, and fireplaces in perspective; but, yielding to the insistent desire for real-life things which audiences have shown these past ten years, our present-day designers have displayed an excess of zeal. They have provided far too many pieces of furniture and made them just as real as could be; but they have failed to realize that these pieces of furniture are never in the proper proportions to the set, and that flawless staging would require furniture built in perspective.

Moreover, we have to struggle against two of the basic improbabilities of our modern stage settings: the height of the set, which we cannot lower without risking the danger that spectators in the upper balconies will not see part of the play, and the width of the frame. There used to be a third difficulty, which fortunately is fast disappearing from all our theaters: the deadly proscenium arch! Soon it will be nothing but a sad memory, and the nightmare of scene designers.

In using furniture, we must devise ways of eliminating that peculiar impression of emptiness which comes from frameworks that are too wide. In this field, at least, we have made much progress with the means at hand. Memories of the classical theater no longer paralyze us; we have gone far beyond the single-table set in *Tartuffe*.

The question of painted props has also been successfully solved. Today, an object painted on a flat disturbs and distracts the eye of even the most inexperienced theatergoer. Occasionally, it still happens that some of our scene designers surreptitiously slip vines, simulated flowers, or shrubbery into a landscape or outdoor set. But directors are on guard against such practices. How often have geraniums or creeping vines been eliminated from an attractive set just as soon as they were discovered!

In our interior sets, we must not be afraid of an abundance of little objects, of a wide variety of small props. Nothing makes an interior look more lived in. These are the imponderables which give a sense of intimacy and lend authentic character to the environment the director seeks to re-create.

Among so many objects, and with the complicated furnishings of our modern interiors, the performers' acting becomes, without their realizing it and almost in spite of themselves, more human, more intense, and more alive in attitudes and gestures.

And now the lights!

Here there is always a lively controversy, which still makes the ghost of Sarcey shudder. Most of our directors still favor the crude, glaring light of footlights and spotlights—except for a few night effects obviously called for in the script.

Nevertheless, our lighting equipment is markedly improving every day. We have come a long way from the sorry-looking candles, tapers, oil lamps, and gaslights—in this field we have made steady, uninterrupted progress.

For light is the life of the theater, the good fairy of the *décor,* the soul of the staging. Light alone, intelligently handled, gives atmosphere and color to a set, depth and perspective. Light acts physically on the audience: its magic accentuates, underlines, and marvelously accompanies the intimate meaning of a dramatic work. To get excellent results from light, you must not be afraid to use and spread it unevenly.

The audience, even though it is thrilled by a beautiful stage set skillfully lighted, is not yet at the point where it can forego discerning clearly the face and the slightest gestures of a favorite actor. We know your aversion for those carefully prepared effects in half darkness; yet far from spoiling your impression, these effects really safeguard it, without your suspecting it. So we directors must stand our ground and make no concessions in that respect. One day we shall be right: the broad public will finally realize or feel that, to create a stage picture, values and harmonies are needed which we cannot obtain without sacrificing certain parts. The audience will realize that it gains thereby a deeper and more artistic general impression. . . .

Now the second part of our work begins. We can now bring on the characters: their home is ready, full of life and brightness.

But here, in the guise of traditions, we are going to encounter all the routines, all the resistances, the whole crippling heritage of the past. They have given us statues—and we need living, moving human beings. We have to make characters live their daily lives—and we get men and women who have been taught that in the theater, as contrasted with real life, one must never speak while walking. So they insist on speaking out at the audience, just as they did two hundred and fifty years ago; they get out of character to comment on or emphasize what the playwright has put in their mouth. They have been taught (in that same old pompous style!) that they must have the proper inflection, declaim according to the rules, recite their lines elegantly so as not to sound vulgar and familiar. They have learned to play up effects of detail, even though these have no interest or meaning in the over-all picture, and they strive with all their might to win applause from the audience by using every device and trick of the trade.

To interpret the character they are supposed to portray, they have only two instruments at their disposal: voice and face. The rest of their body does not participate in the action. They wear gloves and are always superbly groomed; and, since they no longer have the elaborate or majestic costumes of a former age, they wear rings or a flower in their buttonhole.

Rigorously trained in the primitive and rudimentary movements of our classical theater, ruined forever by scenes of "furies" and "dreams," they ignore the complexity, the variety, the nuances, the life of modern dialogue—its turns of phrase, its subtle intonations, its overtones, its eloquent silences.

That is a true picture of almost all our beginners after they have finished their course in dramatic art. Every year we see dozens of them graduate and bury themselves in some small town, loaded down with this outmoded baggage which will plague them for the rest of their career.

The best of our acting personnel (I am not, of course, speaking of the Comédie Française, whose artists are trained solely, and rightfully so, to interpret the classics) are recruited from among actors who have risen in the ranks. They have developed themselves, by contact with audiences and in the serious work of laborious rehearsals. They may stammer, as did Dupuis, Réjane, or Huguenet; but they do not "recite." They live their parts; and they are the marvelous interpreters of our contemporary drama.

These actors know:

That movement is the actor's most intense means of expression;

That their whole physical make-up is part of the character they represent, and that at certain moments in the action their hands, their back, and their feet can be more expressive than any oral ranting;

That every time the actor is revealed beneath the character, the dramatic continuity is broken;

And that by emphasizing a word, they often destroy its effect.

They know too that every scene in a play has a movement all its own, subordinated in turn to the general movement of the play; and that nothing must disturb a group effect—neither a glance at the prompter nor any attempt at individual "mugging."

Finally, they make their characters come alive before our eyes; they faithfully depict for us every aspect of their characters, the material as well as the spiritual.

The high-flown style, that everlasting curse of all the arts, which has always been opposed to truth and life, is no longer here to plague us; and the theater of manners, the comedies of character, and the social plays of our time have found their true interpreters in these actors.

The stilted teachings of the Conservatoire, indiscriminately inculcated in whole generations of young people whose ambition is a single theater that will not use one out of ten of them, have victimized an untold number of beginners. Such institutions falsify and level tem-

peraments: they take all the young talents of which the modern theater has such an urgent need and stamp them haphazardly in the
mold of their classical heroes.

There are many other things I should have liked to discuss: crowds,
their means of expression, their shouts, the way they are grouped. . . .
But I shall have to refrain. This "chat" has already lasted too long.

I should have liked to express all my admiration for the classical
theater and the amazement I feel when I see that many are seriously
considering the possibility of rejuvenating it by modernizing the
staging of classical plays.[1] I, on the contrary, if ever I have the honor
to direct in a state theater, should like to turn back and restore our
masterpieces within the true framework they require: that of their
own time. I should like to see Racine played with the court costumes
of that period, in simple and harmonious sets, without any external
trappings that might lessen the impact of Racine's genius.

Since Nero speaks of sometimes panting at the feet of Julia, since
Orestes sighs, I should like to redesign for them those majestic costumes which go so well with their frenzies and their passionate loves.

Any attempt at local color or historical accuracy in such masterpieces appears to me futile: in the eyes of a contemporary of Pericles,
Lekain or Talma would have seemed as little a Greek as Baron. I
firmly believe that we change the meaning of those marvelous tragedies when we try to "situate" them—either in the country or the
period in which they arose. I cannot conceive of the exquisite temple
of the Winged Victory sacrilegiously torn out of the context of the
splendid landscape it dominates; and I wish that I could have seen
the "Night Watch" in the smoke-filled hall in which it was hung.
I am sure that it shone more resplendently there than it does now,
mounted beneath a red velvet canopy in the Amsterdam Museum.

Those of us who have not had the great good fortune to be called
and trained to interpret and preserve the theatrical art of the past

[1] This apparent reluctance to modernize the classics is probably due to the fact
that Antoine was seeking the directorship of the Odeon at the time these remarks
were published.

are satisfied to serve, with all that is in us, the theater of today. We must simply strive to do our best by experimenting as much as possible.

If we discover something really solid and lasting, we shall have added to the common heritage. *La Parisienne*—with a husband who talks about his rent, his children's pants, and a job as tax collector—must not be directed and played like *Le Misanthrope*. Yet it is—I hope and I believe—no less a masterpiece in the history of the theater, a glorious link in the endless golden chain.

Translated by Joseph M. Bernstein

OTTO BRAHM

(1856-1912)

Style and Substance

The form in which Sophocles' *Antigone* is now given in the German theater dates back to the 1840's. Frederick William IV gave the initial impulse; Tieck, Felix Mendelssohn, and Böckh directed and backed the production. Played first in the little theater of the New Palace in Potsdam, the piece then went to the Royal Theater and Opera House in Berlin, and from there to other German theaters.

The production at the Deutsches Theater departs in several respects from the tradition established in the 1840's. This involves distinctly different problems: the division into scenes, the chorus, and the performance style as a whole. These changes have proved popular, and many have approved of them; but others—the conservative-minded—have felt that these innovations go "too far." Personally I must confess that, on the contrary, the changes do not strike me as sufficiently radical; I feel that they do not go far enough.

Anyone who has closely followed the productions of the Deutsches Theater will quickly realize that this presentation of *Antigone* is based on the same artistic conception as that of all its previous play productions. This conception is, in a word, realism; and since the *Antigone* of the 1840's was based on an opposing conception, the divergence was bound to arise.

The tragedy, in Tieck's adaptation, was presented on a straight-

Otto Brahm: *Kritische Schriften ueber Drama und Theater.* Berlin: S. Fischer, 1913, 86-93.

line, rectangular, elevated space—supposed to correspond to the ancient Greek stage; it was played across the entire stage, beneath a colonnade. The Deutsches Theater, seeking to eliminate all stiffness and woodenness from its productions of modern drama, has also broken with this symmetrical pattern. It has learned from the Meininger to broaden or narrow its stage artistically; to make it living and livable. Thus, sharp corners have been softened; the wings have been arranged with deliberate asymmetry; the downstage playing area is connected with a second playing area upstage by means of steps. Every device has been used to achieve fullness of life. The sets for *Antigone* flout academic rules: the square in front of the Royal Palace of Thebes is, as Sophocles describes it, really an "open square," not one carefully measured off by a precise gauge; the height and width of the stage are not exactly symmetrical, and space has been left free downstage and on the sides. Trees grow, tapestries decorate the palace walls, and the over-all impression given is: here human beings can live and feel at home. The older setting, however, gave the impression: here we have good acoustics, here actors can recite their lines well.

A second change concerns the chorus. This is not grouped across the entire stage but off to one side; not just around the altar but with free play of movement. Here too it is obvious that practical considerations involving the smallness of the theater have played their part. Mendelssohn's music, however, has been retained, even though that was perhaps the most questionable feature of the older production. I do not mean the musical composition as such but its relationship to the Sophoclean spirit: here there is a disparity that always disturbs me. The fact that Maestro Böckh has finally approved of this arrangement does not set my mind at rest. Sophocles called for a speaking chorus; in the Mendelssohn music choruses are sung. And the music has something bright and gay which contradicts the basic theme of the tragedy; at times (as, for example, in "The foolhardy one atones for his foolhardy word") it sounds even operatic and frequently recurs in that same vein.

But are all our innovations, as conceived or executed, valid? Are they in keeping with the spirit of ancient Greece? Is the performance on the stage of the Deutsches Theater "genuinely" classical? That is the big question that is being asked. It is a big question indeed, for in the answer to it lies the meaning of the tragedy as performed in our theater.

We call those creations classics if they achieve a never-ending, immediate effect across the centuries. They survive the ravages of time. This does not mean, however, that they always have identical meaning for the various generations. Shakespeare's impact on his century was different from his impact on our present-day audiences. Just because he lives, he too changes, along with human beings. As we have often seen, artistic impressions from earlier periods evolve in us and with us (without there being any renewed contact with the themes treated); just as works of art rise or fall in our opinion, simply as a result of the passage of time, so too the creations of the great masters develop, as does humanity itself. But what is true of all the arts is especially true of the dramatic art; it strives to make an immediate impression on receptive but naïve audiences, who come to the theater without any complicated pretensions at literary culture. And what truer, more genuine, more striking impression can it make than if it is imbued with the same spirit as that which dominates its contemporary world? Dramatic art can only be modern—whether it presents Shakespeare or Schiller, Sophocles or Kleist. Today the realistic style is valid for all; only within this style can the nuances between previous periods and our own be skillfully brought out.

Purely practical, not theoretical, considerations lead us to this point of view. What is valid for us in the works of the classics—in *Antigone,* for example? We see that our deepest impressions are not the same as those of the ancient Greeks. *Antigone* is the nearest to us of all the Greek tragedies because within ourselves we find the same conflict as that which permeates the play: the conflict between the rights of the individual and the rights of the community, between individual emotions and reasons of state. In *Antigone* we see two equally justified attitudes opposing each other, both of them charged with passion, both high-minded and exclusive. Antigone's defiant reverence clashes with Creon's unbending rule; and the excess of her zeal proves tragic to both. But we do not see the tragedy as the Greeks did: to them, Antigone and Creon were not heroes of equal stature. Their sympathies belonged to Antigone; Creon was only the foil, the figure needed as a contrast to the protagonist. He was not a significant character in his own right. A glance at the other two plays in the trilogy confirms this: in *Oedipus Rex* and *Oedipus at Colonus,* Creon is not the powerful ruler. He is the intriguer "with spiteful mouth"; the man with "ever-nimble tongue, cunningly contriving to give everything the appearance of truth." In these plays he is nothing in and of himself; he is merely Oedipus' foil, as he was that of Antigone. To Greek audiences he could not be considered of equal rank because he was played by "the third actor," whereas Antigone's role was taken by the first actor (the *protagonist*). And just as a modern actor, playing the part of an underling, for example, can never hope to win applause from the naïver members of the audience, with the gallery gods ever ready to hiss him because of the role he portrays, so contrariwise Greek audiences were prejudiced in advance against the *tritagonist* ("the third actor") as soon as he appeared on stage to play his role.

To us the basic theme of the tragedy is quite a different one. The climax of the tragedy affects us in a wholly un-Greek way, when we witness the change of mood wrought in Creon by Tiresias the seer and view sympathetically the ruler's collapse. This transformation was what alienated Greek audiences most: in fact, only the third actor was allowed to portray such changes. In his *Technique of the Drama,* a book of finely reasoned comments which has helped shape my own thinking on the matter, Gustav Freytag writes: "The Greeks were very sensitive to vacillations of the will. The greatness of their heroes lay above all in their steadfastness. The first actor would have found it difficult to portray a character who, in any major situation, allowed himself to be dominated by other persons in the play." But we, in our Deutsches Theater production, are deeply moved when Creon, shattered by the terrible words of the seer, goes to pieces and cries out: "Woe! Woe!" at the prospect of the downfall of his dynasty.

The powerful realistic coloring of the production reinforces this impression. And we offer still another simple observation in support of our frankly modern style of presentation. To present the classics in a classical manner—is that really possible? As far as the Greek theater is concerned, the question is easily answered: no one wants to transfer the mask and buskin of the antique stage to our contemporary scene. But can we really present Shakespeare in the style of his actors; can we enjoy a Hamlet as Burbage played him? Today we do not even see our own German dramatists—Goethe and Schiller, for example—the way their contemporaries and the next generation after that saw them. We hear them, not in the accents of Esslair and Emil Devrient, but in those of Sonnenthal and Kainz. The former were modern in their day, the latter modern in our day; and when Frau Crelinger and Frau Jachmann played Antigone with sweeping gestures and resounding voice, they were not acting in the Greek style, as they thought, but in the style of their time—only at that time the Weimar style prevailed, and today's theater calls for the realistic style. But reactionaries in the theater, intent on clinging to the outworn, get bogged down in hollow conventions and so miss the truth of life.

In that sense the *Antigone* production of the Deutsches Theater offered too little, not too much, realism. The movements of Antigone and Ismene still showed the influence of the Weimar school of acting: at times the actresses flung their arms out wide, at times they assumed rigid poses, like "frozen statues." Incidentally, it is wrong to think of these gestures as antique; as a matter of fact, stage rules forbade the Greek players to bring their arms higher than their face; and to fling them into the air was considered inexpressive. At the beginning of the play, moreover, Fräulein Gessner and Fräulein Jürgens were permitted to use Teschendorff's well-known painting as a model for their positions—in other words, a picture which certainly cannot be said to convey a genuine conception of the ancient world. It is not by these conventional gestures that Fräulein Gessner achieves her effect; it is by a very personal acting style in which, half unconsciously, her dynamic stage personality comes alive. When she wrings her hands in woe; when, summoned by Creon, she tosses her head high; when, as death approaches, her body begins suddenly to shudder—all this shows that she is completely in the part. This actress's body is more eloquent than her voice: in the latter she still has much to learn, in the way in which she builds her speeches as well as in an intelligent use of her rich organ. At the present time, she often forces her voice; and if we criticize it, it is not because it is a question of *Antigone* but because it is unaesthetic in any play. Nor has Herr Pohl as Creon mastered his diction; he falls easily into a fatal singsong. He lingers over certain individual words without any rhyme or reason and pauses at every verse ending, as if facing a barrier. He does not have the breath for the part—in the narrow as well as the broad sense of the term—and he does not convey the ruler's sense of power. But in the climax he is superb; here he becomes impassioned, he shows real feeling, and the result is excellent acting.

Herr Höcker played the Watchman with commendable art. The man's garrulousness and peasant slyness, his crude joy when he is out of danger, and his philistine show of sympathy at the sacrifice— all these traits rang true. His performance and Kainz's fiery Haemon offer the best examples of what the Deutsches Theater can do; they also show that modern realism in presentation and the style of classical drama are not mutually exclusive.

Translated by Joseph M. Bernstein

KONSTANTIN STANISLAVSKY

(1863-1938)

Creative Work with the Actor;
A Discussion on Directing

APRIL 13th AND 19th, 1936

K. S. STANISLAVSKY: . . . I am told that we must create directors, but I must say that this question has never been clear to me. My experience tells me that you cannot create a director—a director is born. It is possible to create a favorable atmosphere in which he can grow. But to take Ivan Ivanovich and make a director out of him is hardly feasible. The true director comprises within his own person a director-teacher, a director-artist, a director-writer, a director-administrator. What can we do if one has these qualifications while another has not?

If the director realizes that "I possess certain elements and lack others, but I shall try to acquire more, and in the meantime give the theater all I have"; if he does this with discernment and helps create a *collective* of directors—this might, to a certain extent, compensate for the absence of all those elements in one man. . . .

One thing is clear to me: there are directors of the *result* and directors of the *root*. We must distinguish one from the other. We need directors of the *root*. This is one of the most important requisites for the Art Theater.

K. S. Stanislavsky: *Stati, Rechi, Besedi, Pisma.* Moscow: Iskusstvo, 1953, 653-688 *passim.*

The first seeks immediate results. . . . He often takes two—three—five substances, mixes them in the retort to see what will happen. Sometimes what happens is not what is required. "How can I, the director, fix it? I can add to these elements the inorganic substance opopanax . . . I can say to the actor 'Make a good try in this passage . . . otherwise they'll blame me as director.'"

This method of work I consider a crime. If you drop opopanax into a retort containing organic substances everything will begin to boil, hiss, stink.

Hence, one or the other—*result* or *root*.

Another thing: "I, as director, produce a play and *that's* all." Or "I produce a play and in the process create an actor." There is a difference. The director might *make* a play without worrying about the actor. He can get the actor full-fledged. However, one must first create an actor's company—the plays and the theater will follow as a matter of course.

It is possible to "make" a play, to "model" a play to prove yourself a director. The actor can pass muster by a certain cleverness . . . but nothing significant will come of it so long as the actor is oblivious of the word "organic." Many have forgotten the difference between the organic and the inorganic, theatrical truth and organic truth. . . .

The question is whether you can prepare an actor with whom I can talk about his role so that, like a piece of clay, he could feel the pressure of my fingers. Not every kind of clay is fit for sculpture and it is not every actor you can talk to about art. But if we set aside this first moment, we start everything by compulsion. If a director foists upon an actor *his own*, the director's thoughts, derived from *his own* personal emotional memories, if he tells him "You must act precisely so," he does violence to the actor's nature. Does he need my emotional memories? He has his own. I must cling to his soul like a magnet and see what it contains. Then cast another magnet. I want to see the material side of him. Aha! Now I understand of what living emotional material he is constituted. There can be no other. . . .

But there is still the sequence and logic of the emotions—what about them? How can we speak of the logic and sequence of the emotions? I do not even know to what university I should turn to learn about the inner logic and sequence of the emotions. How to understand them? How to record them? I say this is *not* necessary. The business of an actor is to act. You play Romeo. *If* you were in love *what* would you *do?* Take your notebook and write "Met her at some spot, she did not look at me, I turned away offended." In this way you can fill a whole volume. You recall your life, you transfer your emotions to your role. This passion, *love,* you analyze into its component moments of logical action. All of them together consti- tute *love.* . . . To all the stages in the unfolding of the emotions there will be corresponding logical sequences. Along these stages you will step into your role, because you took from your own life everything that concerns love and you transfer it to your role. These are not merely *bits of Romeo,* they are *bits of yourself.* . . .

N. N. Litovtzeva: And when do you give the actors the necessary words?

Stanislavsky: That is the most difficult moment. I try at first not to give any words at all—all I need is the plan of the *action.* When the actor has mastered that, a certain line of *action* has matured within him which he begins to feel with his body, his muscles. When this happens the actor realizes where he is going and why. He reaches a moment when he must act *for the sake of something.* That is a very agitating moment. . . . I give them the words when they *have* to act with words. At first they can act only with thoughts. And when I see that they understand these thoughts and that they also grasp the inner logic and sequence of these thoughts, I say: "Now take the words." Then they will have a different relation to the words. They need the words not in order to memorize them by rote but to act them out. They put the words not on the muscles of their tongue, not even in the brain, but into the very soul whence the actor strives toward the *super-objective.*[1] Then the words will become super-effective.

The correct actions and the correct thoughts have been established.

[1] This term, a literal translation from the Russian, has been variously adapted by American directors as *spine* (Kazan), *action* (Clurman), etc.

Now you are nearer to the essence of the role. You have a base on which to stand.

But can you succeed without *through action*? Definitely not. This is achieved gradually, not in a formal but in an absolutely correct sense. . . .

V. G. SAKHNOVSKY: . . . Supposing that a favorable combination of circumstances makes it possible to organize an ensemble. Is it enough to train the group technically and professionally or would you make other demands on it, as for example, that the actors should be capable of analyzing the phenomena of life, that they should be broadly cultured, that they should be abreast of their age?

STANISLAVSKY: I am surprised that such a question is put to me at all. Can there be any doubt about whether we need an actor with a wide or a narrow horizon, an actor who is intelligent or one who is stupid—by all means, the broadest outlook, the most cultured. . . .

E. S. TELESHEVA: Must you explain the *super-objective* to the actor? Do you yourself define it before work begins?

STANISLAVSKY: I am afraid to make a definitive decision prematurely. There must be something of a hint first. I know where I am going—to the right or to the left. But I am looking for a device whose logic itself will lead us by the nose to the point where we must say: this is definitely the *super-objective,* there can be no other.

Suppose you play a certain scene. What is your *objective?* I want to know what you are driving at. I say to the actor: "Start playing and proceed." The first *objective* has been dissolved in the new—it is no longer needed. Let us take the next *fragment.* I discover a new circumstance. Now the foregoing *objective* is no longer useful. It has been dissolved by a more powerful solvent. My attention is already drawn to the fourth *fragment.*

Thus you go through the entire play till you reach the *super-objective.* If you found an actor who was so thoroughly steeped in the *super-objective,* who understood it so profoundly and completely that this *objective* swallowed all the *fragments* and all the subordinate *objectives* of the play, a most powerful *through action* would result and the entire role would be created largely unconsciously. Every great *objective* destroys and absorbs in itself all the preceding smaller *objectives* which recede into the subconscious. They no longer burden your mind. You take the *super-objective* and everything only serves to bring you to it.

LITOVTZEVA: Then the path is from the minor *objective* to the *super-objective?*

STANISLAVSKY: . . . Every important *objective* commands your attention completely. You do not have enough concentration to perform consciously every step of the way. Your own creative nature does it. That is true creativity. Organic nature itself, with which you cannot meddle, is the creator. But not every *super-objective* is capable of awakening our nature to creativeness. Suppose that my *super-objective* in *Hamlet* is to show the profligate mother in conflict with her son who deeply loves his father. Can such a *super-objective* satisfy? No, because I brought it down to a trivial level. I reduced it to a philistine idea. If I base the *super-objective* on a profound conception of life, that is a different thing altogether.

Imagine that I have the following *objective*. I am convinced that I, Hamlet, must cleanse the entire court, the entire world of evil and I must involve in this *objective* all the people around me in order to save my martyred father. I have undertaken an unequalled *objective,* but I fulfill it. You understand what torture, to be unable to fulfill an *objective* which could save my father. This overpowering *objective* facing a man who struggles and tosses about trying to accomplish it will of course move you more strongly than the other. . . .

I say to the actor: "Give me what is in the play, but give it to me so that it is true to the very end." Let him go over it ten times. He can don his costume only when he is one with the role and the role is one with him. But heaven forbid that the image be molded when the actor is not yet warm, not yet pliable. This is harmful to the role. The role is not yet one with him and he is not yet one with the role. That is a moment which we often miss. If, however, you want to achieve a full blending of the actor with his role, then sit him down with you at the table. He will appeal to you himself. "I have a line on the role—I would not like to spoil it—what *given circumstances* do I still lack to breathe more life into the role?"

I. Y. SUDAKOV: To be ready to mount the stage how many of these *given circumstances* does he need?

STANISLAVSKY: He will not enter the room until it is made alive by the *given circumstances*. The actor will beg you for it because he must place himself within the role. He will think: "They say I entered the wrong way. But how should I enter? What should I do? I don't know yet to whom I am going and where I came from."

"Let us talk about where you came from."

"And where did I come to?"

You tell him: "Play so that I can believe you," and he will have to go through the same process all over again.

SUDAKOV: And if he had buried his father that day, he would enter differently.

STANISLAVSKY: If he buried his father—that is one thing. If he returned drunk from a tavern—that's another. If he came from his bride—that is still a third.

He will not know how to drink a glass of tea unless he knows where he came from and why.

SUDAKOV: Then the life of the image will result from the evaluation of the *given circumstances*.

STANISLAVSKY: The result will be the life of the human body. But that is a trap. The question is not in the life of the human body. In order to create the life of the human body we must create the life of the human soul. From it you create the logic of action, you create the inner line, but give it form externally. If you go through three—four acts in a given sequence the appropriate mood will come naturally.

A moment arrives when from the fusion of the actor's personal inner truth with the truth of the role, something transpires. His head swims in the literal sense. "Where am I? Where is the role?" And right there is the beginning of the amalgamation of the actor and his role. The mood is *yours* but it also flows from the *role*. The logic of the mood is inherent in the role. The *given circumstances* are from the role. You cannot tell where you are and where the role is. There is complete amalgamation. And that is the moment of unity. . . .

SUDAKOV: You follow the line of the play.

STANISLAVSKY: I follow the facts of the play. I take the actor as such. He places himself in the *given circumstances* of the role. He has to create a characteristic image. But he remains himself. Whenever he withdraws from himself, he kills the role. You live with your emotions. Remove the emotions and the role is dead. You must remain yourself in the image. If I walk around with a sick leg am I a different man? Am I different if bitten by a bee? These are external circumstances. . . .

We are analyzing all the procedures, all the possibilities which take us to the threshold of the subconscious, which generate the subconscious reactions. The most powerful are *through action* and the *super-objective*. What is our present *objective?* Take two—three—four—five cues. You say: "I want to attract attention" and someone else will say "I try to understand what I am told." The first *objective* has here been swallowed by the second, and the third will swallow the second, and all of them will be swallowed in the end by the *super-objective*.

If now you find an actor who adheres fast to the *super-objective* and follows *through action* all the subordinate *objectives* will be resolved subconsciously.

LITOVTZEVA: It is not clear to me how each preliminary *objective* is swallowed by the subsequent one.

STANISLAVSKY: For example:

"What dost thou say?"

"Nothing, my lord: or if—I know not what."

What is Iago's *objective?*

LITOVTZEVA: To arouse suspicion.

STANISLAVSKY: And Othello's?

LITOVTZEVA: To understand Iago's hint.

STANISLAVSKY: And what is the next *objective?* Othello laughs at

Iago's words "Nothing, my lord." What then happened to the first *objective?* It was swallowed up by the second. Let us go further. You have a powerful *objective:* "to sacrifice life for the ideal woman." If your every sentence supports this *objective* you will realize how ridiculous it is to permit suspicion to fall on Desdemona. How you will laugh! But if you come upon some plausible circumstance cunningly contrived by Iago you will become perplexed. Everything will appear self-evident precisely because I cleave strongly to the *super-objective* and the *through action.* . . .

SAKHNOVSKY: The director read the play as attentively as the actor. Then the director and the actor met and followed the organic line of action which you speak about. What next? Do you go through act after act, scene after scene? What will this lead to? When does the question of the *super-objective* and *through action* arise?

STANISLAVSKY: You indicate approximately some kind of an objective. But the *super-objective* will not be found in a long time. Perhaps only at the twentieth performance. However, you do suggest to the actor a temporary *super-objective.* He will make use of it. This *objective* is not final. It indicates for the moment the necessary direction, not far from the truth, yet not the truth itself which will emerge from the study of the role in one's self and one's self in the role.

SAKHNOVSKY: And when will *through action* appear?

STANISLAVSKY: All the actors in a body will suggest it to you. If you plan it alone it may be right *formally* yet wrong as *living experience.* The actors themselves will prompt you: "Here it is, the *objective,* this is about where we must look for it." Let us look for it together with the actors. . . .

L. M. LEONIDOV: You deduce the *super-objective* from indications by the author. But if we both play the Bailiff must we both have the same *super-objective?*

STANISLAVSKY: The same one but it is somewhat different in your case. Yours is pinkish blue, mine is pinkish green.

LEONIDOV: We walk along different corridors but we arrive at the same spot.

STANISLAVSKY: That spot is in your imagination and mine. The difference is there because each is the result of the difference in our entire lives, in our emotional memories.

LEONIDOV: In the life of the Bailiff?

STANISLAVSKY: It has become your life. In your reflection it will be somewhat different from mine.

LITOVTZEVA: How then can we go on if we do not immediately know where to go? We can lose our way.

STANISLAVSKY (passing a finger around the rim of a tea glass): Here is a circle. In the center is the *super-objective*. It is the circle of your life—the role. Life begins here and death. You take this section of life (indicating part of the circle). You know the past, you have prospects for the future. You must find your way to the *super-objective*. You know it is somewhere around here (points to the center of the glass). You proceed from here, from your simple action. You know that the *super-objective* is somewhere up there in the airless space. Presently you pass around the circle and determine the center. In the final analysis you must explore what constitutes the center, the essence, the soul of your role. . . .

LEONIDOV: Can an actor concentrate the entire length of four acts? Or are there still other factors?

STANISLAVSKY: Great actors like Salvini or Yermolayeva can. Yermolayeva requires no other factors. From beginning to end her attention is concentrated both on the stage and behind the wings.

LEONIDOV: The most important thing is that on the stage no word is to be mumbled. Every sentence must be pregnant with thought. But to what extent is this possible through the length of four acts?

STANISLAVSKY: You may live with the *super-objective* but that need not prevent you from talking to someone between the acts about an unrelated subject. You do not thereby depart from your line. The line of *physical action* has a staying power; you may return to it very easily. Of course, if such a line is lacking, there will be trouble.

I have in my studio only God knows what talents—but they know how to pay attention to their work. When I said to them: "I give you just three problems: you meet, you look each other over, you get married," they told me this lightened their task so much, they had no trouble playing their parts. I found new adjustments, new situations. They made excellent actors.

LITOVTZEVA: Did you give them the *mise en scène?*

STANISLAVSKY: The worst *mise en scène* is the one given by the director. I watched them standing with their back to me doing something. I heard everything and understood everything. I could not invent another *mise en scène* like it.

I want to create a performance without any *mises en scène.* Today this wall is open and when the actor comes tomorrow he will not know which wall might be open. He might come to the theater and find that a pavilion is differently placed than it was yesterday, and all the *mises en scène* are changed. The fact that he has to improvise a *mise en scène* adds much that is unexpected and interesting. No director can invent such *mises en scène.*

Translated by Louis Lozowick

VLADIMIR NEMIROVICH-DANCHENKO

(1858-1943)

The Three Faces of the Director

A *régisseur* is a triple-faced creature:

1. the *régisseur*-interpreter; he instructs *how* to play; so that it is possible to call him the *régisseur*-actor or the *régisseur*-pedagogue;

2. the *régisseur*-mirror, reflecting the individual qualities of the actor;

3. the *régisseur*-organizer of the entire production.

The public knows only the third, because he alone is visible, in everything: in the *mises en scène,* in the design of the director, in the sounds, in the lighting, in the harmony of the crowd scenes. The *régisseur*-interpreter and the *régisseur*-mirror, however, are invisible. They have sunk themselves in the actor. One of my favorite conceptions, which I have often repeated, is the necessity of the *death* of the *régisseur* in the actor's creativeness. However much and richly the *régisseur* instructs the actor, it too often happens that the former plays the whole role to the last detail; it only remains for the actor to imitate and to transmute the whole in himself. In a word, no matter how deep and rich in content the *régisseur's* role may be in the shaping of the actor's creativeness, it is absolutely essential that not a trace of it be visible. The greatest reward that such a *régisseur* can have comes when even the actor himself forgets about what he

Vladimir Nemirovich-Danchenko: *My Life in the Russian Theatre,* translated by John Cournos. Boston: Little, Brown & Co., 1936, 155-161. By permission of Marjorie Barkentin.

has received from the *régisseur,* to such a degree that he enters into the life of all the instructions received from him.

"Except a corn of wheat fall into the ground and die, it abideth alone; but if it die, it bringeth forth much fruit." This Biblical expression, in the deepest sense, applies to the joint creativeness of the *régisseur* and the actor.

Is it necessary to say that for this the *régisseur* should possess the potentiality of an actor? Essentially, it should be said, he ought to be in a profound sense an actor of diverse parts. And if the better *régisseurs* before us—Yablochkin, Agramov—like me did not remain actors, it is evident that we were hindered by the limitation of our external expressiveness and our tremendous demands upon ourselves.

The *régisseur*-mirror's most significant ability is to perceive the individuality of the actor; to follow it uninterruptedly in the process of work; to observe how the intentions of the author and the *régisseur* are reflected in him, what he does well and what he does badly, the direction in which his imagination leads him, his desires, and to what limits it is possible to insist upon one or another solution. Simultaneously it is necessary to watch the actor's will and to direct it, without his being conscious of it; to be able without inflicting humiliation but with love and friendliness to mimic: "This is how you are doing it; is that what you intended?" so that the actor may see himself face to face, as in a mirror.

The *régisseur*-organizer brings within his horizon all the elements of the production, giving first place to the creativeness of the actors, and merges them with the whole setting into one harmonious whole. In this organizing work he is all-powerful. The servant of the actor where it is necessary to submit to his individuality, adapting himself also to the individual qualities of the artist-decorator, constantly taking into account the demands of the direction, he appears in the final reckoning the real dominator of the production.

In this, then, lies the first and most significant difference between the new and the old theater: a single will reigns in our theater. The production is permeated with a single spirit, whereas in the old theater, even to this day, there reigns the fullest divergence of directing

forces. Say, the *régisseur* has sensed the true inwardness of the theatrical essence of all the elements of the performance, say he has fused
the author with the actor—hence success. Again, he has not sensed
this essence, he has entangled himself in it, he has broken it up into
divergent elements; there may be excellent fragments in it, but in a
general way it is at odds with itself, a failure.

As I recall my activities with pupils and actors thirty years ago, I
find that the essence of my method was then what it is now. To be
sure, I have become immeasurably more experienced, my methods
have become more deliberate, more shrewd; a certain "craft" has
developed; but the basis remains the same: it is *intuition* and the
infection of the actor by it. What is this? How is it to be explained
in brief?

Once a short but remarkable dialogue passed between me and
Leonid Andreyev. When I worked over his plays, he, with uncon-
cealed sincerity, was delighted because I had succeeded in revealing
his most sensitive intentions to the actors. "Amazingly accurate. I
couldn't have done better myself!" he exclaimed. And one day he
kept his eyes fixed on me for a long time; then suddenly, with great
earnestness, he asked: "How could you have stopped writing plays
yourself, when you are in the possession of such a gift, of being able to
sense a human being and of analyzing his behavior?"

I answered something like this:

"It is possible that this gift of intuition does not go beyond literature in me, and does not extend to life as it is. It is possible that I—
forgive the high-sounding words—penetratingly see *your* attitude to
the world, your observation of life, as I also see those of Chekhov,
Dostoyevsky, and Tolstoy. It is you, the author, who from the lines
of your play whisper to me your knowledge of life, while I, with
merely a kind of sixth sense, perceive where it is the truth and where
falsehood. It is even possible that I shall enter into a dispute with you
and even prove myself to be in the right. But without your prompting as the author, it is very unlikely that I should have paused before
these living appearances, which I now so excellently analyze. But in
order to create plays oneself, it is necessary oneself to grasp at life."

When, some years afterward, we worked over Dostoyevsky and we invited several scholars from the Psychological Society to the rehearsals, they invariably said that we had nothing to learn from them, but that they had much to learn from us.

Forgive me, reader, for bragging, but in questions of theatrical art this comprehension has such a tremendous significance: true intuition! Without it, all is falsehood, all is a mutilation of the author's intention and style. But as it lends itself only with difficulty to analysis, as "images" prompted by intuition do not allow license and demand a rigid control in the selection of theatrical resources, so to this day the lords of theatrical undertakings are afraid of it and avoid it; often they simply drive it from the theater as though it were the plague. Without it matters are simpler, especially for *régisseurs* with "ingenious ideas," which is the term applied by Heine to all sorts of rubbish that finds its way into men's heads.

This conception—of accurate intuition—has to this day found no scientific formulation in theatrical art. For this reason there remains but the single alternative for rehearsals: to *infect* the actor with the intentions, images, the subtlest nuances, now by means of interpretation, now by the simple method of *showing* the actor how to execute a role.

There is but a single foundation, which very much later I formulated thus: *The law of the inner justification.* But this is far too complex to be discussed here.

Later, after Stanislavsky had transferred his *régisseur's* attention from the outer to the inner, he occupied himself, together with his assistant, *régisseur* Sulerzhitsky, with a precise definition of the elements of the creativeness of the actor. The so-called "method" of Stanislavsky found its approximation at this time. There appeared his now popular expression, "transparent action." It answers the question I have earlier put: where should the actor's temperament be directed? The deepest essence of a play or role was defined in the word "seed," more particularly the seed of scenes, the seed of a fragment.

A role was composed during the rehearsal out of a multitude of conversations of a semi-dilettantish character. At present, during the labors with my actors, I use precise definitions: "atmosphere," in which this or another scene takes place: the "physical self-consciousness" of a given character—gay, sad, ill, somnolent, indolent, cold, hot, etc.: "characterization"—an official, an actress, a society woman, a female telegraphist, a musician, etc.: the "style" of the entire setting—heroic, Homeric, epochal, comical, farcical, lyrical, etc.

But the most important domain of the rehearsing labors was something which, as it happened, Chekhov was the first to hit upon. It was during the rehearsals in St. Petersburg that Chekhov said: "They act too much. It would be better if they acted a little more as in life." In this is contained the most profound difference between the actor of our theater and the actor of the old theater. The actor of the old theater acts either *emotion:* love, jealousy, hatred, joy, etc.; or *words,* underlining them, stressing each significant one; or a *situation,* laughable or dramatic; or a *mood,* or *physical self-consciousness.* In a word, inevitably during every instant of his presence on the stage he is *acting* something, representing something. Our demands on the actor are that he should not act anything; decidedly not a *thing;* neither feelings, nor moods, nor situations, nor words, nor styles, nor images. All this should come of itself from the individuality of the actor, individuality liberated from stereotyped forms, prompted by his entire "nervous organization"—that which our Professor Speransky but lately defined by the word "trophica." For us the individuality of the actor is the immense region of his imagination, his heredity, all that might manifest itself beyond his consciousness in a moment of aberration. To awaken the features of individuality, such is the problem during rehearsal. There is yet another very important requirement: in such a degree to read and incarnate oneself into a role that the words of the author become for the actor his own words; i.e., if I may repeat what I said about the *régisseur,* the author must also be lost in the individuality of the actor.

For in the end, when you watch a performance you must forget not only the *régisseur,* you must forget even the author; you must yield wholly to the actor. He can gratify you, or distress you. The actor speaks, and not the author, and not the *régisseur*. Both one and the other have died in him, even as have died and become resurrected the innumerable observations and impressions experienced by him in the course of his whole life, from childhood to this very evening. All this, as though long since passed away, is resurrected under the pressure of that force which is embodied in a theatrical performance.

DAVID BELASCO

(1859-1931)

Creating Atmosphere

Let us assume that a play has been brought into acceptable form in its manuscript and I have made up my mind to produce it. My first step in the practical work of production is to study out the scenes, which must be constructed as carefully as the play itself, for a skillfully devised scene is always of vital assistance to an episode. In this preliminary work I seldom follow the stage directions on the printed page, either of my own plays or those of other dramatists. I prefer to plan the scenes myself with reference to stage values.

I consider where a window or door, a balcony or a fireplace, will be most effective. The feeling of the scene is always a great factor in determining its arrangement, for symbolism to a certain extent enters the production of every play. For instance, sunlit scenes simply imply happiness, moonlit scenes give a suggestion of romance, while tragedy or sorrow should be played in gloom. It is never advisable to stage comedy scenes, which depend for their interest upon the wittiness of the dialogue, in exterior settings, for the surroundings suggest too great an expanse; if acted in an interior setting the lines become immeasurably more effective.

Such details as these must be carefully thought out, and as I become more familiar with the lines and episodes the scenes gradually form themselves. Then I make a rough sketch, taking into account the

David Belasco: *The Theatre Through Its Stage Door,* edited by Louis V. Defoe. New York: Harper, 1919, 53-89, 165-167, 189-195 *passim.*

necessary arrangement of furniture or other properties and considering how the characters can be maneuvered to best advantage.

When I have settled these matters approximately, I send for my scenic artist. With him seated in front, I take the empty stage and, as far as possible, try to act the whole play, making every entrance and exit and indicating my ideas of the groupings of the characters and their surroundings. This process, which would probably seem farcical to a casual onlooker, will consume perhaps four or five evenings, for not one detail can be left to chance or put aside until I am satisfied that it cannot be improved.

During this process one must treat the play as a human being; it must laugh at certain points, at others it must be sad; lovers must come together in certain lights; and all its changing moods must be blended harmoniously. For the completed play is impressive and fulfills its purpose only to the extent that it carries an audience back to its own experiences. If my productions have had an appealing quality, it is because I have kept this important fact constantly in mind and have tried, while concealing the mechanism of my scenes, to tug at the hearts of my audiences.

Having explained in detail my ideas and turned over a manuscript to him, the scenic artist proceeds to make a drawing of the scenes, following my crude sketches, and thus we reach a definite starting point. In due course of time—it may be a week or a month—the scenic artist will have constructed the actual scene models which are set up in the perfectly equipped miniature theater of my studio. But changes are always suggesting themselves, and often these models, which are about four feet long, have to be taken apart and reconstructed several times.

It is time now to begin to consider what to me is the all-important factor in a dramatic production—the lighting of the scenes. With my electrician I again go over the play in detail, very much according to the method I have previously followed with my scenic artist. When he has thoroughly grasped my ideas and become quite familiar with the play itself, we begin our experiments, using the miniature theater and evolving our colors by transmitting white light through gelatin or silk of various hues. Night after night we experiment together to obtain color or atmospheric effects, aiming always to make them aid the interpretation of the scenes.

Lights are to drama what music is to the lyrics of a song. No other factor that enters into the production of a play is so effective in conveying its moods and feeling. They are as essential to every work of dramatic art as blood is to life. The greatest part of my success in the theater I attribute to my feeling for colors, translated into effects of light. Sometimes these effects have been imitated by other producers with considerable success, but I do not fear such encroachments. It may be possible for others to copy my colors, but no one can get my feeling for them. . . .

If, as I conceive it, the purpose of the theater be to hold the mirror up to nature, I know of no better place to obtain the effects of nature than to go to nature itself. To fulfill this purpose with integrity, to surround the mimic life of the characters in drama with the natural aspects of life, to seek in light and color the same interpretative relation to spoken dialogue that music bears to the words of a song, is, I contend, the real art, the true art of the theater. He who goes direct to nature for the effects he introduces on the stage can never be wrong. It is upon this creed that I base my faith in realism in dramatic art.

The lighting effects on my stages have been secured only after years of experiment and at an expense which many other producers would consider ridiculous. Sometimes I have spent five thousand dollars attempting to reproduce the delicate hues of a sunset and then have thrown the scene away altogether. I recall that when I produced *The Girl of the Golden West,* I experimented three months to secure exactly the soft changing colors of a California sunset over the Sierra Nevadas, and then turned to another method. It was a good sunset, but it was not Californian.

These experiments have always been the most interesting part of my work as a producer, although they have also been the most perplexing and sometimes the most baffling. It is no easy matter, for instance, to indicate the difference between the moon and stars of a Japanese night and the fanciful moon and stars of fairyland. But there is, nevertheless, a difference which an audience must be made to feel, without detecting the mechanism, just as one is conscious of heat, yet does not see it, on entering a warm room. . . .

The scene models having been approved and the very important matter of the lighting being well under way, it is time now to begin the building of the actual scenes. I turn my carpenters over to my scenic artist, who furnishes to them the plans. They then construct the scenery in my own shops, for I never have such work done by contract. I will allow nothing to be built out of canvas stretched on frames. Everything must be real. I have seen plays in which thrones creaked on which monarchs sat, and palace walls flapped when persons touched them. Nothing so destructive to illusion or so ludicrous can happen on my stage. . . .

I generally prefer to leave the costuming until after the first week of rehearsals, when I am reasonably sure of my actors, unless it happens to be a costume play which I am producing. If it demands other than modern clothes, I write a full description for the characters, deciding whether their hair shall be smooth or shaggy and whether they shall or shall not wear beards, and then call a costume designer into consultation. All this is very necessary in a costume play, in order to preserve the color harmonies of my scenes. If, on the other hand, it be a modern play that I am producing, I send my actors, when the proper time comes, to the various shops to be fitted for their clothing.

. . . In order to keep in my own complete control this important detail of a dramatic production, I provide all the clothing worn by the people in my companies. It is the ordinary practice, in the case of fancy costumes, for the producer to supply them, but so-called modern clothing is expected to be furnished by the actors themselves. But I have found it advisable to regulate every detail which enters into productions on my stage, and the advantage I gain by such caution greatly outweighs the expense. . . .

When I produced *The Darling of the Gods* I sent to Japan for the costumes of my principal actors, as well as for the paraphernalia of its scenes. When I presented *Du Barry* I sent a commissioner to

France, where he purchased the rich fabrics and had them dyed to reproduce exactly the dresses and styles of the Court of Louis XV, as shown by portraits painted during that period.

The problem of obtaining appropriate costumes, however, varies with every play. I have dumfounded a tramp by asking him to exchange a coat on his back for a new one. Sometimes a poor girl of the street has attracted my attention because she was like a character I had in mind. I have sent for her and bought her dress, hat, shoes, and stockings. My wardrobe people have rummaged for weeks through pawnshops and second-hand stores to find a vest or some other article of apparel appropriate to an eccentric character in one of my plays. From fashionable dressmakers and tailors have come bills that would stagger a rich society woman.

While all these various details of the production are moving along, I am hunting everywhere for my cast. In fact, I have been on the lookout for actors and actresses suitable to the various characters from the moment I made up my mind to accept the play. Applicants for parts come to my office in swarms, but generally they are members of the profession who are too familiarly known to the public, since I prefer, as far as possible, to develop my own actors. I ransack the varieties and the cheap stock companies, and I both go to see the people and have them come to see me. If I happen to be producing a play for a star, the organization of the company is somewhat simplified, but in any event I always choose my players with the greatest care. In making my selections I would much prefer to have an actor resemble the character he is to represent than have him depend upon disguise and the assumption of manners, for my motto as a producer has been to keep as close to nature as possible.

I have been dealing, up to this point, with what, to a theater audience, are the impersonal factors in the evolution of a play on my stage. Until my company is fully organized its members, of course, remain scattered. In due course of time—I usually allot about six weeks to rehearsals of a play which does not offer unusual difficulties—notices are sent out for the people to assemble. When they arrive at the theater I always make it a practice to be on hand to receive them. I want them to feel from the outset an intimate relationship to me and to one another. Some have already played together in the same companies; some know one another only by reputations, and some are strangers. I introduce them to one another and treat them as guests in my drawing room, rather than as employees on my stage. After a few moments spent in general conversation I then invite them to accompany me to the reading room, where they find a long, well-lighted table surrounded by comfortable chairs.

When we are all seated—I at the head of the table with the scene models beside me—I invariably give a few preliminary instructions. First of all I caution the members of the company not to discuss the play outside my theater. I impress upon them that the ultimate result of our efforts will depend upon the spirit of co-operation which each brings to it and that the success of the whole is more important to me than any of its parts. I urge that they must not judge the value of their characters by the number of lines allotted to them to speak, but rather by the artistry which the characters permit. Above all, I ask them not to be selfish, but to assist one another because, after all, they are only the component parts of a single picture.

My sermon preached and reiterated, I then read the play from the beginning to end, without interruptions or comments. This ceremony finished, the individual parts are distributed by the prompter. . . .

Talk about stage fright! The suffering of actors at a first public performance is nothing compared to what they undergo when, with no one but myself present, they first read their parts from the manuscript. Each character is closely analyzed as we proceed. Invariably our discussions bring out more of the psychology of the roles than the author ever dreamed his play contained. When the reading is finished we indulge in a little general conversation—the pleasant social relationship of the members of a theatrical company is always important—and then the rehearsal is adjourned until the following morning. . . .

When I am satisfied that the members of the company have in their minds a clear conception of the play and its characters—up to this point they have been only reading and listening, not acting—I make it a rule to turn them over to my stage director, who supervises them during the first rehearsal on the stage. He, in the meantime, has been studying the play and listening to the readings, and knows, roughly at least, what I am aiming to accomplish. I have always found it better to keep out of sight during the first experiments in the real acting, for when I am present the actors stand still and depend upon me for directions.

I always caution the stage director to let them give him everything, that he must give them nothing. In this way they rely upon their own initiative and, so to speak, squeeze themselves dry. Their invention seems to grow when they know they can do as they please. With this confidence gained, I take control of the play again and we go at it in earnest.

Now the period of hardest work has been reached. I have kept my people on the stage twenty hours at a stretch, making some of them read a single line perhaps fifty times, experimenting with little subtleties of intonation or gesture, and going over bits of business again and again. Infinite patience is needed to make others understand the soul of a character as the author or producer conceives it, and such patience, coupled with the knack of communicating his own ideas, must be possessed by every successful producer.

I have never resorted to bullying in order to make my actors do as I wish; I have always found that the best results can be gained by appealing subtly to their imagination. I can convey more to them by a look or a gesture than by a long harangue or a scolding.

Peculiarities in the actors are also disclosed by these experiments. Some may be able to speak their lines more effectively while seated than while standing; some play better on the right side of the stage than on the left, or vice versa; one arrives at his best results deliberately, another by nervous energy; I have even known actors whose work varied according to whether they directly faced the audience or presented their profiles to it. Experience has taught me not to direct my players arbitrarily, but to be guided by what they can best do. Their peculiarities are the results of temperament and personality, which the intelligent stage director should always attempt to preserve. I try to correct mannerisms when they are bad, for bad mannerisms are as destructive to good acting as weeds to a garden; but when mannerisms are indexes of personality they have a distinct value. . . .

All these idiosyncrasies in my actors I try to preserve, when they are not so pronounced that they seem to be affectations. I direct them so that such personal peculiarities will be put to effective uses. This is one of the reasons why I always work with the company before me. Of late there has sprung up a practice of organizing several companies —in some instances half a dozen—and sending them on tour in plays which happen to have met with unusual popularity in New York. There is a great commercial advantage in such a policy, for it permits the profits of a successful play to be quickly gathered and it simplifies the work of the producer, because invariably the secondary companies attempt no more than to imitate the methods of the original organization. For this reason bad art must inevitably result. Therefore I am opposed to it. I have never directed a second company; if I did, I fear I would change all the business of the play, and possibly make alterations in the play itself. I would discover immediately that what one set of players could do most effectively in a certain manner, another set would have to do in a wholly different way, dependent upon the temperament, personality, and technical equipment of each. When actors attempt only to imitate a model, they become automatons and the artistic finish of both the play and its performance is consequently sacrificed.

So we go over the speeches time after time, generally spending a week or ten days on each act. During this period I have insisted that my actors avoid trying to memorize their roles until their conception of them is fully formed and they are actually molded into the characters. Otherwise, with every word glibly at their tongues' ends, they will presently begin to talk like parrots. Furthermore, they are always unconsciously studying and memorizing while rehearsing. . . .

During all the time that rehearsals have been in progress—and perhaps for many weeks or even months before the first reading—other preparations for the production have been going on. Carpenters have been building the scenery in my shop, artists have been painting it at their studios, electricians have been making the paraphernalia for the lighting effects, property men have been manufacturing or buying the various objects needed in their department, and costumers and wig-makers have been at work. All these adjuncts to the play have been timed to be ready when they are needed. At last comes the order to put them together. Then for three or four days my stage resembles a house in process of being furnished. Confusion reigns supreme with carpenters putting on doorknobs, decorators hanging draperies, work-men laying carpets and rugs, and furniture men taking measurements.

Everything has been selected by me in advance. My explorations in search of stage equipment are really the most interesting parts of my work. I attend auction sales and haunt antique shops, hunting for the things I want. I rummage in stores in the richest as well as in the poorest sections of New York. Many of the properties must be especially made, and it has even happened that I have been compelled to send agents abroad to find exactly the things I need. . . .

When I produced *The Easiest Way* I found myself in a dilemma. I planned one of its scenes to be an exact counterpart of a little hall bedroom in a cheap theatrical boardinghouse in New York. We tried to build the scene in my shops, but, somehow, we could not make it look shabby enough. So I went to the meanest theatrical lodging-house I could find in the Tenderloin district and bought the entire interior of one of its most dilapidated rooms—patched furniture, threadbare carpet, tarnished and broken gas fixtures, tumbledown cupboards, dingy doors and window casings, and even the faded paper on the walls. The landlady regarded me with amazement when I offered to replace them with new furnishings.

While the scenery and properties are being put together I lurk around with my notebook in hand, studying the stage, watching for defects in color harmonies, and endeavoring to make every scene con-form to the characteristics of the people who are supposed to inhabit them. However great the precaution I may have observed, I generally decide to make many more changes. Then, when the stage is furnished to my satisfaction, I bring my company up from the reading room and introduce them to the scenes and surroundings in which they are to live in the play.

There is a vast difference between rehearsing a company on an empty stage and in the fully equipped settings of a play. The change involves retracing many steps which have already been taken, and undoing many things which seemingly have been done well; but I have been unable to discover a way to avoid it. Now we have the actual width and depth of the stage to guide us and we are able to time with mathematical exactness entrances and exits and the movements of the actors from one place to another. When the characters are put into the permanent scenes, the stage director must also consider them from a somewhat different point of view. The players must be adapted to the scene, not the scene to the players, for the effort should always be to lose the identity of the scene and intensify the identity of the characters. I have always been a strong advocate of stage settings which stimulate the imagination of my audiences and at the same time adorn my plays, but first, last, and always I try not to attract the eye when attention should be fixed upon the dialogue. . . .

At last, when every little imperfection in the interpretations of the characters has been detected and perfected, I set apart one performance at which I try not to consider the acting, but the play itself. I am on the lookout for repetitions in the dialogue that may have escaped me, unduly emphatic speeches and climaxes that have not been consistently approached. I keep a stenographer beside me taking down notes and suggestions, for I try not to interrupt the performance or interfere with the inspiration of the players. These final changes made, the company are bidden to become letter-perfect in their roles as they are now developed. This task of unlearning and learning again is one of the hardest that an actor is called upon to perform. It needs a trained mind to do it quickly and successfully. . . .

At about this time, if all the costumes are ready, I hold what I call my "dress parade." I have my actors dress exactly as they are to be seen in the play, with every detail of clothing—shoes, gloves, neckties, wigs, beards, and cosmetics complete—and march them back and forth across the stage. It frequently happens that changes will be advisable in the appearance of some of them, and the time to decide such matters is now. I supply every detail of the wardrobe which actors wear on my stage, whether I am producing a costume drama or a modern comedy. In every respect the production and all that pertains to it must be in perfect harmony. I take pains to caution the players to "make up" with reference to the predominating tone of the lighting of the stage. In my own theaters the dressing rooms are equipped with rows of electric bulbs of every hue, so that the actors may gauge the exact effect of the pigments which they put on their faces. But when, occasionally, I have produced plays in other houses than my own, this important precaution has not been possible, and sometimes it has led to grave defects in the appearance of some of the characters. . . .

The dress parade over, and the time for the dress rehearsals being at hand, I give my attention to a curtain rehearsal. One who is not familiar with the little touches, apart from the play itself, which aid the general effect of a dramatic production may not realize how important it is to have the curtain work in harmony with the feeling of the scene upon which it rises and falls. I have sometimes experimented with a curtain fifty times, raising or lowering it rapidly, slowly, or at medium speed. The curtain men must be taught to feel the climaxes as keenly as the actors and to work in unison with them. This is a good time, also, if the play has a musical accompaniment, to rehearse the score with my orchestra leader and musicians, and weld them into parts of the completed whole.

We are ready for the final dress rehearsals now. The production, which has been developing day by day for six weeks or more, has become as complete and its performance is as spontaneous as if it were being given before a crowded audience.

The stage is ordered cleared, the actors are sent to their dressing rooms to get themselves ready, and I take my place, with my scenic artists and others attached to my staff, in front of the empty theater. The people are likely to be more nervous than on a real opening night, for they are conscious that they are to be subjected to concentrated criticism from which there is no appeal. In a crowded theater they are sure of pleasing at least a part of the audience; it is a different affair when they are trying to meet the approval of only one person. The introductory music, if there be music, is played, up goes the curtain, and the performance begins.

I try not to interrupt if it can possibly be avoided, preferring to reserve my criticisms until the end. But if indefensible mistakes occur—if, for instance, a character on leaving a drawing room forgets his hat or stick or gloves—I am cruel enough in my comments to make sure that the blunder will never occur again. It is too late now for praising, coaxing, or cajoling. I go on the principle that the good things will take care of themselves, but that not a single flaw must be left undetected. The dress rehearsal ended, I commend the company when I can, reprove them when I must, and generally discuss tempo, deportment, and elocution—everything, in fact, that suggests itself to me. Then the curtain is lowered, the scene is "struck," and we go over the play again and again until, so far as I can judge, nothing more remains to be done. . . .

Any play worth producing at all is entitled to the most perfect interpretation that can be secured for it. Any means that aids the audience's grasp and understanding of it, or that appeals to the aesthetic sense, is useful and legitimate in the theater—provided the stage director never loses sight of the fact that, when all is said and done, the play itself is the main thing, that the actors are always the chief instruments through which the story is to be told, and that the scene is only a background against which the dramatist's work is being projected.

If for however brief a time scenery, accessories, or any of the details of the environment, no matter how clever they be in themselves, distract the audience's attention from the play proper or cease to be other than mere assisting agencies, their value is destroyed and they become more a hindrance than an aid and, consequently, an inartistic blunder. One must remember that in nature the glory and beauty of the stars are never obliterated by the background of the sky. . . .

But all these adjuncts of lighting, color, and costumes, however useful they may be, and however pleasing to an audience, really mark the danger point of a dramatic production. No other worker in the American theater has given so much time and energy to perfecting them as I; nevertheless, I count them as valuable only when they are held subordinate to the play and the acting. The stage always accomplishes more through the ability of its actors than through the genius of its scenic artists and electrical experts. And if the theater in this country now is in a state of decline, it is because too much attention is being paid to stage decoration, important as it is when held in its proper place, and too little to the work of the players.

It is at once significant and deplorable that our scenic artists study continually, our actors seldom. And it is a fact that, except in the rarest cases, the more indifferent the quality of the acting the more elaborate is likely to be the surroundings in which it is found. If the artistic success of a play depended principally upon its scenery and decorations, anyone who could afford to engage a good painter might become a dramatic producer almost overnight. And if this be the end sought by dramatic art, then we have had no past theater. Shakespeare would doubtless have utilized every accessory and aid known to our modern stage, yet the greatness of his dramatic genius was established without them.

Only when the stage director is resolved that the play shall stand first in importance in a theater production can he safely employ the countless pictorial aids which contribute to its effect and its appeal. Only when he relies upon his actors as the chief means of its interpretation should he venture upon those other agencies which help to bring it into closer relation with life and nature.

In short, to paraphrase Hamlet's words, the play must always be the thing, whether to stir the aesthetic impulse of the public or to catch the conscience of the king.

ADOLPHE APPIA

(1862-1928)

Light and Space

For some years now dramatic art has been in a process of change. Naturalism on the one hand, Wagnerianism on the other, have violently displaced the old landmarks. Certain things which, twenty years ago, were not "of the theater" (to use an absurdly hallowed expression) have almost become commonplace. This has resulted in some confusion: we no longer know to which type a given play belongs; and the fondness we have for foreign productions fails to give us guidance.

This would not, however, create serious difficulties if our stages adapted themselves to every new effort. Unfortunately, this is not the case. The author with his manuscript—or the composer with his score—may be in agreement with the actors; but once on the stage, in the blaze of the footlights, the new idea slips back into its old framework—and our directors ruthlessly cut anything that goes beyond that.

Many assert that it cannot be otherwise, that the conventions of scene design are rigid, etc. I say just the opposite. And in the following pages I have tried to formulate the basic elements of staging which, instead of paralyzing and stifling dramatic art, will not only be faithful to it but will also be a source of inexhaustible suggestion for the playwright and his interpreters.

Adolphe Appia: "Comment reformer notre mise en scène," *La Revue (Revue des Revues)*, L, No. ii, June 1, 1904, 342-349.

I trust that the reader will bear with me during this difficult résumé.

Our modern staging is entirely the slave of painting—the painting of sets—which purports to give us the illusion of reality. But this illusion is itself an illusion, because the physical presence of the actor contradicts it. In fact, the principle of the illusion achieved by painting on vertical pieces of canvas ("flats") and that of the illusion achieved by the plastic, living body of the actor are in contradiction. So it is not by developing in isolation the play of these two kinds of illusions—as is done on all our stages—that we shall obtain an integrated and artistic performance.

Let us therefore examine modern stagecraft from these two points of view in turn.

It is impossible to set up on our stages real trees, real houses, etc:; besides, that would hardly be desirable. Hence we feel that we must *imitate* reality as faithfully as possible. But to render things plastically is difficult, often impossible, and in any case very expensive. That forces us, it would seem, to reduce the number of things represented. Our directors, however, are of a different mind. They consider that the stage set must represent anything they want it to; consequently, what cannot be rendered plastically must be painted. Undoubtedly, painting allows one to show the audience a countless number of things. Thus it seems to give to staging a much-sought freedom; so our directors stop right there. But the basic principle of painting is to reduce everything to a flat surface. How then can it fill a three-dimensional space—the stage? Without any attempt to solve the problem, the directors have decided to cut up the painting and to set up these "cut-outs" on the floor of the stage. It means therefore giving up any attempt to paint the lower part of the stage picture; if it is a landscape, for example, the top will be a dome of forest scenery; to the right and left there will be trees; at the rear there will be a horizon and a sky—and at the bottom, the floor of the stage! This painting, which was supposed to represent everything, is forced from the very outset to renounce representing the ground; because the illusory forms it depicts must be presented to us

vertically, and *there is no possible relationship* between the vertical
flats of the set and the stage floor (or the more or less horizontal canvas covering it). That is why our scene designers cushion the base
of the flats.

So the ground cannot be reproduced by painting. But that is precisely where the actor moves! Our directors have forgotten the actor:
they want to produce a *Hamlet* without Hamlet! Are they willing to
sacrifice a bit of the dead painting in favor of the living, moving body
of the actor? Never! They would rather give up the theater! But
since it is nonetheless necessary to take into account this quite living
body, painting consents to place itself here and there at the actor's
disposition. At times it even grows generous, although by so doing
it looks quite ridiculous; at other times, however, when it has refused
to yield a single inch, it is the actor who becomes ridiculous. The
antagonism is complete.

We have begun with painting. Now let us see what direction the
problem would take if we began with the actor, with the plastic, moving human body, seen solely from the point of view of its effect on the
stage—as we have done with stage setting.

An object becomes plastic for our eyes only by the light that strikes
it—and its plasticity cannot be artistically produced except by an
artistic use of light. That is self-evident. So much for form. The
movement of the human body requires obstacles in order to express
itself; all artists know that the beauty of the body's movements depends on the variety of the points of support afforded by the ground
and other objects. The actor's mobility cannot therefore be improved
artistically except by an integrated relationship with other objects
and the ground.

Hence the two basic conditions for an artistic presentation of the
human body on the stage are: lighting that brings out its plasticity,
and a harmonizing with the setting which brings out its attitudes and
movements. Here we are a long way from painting indeed!

Dominated by painted sets, the *décor* sacrifices the actor and, more
than that, as we have seen, a good deal of its pictorial effect, since it
must cut up the painting. This is contrary to the essential principle

of the art of painting. Moreover, the stage floor cannot share in the illusion offered by the flats. But what would happen if we subordinated it to the actor!

First of all, we would make lighting free again! As a matter of fact, under the domination of the painted set, the lighting is completely absorbed by the *décor*. The things represented on the flats must be *seen:* so lights are lit and shadows are painted. . . . Alas! It is from this kind of lighting that the actor must take what he can get! Under such conditions it cannot be a question either of true lighting or of any plastic effect whatever! Lighting in itself is an element the effects of which are limitless; once it is freed, it becomes for us what the palette is for the painter. All the color combinations become possible. By simple or complex searchlights, stationary or moving, by partial obstruction, by different degrees of transparency, etc., we can achieve infinite modulations. Lighting thus gives us a means of externalizing in some way most of the colors and forms that painting freezes on the canvas and of distributing them dynamically in space. The actor no longer walks *in front of* painted lights and shadows; he is immersed in an atmosphere *that is destined for him.* Artists will be quick to grasp the scope of such a reform.[1]

Now comes the crucial point: the plasticity in the *décor* necessary for the actor's harmony of attitudes and movements. Painting has gained the upper hand on our stages, replacing everything that could not be realized plastically, and it has done this with the sole aim of giving the illusion of reality.

But are the images it piles up thus on the vertical flats indispensable? Not at all: there is not one play that needs even a hundredth part of them. For note this well: these images are not living, they are *indicated* on the canvas like a kind of hieroglyphic language. They *signify* only the things they purport to represent—and all the more so because they cannot enter into real, organic contact with the actor.

[1] A well-known artist in Paris, Mariano Fortuny, has invented a completely new system of lighting, based on the properties of *reflected light.* The results have been extraordinarily successful—and this far-reaching invention will bring about a radical transformation in staging in all the theaters . . . in favor of lighting.

The plasticity required by the actor aims at an entirely different effect: the human body does not seek to produce the illusion of reality *since it is itself reality!* What it demands of the *décor* is simply to set in relief this reality. This results inevitably in a shift in the aim of the stage set: in the one case it is the real appearance of *objects* that is sought; in the other, it is the highest possible degree of reality of the human body.

Since these two principles are technically opposed, it is a question of choosing one or the other. Is it to be the accumulation of dead images and decorative richness on the vertical flats, or is it to be the spectacle of the human being in all its plastic and mobile manifestations?

Can there be any possible hesitation in our answer? Let us ask ourselves what we are looking for in the theater. We have beautiful painting elsewhere, and fortunately not cut up. Photography allows us to sit in our armchair and view the whole world; literature evokes the most fascinating pictures in our imagination; and very few people are so devoid of feeling that they are not able from time to time to contemplate a beautiful sight in nature. We come to the theater in order to witness a dramatic *action*. It is the presence of the characters on the stage that motivates this action; without the characters there is no action. So it is the actor who is the essential factor in staging; it is he whom we come to *see,* it is from him that we expect the emotion, and it is for this emotion that we have come. Hence it is above all a question of basing our staging on the actor's presence. To do this, we must free staging of everything that is in contradiction with the actor's presence.

This, then, is the way we must frankly pose the technical problem.

Some may object that this problem has at times been rather successfully solved on several of our Paris stages—at the Théâtre Antoine, for example, or elsewhere. No doubt; but why has this always happened with the same type of plays and settings? How would those directors go about staging *Troilus and Cressida* or *The Tempest, The Ring of the Nibelung* or *Parsifal?* (At the Grand Guignol Théâtre, they are adept at showing us a concierge's lodging; but what happens, for example, when they want to depict a garden?)

Our staging has two distinct sources: opera and the spoken drama. Up to now, with very few exceptions, opera singers have been considered glorified machines for singing, and the painted set has been the outstanding feature of the spectacle. Hence its impressive development. The evolution of the spoken play has been different: the actor of necessity comes first, since without him there is no play; and if the director occasionally feels that he has to borrow some of the trappings of opera, he does so prudently and without losing sight of the actor. (Let the reader compare in his memory the decorative effect of such a lavish play production as *Theodora* with that of any opera.) Yet the principle of stage illusion remains the same for the spoken play as for the opera, and it is that principle which is the most seriously violated. Besides, dramatists are well acquainted with two or three combinations in which modern staging can achieve a little illusion despite the presence of the actor; and so they never venture beyond them.

During the last few years, however, things have changed. With the Wagnerian music-dramas, opera has come closer to the spoken play, and the latter (apart from the plays of naturalism) has sought to overcome its former limitations, to come nearer to the music-drama. Then, strangely enough, it turns out that our staging no longer fits the needs of either the one or the other! The ostentatious display that opera makes of painting no longer has anything to do with a Wagner score (the Wagnerian directors, at Bayreuth and elsewhere, do not yet seem to realize this); and the monotony of the settings in the spoken drama no longer satisfies the sharpened insight of the dramatists. Everyone feels the need of a reform, but the power of inertia keeps us in the same old rut.

In such a situation theories are useful, but they do not lead far. We must come directly to grips with stage design and, little by little, transform it.

The simplest method perhaps would be to take one of our plays exactly as it is, *already completely set,* and to see what could be done with its staging if it were based on the principle elaborated above. Of course we would have to choose carefully a play written especially for modern staging, or an opera that adapts itself perfectly to it. The *décors* in our traditional theaters are of no help to us. On the contrary, we must choose a dramatic work whose requirements obviously do not jibe with our present-day means: a play by Maeterlinck, or some other play of the same type, or even a Wagnerian music-drama. The latter is preferable because music, by definitely delimiting the duration and intensity of the emotion, can be a valuable guide. Besides, the sacrifice of illusion would be less conspicuous in a Wagnerian music-drama than in a spoken play. We shall then see everything in the fixed set which runs counter to our efforts; we shall be forced to make concessions that are quite revealing. The question of lighting will concern us first of all: on this point we will have an example of the tyranny of painted flats; and we shall understand—no longer theoretically but in a thoroughly concrete manner—that immense harm still being done to the actor and, by him, to the dramatist.

No doubt that would only be a modest effort; but it is extremely difficult to accomplish such a reform all at once, because it is as much a question of reforming the audience's taste as it is of transforming our staging. Moreover, the results of material and technical work *on ground that is already familiar* are perhaps surer than those arising from a radical reform.

Take, for example, the second act of *Siegfried*. How are we to represent a forest on the stage? First of all, let us be clear as to the following: is it *a forest* with characters, or rather *characters* in a forest? We are at the theater to witness a dramatic action. Something takes place in this forest which apparently cannot be expressed by painting. Here then is our point of departure: So and So does this and that, says this and that, in a forest. To design our set we do not have to try to visualize a forest; but we must depict in detailed and logical sequence everything that takes place in this forest. Hence perfect knowledge of the score is indispensable, and the director's source of inspiration is thus completely different: his eyes must remain *riveted on the characters.* Then if he thinks of the forest, it will be as a kind of special atmosphere surrounding and hovering above the actors— an atmosphere which he can grasp only *in its relation* to the living, moving actors from whom he must not avert his eyes. At no point in his conception, therefore, will the stage picture remain a lifeless arrangement of painting; it will always be alive. In that way the staging becomes the creation of a stage picture in its time-flow. Instead of starting with a painted set ordered by somebody or other from somebody else, with the actor then getting along as best he can with shoddy props, we start with the actor. It is his art we wish to highlight and for which we are ready to sacrifice everything. It will be: Siegfried here and Siegfried there—and never: the tree for Siegfried, the road for Siegfried. I repeat: we no longer seek to give the illusion of *a forest* but that of *a man* in the atmosphere of a forest. Reality here is a man, alongside whom no other illusion matters. Everything this man touches must be part of his destiny—everything else must help create the appropriate atmosphere around him. And if we look away from Siegfried for a moment and raise our eyes, the stage picture does not of necessity have to give us an illusion: the way it is arranged has *only* Siegfried in mind; and when a slight rustling of the trees in the forest attracts Siegfried's attention, we the spectators *will look at Siegfried* bathed in the moving lights and shadows; we will not look at parts of the *décor* set in motion by backstage manipulation.

Scenic illusion is the living presence of the actor.

The setting for this act, as it is now presented to us on stages throughout the world, fails woefully to live up to our conditions. We must simplify it a great deal, give up lighting the painted flats as is now the rule, institute a complete reform in the arrangement of the stage floor and, above all, provide for our lighting by installing a wealth of electrical equipment regulated in great detail. The footlights—that astonishing monstrosity—will hardly be used. Let us add that most of this work of re-creation will be with the characters, and the production will not be finally set until after several rehearsals with the orchestra (indispensable conditions which may now seem exorbitant yet are elementary!).

An attempt along these lines cannot fail to teach us the course to follow in transforming our rigid and conventional staging into living, flexible, and artistic material, suitable for any dramatic creation whatever. We shall even be surprised that we have so long neglected so important a branch of art and have consigned it, as unworthy of our personal attention, to men who are not artists.

As far as staging is concerned, our aesthetic feeling is still in a state of paralysis. A person who would not tolerate in his own apartment an object that was not of the most exquisite taste, finds it quite natural to buy a high-priced seat in a hall that is ugly and built in defiance of good sense, and to sit there for a couple of hours watching a play alongside which the worst chromos from an antique dealer are delicate works of art.

Methods of staging, like methods in the other arts, are based on forms, light, and colors. These three elements are at our disposal; consequently we can use them in the theater, as elsewhere, in an artistic manner. Up to now it was felt that staging should achieve the highest possible degree of illusion—and it is this principle (an unaesthetic principle if ever there was one!) that has paralyzed our efforts. I have endeavored to show in these pages that the art of scene design must be based on the only *reality* worthy of the theater: the human body. We have seen the first and elementary consequences of this reform.

The subject is a difficult and complex one, particularly in view of the misunderstandings surrounding it and the bad habits we have formed from frequenting present-day plays. To be thoroughly convincing, I would have to develop this idea a good deal further. I would have to discuss the brand-new task that is incumbent on the actor; the influence that a flexible and artistic scene design would inevitably exert on the dramatist; the stylizing power of music on a stage production; the changes that will be required in building new stages, new theaters, etc. It is impossible for me to do that here;[2] but perhaps the reader will have found in my aesthetic desire something approaching his own. In that case, it will be easy for him to continue this work by himself.

Translated by Joseph M. Bernstein

---

[2] I have published a complete study of the subject in Germany with the publishing house of Bruckmann in Munich. The volume, illustrated with sketches, is called: *Die Musik und die Inscenierung.*

GORDON CRAIG

(b. 1872)

The Artist of the Theater

STAGE-DIRECTOR: You have now been over the theater with me, and have seen its general construction, together with the stage, the machinery for manipulating the scenes, the apparatus for lighting, and the hundred other things, and have also heard what I have had to say of the theater as a machine; let us rest here in the auditorium, and talk awhile of the theater and of its art. Tell me, do you know what is the Art of the Theater?

PLAYGOER: To me it seems that Acting is the Art of the Theater.

STAGE-DIRECTOR: Is a part, then, equal to a whole?

PLAYGOER: No, of course not. Do you, then, mean that the Play is the Art of the Theater?

STAGE-DIRECTOR: A play is a work of literature, is it not? Tell me, then, how one art can possibly be another?

PLAYGOER: Well, then, if you tell me that the Art of the Theater is neither the acting nor the play, then I must come to the conclusion that it is the scenery and the dancing. Yet I cannot think you will tell me this is so.

STAGE-DIRECTOR: No; the Art of the Theater is neither acting nor the play, it is not scene nor dance, but it consists of all the elements of which these things are composed: action, which is the very spirit of acting; words, which are the body of the play; line and color, which

Edward Gordon Craig: *The Art of the Theatre.* London: T. N. Foulis, 1905.

are the very heart of the scene; rhythm, which is the very essence of dance.

PLAYGOER: Action, words, line, color, rhythm! And which of these is all-important to the art?

STAGE-DIRECTOR: One is no more important than the other, no more than one color is more important to a painter than another, or one note more important than another to a musician. In one respect, perhaps, action is the most valuable part. Action bears the same relation to the Art of the Theater as drawing does to painting, and melody does to music. The Art of the Theater has sprung from action-movement-dance. . . .

The reason why you are not given a work of art on the stage is not because the public does not want it, not because there are not excellent craftsmen in the theater who could prepare it for you, but because the theater lacks the artist—the artist of the theater, mind you, not the painter, poet, musician. The many excellent craftsmen are, all of them, more or less helpless to change the situation. They are forced to supply what the managers of the theater demand, but they do so most willingly. The advent of the artist in the theater world will change all this. He will slowly but surely gather around him these better craftsmen of whom I speak, and together they will give new life to the art of the theater.

PLAYGOER: But for the others?

STAGE-DIRECTOR: The others? The modern theater is full of these others, these untrained and untalented craftsmen. But I will say one thing for them. I believe they are unconscious of their inability. It is not ignorance on their part, it is innocence. Yet if these same men once realized that they were craftsmen, and would train as such—I do not speak only of the stage-carpenters, electricians, wigmakers, costumers, scene-painters, and actors (indeed, these are in many ways the best and most willing craftsmen)—I speak chiefly of the stage-director. If the stage-director was to technically train himself for his task of interpreting the plays of the dramatist—in time, and by a gradual development he would again recover the ground lost to the theater, and finally would restore the Art of the Theater to its home by means of his own creative genius.

PLAYGOER: Then you place the stage-director before the actors?

STAGE-DIRECTOR: Yes; the relation of the stage-director to the actor is precisely the same as that of the conductor to his orchestra, or of the publisher to his printer.

PLAYGOER: And you consider that the stage-director is a craftsman and not an artist?

STAGE-DIRECTOR: When he interprets the plays of the dramatist by means of his actors, his scene-painters, and his other craftsmen, then he is a craftsman—a master craftsman; when he will have mastered the uses of actions, words, line, color, and rhythm, then he may become an artist. Then we shall no longer need the assistance of the playwright—for our art will then be self-reliant.

PLAYGOER: Is your belief in a Renaissance of the art based on your belief in the Renaissance of the stage-director?

STAGE-DIRECTOR: Yes, certainly, most certainly. Did you for an instant think that I have a contempt for the stage-director? Rather have I a contempt for any man who fails in the whole duty of the stage-director.

PLAYGOER: What are his duties?

STAGE-DIRECTOR: What is his craft? I will tell you. His work as interpreter of the play of the dramatist is something like this: he takes the copy of the play from the hands of the dramatist and promises faithfully to interpret it as indicated in the text (remember I am speaking only of the very best of stage-directors). He then reads the play, and during the first reading the entire color, tone, movement, and rhythm that the work must assume comes clearly before him. As for the stage directions, descriptions of scenes, etc., with which the author may interlard his copy, these are not to be considered by him, for if he is master of his craft he can learn nothing from them.

PLAYGOER: I do not quite understand you. Do you mean that when a playwright has taken the trouble to describe the scene in which his men and women are to move and talk, that the stage-director is to take no notice of such directions—in fact, to disregard them?

STAGE-DIRECTOR: It makes no difference whether he regards or disregards them. What he must see to is that he makes his action and scene match the verse or the prose, the beauty of it, the sense of it. Whatever picture the dramatist may wish us to know of, he will describe his scene during the progress of the conversation between the characters. Take, for instance, the first scene in *Hamlet*. It begins:

> Ber.   Who's there?
> Fran. Nay, answer me; stand and unfold yourself.
> Ber.   Long live the king!
> Fran. Bernardo?
> Ber.   He.
> Fran. You come most carefully upon your hour.
> Ber.   'Tis now struck twelve; get thee to bed, Francisco.
> Fran. For this relief much thanks, 'tis bitter cold,
>   And I am sick at heart.
> Ber.   Have you had quiet guard?
> Fran. Not a mouse stirring.
> Ber.   Well, good night.
>   If you do meet Horatio and Marcellus,
>   The rivals of my watch, bid them make haste.

That is enough to guide the stage-director. He gathers from it that is it twelve o'clock at night, that it is in the open air, that the guard of some castle is being changed, that it is very cold, very quiet, and very dark. Any additional "stage directions" by the dramatist are trivialities.

PLAYGOER: Then you do not think that an author should write any stage directions whatever, and you seem to consider it an offense on his part if he does so?

STAGE-DIRECTOR: Well, is it not an offense to the men of the theater?

PLAYGOER: In what way?

STAGE-DIRECTOR: First tell me the greatest offense an actor can give to a dramatist.

PLAYGOER: To play his part badly?

STAGE-DIRECTOR: No, that may merely prove the actor to be a bad craftsman.

PLAYGOER: Tell me, then.

STAGE-DIRECTOR: The greatest offense an actor can give to a dramatist is to cut out words or lines in his play, or to insert what is known as a "gag." It is an offense to poach on what is the sole property of the playwright. It is not usual to "gag" in Shakespeare, and when it is done it does not go uncensured.

PLAYGOER: But what has this to do with the stage directions of the playwright, and in what way does the playwright offend the theater when he dictates these stage directions?

STAGE-DIRECTOR: He offends in that he poaches on their preserves. If to gag or cut the poet's lines is an offense, so is it an offense to tamper with the art of the stage-director.

PLAYGOER: Then is all the stage direction of the world's plays worthless?

STAGE-DIRECTOR: Not to the reader, but to the stage-director, and to the actor—yes.

PLAYGOER: But Shakespeare—

STAGE-DIRECTOR: Shakespeare seldom directs the stage-director. . . . Would you like to hear what scene directions Shakespeare actually wrote for *Romeo and Juliet?* He wrote: *"Actus primus. Scaena prima."* And not another word as to act or scene throughout the whole play. And now for *King Lear.*

PLAYGOER: No, it is enough. I see now. Evidently Shakespeare relied upon the intelligence of the stage-men to complete their scene from his indication. . . . But is this the same in regard to the actions? Does not Shakespeare place some descriptions through *Hamlet,* such as "Hamlet leaps into Ophelia's grave," "Laertes grapples with him," and later, "The attendants part them, and they come out of the grave"?

STAGE-DIRECTOR: No, not one word. All the stage directions, from the first to the last, are the tame inventions of sundry editors, Mr. Malone, Mr. Capell, Theobald and others, and they have committed an indiscretion in tampering with the play, for which we, the men of the theater, have to suffer.

PLAYGOER: How is that?

STAGE-DIRECTOR: Why, supposing any of us reading Shakespeare shall see in our mind's eye some other combination of movements contrary to the "instructions" of these gentlemen, and suppose we represent our ideas on the stage, we are instantly taken to task by some knowing one, who accuses us of altering the directions of Shakespeare—nay more, of altering his very intentions.

PLAYGOER: But do not the "knowing ones," as you call them, know that Shakespeare wrote no stage directions?

STAGE-DIRECTOR: One can only guess that to be the case, to judge from their indiscreet criticisms. Anyhow, what I wanted to show you was that our greatest modern poet realized that to add stage directions was first of all unnecessary, and secondly, tasteless. We can therefore be sure that Shakespeare at any rate realized what was the work of the theater craftsman—the stage-director, and that it was part of the stage-director's task to invent the scenes in which the play was to be set.

PLAYGOER: Yes, and you were telling me what each part consisted of.

STAGE-DIRECTOR: Quite so. And now that we have disposed of the error that the author's directions are of any use, we can continue to speak of the way the stage-director sets to work to interpret faithfully the play of the dramatist. I have said that he swears to follow the text faithfully, and that his first work is to read the play through and get the great impression; and in reading, as I have said, begins to see the whole color, rhythm, action of the thing. He then puts the play aside for some time, and in his mind's eye mixes his palette (to use a painter's expression) with the colors which the impression of the play has called up. Therefore, on sitting down a second time to read through the play, he is surrounded by an atmosphere which he proposes to test. At the end of the second reading he will find that his more definite impressions have received clear and unmistakable corroboration, and that some of his impressions which were less positive have disappeared. He will then make a note of these. It is possible that he will even now commence to suggest, in line and color, some of the scenes and ideas which are filling his head, but this is more likely to be delayed until he has re-read the play at least a dozen times.

PLAYGOER: But I thought the stage-director always left that part of the play—the scene designing—to the scene painter?

STAGE-DIRECTOR: So he does, generally. First blunder of the modern theater.

PLAYGOER: How is it a blunder?

STAGE-DIRECTOR: This way: *A* has written a play which *B* promises to interpret faithfully. In so delicate a matter as the interpretation of so elusive a thing as the spirit of a play, which, do you think, will be the surest way to preserve the unity of that spirit? Will it be best if *B* does all the work by himself? Or will it do to give the work into the hands of *C, D,* and *E,* each of whom see or think differently to *B* or *A?*

PLAYGOER: Of course the former would be best. But is it possible for one man to do the work of three men?

STAGE-DIRECTOR: That is the only way the work can be done, if unity, the one thing vital to a work of art, is to be obtained.

PLAYGOER: So, then, the stage-director does not call in a scene painter and ask him to design a scene, but he designs one himself?

STAGE-DIRECTOR: Certainly. And remember he does not merely sit down and draw a pretty or historically accurate design, with enough doors and windows in picturesque places, but he first of all chooses certain colors which seem to him to be in harmony with the spirit of the play, rejecting other colors as out of tune. He then weaves into a pattern certain objects—an arch, a fountain, a balcony, a bed—using the chosen object as the center of his design. Then he adds to this all the objects which are mentioned in the play, and which are necessary to be seen. To these he adds, one by one, each character which appears in the play, and gradually each movement of each character, and each costume. He is as likely as not to make several mistakes in his pattern. If so, he must, as it were, unpick the design, and rectify the blunder even if he has to go right back to the beginning and start the pattern all over again—or he may even have to begin a new pattern. At any rate, slowly, harmoniously, must the whole design develop, so that the eye of the beholder shall be satisfied. While this pattern for the eye is being devised, the designer is being guided as much by the sound of the verse or prose as by the sense or spirit. And shortly all is prepared, and the actual work can be commenced.

PLAYGOER: What actual work? It seems to me that the stage-director has already been doing a good deal of what may be called actual work.

STAGE-DIRECTOR: Well, perhaps; but the difficulties have but commenced. By the actual work I mean the work which needs skilled labor, such as the actual painting of the huge spaces of canvas for the scenes, and the actual making of the costumes.

PLAYGOER: You are not going to tell me that the stage-director actually paints his own scenes and cuts his own costumes, and sews them together?

STAGE-DIRECTOR: No, I will not say that he does so in every case and for every play, but he must have done so at one time or another during his apprenticeship, or must have closely studied all the technical points of these complicated crafts. Then will he be able to guide the skilled craftsmen in their different departments. And when the actual making of the scenes and costumes has commenced, the parts are distributed to the different actors, who learn the words before a single rehearsal takes place. (This, as you may guess, is not the custum, but it is what should be seen to by a stage-director such as I describe.) Meantime, the scenes and costumes are almost ready. I will not tell you the amount of interesting but laborious work it entails to prepare the play up to this point. But even when once the scenes are placed upon the stage, and the costumes upon the actors, the difficulty of the work is still great.

PLAYGOER: The stage-director's work is not finished then?

STAGE-DIRECTOR: Finished? What do you mean?

PLAYGOER: Well, I thought now that the scenes and costumes were all seen to, the actors and actresses would do the rest.

STAGE-DIRECTOR: No, the stage-director's most interesting work is now beginning. His scene is set and his characters are clothed. He has, in short, a kind of dream picture in front of him. He clears the stage of all but the one, two, or more characters who are to commence the play, and he begins the scheme of lighting these figures and the scene.

PLAYGOER: What, is not this branch left to the discretion of the master electrician and his men?

STAGE-DIRECTOR: The doing of it is left to them, but the manner of doing it is the business of the stage-director. Being, as I have said, a man of some intelligence and training, he has devised a special way of lighting his scene for this play, just as he has devised a special way of painting the scene and costuming the figures. If the word "harmony" held no significance for him, he would of course leave it to the first comer.

PLAYGOER: Then do you actually mean that he has made so close a study of nature that he can direct his electricians how to make it appear as if the sun were shining at such and such an altitude, or as if the moonlight were flooding the interior of the room with such and such an intensity?

STAGE-DIRECTOR: No, I should not like to suggest that, because the reproduction of nature's lights is not what my stage-director ever attempts. Neither should he attempt such an impossibility. Not to *reproduce* nature, but to *suggest* some of her most beautiful and most living ways—that is what my stage-director shall attempt. The other thing proclaims an overbearing assumption of omnipotence. A stage-director may well aim to be an artist, but it ill becomes him to attempt celestial honors. This attitude he can avoid by never trying to imprison or copy nature, for nature will be neither imprisoned nor allow any man to copy her with any success.

PLAYGOER: Then in what way does he set to work? What guides him in his task of lighting the scene and costumes which we are speaking about?

STAGE-DIRECTOR: What guides him? Why, the scene and the costumes, and the verse and the prose, and the sense of the play. All these things, as I told you, have now been brought into harmony, the one with the other—all goes smoothly—what simpler, then, that it should so continue, and that the director should be the only one to know how to preserve this harmony which he has commenced to create? . . .

We have passed in review the different tasks of the stage-director—scene, costume, lighting—and we have come to the most interesting part, that of the manipulation of the figures in all their movements and speeches. You expressed astonishment that the acting—that is to say, the speaking and actions of the actors—was not left to the actors to arrange for themselves. But consider for an instant the nature of this work. Would you have that which has already grown into a certain unified pattern, suddenly spoiled by the addition of something accidental?

PLAYGOER: How do you mean? I understand what you suggest, but will you not show me more exactly how the actor can spoil the pattern?

STAGE-DIRECTOR: *Unconsciously* spoil it, mind you! I do not for an instant mean that it is his wish to be out of harmony with his surroundings, but he does so through innocence. Some actors have the right instincts in this matter, and some have none whatever. But even those whose instincts are most keen cannot remain in the pattern, cannot be harmonious, without following the directions of the stage-director.

PLAYGOER: Then you do not even permit the leading actor and actress to move and act as their instincts and reason dictate?

STAGE-DIRECTOR: No, rather must they be the very first to follow the direction of the stage-director, so often do they become the very center of the pattern—the very heart of the emotional design.

PLAYGOER: And is that understood and appreciated by them?

STAGE-DIRECTOR: Yes, but only when they realize and appreciate at the same time that the play, and the right and just interpretation of the play, is the all-important thing in the modern theater. Let me illustrate this point to you. The play to be presented is *Romeo and Juliet*. We have studied the play, prepared scene and costume, lighted both, and now our rehearsals for the actors commence. The first movement of the great crowd of unruly citizens of Verona, fighting, swearing, killing each other, appalls us. It horrifies us that in this white little city of roses and song and love there should dwell this amazing and detestable hate which is ready to burst out at the very church doors, or in the middle of the May festival, or under the windows of the house of a newly born girl. Quickly following on this picture, and even while we remember the ugliness which larded both faces of Capulet and Montague, there comes strolling down the road the son of Montague, our Romeo, who is soon to be lover and the loved of his Juliet. Therefore, whoever is chosen to move and speak as Romeo must move and speak as part and parcel of the design—this design which I have already pointed out to you as having a definite form. He must move across our sight in a certain way, passing to a certain point, in a certain light, his head at a certain angle, his eyes, his feet, his whole body in tune with the play, and not (as is often the case) in tune with his own thoughts only, and these out of harmony with the play. For his thoughts (beautiful as they may chance to be) may not match the spirit or the pattern which has been so carefully prepared by the director.

PLAYGOER: Would you have the stage-director control the movements of whoever might be impersonating the character of Romeo, even if he were a fine actor?

STAGE-DIRECTOR: Most certainly; and the finer the actor the finer his intelligence and taste, and therefore the more easily controlled. In fact, I am speaking in particular of a theater wherein all the actors are men of refinement and the director a man of peculiar accomplishments.

PLAYGOER: But are you not asking these intelligent actors almost to become puppets?

STAGE-DIRECTOR: A sensitive question! which one would expect from an actor who felt uncertain about his powers. A puppet is at present only a doll, delightful enough for a puppet show. But for a theater we need more than a doll. Yet that is the feeling which some actors have about their relationship with the stage-director. They feel they are having their strings pulled, and resent it, and show they feel hurt—insulted.

PLAYGOER: I can understand that.

STAGE-DIRECTOR: And cannot you also understand that they should be willing to be controlled? Consider for a moment the relationship of the men on a ship, and you will understand what I consider to be the relationship of men in a theater. . . . It will not be difficult for you to understand that a theater in which so many hundred persons are engaged at work is in many respects like a ship, and demands like management. And it will not be difficult for you to see how the slightest sign of disobedience would be disastrous. Mutiny has been well anticipated in the navy, but not in the theater. The navy has taken care to define, in clear and unmistakable voice, that the captain of the vessel is the king, and a despotic ruler into the bargain. Mutiny on a ship is dealt with by a court-martial, and is put down by very severe punishment, by imprisonment, or by dismissal from the service.

PLAYGOER: But you are not going to suggest such a possibility for the theater?

STAGE-DIRECTOR: The theater, unlike the ship, is not made for purposes of war, and so for some unaccountable reason discipline is not held to be of such vital importance, whereas it is of as much importance as in any branch of service. But what I wish to show you is that until discipline is understood in a theater to be willing and reliant obedience to the director or captain no supreme achievement can be accomplished.

PLAYGOER: But are not the actors, scene-men, and the rest all willing workers?

STAGE-DIRECTOR: Why, my dear friend, there never were such glorious-natured people as these men and women of the theater. They are enthusiastically willing, but sometimes their judgment is at fault, and they become as willing to be unruly as to be obedient, and as willing to lower the standard as to raise it. As for nailing the flag to the mast—this is seldom dreamed of—for *compromise* and the vicious doctrine of compromise with the enemy is preached by the officers of the theatrical navy. Our enemies are vulgar display, the lower public opinion, and ignorance. To these our "officers" wish us to knuckle under. What the theater people have not yet quite comprehended is *the value of a high standard and the value of a director who abides by it.*

PLAYGOER: And that director, why should he not be an actor or a scene-painter?

STAGE-DIRECTOR: Do you pick your leader from the ranks, exalt him to be captain, and then let him handle the guns and the ropes? No; the director of a theater must be a man apart from any of the crafts. He must be a man who knows but no longer handles the ropes.

PLAYGOER: But I believe it is a fact that many well-known leaders in the theater have been actors and stage-directors at the same time.

STAGE-DIRECTOR: Yes, that is so. But you will not find it easy to assure me that no mutiny was heard of under their rule. Right away from all this question of positions there is the question of the art, the work. If an actor assumes the management of the stage, and if he is a better actor than his fellows, a natural instinct will lead him to make himself the center of everything. He will feel that unless he does so the work will appear thin and unsatisfying. He will pay less heed to the play than he will to his own part, and he will, in fact, gradually cease to look upon the work as a whole. And this is not good for the work. This is not the way a work of art is to be produced in the theater.

PLAYGOER: But might it not be possible to find a great actor who would be so great an artist that as director he would never do as you say, but who would always handle himself as actor, just the same as he handles the rest of the material?

STAGE-DIRECTOR: All things are possible, but firstly, it is against the nature of an actor to do as you suggest; secondly, it is against the nature of the stage-director to perform; and thirdly, it is against all nature that a man can be in two places at once. Now, the place of the actor is on the stage, in a certain position ready by means of his brains to give suggestions of certain emotions, surrounded by certain scenes and people; and it is the place of the stage-director to be in front of this, that he may view it as a whole. So that you see even if we found our perfect actor who was our perfect stage-director, he could not be in two places at the same time. Of course we have sometimes seen the conductor of a small orchestra playing the part of the first violin, but not from choice, and not to a satisfactory issue; neither is it the practice in large orchestras.

PLAYGOER: I understand, then, that you would allow no one to rule on the stage except the stage-director?

STAGE-DIRECTOR: The nature of the work permits nothing else.

PLAYGOER: Not even the playwright?

STAGE-DIRECTOR: Only when the playwright has practiced and studied the crafts of acting, scene-painting, costume, lighting, and dance, not otherwise. But playwrights, who have not been cradled in the theater, generally know little of these crafts. Goethe, whose love for the theater remained ever fresh and beautiful, was in many ways one of the greatest of stage-directors. But, when he linked himself to the Weimar theater, he forgot to do what the great musician who followed him remembered. Goethe permitted an authority in the theater higher than himself, that is to say, the owner of the theater. Wagner was careful to possess himself of his theater, and become a sort of feudal baron in his castle.

PLAYGOER: Was Goethe's failure as a theater director due to this fact?

STAGE-DIRECTOR: Obviously, for had Goethe held the keys of the doors that impudent little poodle would never have got as far as its dressing-room; the leading lady would never have made the theater and herself immortally ridiculous; and Weimar would have been saved the tradition of having perpetrated the most shocking blunder which ever occurred inside a theater.

PLAYGOER: The traditions of most theaters certainly do not seem to show that the artist is held in much respect on the stage.

STAGE-DIRECTOR: Well, it would be easy to say a number of hard things about the theater and its ignorance of art. But one does not hit a thing which is down, unless, perhaps, with the hope that the shock may cause it to leap to its feet again. And our Western theater is very much down. The East still boasts a theater. Ours here in the West is on its last legs. But I look for a Renaissance.

PLAYGOER: How will that come?

STAGE-DIRECTOR: Through the advent of a man who shall contain in him all the qualities which go to make up a master of the theater, and through the reform of the theater as an instrument. When that is accomplished, when the theater has become a masterpiece of mechanism, when it has invented a technique, it will without any effort develop a *creative art* of its own. But the whole question of the development of the craft into a self-reliant and creative art would take too long to go thoroughly into at present. There are already some theater men at work on the building of the theaters; some are reforming the acting, some the scenery. And all of this must be of some small value. But the very first thing to be realized is that little or no result can come from the reforming of a single craft of the theater without at the same time, in the same theater, reforming all the other crafts. *The whole Renaissance of the Art of the Theater depends upon the extent that this is realized.* The Art of the Theater, as I have already told you, is divided up into so many crafts: acting, scene, costume, lighting, carpentering, singing, dancing, etc., that it must be realized at the commencement that ENTIRE, not PART reform is needed; and it must be realized that *one* part, one craft, has a *direct* bearing upon each of the other crafts in the theater, and that no result can come from fitful, uneven reform, but only from a systematic progression. Therefore, the reform of the Art of the Theater is possible to those men alone who have studied and practiced all the crafts of the theater.

PLAYGOER: That is to say, your ideal stage-director.

STAGE-DIRECTOR: Yes. You will remember that at the commencement of our conversation I told you my belief in the Renaissance of the Art of the Theater was based in my belief in the Renaissance of the stage-director, and that when he had understood the right use of actors, scene, costume, lighting, and dance, and by means of these had mastered the crafts of interpretation, he would then gradually acquire the mastery of action, line, color, rhythm, and words, this last strength developing out of all the rest. . . . Then I said the Art of the Theater would have won back its rights, and its work would stand self-reliant as a creative art, and no longer as an interpretive craft.

PLAYGOER: Yes, and at the time I did not quite understand what you meant, and though I can now understand your drift, I do not quite in my mind's eye see the stage without its poet.

STAGE-DIRECTOR: What? Shall anything be lacking when the poet shall no longer write for the theater?

PLAYGOER: The play will be lacking.

STAGE-DIRECTOR: Are you sure of that?

PLAYGOER: Well, the play will certainly not exist if the poet or playwright is not there to write it.

STAGE-DIRECTOR: There will not be any play in the sense in which you use the word.

PLAYGOER: But you propose to present something to the audience, and I presume before you are able to present them with that something you must have it in your possession.

STAGE-DIRECTOR: Certainly; you could not have made a surer remark. Where you are at fault is to take for granted, as if it were a law for the Medes and Persians, that that *something* must be made of words.

PLAYGOER: Well, what is this something which is not words, but for presentation to the audience?

STAGE-DIRECTOR: First tell me, is not an idea something?

PLAYGOER: Yes, but it lacks form.

STAGE-DIRECTOR: Well, but is it not permissible to give an idea whatever form the artist chooses?

PLAYGOER: Yes.

STAGE-DIRECTOR: And is it an unpardonable crime for the theatrical artist to use some different material to the poet's?

PLAYGOER: No.

STAGE-DIRECTOR: Then we are permitted to attempt to give form to an idea in whatever material we can find or invent, provided it is not a material which should be put to a better use?

PLAYGOER: Yes.

STAGE-DIRECTOR: Very good; follow what I have to say for the next few minutes, and then go home and think about it for a while. Since you have granted all I asked you to permit, I am now going to tell you out of what material an artist of the theater of the future will create his masterpieces. Out of ACTION, SCENE, and VOICE. Is it not very simple?

And when I say *action,* I mean both gesture and dancing, the prose and poetry of action.

When I say *scene,* I mean all which comes before the eye, such as the lighting, costume, as well as the scenery.

When I say *voice,* I mean the spoken word or the word which is sung, in contradiction to the word which is read, for the word written to be spoken and the word written to be read are two entirely different things.

And now, though I have but repeated what I told you at the beginning of our conversation, I am delighted to see that you no longer look so puzzled.

VSEVOLOD MEYERHOLD

(1874-1942)

The Theater Theatrical

The Naturalistic Theater and the Theater of Mood

The Moscow Art Theater has two visages: the Naturalistic Theater and the Theater of Mood. The naturalism of the Moscow Art Theater is a naturalism borrowed from the Meiningen players. *Accuracy in reproducing nature* is its basic principle. On the stage everything has to be as real as possible—the ceilings, the stucco cornices, the stones, the wallpaper, the little stove doors, the ventilation holes, and so on. . . .

The actor's make-up is *overly realistic*—real faces as we see them in real life, an exact copy. The Naturalistic Theater considers the face an actor's main expressive tool and consequently overlooks all other means of expression. The Naturalistic Theater does not know the advantages of plasticity and does not compel its actors to train their bodies. The schools connected with the Naturalistic Theater do not realize that physical sport should be a basic training, especially for plays such as *Antigone* and *Julius Caesar,* plays which because of their music belong to *another* kind of theater.

Many excellently made-up faces remain in one's mind, but no pos-

Vsevolod Meyerhold: "From *On the Theater*" (a translation by Nora Beeson of the essay, "On the History and Technique of the Theater," 1906), *Tulane Drama Review*, IV, May 1960, 134-147 *passim*. By permission of Nora Beeson.

tures or rhythmic movements. During a performance of *Antigone* the director somehow unconsciously arranged his actors to resemble frescoes and vase paintings, but he was not able to *synthesize* or *stylize* what he had seen on archeological remains; he could only photograph. On the stage before us we saw a series of groupings, like a row of hill tops, but realistic gestures and movements, like ravines, disturbed the internal rhythm of the reproduction.

The actor in the Naturalistic Theater is extremely nimble at transforming himself, but his methods do not originate from *plastic* action but from make-up and an onomatopoeic imitation of various accents, dialects, and voices. Instead of developing his esthetic sense to exclude all coarseness, the actor's task is to lose his self-consciousness. A photographic sense of recording daily trivia is instilled in the actor. . . .

The Naturalistic Theater denies that the spectator has the ability to finish a painting in his imagination, or to dream as he does when listening to music. And yet the spectator possesses such an ability. In the first act of Iartsev's play *At the Monastery* the interior of a monastery was shown and curfew bells were heard. No window was shown on stage, but from the sound of the bells the playgoer imagined a courtyard covered with piles of bluish snow, fir trees as in the paintings by Nesterov, little paths leading from cell to cell, and the golden cupolas of a church. One spectator imagined such a picture, the second another, and the third still another. Mystery had taken hold of the playgoer and was transporting him into a world of dreams. In the second act a window overlooked the courtyard of the monastery but no cells, heaps of snow, or colored cupolas were visible. And the spectator was disenchanted and even enraged for Mystery had disappeared and dreams were abused. . . .

"A work of art can function only through the imagination. Therefore a work of art must constantly arouse the imagination, not just arouse, but activate." To arouse the imagination "is a necessary condition of an esthetic phenomenon, and also a basic law of the fine arts. It therefore follows that an artistic work must *not* supply everything to our senses but only enough to direct our imagination onto the right path, leaving the last word to our imagination."[1] . . .

The Naturalistic Theater not only denies that the playgoer has the ability to dream, but even that he has the ability to understand intelligent conversation on stage. All the scenes in Ibsen's plays are submitted to a tedious analysis which transforms the work of the Norwegian dramatist into something boring, dragging, and doctrinaire. Especially in the performance of Ibsen plays the method of the naturalistic stage director is clearly demonstrated. Each play is divided into a series of scenes, and each separate part is *minutely analyzed*. This painstaking analysis is applied to the tiniest scenes of the drama. With these various, thoroughly digested parts the whole is glued together again. This piecing together of the whole from its parts is called the art of the director, but I think the analytical work of the naturalist-director, this pasting together of the poet's, the actor's, the musician's, the painter's, or even the director's work, will never result in a unified whole.

The famous critic of the eighteenth century, Alexander Pope, in his didactic "Essay on Criticism" (1711), enumerates the reasons which prevent critics from giving sound judgment, and among other reasons, points out their habit of examining parts of a work when the critics' first duty should be to look from the point of view of the author at a work *as a whole*.

The same could be said for the stage director. The naturalistic director, profoundly analyzing each separate part of a work, does not see the picture as a whole; fascinated by his filigree work—the embellishment of some scenes with his pearls of "characterization"—he destroys the balance, the harmony of the whole. . . .

In Chekhov's *Cherry Orchard*, as in the plays of Maeterlinck, an unseen hero exists on stage whose presence is felt whenever the curtain drops. When the curtain closed on the Moscow Art Theater's performance of *The Cherry Orchard*, the presence of such a protagonist was not felt. Only types were remembered. To Chekhov the characters of *The Cherry Orchard* were a means to an end and not a

---

[1] Schopenhauer

reality. But in the Moscow Art Theater the characters became real and the lyrical-mystic aspect of *The Cherry Orchard* was lost.

If in the Chekhov plays the particulars distracted the director from the *whole* because the impressionistically drawn figures of Chekhov lent themselves well to precise characterization, similarly, in the plays by Ibsen, the director had to explain to the public what seemed incomprehensible to him.

The performances of Ibsen plays above all aimed to *enliven the "boring" dialogue* with something—with eating a meal, arranging a room, introducing scenes of packing, moving about furniture, and so forth. In *Hedda Gabler,* when Tesman and Aunt Julia eat breakfast together, I remember well how awkwardly the actor playing Tesman ate, but I hardly heard the thesis of the play. . . .

Stanislavsky felt that a theatrical sky could be made real to an audience, and the entire staff worried about how to raise the roof of the theater. No one felt that rather than altering the stage, the foundation of the Naturalistic Theater might be more profitably changed. For no one believed that the wind blowing the garlands in the first scene of *Julius Caesar* was not the stagehand, especially as the costumes of the actors were not moving. In the second act of *The Cherry Orchard* the actors walked in "real" ravines, over "real" bridges, near a "real" chapel, and in the sky hung two great lumps covered with blue cloth the likes of which had never been seen in any sky. The hills on a battlefield (in *Julius Caesar*) were built so as to diminish gradually toward the horizon, but why did the actors not diminish in size as they moved in the same direction as the hills? . . .

Naturalism introduced a more complex staging technique in the Russian theater, yet it is the theater of Chekhov, the second style of the Moscow Art Theater, which demonstrated the power of *mood;* without this mood, or atmosphere, the theater of the Meiningers would have perished long ago. But the development of the Naturalistic Theater was not aided by this *new mood* originating from Chekhov's plays. The performance of *The Seagull* in the Alexandrinsky Theater did not dispel the author's mood, yet the secret was not to be found in the chirping of crickets, the barking of dogs, or

in realistic doors. When *The Seagull* was performed in the Hermit-
age building of the Moscow Art Theater, the *machinery* was not
working perfectly, and technique did not yet extend its feelers into
all corners of the theater.

The secret of Chekhov's mood lies in the *rhythm* of his language.
This rhythm was felt by the actors of the Art Theater during the
rehearsals of the first Chekhov play, was felt because of their love
for Chekhov.

The Moscow Art Theater would never have attained its second
style without the rhythmicality of Chekhov's words; the Theater of
Mood became its real character and was not a mask borrowed from
the Meiningen players.

That the Art Theater could under one roof shelter the Naturalistic
Theater and the Theater of Mood was due, I am convinced, to A. P.
Chekhov, who personally attended the rehearsals of his plays and
who, with the charm of his personality and frequent conversations,
influenced the actors, their tastes, and their ideas about the problem
of art.

This new kind of theater was created chiefly by a group known as
"Chekhovian actors." They performed all the Chekhov plays and
can be considered the originators of the Chekhovian rhythmic diction. Whenever I remember the active part these actors took in creating *The Seagull's* characters and mood, I understand why I believe
so strongly that the actor is the most important element on a stage.
Neither the sets, nor the crickets, nor the horses' hoofs on the boards
could create *mood*, but only the extraordinary musicality of the performers who understood the rhythm of Chekhov's poetry and could
veil his work in lunar mist.

In the first two productions (*The Seagull* and *Uncle Vanya*) the
actors were perfectly *free* and the harmony was not disrupted. But
later, the naturalistic director made the ensembles more important
and lost the key to a Chekhov performance. Once the ensembles
became important, the work of the actors became passive; but instead
of encouraging the lyricism of this *new key,* the naturalistic director

created atmosphere with external devices such as darkness, sounds, accessories, and characters, and soon lost his sense of direction because he did not realize how Chekhov changed from subtle realism to mystic lyricism.

Once the Moscow Theater had decided how to produce Chekhov plays, it applied the same pattern to other authors. Ibsen and Maeterlinck were performed "in the manner of Chekhov." . . .

The Art Theater could have extricated itself from the impasse in which it found itself by using Chekhov's lyrical talent. But instead it used more and more elaborate tricks, and finally even lost the key to performing its very own author, just as the Germans had lost the key to performing Hauptmann, who, aside from his realistic plays, had written dramas which demanded an entirely different approach. . . .

The First Experiments of the Theater of Convention

The Theater Studio, heeding the advice of Maeterlinck and Bruisov, was the first theater to experiment with a conventionalized, stylized technique. And as the Studio with its production of Maeterlinck's tragedy, *La Mort de Tintagiles,* came very close to realizing the ideals of the Stylized Theater, it seems to me not out of place to describe the method of work employed by the directors, actors, and painters on this play, and to recount the experiences gained.

In the theater a discord always exists between the creative artists who collectively present their work to the public. Author, director, actor, designer, musician, and property man are never ideally united in collectively creative work. For that reason I do not feel that Wagner's synthesis of art is possible. Both the painter and the musician are handicapped, the former in a decorative theater where he is only able to paint scenery for the stage at night instead of for a painting exhibit in daylight, and the latter because his music always plays a subservient role in the dramatic theater.

Already at the beginning of our work on *La Mort de Tintagiles* the question of creative difference worried me. If the designer or the musician were not able to fit into the total scheme—with each one trying to pull in his direction—then it seemed to me that at least the author, director, and actor should work closely together. But these three, who form the foundation of any theater, *could join their efforts* only under the conditions existing in the Theater Studio during the rehearsals of *La Mort de Tintagiles.*

Following the usual practice of "talking" about the play (preceded, of course, by the director being acquainted with everything written about the play), the director and actor then read some poetry by Maeterlinck, fragments from those of his plays which had scenes similar in mood to *La Mort de Tintagiles.* This was done so as not to make the play into an exercise. Each actor in turn read some verses or excerpts. This work was for the actor what a sketch is for the painter or an exercise for the musician.

Such exercises polished technique; a painter can begin a picture only after technique has been mastered. Not only the director but all those listening made suggestions. This work was aimed at finding how the author "sounded" best. When in this collective work an author's text begins to "sound," then the audience will proceed to analyze the means which convey the style of a given author.

But before giving an insight into our new ideas I want to point out *two methods of directing a play* which in different ways establish the relationship between the actor and the director: one system restrains the creative freedom of both the actor and the spectator, and the other liberates both actor and spectator, permitting the latter to use his imagination actively rather than merely to contemplate. These two systems are best understood if the four fundamentals of the theater—the author, director, actor, and spectator—are graphically represented as follows:

1) A triangle with the apex representing the director, and the bases the author and the actor. The playgoer sees the work of the author and actor through the *work of the director.* (Graphically the "spectator" is at the top of the triangle.) This is one kind of theater—the "triangular theater."

SPECTATOR

DIRECTOR

AUTHOR ×   × ACTOR

2) A straight, horizontal line where the four fundamentals of the theater are represented from left to right: author, director, actor, spectator. This is the other kind of theater—the "straight theater." The actor freely reveals his soul to the spectator after having incorporated the work of the director, just as the director had incorporated the work of the author.

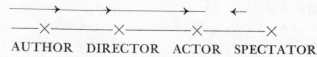

AUTHOR   DIRECTOR   ACTOR   SPECTATOR

In the "triangular theater" the director, after having discussed his plan in great detail, will rehearse until his conception is simply reproduced, until he hears and sees the play as he had heard and seen it by himself. A symphony orchestra is an example of this "triangular theater" and the conductor is like the stage director. However, the theater, architecturally speaking, does not permit the director to use a conductor's stand, and therefore the difference between the methods of a director and a conductor is obvious.

Yes, but it so happens that a symphony orchestra can play without a conductor. Nikisch, for example, performs with an orchestra which he has conducted for many years with hardly a change in its personnel. Some music the orchestra performs year after year. Could not the orchestra bring to life Nikisch's conception without his being on the conductor's stand? Yes, this could happen, yet the audience would nevertheless hear the music as interpreted by Nikisch. But there is another question—would the music be played exactly the same as if Nikisch had conducted? The performance would have been less good, but we still would have heard Nikisch's interpretation of the piece.

I think a symphony orchestra without a conductor is possible; but it is not possible to draw a parallel between an orchestra without a conductor and a theater in which the actors perform on stage completely without a director. A symphony orchestra without a conductor is possible, but without rehearsals the audience will not be moved, and an orchestra can only convey the interpretation of this or that conductor. The actor's work must do more than acquaint the audience with a director's conception. An actor can inspire an audience only if he transforms himself into the author and director.

The main virtue of a player in a symphony orchestra is to possess a virtuoso technique and to follow accurately the dictates of a conductor. Like a symphony orchestra, the "triangular theater" must admit actors with a less individualistic virtuoso technique.

In the "straight theater" the director takes the part of the author, and makes the actor see his work (author and director are one). After incorporating the author's work by way of the director, the actor comes face to face with the spectator (author and director at the actor's back), and acts *freely* while enjoying the give and take between the two main elements of a theater—the player and the playgoer. The director *alone* must set the tone and style of a performance so that the "straight theater" may not become chaotic,[2] and yet the acting will remain free and unrestrained.

The director reveals his *plan* in *talking* about the play. The play is colored by the director's point of view. Captivating the actors with his love for the play, the director infuses them with the spirit of the author. But *after his explanations* all artists have complete independence. Then the director again calls them together to unify the different parts. *He does not want an exact recreation of his conception,* which existed solely to give unity to the whole, but waits for the

[2] Alexander Blok (in *Pereval*, 1907) feared that the actors of such a theater "might burn the ship of the play," but I think differences of opinion occur only when free interpretation is permitted. The danger is removed when the director gives good explanations to the actor, and the latter in turn has really understood his director.

moment when he can hide in the wings letting the actor either "burn his ship" (if the actor is at odds with the director or with the author, especially when the actors does not belong to the "new School"[3]) , or act freely in an almost improvisational manner, of course keeping to the text, but revealing the play to the audience through the prism of the actor's technique which has assimilated both the author's and the director's concepts. *Theater is acting.*

In the works of Maeterlinck, in his poetry and plays, his introduction to the latest edition, and his little book, *The Treasure of the Humble,* where he speaks of the static theater we see clearly that the author did not want to bring horror onto the stage, did not want to annoy the spectator with historical wailing, or make the public recoil in terror. Quite the contrary—he wanted to instill in the spectator a trembling but wise contemplation of the inevitable, to make the spectator weep and suffer but simultaneously move him and bring him to a state of peace and felicity. The basic task which the author sets himself is "to alleviate our sorrows by sowing hope long extinct." Human life with all its passions begins to flow again when the playgoer leaves the theater, but these passions no longer seem *vain;* life continues with its joys and sorrows, with its obligations, all of which now assume a greater meaning: either we find a way out of the darkness, or learn to endure life without bitterness. Maeterlinck's art is healthy and vivifying. He causes us to contemplate the greatness of Destiny, and his theater becomes a temple.

I think our predecessors when performing Maeterlinck made a mistake in frightening the spectator without revealing the inevitability of fate. "At the basis of my dramas," wrote Maeterlinck, "is the idea

[3] The "triangular theater" needs actors without individuality but with virtuosity. In the "straight theater" the individual acting talent is very important, and so a *new school* is needed. A new school is not one in which new techniques are taught, but one which arises only when a new, free theater is born.

The "straight theater" grows but once from a school, a single school, just as from each seed grows only one plant. And just as for the next plant a new seed has to be sown, so a new theater must grow each time from a new school. The "triangular theater" tolerates many schools, but the task of these schools is to fill vacant positions with a group of candidates who have been trained to imitate the great actors of the established theaters. I am convinced that especially these schools are to be blamed for the lack of real talent on our stages.

of a Christian God together with the idea of ancient fate." The author perceives people's words and tears as a dull rumble, as if in a deep, bottomless well. He sees people from a great distance, and they seem to him weakly shimmering sparks. And he wants to overhear words of meekness, hope, compassion, and fear, and show the might of that Destiny which controls our fates.

We tried in our performances of Maeterlinck to awaken in the spectator the same feeling Maeterlinck tried to arouse. Maeterlinck's plays are mysteries either of hardly perceptible harmony of voices, of quiet tears, of restrained sighs and tremors of hope (as in *La Mort de Tintagiles*), or of ecstasy calling for universal religious belief, for dancing to the sounds of pipe and organ, for a Bacchanalia of the great working of a Miracle (as in the second act of *Beatrice*). Maeterlinck's dramas are "above all a revelation and a purification of the soul. His dramas are of spirits singing *mezza voce* of suffering, love, beauty, and death." Artlessness leading from earth to the world of dreams. Harmony arousing quiet. Or ecstatic joy. These are the spiritual feelings which we brought to Maeterlinck's theater in our rehearsal studio. . . .

After taking into consideration Maeterlinck's writings and my work with the actors in the rehearsal studio, I intuitively reach the following conclusions:

I. Concerning diction:

1. Needed is a cold minting of words, absolutely free from any vibration (tremolo) or weeping. Complete absence of tension or gloom.

2. The sound must always have support, and the words must fall like drops in a deep well; the clear impact of the drops is heard without the vibration of the sound in space. No indistinctness in the sound, no words with howling endings as when reading "decadent" verses.

3. A mystic tremor is more forceful than the old-style temperament which was always uncontrolled, externally coarse (swinging of arms, beating of breast and thighs). The inner thrill of the mystic tremor is reflected in the eyes, on the lips,

in sounds, in the pronunciation of words; an outer calm during volcanic experiences. And all without tension, lightly.

4. Spiritual emotions, all their tragedy, are **indissolubly connected** with form which in turn is inseparable from content,
just as content dictates a particular, and no other, form in
Maeterlinck.[4]

5. Never fast patter which is permissible only in neurasthenic
kinds of plays, in those which have a row of dots. Epic calm
does not exclude a tragic experience. Tragic experiences are
always majestic.

6. Tragedy with a smile.

I fully understood these intuitive ideas only after reading the words
of Savonarola:

Do not think that Mary at the death of her son cried out, walked the streets
tearing her hair and acting like a mad woman. She came for her son with
meekness and great humility. She undoubtedly cried tears, but from her
external appearance she seemed not sad, but simultaneously *sad and joyful*. At the descent from the Cross she was both sad and joyful, absorbed in
the secret of the great blessedness of God.

To create an impression on the audience, the actor of the old school
shouted, wept, groaned, and beat his chest with his fists. But the new
actor must express tragedy like the sad, yet joyful, Mary: externally
calm, almost *cold,* without shouts and weeping, without tremulous
sounds, yet still profound.

II. Concerning plastic ideas:

1. Richard Wagner with his orchestra provided inner tension;

---

[4] Practice raised a question the answer to which I will not take upon myself,
but I only want to propose one: should an actor at first expose the inner content
of a role, show bursts of temperament, and only then clothe his experience with
this or that form? Or vice versa? At first we adhered to this method: not to show
temperamental outbursts until we had mastered the form. I think this is right.
But you will justly complain that form then enchains temperament. No, this is
not so. The old, naturalistic actors, our teachers, said: if you don't want to ruin
the role for yourself, begin to read it, not out loud, but to yourself, and only when
the part begins to sound in your heart, then speak it aloud. To approach a realistic role by silently reading the text, and a nonrealistic part by first mastering the
rhythm of the language and movement—that is the only true method.

the music sung by the singers seemed insufficiently powerful to convey the inner experiences of his heroes. Wagner called on his orchestra for help, feeling that only an orchestra could reveal Mystery to the audience. In "Drama," likewise, the *word* is not sufficiently strong to bring out the inner meaning. Pronunciation, even good pronunciation, does not mean speaking. It is necessary to seek new ways of expressing the inexpressible, and to reveal what is concealed.

As Wagner makes his orchestra speak about the spiritual experiences of his heroes, so I make plastic movements express inner feelings.

Plastic gestures are not new. Salvini in *Othello* or *Hamlet* always used plastic movements. True, this was also plastic art, but I am not talking about that kind of plasticity. Salvini's gestures closely corresponded to the words and their pronunciation. I mean that plasticity which exists aside from words.

What does plasticity aside from words mean?

Two men are holding a conversation about the weather, about art, or about apartments. A third bystander observing them, if he is more or less sensitive, can decide quite accurately who these two men are—friends, enemies, or lovers—from their conversation about subjects which do not reveal their personal relationships. From the way these two conversing men move their hands, take certain poses, lower their eyes, an observer can decipher their relationship, because in talking about the weather or art these two men use gestures which do not necessarily explain their words. And from these movements which are not related to the words, an observer can decide whether friends, enemies, or lovers are conversing.

A director builds a bridge from the spectator to the actor. Following the dictates of the author, and introducing onto the stage friends, enemies, or lovers, the director with movements and postures must present a certain image which will aid the spectator not only to hear the words, but to guess the inner, concealed feelings. And if the director, absorbed in the author's theme, hears the inner music, then he will propose to the actors plastic movements which will enable the spectator to hear this inner music.

Gestures, postures, glances, and silences depict the truthful relationship among people. Words do not tell the whole story. A pattern
of movement is needed on the stage which will force the spectator
into the position of being a keen observer, just as the third observer
of the two talking figures was able to divine their internal thoughts.
Words are for hearing, movement for seeing. In this manner the
spectator's imagination is aroused by two sensations—the visual and
auditory. The difference between the old and the new theater is that
in the latter movement and words are subordinate each to its own
rhythm. It does not necessarily follow that movement must never
correspond to words. Some phrases need to be illustrated by movement, but this must be as natural as the logical stresses in poetry.

    2. Maeterlinck's pictures have an archaic quality, as in icons.
       Arkel, as from a painting by Ambrogio Borgonione. Gothic
       arches. Wooden statues shining like rose wood. And the
       actors symmetrically arranged to express holiness, as in a
       Perugino painting.

"Women, effeminate boys, and languid, gentle old men can best express sweet dreaminess"; this was Perugino's aim. And does it not
also express Maeterlinck?

    The New Theater changed the absurd ornateness of the naturalis-
tic theaters into a structural plan based on rhythmic, linear movement and musical harmony of colors.

    An iconographic style was used in the sets (since we had not yet
abolished scenery altogether). And just as plastic movements were
used to bring out inner feelings, so scenery was painted which would
not detract from these movements. The spectator's concentration
had to be focused on motion; for that reason *La Mort de Tintagiles*
used only one backdrop. This tragedy was rehearsed against a background of simple canvas and made a very strong impression because
the pattern of the gestures stood out clearly. The play would have
been lost had the actors performed in scenery with space and air.
Therefore, a decorated panel. But after some experiments with
painted panels (as in *Beatrice, Hedda Gabler*), it seemed that they
were as unsuitable as the old type of scenery which had blurred move-

ment. In Giotto's paintings nothing marred the smoothness of his lines because he did not adhere to a naturalistic, but rather to a decorative, point of view. But the theater must not turn toward a "decorative" style (unless treated as in the Japanese theater).

A decorated panel, like a symphony, has a special function; and if figures are necessary then they should be cardboard puppets, not wax, wood, or cloth. For a painted flat has only two dimensions and demands figures of two dimensions.

The human body and the accessories surrounding it—tables, chairs, beds, and dressers—are all three-dimensional, and therefore a theater where the actor is the most important factor must be based on the plastic arts and not on painting. A *plastic statuesqueness* should be fundamental to acting.

This was the result of the first cycle of experiments in the New Theater. The historically inevitable circle was completed; experiments in stylized staging had raised new ideas concerning the decorative arts in the dramatic theater.

By rejecting a decorative style, the New Theater did not negate the new stylized staging nor Maeterlinck's iconographic notions. But the means of expression were architectural rather than painted. All the concepts of a stylized performance were kept inviolate in *La Mort de Tintagiles, Hedda Gabler,* and *Soeur Beatrice,* but the painter was employed without hindering the actors or the objects.

Staging a Classic

When I spoke of the methods open to the stage director who sought to reconstruct the characteristic stages of model theatrical epochs, when I discussed the two methods at the disposal of the director who contemplated the production of a play from an old theater, I failed to mention one possible exception. In the production of a play from the old theater, it is not at all necessary to subordinate the staging to *methods of archaeology*. In the matter of reconstruction the stage director need have no worry over the faithful reproduction of the architectural features on the antique stage. The production of a genuinely old play may be done in *free composition* in the spirit of primitive stages but on one indispensable condition: to take from the old stage the *essence* of those architectural features which would be most appropriate to the spirit of the work in production.

In order to produce, for example, *Don Juan* by Molière, it would be a mistake to attempt an exact replica of any contemporary stage of Molière's time: Palais Royal or Petit-Bourbon.

If we probe into the spirit of Molière's work we will discover that he strove to expand the framework of the contemporary stage which had been more suitable to the pathos of Corneille than to plays which had evolved out of elements of folk art.

The academic theater of the Renaissance which failed to utilize the possibilities inherent in the forward thrust of the forestage, set apart at a respectable distance from each other the actor and the

Vsevolod Meyerhold: *O Teatr*. Petrograd: 1913, 121-128. This excerpt translated by Louis Lozowick. The staging of *Don Juan* discussed here is a description of Meyerhold's production at the Alexandrinsky Theater, St. Petersburg, in 1910.

public. The first rows of seats were pushed back not only to the center of the orchestra but further still to the wall opposite the stage.

Could Molière acquiesce in this separation of actor and audience? Could Molière's overflowing gaiety find full release in such circumstances? Could the full breadth of his bold and true strokes be seen to advantage? Could the author, hurt by the suppression of *Tartuffe,* hurl his denunciatory soliloquies across that stage? Were not the columns in the wings a hindrance to the free gestures and gymnastic movements of Molière's actors?

Molière was the first theatrical master under *Le Roi Soleil* who strove to carry the action forward from the depth and the center of the stage to the *proscenium,* to its very edge.

Both the stage of antiquity and the popular stage of Shakespeare's time required no illusory sets like ours. Nor was the actor a source of stage illusion. With his gestures, facial expression, plastic movements, the actor was the *sole* vehicle for the realization of the dramatist's idea.

This was also the case in medieval Japan. In the *Nō* plays with their exquisite ceremonial, in which action, dialogue, song were rigidly stylized, in which the chorus performed a role similar to that of the Greek chorus, in which the wild fury of the music tended to transport the public into a world of hallucination, the stage director placed the actors so close to the edge of the platform that their dances, movements, gesticulation, mimicry, poses were in full view.

Speaking of the production of *Don Juan* it was not by accident that I mentioned the methods of the old Japanese theater.

From descriptions of Japanese theatrical performances approximately contemporaneous with Molière's predominance on the French stage, we learn that special attendants, so-called Corumbo in black cloaks, like priestly cassocks, would prompt the actors in view of the audience. Whenever the costume of a female character (played by a male) fell into disarray in a moment of high exaltation, Corumbo would hasten to arrange his train into beautiful folds and put his hair dress in order. It was part of his duty to pick up objects which the actors had dropped or forgotten on the stage. After a scene of battle he would remove from the stage lost headgear, weapons, cloaks. When a hero died Corumbo would throw a black cloth over the corpse under the cover of which the actor disappeared from the stage. When action required total darkness Corumbo would kneel down at the feet of the hero and throw light on his face by a candle attached to a long rod.

The Japanese have preserved to this day the mannerisms of the actors dating back to the creators of Japanese drama, Onono-Otsu (1513-1581), Satsumo-Joun (b. 1595) and the Shakespeare of Japan, Chikamatsu-Monzaimon.

Is not there something analogous in the present attempts of the Comédie Française to revive the methods of Molière's comedians?

In the extreme west of Europe (France, Italy, Spain, England) as in the extreme east of Asia (Japan) within the limits of one epoch (second half of the sixteenth and the whole of the seventeenth centuries) the theater resounded with the tinkling bells of pure theatricality.

Is it not clear why each device on every stage of that brilliant theatrical epoch was adopted precisely on the wonderful platform called the proscenium?

And, what about the proscenium?

Like a circus arena pressed on all sides by a circle of spectators, the proscenium is brought close to the public so that not a single gesture, not a single act, not a single facial expression shall be lost in the dust of the wings. And mark well how resourcefully planned are these gestures, actions, postures, expressions. Indeed—could the pompous affectations, the lack of plasticity in bodily movement be suffered by a public placed as close to the actor as was made necessary by the proscenium of the old English, Spanish, Italian, Japanese stages?

This proscenium so skillfully employed by Molière was the best insurance against the aridity of Corneillian methods which had been nursed in the Court of Louis XIV.

Furthermore—how notable have been the gains for Molière's work when performed on the proscenium although created in the wholly unfavorable climate of the contemporary stage! How spontaneously alive are the grotesque figures of Molière moving unhampered on the protruding forestage! The atmosphere of this space is not cramped by columns, while the light flooding this dustless atmosphere plays only on the lithe figures of the actors. Everything around seems especially made to increase the play of light both from the candles on the stage and the candles in the auditorium which throughout the performance is never darkened.

While rejecting the obligatory use of detail typical only of the stage of Louis XIV (curtain with cutout for head of announcer) could the stage director ignore the entourage associated with the style of the time which reared the theater of Molière?

There are plays like *Antigone* by Sophocles or *Woe from Wit* by Griboyedov which can be appreciated by a modern spectator through the prism of his own time. *Antigone* and *Woe from Wit* might even be performed in modern dress. The hymn to liberty in the former, the conflict of two generations in the latter play are expressed with such clear and insistent emphasis that their message can be transmitted in any environment.

There are on the other hand plays whose cardinal idea will be fully appreciated by a modern spectator only if in addition to grasping the fine subtleties of the plot he will be made aware of that elusive climate which in a bygone age surrounded the actors, the theater and the audience. There are plays which cannot be comprehended otherwise than if they are presented in a way intended to arouse in the spectator a receptivity to the action on the stage by setting it in a milieu analogous to the one that surrounded the audience of a specific past. Such a play is *Don Juan* by Molière. The public will only then appreciate the full subtlety of this charming comedy if it enters at once into a rapport with the smallest facets of the epoch in which the work was created. That is why the director who would undertake to stage *Don Juan* must first of all fill the stage and the auditorium with such an atmosphere that the dramatic action could not be grasped otherwise than through the prism of that atmosphere.

If one reads *Don Juan* by Molière without knowing the epoch which created his genius, how boring it appears! How indifferently the plot is developed compared with, say, the plot of *Don Juan* by Byron, not to speak of *El Burlador de Sevilla* by Tirso de Molina.

When we read *Woe from Wit* by Griboyedov chords of our own time
seem to be echoed from every page, and this makes the play especially
significant for the contemporary public. When, however, we read
the lengthy monologues of Elvire (Act I) or the long soliloquy of Don
Juan, flaying hypocrisy (Act V), our attention flags. In order to make
the modern spectator listen to these perorations without getting
bored, in order to make him follow a whole series of dialogues without finding them remote, it is necessary to remind him insistently
throughout the play of all those thousands of looms of the Lyonnaise
manufactories which supplied the silk for the monstrously large
Court of Louis XIV, of the Hôtel des Gobelins, that veritable city
of painters, sculptors, jewelers, cabinet-makers, of the furniture built
under the superintendence of the outstanding artist Le Brun, of all
those craftsmen who made mirrors and lace according to the Venetian
models, stockings according to the English, cloth according to the
Dutch, tin and copper according to the Germans.

Hundreds of wax candles in three chandeliers above and two can-
delabra on the proscenium. Blackamoors inundating the stage with
intoxicating perfumes, which flow drop by drop from a crystal flask
onto a red-hot plate. Blackamoors flitting over the stage to pick up a
lace handkerchief dropped by Don Juan or offer a chair to a tired
actor. Blackamoors tying the laces on the shoes of Don Juan as he
argues with Sganarelle. Blackamoors passing lanterns to the actors
when the stage is in semidarkness. Blackamoors removing from the
stage the cloaks and sabers after the desperate fight between Don
Juan and the brigands. Blackamoors crawling under the table when
the statue of the Commander appears. Blackamoors ringing a silver
bell to summon the audience and in the absence of a curtain, announcing intermissions—all these are not stage tricks for the diversion
of snobs; all this is in support of the main idea: to reveal as behind
an incense-laden veil the perfumed and gilded realm of Versailles.

And the more resplendent the costumes and accessories (even if the
architecture of the stage is extremely simple) the greater the contrast
between Molière's temperament as comedian and the solemn affectation of Versailles.

Was it the vagabondage over the provinces that put such a sharp stamp of forthrightness on the character of Molière? Or life in jerry-built stroller's stalls? Perhaps the struggle against hunger? Or was his defiant tone born amid the love-making actresses who cast the poet into such gloom and disappointment? In any case, after a period of friendly relations with Molière, Louis XIV seems to have found ample reason for growing cool.

The discord between *Le Roi Soleil* whose image is suggested in the lavish decorations on the proscenium, the discord between the King and the poet who in this pompous atmosphere makes Sganarelle complain of a stomach-ache (contrast of precious background versus Molière's mordant grotesques)—would not this discord now fuse into such a harmony that the spectator will inevitably fall under the spell of Molière's theater? And would any detail of this creative genius be lost upon the spectator?

Don Juan is being performed without a curtain. There was none in the theaters of Palais Royal or of Petit-Bourbon.

But why remove the curtain? The spectator is usually indifferent in front of a curtain however well painted by whatever gifted artist. The spectator who came to see what is behind the curtain awaits its rise with apathy. And when it is up, how long will it be before he absorbs the full enchantment of the atmosphere surrounding the players. It is quite otherwise when the stage is open from beginning to end, when the extras with their own peculiar pantomime prepare the stage in sight of the audience. Long before the actor appears on the boards the spectator has already inhaled deeply the air of an epoch. And then that which in the reading of the play seemed superfluous or boring is now seen in a totally different light.

And it is unnecessary to darken the stage either during the intermission or in the course of the performance. Bright light infects with a festive mood those who come to the theater. The actor noting a smile on the lips of the spectator begins to enjoy his own sight as in a mirror. The actor who wears the mask of Don Juan will win the hearts not only of the masked Mathurine and Charlotte but also of the owners of those beautiful eyes whose sparkle he will detect in the auditorium as an answer to the smile in his own role.

EUGENE VAKHTANGOV

(1883-1922)

Fantastic Realism

APRIL 10, 1922

VAKHTANGOV: Meyerhold understands theatricality as a performance at which the audience does not forget for a single moment that it is in a theater. Stanislavsky demanded exactly the reverse: that the audience forget that it is in the theater, that it come to feel itself living in the atmosphere and milieu in which the characters of the play live. He rejoiced in the fact that the audience used to come to the Moscow Art Theater to *The Three Sisters,* not as to a theater, but as if invited to the Prosorov house. This he considered to be the highest achievement of the theater. Stanislavsky wanted to destroy theatrical banality, he wanted to put an end to it at once. Whatever reminded him of the old theaters, even to the slightest extent, he branded with the word "theatrical," this word having become a term of abuse in the Moscow Art Theater. To be sure, what he was berating was vulgar indeed, but carried away by the need for ferreting out vulgarity, Stanislavsky also removed a certain genuine, necessary theatricality, and genuine theatricality consists in presenting theatrical works in a theatrical manner. . . .

Stanislavsky bore down on vulgarity, began to drive it out, began to

Eugene Vakhtangov: *Zapiski, Pisma, Stati*. Moscow: Iskusstvo, 1939, 254-262 *passim*. Excerpts from stenographic reports of two conversations between Eugene Vakhtangov and his disciples Boris E. Zakhava and K. I. Kotlubai during his final illness.

search for the truth. This quest after truth led him to the truth of inner experiences, that is, he began to demand a genuine, natural inner experience upon the stage, forgetting that the actor's inner experience must be conveyed to the auditorium with the help of theatrical means. And Stanislavsky himself was compelled to use theatrical means. You know there is not a production of Chekhov's plays without a backstage language of its own—none of them takes place without the sound of the cricket, the noise of the street, the shouting of the hucksters, the striking of a clock. And all those are theatrical means found for Chekhov's plays.

K. I. KOTLUBAI: And what is a mood? Isn't this a theatrical achievement?

VAKHTANGOV: No, there should be no moods in the theater. There should be pure joy and no moods. Altogether there is no such thing as theatrical moods. When you look at a naturalistic picture are you possessed then by a "mood"? It impresses you with its content, but you forget the craftsmanship. I remember the impression made upon me by Repin's "John the Terrible Killing His Son." I stood there for hours. I was afraid to come close to the picture, but I evaluated it only from the point of view of its content. Blood, John's eyes, and especially the eyes of the murdered son. But now I look at the picture and it produces within me a feeling of revulsion. But to go back to our subject.

Meyerhold is the only one of all the Russian directors who has the feel of theatricality. He was a prophet at one time and was not accepted. He was ten years ahead of his time. Meyerhold did the same thing as Stanislavsky. He also destroyed theatrical banality, but he did it with the aid of theatrical means. Stanislavsky in his enthusiasm for real truth, brought naturalistic truth to the stage. He sought theatrical truth in the truth of life. Meyerhold, carried away by theatrical truth, removed the truthfulness of feelings, and truth there must be in both—the theaters of Meyerhold and Stanislavsky.

Feeling is the same in theater and life, but the means and methods of presenting them are different. The grouse is the same, whether served in the restaurant or at home. But in the restaurant it is served and prepared in such a manner as to have a theatrical ring to it, while at home it is just a homemade piece of meat. Stanislavsky served the truth with truth, water with water, grouse with grouse, while Meyerhold removed truth altogether, that is, he left the dish, the method of preparing it, but he prepared paper and not a grouse. And so he obtained paper feelings. Meyerhold was a high-grade master and he served his dish in a masterful restaurant-like manner, but it was not fit to eat. The removal of theatrical banality with the means of the conventional theater led Meyerhold to genuine theatricality, to the formula: the audience should not forget for one single second that it is in a theater. Stanislavsky arrived at the formula: the audience has to forget that it is in the theater.

A perfect work of art is everlasting. A perfect work of art is one in which is present a harmony of content, form and material. Stanislavsky found only a harmony with the mood of the Russian society of his period, but not everything that is contemporary is eternal. But whatever is eternal is always contemporaneous. Meyerhold never felt the "today" but he did feel the "tomorrow." Stanislavsky never felt the "tomorrow," but always felt the "today." But one has to feel "the today in the morrow," and the morrow in the "present day."

APRIL 11, 1922

VAKHTANGOV: Well, gentlemen, I am ready for questions.

B. ZAKHAVA: I believe we should speak about theatricality, genuine theatricality.

VAKHTANGOV: All right. I seek in the theater modern methods of solving the problem of play production in a form which would have a theatrical ring to it. Let us take, for instance, the problems of locale. I am trying to solve them in a manner different from the Moscow Art Theater—that is, not by reproducing the locale upon the stage, by giving it the truth of life. The method of solving the problems of locale by the Moscow Art Theater does not give birth to artistic works, for creativeness is absent there. There is only a refined, skill-ful, keen result of one's observations of life. I should like to call the work I do upon the stage "fantastic realism."

K. I. KOTLUBAI: What you call "fantastic realism" is to me pure and simple realism.

VAKHTANGOV: Let us try now to point out the difference between naturalism and realism.

ZAKHAVA: In my opinion, naturalism reproduces precisely what the artist observes in actuality. Naturalism is photography. But the artist who is a realist distills from the actual only what appears to his eyes as the most important, the most essential. He rejects minutiae, selects the typical and important. But in the process of his creative work he operates all the time with the very materials of actuality. Such an art exists and it should not be confused with naturalism or what Vakhtangov is seeking now. If you name it just pure and simple "realism" what will you put in place of the form intermediary be-tween naturalism and what Vakhtangov is seeking?

VAKHTANGOV: I might name the thing I am seeking not fantastic realism, but theatrical realism, but that is worse. In the theater every-thing should be theatrical. This is taken for granted.

K. I. KOTLUBAI: I am convinced that somewhere there is a well-formulated definition of realism. Zakhava says that the artist who is a realist separates the important from the nonimportant. That is not so, as far as I see it. To me realism in art, and particularly in the theater, is the ability on the part of the artist to create anew whatever he gets from the material by which he is inspired. The material gives the master realist a definite impression, a definite idea, with which he then creates with the aid of means germane to his specific art.

VAKHTANGOV: So you say that Zakhava gave us a wrong definition of realism. Let's discuss specific examples. What is Andreyev's *Life of Man* upon the stage of the Moscow Art Theater?

K. I. KOTLUBAI: From my point of view it is not true realism for the following reason: it is an attempt to carry over the symbolistic content of the play with the aid of the very symbolistic means that are given by the author. It is not creating anew a symbolic play upon the stage. Whatever Andreyev wrote has been carried over to the stage in its pure form.

VAKHTANGOV: This is not so. All the acting characters were created by the director and not by Andreyev. Andreyev did not write that such and such a character is fat. He wrote a text. And the artist actor makes the figure, dresses it the way he feels, imparts to it a definite (in this case schematic) movement, tries to find out how it should walk, speak, sit, etc. *A Man's Life* and *The Drama of Life* are fantastic realism.

ZAKHAVA: And *The Lower Depths?* What do you hold that to be? Naturalism?

VAKHTANGOV: Of course that is pure realism. In my opinion, the theater did not interpret Gorky in the right manner. Gorky is a romantic, and the theater interprets him not romantically, but naturalistically.

Kotlubai says that what we are seeking is realism. Here is an example of our work: In the wedding scene of *The Dybbuk* we had to insert a small scene which would justify an interval. It was necessary for the audience to believe that the orchestra was successful in finding the bridegroom, otherwise it would appear as if the orchestra just left and then came back. That is why I inserted a scene of two girls watching the orchestra and performing all kinds of stunts in the Chekhov style—jumping upon benches, gloating, clapping their hands. It made a wonderful scene which was greatly liked by the actors. They themselves came to feel something of Chekhov in it. However, the scene had to be thrown out, since it clashed with the rest of the play. Now we even have a special term—"the Dybbuk method."

And what, for instance, would you say of *Turandot?*

KOTLUBAI: That is true realism.

VAKHTANGOV: That is fantastic realism. Meyerhold's staging of *The Booth* by Blok was similar to *Turandot*. There you had only the external portrayal of the theater, that is, the side scenes were there and so was the prompter's box. But all that was pointed out by the author. The actors were the impersonators of the characters drawn by the author. This kind of histrionics could be found in the older theaters—those of Shakespeare, Molière. Now we have only a few great actors—Duse, Chaliapin, Salvini—who in acting *show* that they act.

Realism takes from life everything but what it needs for the reproduction of a given scene, that is, it brings to the stage only that which has a histrionic value. It takes life, truth and gives genuine feelings. Sometimes it even gives the minutiae of life, then we have naturalism, for minutiae is photography. The Pushkin production in the Moscow Art Theatre is realism. Did you ever notice there or in *Czar Fyodor* any minute details? And still, in *Czar Fyodor,* you may see certain details in the presentation of the character of a Boyar which will be naturalism. The author overlooks certain minute details but the director-naturalist introduces them: if the character enters from the street where it is snowing, the director will invariably make him shake off the snow in the hall, etc.

Attempts are made to approach the opera in a naturalistic, or rather a realistic manner. I would approach it in the way it sometimes is by talented singers. The audience should never be deceived. The singers should always stress: I am singing and that is why I am performing out on the forestage. Stanislavsky produces operas in a realistic manner. He will not permit the singer to come out to the footlights.

Now, in *Anthony* we have mixed forms: the convention of external setting, realism and fantastic realism. Naturalism is completely absent. Of outstanding importance for fantastic realism is the solving of the means and the form. The means must be theatrical. It is very difficult to find a form harmonizing with the content and presented with the aid of the right means. If we begin to work upon marble with wooden mallets, nothing will come of it. Marble demands an instrument adequate to its structure.

Why was *Turandot* successful? Because harmony was achieved in it. The Third Studio performs an Italian fairy tale by Gozzi on the 22nd of January, 1922. The methods are modern and theatrical. The form and content harmonize like a musical chord. It is fantastic realism, it is a new trend in the theater.

Gogol's world is the world of fantastic realism. In the Moscow Art Theater production of *The Inspector General* we have Volkov playing the role of Osip as a naturalistic character, Lilina and others as realistic, but Khlestakov acted by Chekhov is already a character interpreted with the methods of fantastic realism. Volkov is not theater, but Chekhov is.

In the theater there should be neither naturalism nor realism, but fantastic realism. Rightly found theatrical methods impart genuine life to the play upon the stage. The methods can be learned, but the form must be created. It has to be convinced by one's fantasy. That is why I call it fantastic realism. Such a form exists and should exist in every art.

GEORGE BERNARD SHAW

(1856-1950)

The Art of Rehearsal

My dear McNulty,

As to stage technique, there are several stage techniques; and people may be very clever in one or more of them without being good at them all, and may even—especially in acting—know bits of them and not the rest. The beginning and end of the business from the author's point of view is the art of making the audience believe that real things are happening to real people. But the actor, male or female, may want the audience to believe that it is witnessing a magnificent display of acting by a great artist; and when the attempt to do this fails, the effect is disastrous, because then there is neither play nor great acting: the play is not credible nor the acting fascinating. To your star actor the play does not exist except as a mounting block. That is why comparatively humble actors, who do not dare to think they can succeed apart from the play, often given much better representations than star casts.

Many star actors have surprisingly little of what I call positive skill, and an amazing power of suggestion. You can safely write a play in which the audience is assured that the heroine is the most wonderful creature on earth, full of exquisite thoughts, and noble in

George Bernard Shaw: *The Art of Rehearsal; a Private Letter to an Irish Colleague in Response to a Request for Advice and Information.* New York: Samuel French, 1928. Copyright, 1928, by Bernard Shaw. By permission of the Public Trustee and The Society of Authors.

character to the utmost degree, though, when it comes to the point, you find yourself unable to invent a single speech or action that would surprise you from your aunt. No matter: a star actress at £250 a week will do all that for you. She will utter your twaddle with such an air, and look such unutterable things between the lines, and dress so beautifully and move so enigmatically and enchantingly, that the imagination of the audience will supply more than Shakespeare could have written.

This art of suggestion has been developed to an abnormal degree by the emptiness of the mechanical "well-made play" of the French school. And you may be tempted to say, "If this woman is so wonderful when she is making bricks without straw, what heights would she not reach if I were to give her straw in abundance?" But if you did you would be rudely disillusioned. You would have to say to the actress: "Mere suggestion is no use here. I don't ask you to suggest anything: I give you the actual things to do and say. I don't want you to look as if you could say wonderful things if you uttered your thoughts: I give you both the thoughts and the words; and you must get them across the footlights." On these conditions your star might be dreadfully at a loss. She might complain of having too many words. She would certainly try hard to get in her old suggestive business between the lines; to escape from the play; to substitute a personal performance of her own for the character you wanted to make the audience believe her to be; and thus your trouble with her would be in direct proportion to her charm as a fashionable leading lady.

The success of the Dublin Abbey Street Theatre was due to the fact that when it began none of the Company was worth twopence a week for ordinary fashionable purposes, though some of them can now hold a London audience in the hollow of their hands. They were held down by Yeats and Lady Gregory ruthlessly to my formula of making the audience believe that real things were happening to real people. They were taught no tricks, because Yeats and Lady Gregory didn't know any, having found out experimentally only what any two people of high intelligence and fine taste could find out by sticking to the point of securing a good representation.

Now as to your daily business in the theater. It will be more laborious than you expect. If before you begin rehearsing you sit down to the manuscript of your play and work out all the stage business; so that you know where every speech is to be spoken as well as what it is to convey, and where the chairs are to be and where they are to be taken to, and where the actors are to put their hats or anything else they are to take in their hands in the course of the play, and when they are to rise and when they are to sit, and if you arrange all this so as to get the maximum of effect out of every word, and thus make the actors feel that they are speaking at the utmost possible advantage —or at worst that they cannot improve on your business, however little they may like it—and if you take care that they never distract attention from one another; that when they call to one another they are at a due distance; and that, when the audience is looking at one side of the stage and somebody cuts in on the other, some trick (which you must contrive) calls the attention of the audience to the new point of view or hearing, etc., then you will at the first rehearsal get a command of the production that nothing will shake afterwards. There will be no time wasted in fumbling for positions, and trying back and disputing.

When you have put your actors through an act for the first time in this way, go through it again to settle the business firmly in their memory. Be on the stage, handling your people and prompting them with the appropriate tones, as they will, of course, be rather in the dark as to what it is all about, except what they may have gathered from your reading of the play to them before rehearsal. Don't let them learn their parts until the end of the first week of rehearsal: nothing is a greater nuisance to an actor who is trying to remember his lines when he should be settling his positions and getting the hang of the play with his book in his hand.

One or two acts twice over is enough for each preliminary rehearsal. When you have reached the end of the first stage, then call "perfect" rehearsals (that is, without books). At these you must leave the stage and sit in the auditorium with a big notebook; *and from that time forth never interrupt a scene, nor allow anyone else to interrupt it or try back.* When anything goes wrong, or any improvement occurs to you, make a note; and at the end of the act go on the stage and explain your notes to the actors. Don't criticize. If a thing is wrong and you don't know exactly how to set it right, say nothing. Wait until you find out the right thing to do, or until the actor does. It discourages and maddens an actor to be told merely that you are dissatisfied. If you cannot help him, let him alone. Tell him what to do if you know: if not, hold your tongue until it comes to you or to him, as it probably will if you wait.

Remember that when the "perfect" rehearsals begin, the whole affair will collapse in apparent and most disappointing back-slidings for at least a week as far as the long parts are concerned, because in the first agony of trying to remember the words everything else will be lost. You must remember that at this stage the actor, being under a heavy strain, is fearfully irritable. But after another week the words will come automatically; and the play will get under way again.

Remember (particularly during the irritable stage) that you must not tell an actor too much at once. Not more than two or three important things can be borne at one rehearsal; and *don't* mention trifles, such as slips in business or in words, in a heart-broken desperate way, as if the world were crumbling in ruins. Don't mention anything that doesn't really matter. Be prepared for the same mistake being repeated time after time, and your directions being forgotten until you have given them three or four days running.

If you get angry and complain that you have repeatedly called attention, etc., like a schoolmaster, you will destroy the whole atmosphere in which art breathes, and make a scene which is not in the play, and a very disagreeable and invariably unsuccessful scene at that. Your chief artistic activity will be to prevent the actors taking their tone and speech from one another, instead of from their own parts, and thus destroying the continual variety and contrast which are the soul of liveliness in comedy and truth in tragedy. An actor's cue is not a signal to take up the running thoughtlessly, but a provocation to retort or respond in some clearly differentiated way. He must, even on the thousandth night, make the audience believe that he has never heard his cue before.

In the final stage, when everybody is word perfect, and can give his or her whole mind to the play, you must watch, watch, watch, like a cat at a mouse hole, and make very well-considered notes. To some of them you will append a "Rehearse this"; and at the end of the act you will ask them to go through the bit to get it right. But *don't* say when it doesn't come right: "We must go on at this until we get it, if we have to stay here all night": the schoolmaster again. If it goes wrong, it will go wronger with every repetition on the same day. Leave it until next time.

At the last two rehearsals you ought to have very few notes: all the difficulties should have been cleared away. The first time I ever counted my notes was when I had to produce *Arms and the Man* in ten rehearsals. The total was 600. That is a minimum: I have run into thousands since. Do not forget that though at the first rehearsal you will know more about the parts than the actors, at the last rehearsal they ought to know more about them (through their undivided attention) than you, and therefore have something to teach you about them.

Be prepared for a spell of hard work. The incessant strain on one's attention (the actors have their exits and rests; but the producer is hard at it all the time), the social effort of keeping up everyone's spirits in view of a great event, the dryness of the previous study of the mechanical details, daunt most authors. But if you have not enough energy to face all that, you had better keep out of the theater and trust to a professional producer. In fact, it sometimes happens that the author has to be put out. Unless he goes through the grind I have described, and which I face with greater reluctance as I grow older, he simply bothers and complains and obstructs, either saying that he does not like what the actors are doing without knowing what he wants instead, or at the first rehearsal expecting a perfect performance, or wanting things that can't be done, or making his suggestions ridiculous by unskillful demonstrations, or quarrelling, or devil knows what not.

Only geniuses can tell you exactly what is wrong with a scene, though plenty of people can tell you something is wrong with it. So make a note of their dissatisfaction; but be very careful how you adopt their cure if they prescribe one. For instance, if they say a scene is too slow (meaning that it bores them), the remedy in nine cases out of ten is for the actors to go slower and bring out the meaning better by contrasts of tone and speed.

Never have a moment of silence on the stage except as an intentional stage effect. The play must not stop while an actor is sitting down or getting up or walking off the stage. The last word of an exit speech must get the actor off the stage. He must sit on a word or rise on a word; if he has to make a movement, he must move as he speaks and not before or after; and the cues must be picked up as smartly as a ball is fielded in cricket. This is the secret of pace, and of holding an audience. It is a rule which you may set aside again and again to make a special effect; for a technical rule may always be broken on purpose. But as a rule of thumb it is invaluable. I once saw a fine play of Masefield's prolonged by half-an-hour and almost ruined because the actors made their movements in silence between the speeches. That does not happen when his plays are produced by Granville-Barker or by himself.

Remember that no strangers should be present at a rehearsal. It is sometimes expedient that strangers, and even journalists, be invited to witness a so-called rehearsal; and on such occasions a pre-arranged interruption by the producer may take place to affirm the fact that the occasion is only a rehearsal. But the interruption must be addressed to the mechanical staff about some mechanical detail. No direction should ever be given to an actor in the presence of a stranger; and the consent of every actor should be obtained before a stranger is admitted. The actor, of course, is bound to the same reticence. A stranger is a non-professional who is not in the theater on business. Rehearsals are absolutely and sacredly confidential. The publication of gossip about rehearsals, or the disclosure of the plot of the play, is the blackest breach of stage etiquette.

I have tumbled all this out at express speed, as best I can do for you out of my own experience, in reply to your innocent question about technique. I hope it is intelligible and may be useful.

HARLEY GRANVILLE-BARKER

(1877-1946)

Diversity into Unity

An essential quality of any work of art is its homogeneity. For a staged play, then, to make good its claim to be one it would seem to follow that the actors must continue what the dramatist has begun by methods as nearly related to his in understanding and intention as the circumstances allow. And it is probably true that the staged play is a satisfying work of art to the very degree that this homogeneity exists. We have insisted time and again upon the secondary importance of the physical side of the play's interpretation, for all that in the end it seems to dominate the entire business, to the exclusion even, in innocent eyes, of the dramatist's own share. It would be an exaggeration to say that it stands for no more than does the pen, ink, and paper by which the play was recorded, but quite just to compare it to the technical knowledge of play-making that the dramatist has come to exercise almost unconsciously. And it is likely that the near relation of method, which we want to establish, does lie in this mysterious preliminary process by which the actor "gets into the skin of his part"; for, indeed, all else that he does in performing it can be related to mere technique of expression. It is this mystery, then, that we must investigate and attempt to explain.

To begin with, how does the dramatist work? He may get his play on paper quickly or slowly, but the stuff in it is the gradual, perhaps the casual, accretion of thoughts and feelings, formed long before

Harley Granville-Barker: *The Exemplary Theatre*. Boston: Little, Brown, 1922, 226-246 *passim*.

and now framed in words, or arranged into action, for the first time. How much of this process is conscious, and how much unconscious or subconscious, he probably could not tell you. If we say that the experiences are unconsciously or subconsciously selected and consciously shaped we may not be far wrong. Wherein does the actor's method follow this? Certainly no such process is to be found in the stuffing of his memory with words, and the whipping up and out of whatever emotions his repetition of them happens to suggest during the half-drill, half scramble of the three or four weeks' rehearsing, while he fits himself as best he can—his corners into all the other arbitrary corners—of that strange shifting Chinese puzzle which is called today an efficient and businesslike production. As a matter of fact no actor worth his salt relies upon this sort of preparation; he has other resources within himself. If he worked, as does the dramatist, in solitude, if he too were a fountain-head, his methods would be of only theoretical interest, our care but for the result. But his job is derivative and cooperative both. Therefore we must know the rules, if rules there are.[1]

[1] That this creative collaboration among actors and between them and the dramatist can be brought to a high pitch we can have evidence by comparing performances of a play that differ, not in brilliance of execution, but absolutely in the meaning extracted from the play and in the observable addition of dramatic values. I have seen a performance of Chekhov's *Cherry Orchard* in Moscow, and to read the play afterwards was like reading the libretto of an opera—missing the music. Great credit to the actors; no discredit to Chekhov. For—and this is what the *undramatic* writer so fails to understand, though in Chekhov he may find a salient example—with the dramatist the words on paper are but the seeds of the play. How be sure, as he writes, as he plants them, that each seed will be fertile? Well, that is the secret of his craft. How to cultivate and raise the crop? That is the secret of the actor's art. There is demanded, no doubt, something *more* than acting, if by acting one only means the accomplishment, the graces, or the sound and fury of the stage. For these externals of the business may spring from nothing purposeful, be independent of any dramatic meaning, and then, for all their charm and excitement, they come to nothing in the end. It is only when they are the showing of a body of living thought and of living feeling, are in themselves an interpretation of life itself, when, in fact, they acquire *further* purpose, that they rank as histrionic art. That there are rules for so incorporating them in this creative process of collaboration we may learn from the Art Theater in Moscow, where they have to some extent elaborated them, though without pretense at finality, only for the convenience of mutual understanding. Much that follows, indeed, was suggested to me by my memory of a talk with Stanislavsky. And I have, by the way, seen a performance of *The Cherry Orchard* elsewhere.

We must consider certain constituents of the problem. With but a three hours' traffic in which to maneuver all the material of a play, the longest part can but appear on the stage for a comparatively few informing and effective passages. To find the inferential knowledge of it that he needs the actor must search, so to speak, behind the scenes, before the rise of the curtain and even after its fall. This is a commonplace; and all actors who can be said to study their parts at all, not merely to learn them, do, instinctively if not deliberately, work in this way. But unless they do so in concert with their fellows they really more often harm the rest of the play than help the whole. For an isolated performance, of however great interest—if the rest of the acting is sagging, vague, helpless, unattached, or perversely at cross purposes—must distort the play's purpose. No matter if the one seems to be right and all the others wrong. Nothing is right unless the thing as a whole is right. A play is founded upon conflict; the dramatist, to get the thing going at all, must bring his characters into collision, among themselves or with fate or circumstances. He must keep them all in an equally effective fighting trim; if he betrays one of them, denies him his best chance in argument or action, for all that it may open an easy way out of a difficulty, end a scene quickly, bring a curtain down with effect, the fabric will be weakened, the play's action may be dislocated altogether. It seems obvious, therefore, that the play's interpretation must be founded upon corporate study by the actors, which should begin as an argumentative counterpart of this struggle and develop through the assumption of personality into the desired unity with the play itself. Let us now consider how the unity is to be achieved.

It is to be hoped that the very subsidiary matter—which now bulks so largely—of learning the words of the play would be swamped in the process of argument. Words should never be learnt, for the result —as with action, if the play is brought to that prematurely—is that they harden in the mind as actualities when they should merely come to it as symbols. All solitary study whatever is (once again) to be deprecated. For to study the play, apart from studying your fellow-actors in the play, is to prefer dry bones to flesh and blood. There is much to be said for the method of the seventeenth-century music teacher, who locked up the instrument upon his departure for fear that his pupil might practice. Actors might well leave their books behind them on the table. It is in the untroubled intervals between meetings that ideas may make good growth and opposing points of view tend to reconciliation. That sort of solitary study by which, so to speak, with your mind quiescent, the matter in hand seems to study *you* is profitable enough. It is even, for most memories, the easiest way of assimilating the dialogue. A sensitive mind rebels against nothing so much as getting words by rote.

And one hopes that even the most expert actors would not come to argue their way very slickly through this preliminary period. No play should move in an efficient straight line between first rehearsal and performance. This time of survey and discovery is the time, too, when the first tendons are being formed which will come to unite the actor's personality with the crescent figure of the character itself. Here is the mystery; the gestation of this new being that is not the actor's consistent self though partaking of it; that is not the character worn as a disguise; individual, but with no absolute existence at all, a relative being only, and now related alike to the actor as to the play. It will be slow in coming to birth: the more unconscious the process the better, for it does not work alike with everyone, never at the same pace, never to the same measure. Wherefore the producer may discover that, to rally his team and to save them from a premature awareness of themselves and each other, it may be well once or twice to move from the table to the stage and engage in the business of a scene or two. This exercise should not last too long, nor should the scenes that are tried follow too much in sequence; for, above all things, the physical action of the play must not be defined while the thought and feeling that should prompt it are still unsure. But the shock of the change will be refreshing. It will check the too easy growth of an agreement, the creation of a unity of purpose based only upon words, whether they be the play's or the actors' arguments round and about the play. Quite literally the company should be allowed to feel their feet in the play, to stamp up and down and restore the circulation which too much talk may have slackened.

Having got thus far by the aid of two minor negatives, let us play down a major one. The production itself must never be shaped before its natural form has declared itself. By shaping we are to understand, of course, not only the physical action of the scenes, but their mental and emotional action as well—everything, indeed, that could be regulated, were our play an orchestral symphony, by time signatures, metronome markings, sforzandi, rallentandi, and the rest, even by the beat of the conductor. It is tempting to compare conductor and producer, but one must do so mainly to remark that their powers, if not their functions, are very different. To wield a baton at rehearsals only, and even then to have neither terms nor instruments of precision for explanation or response—the limitation is severe. It is better to remember that compared to music—and to a far greater degree in comparison with painting, sculpture, and poetry—acting is hardly capable of verbal definition. For by admitting the weakness, by abjuring fixation and finality, one can the better profit by the compensating strength, the ever fresh vitality of the purely human medium; and so the art will gain, not lose. Some fixity, however, there must be, for the practical reason, if for no other, that cooperation would be impossible without it. But there is the aesthetic reason too, and the theater's problem is concisely this: how to attain enough definition of form and unity of intent for the staged play to rank as a homogeneous work of art and yet preserve that freedom of action which the virtue of the human medium demands.

Nothing is easier than to play out a production in elaborate mechanical perfection, to chalk the stage with patterns for the actors to run upon, to have the dialogue sung through with a certain precision of pitch, tone, and pace, to bring the whole business to the likeness of a ballet. But nothing will be less like a play as a play should be. Here, too, it is the letter that killeth and only the spirit that giveth life. Even when such a poetical symphony as *A Midsummer Night's Dream* demands for its interpretation a rhythm of speech matched by rhythm of movement—individual, concerted, contrasted—which can only be brought by skillful hard practice to the point where it will defy forgetfulness, all this must still be taken the step further to the point where its cumbering recollection is defied, too. Rehearsals, be it noted, have always this main object of enabling an actor to forget both himself and them in the performance.

But preparation having been brought by one means and another to the stage when the play—now a grown, or half-grown, but still unshaped combination of the work of dramatist, producer, actors—has acquired life enough to be about to go forward by its own momentum, our *positive* rules (if they are discoverable) must begin to apply.

We must now divide the action (using the word comprehensively) into two categories. To the first will belong everything that can be considered a part of the main structure of the play (again using the word comprehensively to express the play, not as the dramatist left it, but as it has been so far brought to fuller being.) And everything so included must be capable of clear definition: its execution must not vary, it must rank for constancy with the dialogue itself. It is obvious, for instance, that the characters must come on and leave the stage at particular moments·in particular ways; we may take it for granted, too, not only that at certain fixed times in fixed places certain things must be done, but done always with the same emphasis and intention. This is common form. And thus far (the inconstancy of its human medium always allowed for) the drama moves in line with the more static arts. Into this first category, then, will fall all ceremonial—the whole movement, for instance, of such a play as the *Agamemnon*. It will also hold the broad relation in tone and time between act and act, between scene and scene, and the emotional, no less than the physical, structure of the action of each scene, its muscular system, so to speak, as apart from its integument, blood and nerves. We should be right to rule into this category any features of the play's interpretation which we hold must be common to every production of it. We might well include, too, all features which, peculiar to this one, called for and were capable of any definition which could be genuinely agreed upon by the interpreters concerned; the greater the number of them the greater the need of agreement, but the less easy its achievement. . . .

If the first [category], for the sake of a single adjective, is to include all the conscious action of the play, the second may be said to hold all the unconscious or—deferring to the psychologist's lingo—the sub-conscious action. Into it, then, we are to bring everything in the play's acting—movement, expression, emotion, thought—which may, without disturbance of the production's structure or to the distraction of fellow actors, be carried forward in any one of fifty different ways. We say fifty, as we might say a dozen or a hundred, simply for comparison with the single way of the first category. And there may be in theory as good an aesthetic reason for exactly enumerating the fifty as there is for prescribing the one. There will appear, indeed, in our plan an indirect method of prescription of the fifty; for the sub-conscious self has still to be regulated. But practically what we are after is a consciousness of complete freedom. And though the freedom can never be quite complete, neither can any action in the first category be made perfectly accurate, for in each case the work is done in the incalculable human medium which defies (and perhaps despises) exactitude. We aim, then, through this freedom at an appearance of spontaneity. This may seem to some people a very little thing; if it does they have not a very discriminating taste for acting. That spontaneity itself is unattainable a ha'porth of knowledge of the art will inform us. The task of ensuring its appearance has exercised other writers than Diderot, and this and the many underlying problems are in one way or another stumbling-blocks to every actor worth the name.

ARTHUR HOPKINS

(1878-1950)

Capturing the Audience

The chief criticism of temporary producing is that it lacks either policy or design. The average production is the result of no fixed co-ordination. It has frequently been said of my productions, that they conveyed a certain sustained illusion that seemed not to be of the theater. I believe this in a sense to be true, for it is the result of a definite experimental policy which I have followed vigorously, bringing it more and more to bear in each new production.

What was originally experimental has now become a fixed method, and I hope definitely to demonstrate that there is a way to insure invariably the projection of nearly all the values a play may possess.

From the very beginning I had an abhorrence of all that is generally termed theatric. It seemed cheap and tawdry, the trick of the street fakir. I thought for a long time that my prejudice was personal and not well founded. But, finally, all protest and all new seeking began naturally to fall into line with a theory of direction that had slowly been evolving in my mind—the theory which for the want of a better term I have defined as Unconscious Projection.

Briefly, the basis of the theory is this: Complete illusion has to do entirely with the unconscious mind. Except in the case of certain intellectual plays the theater is wholly concerned with the unconscious mind of the audience. The conscious mind should play no part.

Arthur Hopkins: *How's Your Second Act?* New York: Philip Goodman Company, 1918, 23-33, 34-36, 45-50 *passim.*, 58-61.

The theater is always seeking unanimous reaction. It is palpably evident that unanimous reaction from conscious minds is practically impossible. Seat a dozen people in a room, present them any problem which you ask them consciously to solve, and you will get nearly as many different reactions as there are people; but place five thousand people in a room and strike some note or appeal that is associated with an unconscious idea common to all of them, and you will get a practically unanimous reaction. In the theater I do not want the emotion that rises out of thought, but the thought that rises out of emotion. The emotional reaction must be secured first.

The problem now arises: "How can we in the theater confine ourselves to the unconscious mind?" The hypnotist has supplied us with the answer: "Still the conscious mind." The hypnotist's first effort is to render inoperative the conscious mind of the subject. With that out of the way he can direct his commands to an undistracted unconscious and get definite reactions. The subject has no opportunity to think about it.

In the theater we can secure a similar result by giving the audience no reason to think about it, by presenting every phase so unobtrusively, so free from confusing gesture, movement and emphasis, that all passing action seems inevitable, so that we are never challenged or consciously asked why. This whole treatment begins first with the manuscript, continues through the designing of the settings, and follows carefully every actor's movement and inflection. If, throughout, this attitude of easy flow can be maintained the complete illusionment of the audience is inevitable.

At first glance one might say that any method which discards conscious digestion must necessarily be limited in scope. The answer is that we begin by discarding conscious irritation, proceed to an unconscious introduction, and then abide by the conscious verdict, for, inevitably, all the unconscious reaction is wasted if the conscious ultimately rejects us. Or to put it more simply, if you give our story complete attention and then reject us, we have no complaint; but if we feel that you have not properly felt our story because of confusing distractions, we must necessarily feel guilty as to our way of projection.

This method entails sweeping readjustments. To begin with, author, director, scene designer and actor must become completely the servants of the play. Each must resist every temptation to score personally. Each must make himself a free, transparent medium through which the whole flows freely and without obstruction. No one at any moment can say, "Ah, this moment is mine! I shall show what can be done with it." There is no part of the play that is done for the benefit of anyone. It must all be inevitable, impersonal and untrammelled. It requires a complete surrender of selfishness. In fact, it demands of everyone the honest rigidity of the true artist, who will stoop to nothing because it is effective or conspicuous or because "it goes."

It is the opposite of all that has become traditional in the theater. It is the establishing of the true community spirit in a work that is essentially community work, and it is not the glorious adoption of an ideal, but the stern necessity for self-preservation which the very method impresses. For woe be unto the one person who is out of key with the scheme once it has been set in operation! He will inevitably make himself look hopelessly out of place, and the more he struggles to stand out the farther aloof and more hopelessly adrift will he become.

It commands honesty and unselfishness, and nothing recommends it to me more than this—nothing could be more convincing proof of its rightness.

The note of unconscious projection must first be struck by the director. If he cannot get his effects in this way, he can scarcely hope that the people with him will succeed. It is always my aim to get a play completely prepared without anyone realizing just how it was done. I want the actors to be unconscious of my supervision. I want whatever direction they require to come to them without their realization. I want them to be unconscious of the movement and the "business" of the play. I want it all to grow with them so easily that when time for the first performance comes they scarcely realize that anything in particular has been done.

The first step in unselfishness must be taken by me. I must renounce at the outset all temptation to be conspicuous in direction, to issue commands, to show how well I can read a line or play a scene, or slam a door; to ridicule or get laughs at a confused actor's expense, to criticize openly. I must renounce all desire to be the boss, or the great master, or the all-knowing one. I must guide the ship by wireless instead of attempting to drag it through the water after me. There are any number of actors who have been with me who firmly believe that they received practically no direction, and that is exactly as it should be. When I discover that an actor is becoming conscious of me I know there is something wrong some place, and it is usually with me.

The two essentials in this kind of direction are for the director to know exactly what he wants and to make sure that he can get what he wants from the people he has selected. These two conditions put an end to all confusion at the outset.

Uncertainty in direction must inevitably result in uncertainty in performance. When actors discover that a director cannot make up his mind just how a scene should be played, and when they see him experimenting with them they instantly become conscious of something lacking, either in the play itself or in the director. This is a dangerous thought to set up. A company under these conditions becomes wabbly, and the first tendency of a wabbly actor is to overplay. Once an actor believes himself to be on thin ice he invariably steps down harder. A scene that is born in uncertainty is rarely well played.

The director is the guide. The play is the unknown region through which he leads the actor. He must know the paths and the turnings so well that he never hesitates. For once he falters, wondering if he is headed right, the actor inevitably begins to look around for his own way out.

My feeling about the birth of a play is that it gradually becomes an individuality, that it becomes a personality of which the different actors are organs or members. I do not see ten or twenty individuals moving about. I see only one thing made of ten or twenty parts that is moving. So long as it moves properly I am totally unconscious of its parts. The moment I become conscious of a part and lose the movement of the whole I know that something is wrong. It is the unfamiliar sound in the engine that warns one that some part is not functioning properly. That is the time to stop the play and investigate. It may be a very tiny thing—a movement at a time when all should be still—a speech when there should be silence—a pause when something should be happening—an unwarranted change of tempo, or any one of a hundred minor or major things that removes concentration from the whole.

The stripping process begins early. I eliminate all gesture that is not absolutely needed, all unnecessary inflections and intonings, the tossing of heads, the flickering of fans and kerchiefs, the tapping of feet, drumming of fingers, swinging of legs, pressing of brows, holding of hearts, curling of mustaches, stroking of beards and all the million and one tricks that have crept into the actor's bag, all of them betraying one of two things—an annoying lack of repose, or an attempt to attract attention to himself and away from the play.

Every moment on the stage should mean something. The spectator follows every movement, and no movement has any right to his attention unless it has some significance.

I never plan the "business" of a play in advance. I know where the entrances are as the scene is first designed, but frequently after going over an act once these are changed.

I am opposed to the old method of marking out the "business" in advance, because at the outset it confines the movement and tends to a fixity that hampers free flow. The first two or three times through an act I let the actors roam about the scene and invariably the "business" solves itself. The movement arrived at in this way has the advantage of having been born in action, and there is essentially a feeling of life about it that one cannot get by marking directions in a manuscript. Automatically all falseness of movement is denied admission, all crosses, dropping downstage, falling upstage, exchanging chairs, circling pianos, wrestling with furniture, and all the strange conduct that directors of past years have relied upon to keep actors busy. The police crusade of some time ago that kept actors moving along Broadway was only an open-air phase of stage direction, as most actors have suffered it for years.

Extreme simplification—that is what I strive for incessantly—not because I like simplicity. It isn't a matter of taste or preference—it is a working out of the method of Unconscious Projection. It is the elimination of all the nonessentials, because they arouse the conscious mind and break the spell I am trying to weave over the unconscious mind. All tricks are conscious in the mind of the person who uses them, and they must necessarily have a conscious appeal. I want the unconscious of the actors talking to the unconscious of the audience, and I strive to eliminate every obstacle to that. I finally become a censor. I must say what shall not pass—and therein I believe lies the whole secret of direction.

The true test of performance is the ease with which it is accomplished. My chief objection to all theatric devices is that they indicate a straining for effect which defeats itself. The strain is a thing personal to the author, actor or director, and it instantly distracts the audience from the effect to the effort. Just as an audience suffers for a singer who is struggling for a note that seems dangerously out of reach, it suffers for an actor who stresses himself for an effect. An actor should be given nothing to do that he cannot do easily, and furthermore he should find the very easiest way he can accomplish whatever is assigned to him. This is an essential part of his self-elimination. He must think of the play as a clean ball. Whenever it is tossed to him he should pass it on without smearing it with his perspiration. An ideal company would end the performance with a spotless ball. An actor must say to himself, "How can I do this without being noticed?" instead of, "What can I do to make myself stand out?" With the latter query he begins to try, and with trying comes strain, and with strain artificiality and discomfort. He accomplishes what he set out to do. He stands out much as a carbuncle does.

The whole system of personal emphasis in the American theater has led to the present unadvanced state of the actor. There is no greater proof of its fallacy than its failure. All are straining for personal success. If they only knew that the greatest success will come to those who can most completely submerge the personal. Theirs is essentially an art where they must serve unreservedly, and the great vacancies in the theater are awaiting actors big enough in mind and character to surrender themselves completely, strip themselves of every conscious trick, disdaining to court approval by commanding it by the very honesty of their aims.

I firmly believe that an actor's mental attitude is instantly conveyed to an audience. I further believe that an audience unconsciously appraises his character. It soon discovers if he is all actor or part man, and its appraisal of his performance is more determined by its unconscious exploration of his unconscious than by any particular thing he does. Invariably the actors whom the public has loved have been people, who, in themselves, possessed great lovable qualities. They were not people who in their roles assumed a lovable nature.

We cannot give actors qualities they do not possess, but I am only seeking to point out that the audience usually gets what is inside of an actor much more clearly than what he actually does, and an actor cannot approach his work selfishly without conveying his attitude to the public. We let all of this pass under the vague terms of personality and magnetism, but I do not believe there is anything vague or mysterious about it. I believe unconscious appraisal reveals to us the character of many people we do not know in the least. We get their intent from what they do, and it is by their intent that we know them. . . .

As to the "new" scenery, much has been said and written, and most of it beside the point.

One's position in the matter is entirely determined by which mind he thinks the stage has to do with, the conscious or the unconscious.

Realistic settings are designed wholly for conscious appeal. An attempt at exact reproduction challenges the conscious mind of the audience to comparison. Comparison of the scene as it is offered with the auditor's conscious knowledge of what it is supposed to reproduce. If a Childs Restaurant in all its detail is offered it remains for the audience to recall its memory photograph of a Childs Restaurant and check it up with what is shown on the stage. If the batter-cake stove is in place and the "Not Responsible for Hats" sign is there, and if the tiling is much the same, then the producer has done well. He has been faithful to Childs, and whatever credit there is in being faithful to Childs should be unstintedly awarded him.

Unfortunately while the audience has been doing its conscious checking up, the play has been going, and going for nothing, since any form of conscious occupation must necessarily dismiss the play. Further than that the result of the whole mental comparing process is to impress upon the auditor that he is in a theater witnessing a very accurate reproduction, *only remarkable because it is not real.* So the upshot of the realistic effort is further to emphasize the unreality of the whole attempt, setting, play and all. So I submit that realism defeats the very thing to which it aspires. It emphasizes the faithfulness of unreality.

All that is detail, all that is photographic, is conscious. Every unnecessary article in a setting is a continuing, distracting gesture beckoning constantly for the attention of the audience, asking to be noticed and examined, insisting upon its right to scrutiny because it belongs. . . .

Detail has been the boon of the American theater for twenty years, detestable, irritating detail, designed for people with no imagination —people who will not believe they are in a parlor unless they see the family album.

And on the other side of the world the unenlightened Chinese for centuries have been presenting drama to unimaginative people wherein scenes were never changed, and palaces, forests, legions and hordes were summoned by the wave of a property man's bamboo stick.

But, thank Heaven, there was a Gordon Craig, who brought the imagination of the Orient to England, and of course England would have none of him. Germany swallowed him through the gullet of Max Reinhardt, and the "new" movement was on. It spread to Russia, to France, to Italy, to America, to every place but England, where it was born.

Here we have failed to grasp its full significance. There is still a feeling that it is some sort of affectation. It would be like us to call a revolt from affectation affectation.

What is all the discussion about? How can there be any discussion? Isn't it a palpable fact that the only mission of settings is to suggest place and mood, and once that is established let the play go on? Do we want anything more than backgrounds? Must we have intricate woodturning and goulash painting? If so, we have no right in the theater. We have no imagination. And a theater without imagination becomes a building in which people put paint on their faces and do tricks, and no trick they perform is worth looking at unless they take a reasonable chance of being killed in the attempt.

The whole realistic movement was founded on selfishness—the selfish desire of the producer or scene painter to score individually, to do something so effective that it stood in front of the play and shrieked from behind it.

It was my good fortune to find an unselfish artist, Robert Edmond Jones. Jones hopes only for one thing for his settings—that no one will notice them, that they will melt into the play. Naturally for this very reason they were conspicuous at first not because of what they were, but because of what people had been accustomed to. But gradually his work is being noticed less and less, and Jones knows that that means he is succeeding. That's the size man he is. And when the day comes that no one ever mentions his settings, he will breathe deeply and say, "I have done it."

He is the true artist. He wants nothing for Jones. He wants what is right for the thing we are doing. Given twenty actors with a spirit as fine as his, and I will promise you a reaction such as is now only a dream.

JACQUES COPEAU

(1878-1949)

Dramatic Economy

Every work intended for performance on the stage involves direct-ing. Since there are various types of drama, there is a directing style and method corresponding to each of these types and—within a given type—to the specific nature of each individual work. Directing is the sum-total of artistic and technical operations which enables the play as conceived by the author to pass from the abstract, latent state, that of the written script, to concrete and actual life on the stage.

The freer of stage directions a script is, and the more it aims at producing nothing but immediate effects, the more leeway it allows the directing—in the material sense of the term. This means a great many sets, a profusion of light and color, elaborate costumes, striking ornaments, and a large number of actors and supers.

Realism brings to the stage separate segments of the world. It seeks to make us believe in a pasteboard universe. It indulges in ingenious make-believe, inspired by the art of the painter, the archi-tect, and the scene designer, in order to reproduce vast buildings, streets and squares, and broad expanses in nature: plains, mountains, sea and sky. It makes the sun set, the moon rise, the night fall, or the day dawn. It lets loose storm, flood, fire, the movement of crowds, the clash of armies; it shows boats on the high seas, trains in motion, planes in flight.

Jacques Copeau: "La mise en scène," *Encyclopédie Française,* December 1935.

Fantasy presents, as if they were realities perceived by the senses, objects which the human mind usually evokes only in imagination: creatures of fantasy, monsters, gods and goddesses, the world of fairyland. A dreamlike atmosphere envelops them; the lands they inhabit change before our eyes.

These material refinements in staging, which the antique theater did not have, were made possible by the inventions of Italian scene designers of the Renaissance. This was particularly true in ballet, pantomime, and opera. In our day they have been heightened by the advances in machinery and electricity, with the use of revolving stages, elevators, cycloramas, and spotlights.

But these refinements, pushed to extremes and too much at the beck and call of the engineer, risk becoming an endless game, a kind of plaything which intrigues us with its endless combinations, surprises, and tricks. When used in performances in the music hall, they achieve effects which are quite appropriate. But I fear they are contaminating some types of drama where they do not belong. Perhaps they will one day be held in check—as already seems to be somewhat the case—by improvements in the cinema, in which technicians have at their disposal more subtle, varied, and powerful means both of capturing the external world and of transforming it into a world of fantasy.

The modern trend in scenic design is in the direction of artistic simplification, in pictorial effect as well as in the choice of elements that constitute a *décor*. Our designers prefer an intelligently interpreted portrait to a photographic image; they aim at impressions rather than descriptions. They strive to evoke and suggest rather than to depict. They single out a part in order to indicate the whole: a tree instead of a forest, a pillar instead of a temple. Stylized elements replace the wealth of detail which, in the older method, went counter to nature, competing with dramatic action and wearing down the playgoer's attention.

The Role of the Director

The layman, ill-informed as to the secrets of stagecraft in the art of the theater, will probably recognize the director's hand only in the tangible excesses we have described. In reality, however, the richer in literary, poetic, psychological, and emotional content a play is, the more profound it is and the more indefinable its beauty; the greater it is, the more consummate in form and original in style, the more numerous and subtle will be the problems it presents for the director.

Let us now follow the director in the successive phases of his work. He receives a script from a playwright. After his initial reading, the inanimate pages begin to come to life in his fingers. They are no longer symbols written on paper: he adds a sense of life to the meaning of the words. They are voices which speak and fall silent at his bidding, gestures which are made, faces which light up. Place, time, colors, and lights are clearly defined in terms of specific emotions and specific episodes. Later, after more methodical study, the director will deepen these various notions. But at his very first contact, a tiny universe both spiritual and concrete commences to take shape—of which the reader is more or less conscious.

What remains in the director's mind, and not only in his mind but within reach of his senses, so to speak, is a feeling of general rhythm— the breathing, as it were, of the work which is to emerge into life. But since a play is essentially action, and an actor primarily a human being who acts, before going any further our director seeks to delimit the place, form, and dimensions of this action. If it is an interior, he will give it its essential props: chairs and other pieces of furniture. If he is dealing with an open space, he will determine its contours and cubes. This is his staging plan, on which he will locate, as accurately as possible without harming the flow of the action, the actors' places or positions as well as their entrances and exits. For, in interpreting the play and setting it in its proper perspective, it is important that a given actor at a given moment and in a given situation, prompted by a given emotion, approach or draw away from a given point on the stage.

Once the stage is set in accordance with the needs of the action as envisaged in its broad lines, the action itself must be organized, act by act, scene by scene, speech by speech, down to the slightest details. As he devises the action he is going to propose to his actors—their places, their distances from one another, the movements they make, their relations with the stage set, the furniture and the props, the pace of their speeches and their silences, the varying tempo of their entrances and exits—the director bears in mind the truthfulness of the characters, the expression of their emotions, the demand of the script, the logic of events, the positions on stage, the lighting effects, the naturalness of the players, and group symmetry. He aims at achieving clear representation, well-defined movement, varied rhythm, and sustained harmony. All his steps are motivated by a unity of style and guided by an over-all idea. But he must be careful not to allow this idea to become too obvious, not to force it to the point of pedantry and abstraction, both in the stage *décor* and in the playing of the actors—for the triumph of his art is the creation of life.

This personal work on the part of the director is necessary, if he is to avoid losses of time, mistakes, and all sorts of disappointments. Yet it is not always carried through in the way in which we have just described it. But let us assume that it has been. Now the moment has come for the director to begin rehearsals.

Unless time does not permit—that precious time we so often waste because of lack of discipline and poor organization in the theater—the director should first call together his actors around a table and not on a stage: firstly, in order to read the play to them and impress on their minds its meaning and rhythm; secondly, in order to have them read their parts. This phase will last as long as the director is capable of sustaining it, and the actors capable of enduring it. It enables the director to explain the author's intentions and his own, to nip in the bud any incipient misunderstandings, to dwell on the beauties of the script and the basic principles of its interpretation, and perhaps to correct certain mistakes in casting before the actors have entered into their parts and while they are still at ease in their mind.

The first rehearsals on the stage are devoted to the *assigning of places*. That is, the actor, guided by the director, adjusts himself to the mechanics of the action, familiarizing himself with the movements he is called upon to make, trying to understand the reasons for them, accepting them or discussing them. At the same time it gives the director an opportunity to verify his conceptions, to modify them if need be, and to make the necessary revisions in his over-all plan before the sets are built. This period of uncertainty must not be prolonged; it demoralizes the actor. So now the play is clarified, even though in summary fashion, from beginning to end. Actors and directors have an over-all view of the work. They know where they are going before they plunge into the actual interpretation.

This work of interpretation becomes possible on the day that the actor, putting away his "sides," begins to speak his lines from memory and tries to harmonize what he says with what he does. At that moment, even the most gifted actors seem to hesitate. There is a critical period during which the interpreter appears as if to have lost the feel of his initial grasp. He will get it back again, and with an accent of enduring truth, if he is professional enough, if he persists in his work, and if he has sufficient power of concentration and sincerity to identify himself—first physically, then emotionally—with the character he portrays. Here too the director is the actor's guide, teacher, and mainstay. His task is not only to keep the actor in line and within the limits of his part, not only to indicate to him where he is near the truth, and not only to correct his mistakes, but also to understand the difficulties confronting the actor and to show him how to solve these difficulties. He must use tact, authority, and persuasion. But it is by means of sympathetic understanding that he will exert his most active influence, provided that his experience with his actors is long, objective, and profound enough for him to know the specific sensitivity, temperament, and ability of each one of them. It is dangerous to allow the actor too much freedom; but it is even more dangerous to stifle his spontaneity with blind coercion.

Every director has his personal method of influencing the actors. These methods should be studied individually. I believe that the Englishman Granville-Barker has found the correct approach when he says that, in his view, a director should react toward an actor as would an audience—but an ideally critical audience. He has expressed his point of view in the following terms: "The more he can leave initiative to the actors the better. And, when he cannot, let him emulate the diplomat rather than the drill-sergeant, hint and coax and flatter and cajole, do anything rather than give orders; let them if possible still be persuaded that the initiative is theirs, not his. The Socratic method has its use, if there is time to employ it; an actor may be argued by it out of one way of thinking into another. But the immediate effect of this may be depressing, even paralyzing. . . . The actor must then be heartened into starting afresh, and encouraged while he finds his way, and protected from the impatience of his fellow-actors, who have already found theirs." Granville-Barker rightly concludes that the directing of a play is most fruitful and commendable if it "could be, as it should be, fairly adapted to every one of the diverse interests involved, if the finally needed unity were evolved from these and not imposed on them." This ideal achievement presupposes, in addition to professional competence, a great intellectual and moral superiority on the part of the director; and, on the part of the actors, thorough schooling in their art and willing discipline, in order to "realize the unity in diversity and diversity in unity, the freedom compatible with order."

Without discussing the question of the ever-present pressures of the commercial theater, the number of rehearsals depends on the length and difficulty of the work in production, the importance and complexity of its staging, the resourcefulness of the director, the zeal of his assistants, and the talent of the actors. An experienced actor, sure of his calling, rich in inner life, may rehearse for a long time and make continuous progress. A beginner or a mediocre actor quickly reaches a saturation point beyond which he loses both his freshness and his grasp. Individual temperaments and national characteristics must always be taken into account. Disciplined Germans and Russians fanatically devoted to their art can engage in an astonishing number of rehearsals. Italians, born improvisers, hardly rehearse at all. The French occupy an intermediate position. But they are lacking in method and often in seriousness.

The Role of the Stage Manager

All during his work, the director is assisted by one or more stage managers. The functions of the stage manager are closely related and complementary to those of the director, and are as sharply defined as his. For if the director stages the play and gives life to it, the stage manager watches over it and sees to it that "the show must go on." As the play draws nearer to opening night, one may say that it passes out of the hands of the director into those of the stage manager, somewhat in the same way that it has passed out of the playwright's hands into those of the director and his actors. Thus we get a picture of the various operations through which a dramatic work passes from the moment it takes shape in the writer's brain to the moment in which it is played before an audience—when it comes fully alive and flows as easily and naturally as though born upon the stage. That is what makes the theater so difficult and often so risky an art. And that is why it really needs strict, intelligent, completely coherent, and homogeneous organization. Without such organization the playwright's thought and the life of his characters will always be cheapened and betrayed.

The stage manager notes all the various points relating to the staging, as they occur, on a copy of the play called a *promptbook*. He is in charge of the electricians, stagehands, property men, costumers, and in general the entire working crew of the play. He makes sure that the actors are on hand; sees to it that their costumes and make-up are just right; watches for entrances, places, movements, and cues; and keeps order on the stage, backstage, and in the dressing rooms. Every day he draws up a *call bulletin* and posts it on the bulletin board in the greenroom. Here the actors find the general timetable of activities in the theater, announcements from the management, and any comments concerning behavior and breaches of discipline. The stage manager is present at every performance, guides it, sees that it runs smoothly, gives the curtain signal, decides the number of curtain calls to be taken and the length of intermissions, supervises the actual placing of sets and props, checks on the lighting, and, in an emergency, addresses the audience.

The collaboration of a good stage manager is seen to best advantage at dress rehearsals, when the director relies on him for all the practical work of running the show, so that he himself may have a little more perspective and calmly judge the over-all effect before making any last-minute changes. Dress rehearsals should be given under actual performance conditions—that is, with scenery and changes of scenery in the time taken by an actual intermission, with lights, props, costumes, make-up and wigs, music, and supers, if there are any. All the equipment needed for the play should be ordered as soon as rehearsals start and made available while rehearsals are under way, so that as many dress rehearsals as possible can be given in the last few days before opening night.

Necessary Harmony

The director figuratively sets the stage himself (plans and dimensions, entrances and exits, essential elements). As for all the accessories to the production (props, furniture, lights, music), if he does not himself create them, they must in any case be created by artists working under him, accepting his guidance and supervision. He must not allow them to clash with one another, to step on each other's toes, or to interfere in any way with the play. Only in this manner can harmony be achieved within a unified framework. As a rule, this principle is obvious. Few would question it. If it is not always practiced, if it is more often violated than kept, we must nevertheless admit that in our day it has been—if not discovered—at least revived and restored to a signal place of honor.

The interdependence of music, dance, and color has produced masterpieces in the ballet. Wagnerian opera has come close to integral unity in the theories of such a master as Adolphe Appia. Primarily a musician in the broadest sense of the term, Appia sought to make the flow of music, imprisoning action in time, govern action in space in the same way. That is, he strove to make the music build up around it its own acting space, to which the performers had to conform. Just as music creates the spoken phrase and the gesture associated with it, so it creates movement, which it measures in its rises or falls, on a level or uneven surface. Thus music creates an essential *décor*. Appia conceived of the stage in relation to the needs of the action, not in response to the demands of local color. He sacrificed pleasure to rigorous accuracy, virtuosity to inner logic. He rejected illusory *décors,* such as picturesquely painted "flats," and replaced them with genuine three-dimensional *décors*—in other words, purely dramatic and dynamic *décors.* The main reforms in contemporary stage design took off from there. They have been pushed to intellectual extremes, even at times to the point of caricature; but they have achieved a salutary pruning in dramatic style and energy.

We have found that a good script, a play that is well written for acting on the stage, contains time-spans—movements and rhythms—comparable to those in music and, as in music, capable of generating space. The question of what space or playing area to choose in a given play, or in a given scene from a play, is therefore not an unimportant matter. For there is a stage economy that corresponds to dramatic economy, a performing style engendered by a literary style; and indeed, a theater's physical structure may serve to heighten and enhance the intellectual structure of a play or, on the contrary, to distort and destroy it.

This concept, tested by experience, is likewise verified by a study of works of the past. Let us take two very well-known examples. Aeschylus and Shakespeare did not invent their action in a vacuum. The one worked for the Greek stage, the other for the Elizabethan stage—in other words, in terms of two instruments which had their permanent architecture, their traditions, and their established laws. Aeschylus' tragedies and Shakespeare's plays were composed, so to speak, in the image of this architecture and in accordance with its rhythms. They were marked by its traditions and laws. We do not completely understand them as works of art unless we are well informed—or at least as well informed as one can be—concerning the specific techniques employed when they were performed. In our world and time, they cannot really regain their fullness of expression unless they are played on a stage under conditions analogous to those of the Greek or Elizabethan theater in which they were born. I say analogous, because where direction is involved the mind must have some leeway and we must shun any attempt at slavish reconstruction. But it is probable that if the French public today understands Shakespeare better and enjoys his plays more, it is thanks to the efforts our directors have made to recapture the living spirit of the text and the dynamics of its action, by drawing closer to a stage tradition which ignorant or inept adapters had too long neglected.

When we evoke the stylized architecture of the theater of Aeschylus and Shakespeare—just as we could have evoked that of the Chinese and Japanese theaters—we are at the opposite pole from the formless or multiformed stage, with its grandiose productions, such as we described at the beginning of this article. To illustrate more sharply the contrast between the two systems, let me point out that the modern stage, such as it has been handed down to us by the ingenious craftsmen of the Renaissance, a cluttered-up and mechanized theater, is a closed-in space in which mind and matter constantly wage war on each other; whereas on the Elizabethan stage, with its minimum of material encumbrances, mind moves freely. In the first case, we are dealing with a bastardized convention, a compromise between realism and abstraction, which simulates a relativist universe. In the second case, we have a convention which is frank, complete, and self-sufficient, creating a universe in itself—a theatrical universe with its own style and technique, which are invaluable guides for the dramatist's imagination as well as that of the director.

Current Trends

Direction has played so prominent a part in the work of the contemporary theater; it has aroused so much curiosity; it has given rise to so much research, effort, and striving; and it has helped shed light on so many basic problems that it has often—and wrongly—been considered an art in itself. Some have asserted that the director possesses universal talents, ranging from those of the actor to those of the creative writer, and including those of the painter and composer. As a matter of fact, that is a portrait of the ideal director. But this ideal has turned the head of more than one director.

In the cinema as in the theater, there is a conflict between technicians and writers for the realization of unity under the guidance of a master-creator. As cinema techniques develop and improve, and as the cinema establishes its own traditions, the director tends increasingly to take the place of the writer. But that place was left vacant; for one cannot really say that up to now we have had masters of the cinema. We usually say that the dramatist is master in the theater; and at bottom, of course, everything does depend on the creative writer. Thus far there has been no split between creator and realizer: there is perfect unity in simplicity. But an increasing complexity in the means of realization will bring about a division of labor. The unity thus lost will be found again only in exceptional cases.

In principle there is no reason why a first-rate dramatist, with rich experience in the theater, should not also be a first-rate director, capable of admirably directing his plays. Up to a certain point, his experience as a director may usefully influence his concepts of drama. But it must be acknowledged that in our day the playwright is usually a master who has let slip the instrument of his mastery. This has come about for many reasons not all of which are his fault. He writes for the stage; yet the stage may repel him or baffle him. He finds it indispensable to get help from a method of interpretation. So he turns to the specialist in this method: the director.

Hence the director is the playwright's right-hand man or substitute in the matter of producing the play. His work is based on an agreement, a kind of contract which he is able to sign because of his insight and to which he is bound because of his sincerity. But trouble arises the moment he makes use of some of his professional skills to distort the playwright's work, to introduce into the fabric of that work his own ideas, intentions, fantasies, and doctrines.

Technical competence, profound understanding, and genuine enthusiasm can and should develop in the director a second inspiration, which is released when he makes contact with another's work. To this extent he participates in creation. He is also a critic, and often better able than the playwright himself to discern errors in playwriting.

It is easy to understand why a gifted director is tempted to conceal the playwright's lack of skill by means of his own technical resources. Admittedly too he becomes impatient when certain masterpieces are said to be unplayable; so he toys with the idea of revising them or of removing the difficulties in them. It need not surprise us therefore if he proceeds boldly to the very source of creation and convinces himself that he can shape the entire process.

It is true that creating a dramatic work in words and actually mounting it on the stage with live actors are but two phases of one and the same intellectual operation. And it is also true that all great dramatists, from Aeschylus to Shakespeare, from Aristophanes to Molière, and from Racine to Ibsen, have been directors. We could cite many others of lesser genius—Voltaire, Diderot, etc.—who had original ideas about directing. The fusion of dramatist and director, however, is in a *descending* line; it is difficult to see how this order can be reversed.

Let us hope for a dramatist who replaces or eliminates the director, and personally takes over the directing; rather than for professional directors who pretend to be dramatists. (No matter how experienced a craftsman he may be, he is immediately too much the professional.) But since we lack great dramatists who stage their own plays personally and with authority, the great director shows his mettle only when he confronts a written masterpiece, particularly when that masterpiece is considered unplayable. Because he believes in it, he understands it; and because he has insight and respects it, he wrests from it its secret.

Does not perfection in directing arise from the friendly conflict between a great creator and his great interpreter? Whenever this salutary conflict is avoided; whenever the technician of the theater, freed of restraints, visualizes things like an actor and only in terms of the acting, his production thins out and dries up. It resembles that of the musical virtuoso who composes solely for his instrument. He obtains perfection without depth, without nuances, without mystery. An added dimension is lacking. And artistic creation suffers a mortal blow.

Translated by Joseph M. Bernstein

LOUIS JOUVET

(1891-1951)

The Profession of the Director

In an empty theater, alone in the middle of a velvet glacier of empty seats, a man is seated. Tense with concentration, all eyes and ears and nerves, he leans toward the stage where the actors are rehearsing. Eyes fixed on that gaping hole—without scenery and almost without light, where persons in incongruous moods and costumes are going through varied convolutions—he contracts his brow, strains his ears to hear the lines that are still imperfectly pronounced or interpreted. This man is the director, or *metteur en scène*.

In the limbo where the production takes form, in the slow growth during which its features are shaped, where it is foreseen in imagination, where the dramatic leaven is mysteriously at work, the director watches with patience, discretion and tenderness over the straggling elements he has assembled to give life to the playwright's work. His job is accomplished through intuition, understanding, foresight, through a special alchemy composed of words, sounds, gestures, colors, lines, movements, rhythms and silences, and including an imponderable which will radiate the proper feeling of laughter or emotion when the work appears before the public.

The director, or *metteur en scène*, has been called the gardener of spirits, the doctor of sensations, the midwife of the inarticulate, the cobbler of situations, cook of speeches, steward of souls, king of the theater and servant of the stage, juggler and magician, assayer and touchstone of the public, diplomat, economist, nurse, orchestra leader, interpreter, painter and costumer—a hundred definitions, but all of them useless. The director is indefinable because his functions are undefined.

The director, when he is also the producer, first selects the play, distributes the parts to the actors of his choice, designs (or has designed for him) the rough models of the settings and costumes, oversees their making, and during all this time organizes and manages rehearsals. He determines the entrances and exits, the positions of the actors, serving as choreographer to that dance which is the sum of the play's movements; he regulates the off-stage noises, the music, the lighting. In short, he arranges in ensemble and in detail all the generalities and all the particulars of that complex ceremony which the performance will be.

To direct a production is to live in terror, to delight in anguish; it is what Paul Valéry calls "the tragedy of execution." It means administering to the spiritual welfare of the playwright and at the same time taking into account the temporal needs of the theater; establishing the point of view of one evening and of eternity; handling the text of a play, hand in hand with the author, as if it were a magic formula. Directing is the opposite of criticism: the critics, zigzagging between laws and rules on one side and their own pleasure on the other, navigate in the theater by trying to sound their reactions with an old fathom-stick in one hand and with the other sighting the play through a pair of old marine-glasses. Directing a play is the exact opposite of this. It means constantly searching for reasons that will explain liking and admiration. It means living according to poets' rules. It means comporting with the gods of the stage, with the mystery of the theater. It means being honest and straightforward in the art of pleasing. And sometimes, too, it means making mistakes.

The director is the kind of lover who draws his talent, invention and joy in his work from the talent, invention and joy which he borrows from or inspires in others. To direct a production means to gather together all the people and things that make up a performance and to create, through them, a certain atmosphere, arousing and serving their capabilities and their personalities. In the setting—the whole play's material surroundings—such things, for example, as wood, paint, nails and light are not, as one might suppose, lifeless, inorganic things but formidable entities whose favor toward the play and its interpreters is to be won only by a secret and long-premeditated accord.

To direct a production means to help the actors with their memorizing and to mold the text in rehearsals so that it is freed of bookishness and takes on the feeling of the players, to make the actor comfortable and to know how to do this. It means nourishing, sustaining and revitalizing the actors, encouraging and satisfying them and finding their proper theatrical diet; it means bringing forth and raising that family—formed according to a different formula for each new play—which we call a theater company.

To direct a production means serving the playwright with a devotion that makes you love his work. It means finding the spiritual mood that was the poet's at the play's conception and during its writing, the living source and stream which must arouse the spectator, and of which even the author is sometimes unaware. It means realizing the corporal through the spiritual. It is a way of dealing with a work, with the places and properties necessary to the setting, with the performers, with the poet who has conceived it, and, finally, with the audience for which it is destined. Charged with the interests of this audience, the director must unite the stage and the auditorium, the spectacle and the spectators. He must organize that area where the active players on the stage and the passive players in the auditorium meet each other, where the spectators penetrate and identify themselves with the action on the stage, and where the actors satisfy their need to prove and free themselves by reflection in the people who listen and look on.

Jean Giraudoux modestly says that the playwright does not make his play, that the audience makes it out of the elements furnished by the playwright. "The audience," he declares, "hears and composes as it pleases, following its own imagination and feelings." He compares a dramatic work to a piece of pottery painted in false colors, whose true colors and finished design do not appear until after it is fired. A play receives the finishing process of an ordeal by fire through contact with an audience.

One could go on forever analyzing the work of the director but, in trying to define it, I only prove that it is easier to do a job well than to write well about it. To sum it up, the directing of a play is a turn of the hand, a turn of the mind and of the heart, a function of such sensitiveness that everything human can enter into it. No more, and no less. I do not believe in theories, and there is no theory to cover the directing of plays. The method fits a theory only after the fact.

There are two kinds of director: the one who expects everything from the play, for whom the play itself is essential; and the one who expects nothing except from himself, for whom the play is a starting point. That is to say—perhaps too summarily, but in order to be clear—there are two sorts of dramatic works, and two sorts of playwrights.

There is the spectacular or theatrical theater in which entertainment, rhythm, music, lines and appeal to the eye—all the spectacular elements—are the important things, and here the director can indulge himself to his heart's content. In this theatrical theater can be included the mimes of Roman decadence, the theater of the marketplace, a good part of opera and all operetta, ballet, fair-plays, melodrama, and the productions of the majority of present-day foreign directors, in which the actor, the singer, the setting, the machinery, are the essentials of the entertainment.

Then there is the theater of dramatists and poets which makes of dramatic art a literary form of the highest order. Here the important thing is the text, and the spectacular elements are admitted only as side-issues and supplements. The literary theater includes the Greek and Roman dramatists (Aeschylus, Sophocles, Euripides, Seneca); the humanistic renaissance with Shakespeare; the classic with Corneille, Racine, Molière; then Marivaux, Beaumarchais, Musset. These peaks of dramatic art have been defined by one of our directors, somewhat cavalierly, as "men of letters who wrote for the theater."

There are works of lasting character, and others whose value is only momentary. It is an accepted fact that fashion affects the writing of plays and their conception; but whenever one attains universality, where the characters are dealt with purely as human beings, we have what the text-books call a classic. This type of play contains within itself its own method of staging; that is, the work of the director is to observe how the play responds to his suggestions, to make his devices disappear into the text, so incorporating them that the play absorbs his directions without being deformed by them.

In the spectacular theater, on the other hand, external direction is required; the work is swathed in personal contributions and inventions. The text is no more than a pretext or a support for the setting, the actors and the stage devices; and the director, relying heavily on the storehouse of the theater or of his imagination, often rivals the leader of a cotillion. So true is that that we can say that the text of a classic or literary play is written for the audience, the text of the other kind for the actors and the director.

The natural tendency of a director is to see his plays with a definite personal bias that is the index of his temperament. Almost all directors, after a few years of modest service, dream of showing their own stature and the scale of their imagination. And, like the apprentice who thought himself a past master of his trade, like the shoemaker whom the painter Apelles put in his place by advising him not to criticize anything above shoes, they are seized with a violent desire to make over masterpieces and to express at last their own personal conceptions.

As an illustration of this mentality, this professional deformity, I should like to quote a sentence that has been in print, on the film production of *A Midsummer Night's Dream:* one of the greatest directors wrote it: "The dream of my life was to produce a work without having anything hamper my imagination." That in itself is not bad for a man whose profession is to serve others. But he adds, "I have set the condition that this work should represent Shakespeare, and nothing but Shakespeare." I hope you can feel in this avowal both the homage he intended to pay to Shakespeare and the opinion he held—comparatively—of himself. And, as a final touch, he adds, "My dream has just been realized." That is, this dream is at your disposal in the motion-picture houses. You may see Shakespeare adapted to the use of commercial New Year's calendars.

The greatest director will never be able to equal in his achievements the dreams and imagination of the most humble of his audience.

In reality, a play stages itself; the only necessity is to be attentive and not too personal in order to see it take on its own movement and begin to manipulate the actors. Acting on them, mysteriously, it tests them, magnifies or diminishes them, embraces or rejects them, nourishes them, transforms and deforms them. From its first rehearsal a true play comes alive, just as wood warps, wine ferments and dough rises. It gathers impetus and gradually the director, like the sorcerer's apprentice, terrified and enraptured at the same time, sees it sweep over the actors and bring them to life, rejecting or carrying away all his directions like straws in the wind, in a kind of blossoming or birth.

The profession of the director suffers from the disease of immodesty, and even the most sincere do not escape it. Their license to work freely with the plays of other people, to dabble with them and make them over, is an established and accepted convention, and after a few hours of conversation with himself or with a colleague a man must have a steady head and firm foothold to resist the dizziness in which, convinced of what he would like to believe, he approaches the conclusion that Shakespeare or Goethe understood nothing of the theater. Great dramatic art is a mystery. No work can be judged outside of its age, and its transportation into another atmosphere requires long adaptation and very great respect. But here is a formula:

One can recognize a great dramatic work with certainty when the director, deciding in all good faith that it should be otherwise constructed or written, has, nevertheless, nothing more to say; when, in spite of all his desire to make over the play, he accepts it practically as it is written. A conversation I had with a director who confided to me that he was in despair because he had just been working for two months, without any result, on *Le Malade Imaginaire* illustrates this definition. When I expressed astonishment, he said, "Yes, I've just spent my whole summer at it. I've tried lighting it from above, and below, and from the side; I've experimented with settings and movement on the stage. There's nothing, nothing, to be done. It's the perfect play. It is a work of genius."

This was the same man, moreover, who one day defined for me his ideas on staging a play: "My work begins and the play interests me at the moment when the text ends."

I have also heard one of the greatest directors declare, in an impulse of revolt and disgust, "I've had enough! All plays are the same. I get tired and disheartened by my work. I am greater than what I do."

If I had space I would speak here in praise of restraint and success in the theater, and say too that the inner joy necessary to good work should not be confused with the taste for indulging one's own pleasure.

In general, the director follows his instinct and directs the plays he feels and loves, and distorts most of the others to his personal taste. That is the fundamental fault with this authorized intermediary who is so valuable when he directs a theater. It is not because I have a taste for disparagement that I say these things, but because I want to point out everything in the director's function that can be an obstacle to the free development of the theater.

If there is any conclusion to be drawn to this subject of the producer, it should be a commendation of the profession. To be professional is to be authentic. It is the only way of being real, to possess and practice the virtue of truth. For nothing counts unless it be true, unless it has roots. Nothing counts but honesty.

In our time, among so many other errors, there is a social lie which allows the relative and the contingent to pose as authentic. I do not know what kind of commercialism or industrialism it is whereby the middleman, the retailer and the *passe-partout* producer have taken precedence over the craftsman; but the theater has been thrown into disorder by these ill-qualified executives and incapable producers. (It has reached a point where, in the movie industry, the generic name for the man who works and labors is strictly reserved, in unconscious mockery, for the man who does nothing and does not know how to do anything: the producer. The only man in the business who knows exactly nothing about casting, cutting, camera-angles, montage—nothing about anything—is pompously entitled the producer.)

It is perhaps evident by this time that my wish is not to humiliate anyone, but to restore justice and equity by having the true workers become aware once more not only of their dignity but of their rights. In continuing to allow the so-called organizers—the merchants in the temple—to be kings in the kingdom of workers, we are in danger of compromising all we have.

In the short life given to us, there is still time for those whose sincerity and talent are expressed not in gain or glory but in the legitimate satisfaction of their taste for perfection, to recover a serenity as necessary to their inner peace and equilibrium as it is vital for social equilibrium. There is still time for the professional to be set apart, encouraged and protected by the society for which he works, and for the government—God on earth—to give some recognition to its own.

BERTOLT BRECHT

(1898-1956)

A Model for Epic Theater

For a decade and a half after the First World War a relatively new theatrical method was tried out in a few German theaters, a method which was called Epic because of the possibilities of description and reference which it opened up, because of such technical features as commenting choruses and written projections. By means of a none too simple technique, the actor put himself at a distance from the role he played and showed dramatic situations at such an angle of vision that they were bound to become the object of the spectators' criticism. The champions of this Epic Theater claimed that the new subject matter—the complications of class conflict at the moment of their most frightful climax—could more easily be mastered in this way; social processes could be presented along with their casual connections. Nevertheless, these experiments made difficulties for aesthetic theory—many difficulties.

It is relatively easy to set up a model for Epic Theater. When working with actors, I usually chose an event that can happen on any street corner as an example of the simplest, so to say "natural," Epic Theater: someone who has seen a traffic accident shows the crowd that has gathered how the mishap occurred. The bystanders may not have seen the accident, or they may have seen it but "in a different light"—the main point is that the witness brings up the

Bertolt Brecht: "A Model for Epic Theater," translated by Eric Bentley, *The Sewanee Review*, July 1949, 1-12.

behavior of the driver or of the victim or of both in such a way that the bystanders can form a judgment concerning the accident.

This example of the most primitive sort of Epic Theater seems easy to understand. But to take such a demonstration on a street corner as the basic pattern of great theater, the theater of a scientific age? If the reader (or listener) decides to do this, and if he grasps all the implications, he is faced, we found, with astonishing difficulties. *The basic pattern of great theater:* by this is meant that such an Epic Theater can in all its particulars be richer, more complicated, more highly developed, but that it does not require any other fundamental constituents than such a demonstration on the street corner in order to be great theater, and that, conversely, it could not be called Epic Theater if one of the chief constituents of the demonstration on the street corner were lacking. *Such a demonstration provides a sufficient model for great theater:* until the novelty and "untraditionalness" of this claim are comprehended, not to mention the unconditional challenge it offers to criticism, what follows cannot really be comprehended.

Consider. The "event" is manifestly not in the least what we understand by an artistic event. The demonstrator need not be an artist. What he has to do to achieve his aim anyone—for practical purposes—can do. If he cannot make as fast a movement as the victim of the accident whom he is imitating, he need only say by way of explanation: "he moved three times as fast," and his demonstration is not damaged. It loses nothing; rather, a bound is set to its perfection. The demonstration would be interfered with if the man's ability to transform himself into someone else were too noticeable. He must beware of making everyone shout "That's the chauffeur to a 't'! How true to life!" His job is not to cast a spell over anyone. He should not draw anyone out of everyday life into a "higher sphere." He need not possess special powers of suggestion.

The decisive fact is that a chief feature of conventional theater is absent from our scene in the street: the creation of illusion. Our demonstrator's procedure is, essentially, to *repeat* something. The incident *has* taken place, the repetition *is* taking place. If the theatrical scene follows the street scene in this, the theater is no longer concealing the fact that it is a theater, any more than the demonstration at the street corner conceals the fact that it is a demonstration and pretends to be the real incident. The fact that the acting has been rehearsed is quite apparent. So is the fact that the text has been learnt by heart. So is the stage apparatus, the whole preparation. What then has become of the "experience"? Is the actuality which is presented not an "experience" at all? The street scene determines what the experience which the spectator is given has to be like. Undoubtedly, our demonstrator has an "experience" behind him, but he is not out to make his demonstration an "experience" for the audience. Only in part does he use even the experience of the driver and his victim. In no way does he try to make it an enjoyable experience for the spectator, however much alive he may make the demonstration. For example: his demonstration loses none of its value if he does not reproduce the terror which the accident aroused; it would lose, rather, if he did; he is not out to produce mere emotions. To follow him in all this is completely to change the function of the theater. Let that be understood.

Our demonstrator is not, so to speak, *against* all the emotions that produce his own performance, but he does not simply transmit them to the audience. In general, he takes a stand and creates a mood, or frame of mind, suited to his interpretation of the case. Those emotions and interpretations—and they exist—which merely get in his way he combats by interrupting his performance and starting to argue. And then back to the presentation which has thus been kept within the realm of discussion.

Essential to the street scene (and thus to the theatrical scene too, if it is to be regarded as Epic) is the circumstance that the demonstration has a socially practical meaning. Whether our demonstrator wants to show that an accident is inevitable when a pedestrian or a driver behaves in such and such a way, and avoidable when he behaves otherwise, or whether he wants to show who is guilty—his demonstration is practical in its aims, has a social direction.

How complete should his imitation be? It depends wholly on the purpose of the demonstration. Our demonstrator need not copy everything his people do. He need only copy *something*, enough to provide a picture, an image. The theatrical scene in general provides much more complete images, in keeping with the wider range of its interests. What then is the connection between street scene and theater? The voice of the man who was run over (to pick up a single detail) may have played almost no part in the accident. Yet a difference of opinion among the witnesses as to whether the cry "Look out!" which they heard came from the victim or from another passerby can supply the reason for our demonstrator's imitating the voice. The demonstration will show whether the voice is an old man's or a woman's or at least whether it is high or low: and so the question is settled. The answer might, however, depend on whether the voice was that of an educated or an uneducated man. Loud or soft might play a big part in determining whether more or less guilt can be pinned on the driver. A great many things about the victim are relevant to the presentation. Was he preoccupied? Did something distract his attention? If so, what was it—in all probability? What was there in his behavior to show that he could be distracted by just such a circumstance and no other? Etcetera, etcetera. As can be seen, our street-corner exercise provides the opportunity for a rather rich and many-sided picture of men. Nevertheless, a theater that does not wish to go, in essentials, beyond the bounds of our street scene, must acknowledge certain limitations in its imitation of life.[1] The purpose served must justify the price paid.

---

[1] We often come across demonstrations of an everyday sort which are more complete imitations than our street accident needs to be. They are mostly comic. Our neighbor (male or female) may mimic the greedy behavior of our landlord. Imitations of this sort are apt to be abundant, full of variety. A closer investigation will prove, however, that even such a seemingly very complex imitation is just a way of treading on one particular corn. The imitation is a grouping of things, a segment of the total reality, from which the moments when the landlord seems "quite reasonable" are entirely omitted—naturally, there *are* moments of that sort. Our neighbor is very far from giving a complete picture: it wouldn't have a comic effect. The theater, which cuts out a thicker segment, runs here into difficulties which must not be underrated. It, too, enables us to criticize what it demonstrates —but it demonstrates much more complex events. And it must enable us to be both negative and positive critics—at one and the same time. One must understand

Let us suppose that the demonstration is dominated by the question of "damages." The chauffeur has to fear dismissal, the confiscation of his license, imprisonment. The victim has to fear big hospital bills, the loss of his job, lasting deformity, possible unfitness for work. Such is the field which our demonstrator draws his characters from. The victim may have had a companion. The chauffeur may have had his girl on the seat beside him. That would bring the social factor into play all the more. The characters can be more richly portrayed.

A further element essential to the street scene is that our demonstrator derives his characters entirely from their actions. He imitates their actions and thereby permits us to judge them. A theater that follows him in this respect is making a complete break with the practice of conventional theater, which is to derive actions from character. Thus, the conventional theater shields actions from criticism. Actions are presented as proceeding, ineluctably, according to laws of nature, from the character of those who perform them. For our demonstrator, on the other hand, the character of the man demonstrated is a quantity which he does not have to estimate in full. Within certain limits this man can be thus and thus, and it makes no difference. The demonstrator is interested in those things about him which make for, or against, street accidents. (All persons whose character meets the conditions he lays down, who show the features he imitates, will bring about the same situation.) A stage personage may be more definitely an individual. The theater must therefore be in a position to say that its "individual" is a special case and to indicate the surroundings in which the relevant social processes come into existence. The things that our demonstration can demonstrate are limited in number: we chose the model as prescribing to us the narrowest pos-

what it means to win the assent of an audience by *criticizing*. We have models, of course, in our street scene, that is, in all sorts of demonstrations of the most everyday sort. Our neighbor and our demonstrator can render someone's "reasonable" behavior as well as their "unreasonable" behavior in presenting him for our scrutiny. But they especially need *commentary* through which they can change the standpoint of their presentation—in case something crops up during the action, in case the reasonable man becomes unreasonable or vice versa. Here the theater gets us into difficulties. See Brecht: "A New Style of Acting." [B. B.]

sible bounds. If the theater is to be "richer" than our street scene and yet is not, in essentials, to go beyond it, the playwright will have to know how to find much in little. He cannot, as it were, add more gold to his stock, but he can be expert in using all the gold there is. The question of the bounds within which he works—of borderline cases—becomes acute.

To take up a detail. Can our demonstrator render *in an excited tone* the chauffeur's claim to be exhausted by overlong hours? (In general he cannot—any more than a messenger, returning to report to his people an interview with the king, could begin with: "I have seen the bearded king.") A situation must be thought of on the street corner in which such excitedness (about long hours, etc.) plays a special part. This done, the tone not only can, but must, be excited. (Continuing the above example, the situation would permit excitement if, for instance, the king had sworn to leave his beard as it was until he . . . etc.). We have to seek a standpoint from which our demonstrator can hand over his excitedness to criticism. Only when he assumes a very definite standpoint can our demonstrator be in a position to imitate the driver's excited tone, namely, if he, for instance, attacks drivers because they do so little to shorten their working hours. ("He isn't even in a union, but if something goes wrong, he gets excited! 'I've been at the wheel for ten hours!' ").

If the theater is to do this, if, that is, it is able to offer the actor a "standpoint," it will have to resort to a number of expedients. If the theater can cut out a larger segment of life by showing the driver in more situations (and not just in the situation of the street accident) it is still not, in principle, going beyond the model. It is building up another situation of the same sort as the model. A scene of the same sort as the street scene is conceivable in which is demonstrated, with sufficient motivation, how emotions like the driver's arise—or one in which comparisons of voices (as to cadence etc.) are made. To keep within the bounds set by the model, the theater has only to be constantly developing the technique by which the emotions are subordinated to the criticism which the spectator makes of them. This, of course, is not to say that the spectator is, in principle, prevented from sharing certain emotions that are being acted out; but, in taking them over, he criticizes them; in fact, the "taking-over" is a special form (phase, consequence) of criticism. The demonstrator in the theater, the actor, must employ a technique by means of which he can render the tone of the person demonstrated with a certain reserve, with a certain distance (allowing the spectator to say: "Now he's getting excited, it's no use, too late, at last" etc.). In short, the actor must remain a demonstrator. He must render the person demonstrated as a different person. He must not leave out of his presentation the "*he* did this, *he* said that." He must not let himself be completely transformed into the person demonstrated.

An essential element of the street scene consists in the natural attitude which the demonstrator assumes—in a double sense. He always has to reckon with two situations. He behaves naturally as demonstrator (D_1) and he lets the person demonstrated (D_2) behave naturally. He never forgets or lets it be forgotten that he is not D_2 but D_1. That is: what the audience sees is not a fusion of D_1 and D_2, an independent D_3, in which the contours of D_1 and D_2 are lost and from which all contradictions have been eliminated. (This of course is what we are used to in the modern theater: Stanislavsky developed the idea—and very clearly.) The opinions and feelings of D_1 and D_2 are not coordinated.

We come now to one of the special elements of Epic Theater, the so-called A-effect (Alienation-effect).[2] Briefly, it has to do with a technique which confers on the human events to be presented the stamp of the conspicuous, of something requiring an explanation, something not obvious, not simply natural. The aim of the A-effect is to make of the spectator an active critic of society. Can we show that this A-effect has meaning for our demonstrator on the street corner?

We can imagine what happens if he has failed to bring off the A-effect. The following situation might arise. A spectator could say: "If the victim, as you show the thing, stepped off into the street on his right foot, not his left, then. . . ." Our demonstrator could inter-

2 In German, *V-Effekt, Verfremdungseffekt*.

rupt him and say: "I have shown that he stepped off on the left foot." In the dispute as to whether, in his demonstration, he really stepped off on the left (or right) foot and as to what the victim did, the demonstration can be so changed that the A-effect comes about. In that the demonstrator now watches his movements carefully, and executes them carefully, probably at a slower rate, he brings off the A-effect, that is he "alienates" this part of the action, brings it forward in all its importance, makes it remarkable. And so the A-effect proves to be useful even to the demonstrator on the street corner. In other words, it occurs even in this little everyday scene which has little to do with art.

More easily recognizable as an element of any street demonstration is the immediate transition that can be made from presentation to commentary, a transition characteristic of Epic Theater. The demonstrator, as often as seems possible, interrupts his imitation with explanations. The choruses and projected documents of Epic Theater, the turning-directly-to-the-audience of the actors, are interruptions of exactly the same sort.

It will be noted, not without astonishment I trust, that I have not actually called any of the constituents of our street scene—or, it follows, of our theater—artistic. Our demonstrator could carry through his demonstration successfully enough with skills that, for practical purposes, everyone possesses. What about the artistic value of Epic Theater?

It is not an accident that Epic Theater is concerned to construct its model *on the street corner,* that it goes back to the simplest, "natural" theater, to a social undertaking whose causes, means, and ends are practical and earthly. The model can get along without recourse to such explanations of theatrical art as "the urge to self-expression," "making the fates of others your own," "an experience of the soul-life," "the play impulse," "the love of story-telling," etc. Is Epic Theater, then, not interested in art?

It would be wise to put the question differently: can we use artistic skills for the purposes of our street scene and thereby also for those of our theater? Yes, we can. Artistic energies lurk even in the demonstration on the street corner. There is a measure of artistic skill in everyone. It cannot hurt to remember this when talking of great art. Undoubtedly the skills we call artistic can always be called into play within the bounds established by our model. They will function as artistic skills even when they do not overstep these bounds (*e.g.*, when no total transformation of D1 into D2 takes place). Actually, Epic Theater is not conceivable without artists and artistry. Fantasy, humor, sympathy—without these and other such qualities it cannot be practiced. It has to be entertaining and it has to be instructive. Now how, out of the elements of our street scene, without taking any element away, without adding any element, can art be developed? How can you derive a theater—with its invented plot, its trained actors, its elevated speech, its make-up, its combination of many actors? Has the "natural" demonstration to be supplemented by other things if we are to proceed from it to the "artistic" demonstration? Are not the extensions of the model which enable us to arrive at Epic Theater fundamental changes? A moment's thought will convince us that they are not.

Take the plot or story. Our traffic accident was not invented. But the theater as we know it does not deal exclusively with invented material. There is the historical play. But even on the street corner a story can be enacted. Our demonstrator can easily come to say: "The driver was guilty, for the event was as I showed it to be. He would not have been guilty had he done what I will now show." And he can make up an event and "demonstrate" it.

Take the learning-by-heart of a role. Our demonstrator might be a witness in a lawsuit. He can learn by heart and study the exact utterance of the person in court whose behavior he has witnessed. The words having been written out, he can bring before the court a role he has memorized.

Take the prepared acting of a number of demonstrators. Such a combined demonstration has not, in itself and invariably, an artistic purpose. Think of the practice of the French police: they order the chief participants in a criminal case to "recapitulate" certain decisive situations in the police station.

Take make-up and disguise. Little changes in appearance—a

rumpling of the hair, for instance—could easily be used in the orbit of some non-artistic demonstration. Make-up is not used for theatrical purposes alone. The chauffeur's mustache (to return to our street corner) may have a definite significance. It may have influenced the deposition of the girl who we said might have been with him. Our demonstrator can bring this idea into his demonstration by having the driver stroke an imaginary beard when he urges his lady companion to give evidence. Thus the demonstrator can subtract a good deal of value from the witness's deposition. To go from here to the use of a real beard in the theater involves, of course, a little difficulty —which is felt also in the matter of costume. Our demonstrator can under certain circumstances put the driver's cap on—for example, if he wants to show that he was drunk (he had his cap on crooked). Under certain circumstances, but not all—see the above passage about borderline cases. Of course in a combined demonstration by many people (as mentioned) we could have costumes, to enable us to distinguish the persons demonstrated. Costumes, yes—but also within certain limits. The illusion that $D_1 = D_2$ must not be created. (Epic Theater can thwart this illusion through especially exaggerated costumes, clothes that have the stamp of "theater.") Further, we can set up a basic model that in this respect replaces the other, namely, the demonstrations of the so-called "flying street vendors." In selling ties, these people present not only the badly dressed man but also the dandy. With a couple of props and a few tricks, they carry out their little suggestive scene—in which they impose the same limitations on themselves that our accident scene imposes on our demonstrator. (They pick up tie, hat, stick, gloves, and make suggestive "copies" of a man of the world, speaking of him, moreover, as *he*.) Among street vendors we also find verse used within the same framework that our model imposes. They use firm irregular rhythms whether it's newspapers or suspenders that they are selling. See Brecht: "Unrhymed Lyrics in Irregular Rhythms."

Such considerations show that we can get along with our model. There is no basic difference between the natural epic theater and the artistic Epic Theater.

Our theater at the street corner is primitive. In respect of motive, purpose, and means, it doesn't go very far. But it is incontestably a meaningful "event." Its social function is clear. And it is in control of all its parts. The performance is occasioned by an incident which is open to more than one interpretation, which in one form or another can be repeated, and which is not yet a closed book, but which will have consequences. Hence our judgment of it really matters. It is the aim and end of the performance to make a consideration of the incident easier. The means correspond to the end. Epic Theater is a fully artistic theater with a complicated content and, in addition, a social end in view. Setting up the street scene as a model for Epic Theater, we assign to it a clear social function, and set up criteria for Epic Theater according to which we can estimate whether the events under review are meaningful or not. Amid questions (often difficult) about particular passages, amid all the problems, artistic and social, that arise when a performance is in preparation, the model puts directors and actors in a position to *exercise control* in seeing whether the social function of the whole apparatus is clear and intact.

TYRONE GUTHRIE
(b. 1900)

An Audience of One

Producing a play clearly requires the coordinated efforts of many people, and the producer is no more than the coordinator. His work may, and I think should, have creative functions, but not always. The important thing is gathering together the different pieces and welding many disparate elements into one complete unity, which is never, of course, fully achieved in artistic matters.

The work of the producer can be analyzed—indeed has been analyzed—in many different ways. I propose to deal with it under two headings: firstly, the producer in relation to the script of the play, that is to say the raw material of his work; and secondly, the producer in relation to actors and staff, that is animate collaborators.

It seems to me that the producer's business, when faced either with a new script or with being asked to revive a classic or an old play, is first of all to decide what it is about. Clearly, that is not entirely simple. To take an obvious instance, who is really going to give the final word as to what *Hamlet* is about? As we all know, more books have been written about *Hamlet* than almost any other topic under the sun. I am told that, as far as biographies are concerned, the three champions about whom the most has been written are Jesus Christ, Hamlet and Napoleon Bonaparte, in that order. *Hamlet* is an obviously difficult case in which to decide what the play is about, but

Transcript of a talk delivered before the Royal Society of Arts, London, March 10, 1952. By permission of Tyrone Guthrie.

take a nice simple little play called *Charley's Aunt*. What is that about? It is just a question of telling the story, or is it a question of finding a meaning to the story? Are Charley's "Aunt" and all those jolly undergraduates symbols of this or that, or are they to be taken at face value? Is the thing to be—as I have seen it done in Scandinavia—a serious study of English university life, or is it just to be made as funny as possible? Personally, I think the latter; but before you can make it funny you have got to decide why it is funny, what is funny about it, and what the joke is, which is quite a tricky little problem.

I think very often the lighter the play is the more it is composed of thistledown and little else, the more difficult it is to pin down. One has often seen little tiny plays absolutely slain by the great mechanism brought to bear on their own interpretation. An obvious case in point is *Così Fan Tutte*. I do not know whether anyone has seen a satisfactory performance of that. I have seen it a great many times, but it always seems to me that a great many steam hammers in human form are assembled to crack a little jewelled acorn.

With regard to what the script is about, the last person who, in my opinion, should be consulted, even if he is alive or around, is the author. If the author is a wise man, he will admit straight away that he does not know what it is about, unless it is a very perfunctory work indeed. If it is just a little piece of journalism on the minor problems of psychoanalysis, then he probably will know all too well what it is about. But if it has the potentialities of being an important work of art, I am perfectly convinced he will not have the faintest idea of what he has really written. He will probably know what he thinks he has written, but that will be the least important part of it. Were it possible to find out, I would lay any money that Shakespeare had only the vaguest idea of what he was writing when he wrote *Hamlet;* that the major part of the meaning of it eluded him because it proceeded from the subconscious. A great work of art is like an iceberg in that ninety per cent of it is below the surface of consciousness. Therefore, in my opinion, the more important the work of art, the less the author will know what he has written.

I had the great privilege and pleasure to know the late James Bridie extremely well. I worked with him often, but he would never even discuss what his plays were about. He would say, "How should I know? I am the last person you should ask. I am only the author. I have written an armature, inside which, possibly, are the deepest ideas which have never quite formulated themselves in my consciousness. If, as I hope and believe, I am a poet, there will be something in these, but I am the last person to know what it is."

The producer has to decide what he thinks the play is about, and of course I am largely joking when I say that he does not really take the author seriously. Naturally he does, but not as to the deeper, the inner and the over-and-above, the between and through, meaning of the lines. If somebody does not decide at an early stage what the play is about, obviously the casting will be made for the wrong reasons. Ideally, a play should be cast because the actors chosen are people that somebody—be it the producer or be it the manager—thinks will express the play best. In fact, in the exigencies of commercial production and the exigencies of practical affairs, all too often plays are cast because somebody thinks that Mr. X will help to sell the beastly thing, and Mr. X happens to be living with Miss Y so she is a cinch for the leading lady, and all sorts of vulgar and extraneous considerations of that kind which really have nothing whatever to do with art but everything in the world to do with the practical business of putting on a play. I cannot sufficiently differentiate between the two, but seeing that we are speaking in these almost hallowed precincts I am going to try to behave as though we were in an ideal atmosphere and plays were cast solely with artistic considerations in view, or at all events very much in the foreground with practical things far away in the background.

In theory, the artistic way to cast a play is to decide who, of the available actors, seems to be the most like the principal part in the script that we are given, and who would best understand the thing. Let me qualify that. It is not entirely a question of who is the most like the principal character, because very often the last thing that an actor does well is to portray a character that is like himself as one conceives him to be in private life. Very many actors do their best work when they are hiding from themselves behind a mass of hair and make-up and fantasy, when they present something entirely unlike their real selves.

One must think which of the available actors would seem to give the best interpretation of a given part. That is why, at a very early stage, the whole business of producing a play has to move into conference. It is, in my opinion, very unwise for the leading actor not to work step by step from the very earliest stages with the three or four people with whom he is going to collaborate most closely: the manager, or whoever is responsible for the budgetary financial side of the production, the leading actors, and certainly the designer, the man who is ultimately going to be responsible for the pictorial look of the thing. All their work should grow together and should, I think, be the result of a productive exchange of ideas.

Therefore, it is clearly necessary that, if the thing is going to work well, they should be people who can to some extent speak one another's language, who can exchange ideas, who can admit themselves to be wrong without red faces in the company of the others, and so on. So that, long before the thing gets to the stage of rehearsal and parts being read or movements made, there should have been a quite extensive exchange of ideas about the look of the thing, about the sound of the thing, about the shape of the thing in predominantly musical and choreographic terms.

To elaborate that a little, the performance of a play is clearly analogous to the performance of a symphonic piece of music. By the time the play is ready, if it is properly rehearsed, the diverse voices, the group of people who are playing the thing, will have found a music for their parts. Why acting, in my opinion, is so much more interesting than opera singing is that the actors invent the music of their parts to a very great extent. In an operatic score, the composer's intention is made extraordinarily clear. The rhythm, the inflection, the loudness and softness, the pitch and the pace at which the idea is to be conveyed, are all clearly defined in the score. Almost the only creative piece of work left to the conductor and the singers is the color, because so far no form of notation has been found for musical color. The actor has to find nearly all those things for himself. Supposing you are an actor who is playing Hamlet. "To be, or not to be: that is the question: whether 'tis nobler in the mind to suffer . . ."— those infinitely familiar lines. You have to find the inflection, that is to say the tune, to which they are sung or spoken, the pitch, the pace, the rhythm and the color. That is, in fact, very highly creative.

Parallel with the creation of the actor must, I think, come the co-ordination of the producer. Supposing two of us are playing a scene. and one has decided that the scene must be played lightly and forcibly, and the other person takes a different view of the scene and feels that it must be managed in a very dark and very black way with long pauses. It is the business of the producer to coordinate the two without necessarily making either man feel that he has been a fool or stupid. It is a point of view which way the scene should be taken, and somebody has to be the chairman, somebody has to decide. That is really in most cases what the producer is.

I know there is an idea abroad, largely cultivated in popular fiction, about the theater and films, that the producer is a very dominant person who goes around doing a lot of ordering about, saying, "Stand here, stand there, copy me, do it this way, do it that way." Of course, with experienced and accomplished actors that would be complete nonsense. Imagine my saying to Dame Edith Evans, "Do it this way, dear, copy me."

The performance of a play should be able to be observed by anybody who knows it well just like a graph, like a patient's temperature chart, like a graph of the sales statistics of a firm or anything else. One should be able to see the peaks and the hollows, and it should be possible to delineate the shape of each scene in a graph, which helps to make the scene more intelligible, which helps to make it illuminate the scene preceding it and the scene following it, which helps it to contrast, and at the same time to blend with the neighboring scenes; and, while each little scene should have a graph, similarly a graph of the whole act should arise from that.

Now on to the second main heading about production.

First of all, and very briefly, there is the question of organization, discipline and that kind of thing. If the company is any good and if the producer is any good, that is simply a matter of general convenience. I do not think the producer has any difficulty over discipline provided the rehearsals are not boring, and provided they are kept moving not at the pace of the very slowest person present but at a fairly decent tempo.

Then comes the question of coaching. How far is a producer to coach the interpretation? How much is he to say to the actors, "Do it this way"? I do not think one can give a complete answer to that. If you are taking the first production that has ever been done by the dramatic society attached to the Little Pifflington Women's Institute, you will probably have to do a great deal of coaching and coaxing to break down the self-conscious giggling of people who are quite unaccustomed to impersonation and pretending to be someone they are not. But if you have a good professional cast the amount of coaching you have to do is very small.

I do not think one should be at all afraid of saying to actors in a quite dogmatic way, "Play this scene sitting on the sofa, and if you are not comfortable let me know later on, but don't decide until we have done it once or twice. Later on, maybe you would feel like getting up halfway through and going to the window." Otherwise, if the actor is allowed to grope it out too much for himself, there is a waste of time, and the dominant personalities start bullying the milder, more unselfish and cooperative ones, which is what we have to be on the lookout for.

Then comes what I have tried to indicate is very much the main business of the producer, the work of coordination from the departments inwards.

Clearly, the coordinating of an idea, so far as it is concerned with visual matters, lies to a considerable degree in the hands of the person responsible for the lighting. Here, as elsewhere, I feel there should be the minimum of dogmatism. A good designer will have been working from quite an early stage in collaboration with the leading actors. Actors on the whole are sensible people about their clothes.

Most actors have not at all a vain idea of their own appearance, but a very realistic appreciation of their good points and bad points, and they can be very helpful to a designer in suggesting things like the length of their coats or the width of their sleeves. If an actor says, "I want a long sleeve because I think I can do something with it," that should be taken very seriously; and, in my opinion, an actor should never be forced to wear a dress he does not like, unless it is for economic or disciplinary reasons. You could not expect people to feel free, unself-conscious and at ease on the stage in dresses they feel to be unsuitable.

Where I think the producer's work of coordination requires the greatest amount of time and care spent upon it is in the vocal interpretation of the play. As I have already tried to indicate, the performance of a play is, on a smaller scale, a performance of a musical work. The script is, as it were, sung, because speaking and singing are, after all, the same process. Although I am speaking now and not singing, I am uttering a definable tune all the time. Every syllable I utter is on a certain pitch and a musician could say precisely where it was. Every sentence that I phrase is consciously phrased in a certain rhythm. The pauses, although I am not conscious of it, are expressing an instinctive need to pause, not merely to breathe, but for clarity and various other interpretative purposes. This is even more pronounced in the performance of a play, where all that has been most carefully thought out in terms of pace, rhythm, pitch, volume and all the rest of it, to make a certain expressive effect. That is particularly where the coordinating hand of the producer is required, joining up the various songs that are being sung and making them into a unit; and similarly, joining up the various patterns that are being danced, because even in the simplest realistic comedy, in the most ordinary kind of realistic set—the actors have to move, and their movements have to tot up to some kind of choreographic design which expresses the play, which has some meaning over and above the common-sense position in which one would pour tea or put sugar into it. For long stretches of the play the positions have to be guided not at all by anything that is afoot. Of course, it is mere journalism to think that plays are concerned with action. They are not. Plays in the cinema may be, but in the theater the action is a tiny point.

In almost every play for the stage, there is scarcely any action. The movements of the play are almost all concerned with the expression of ideas and not of action. If there is action, it is very short-lived and very brief. The choreography is much more concerned with the subtle delineation of emotions by the way people are placed, with the subtle changes of emphasis by putting people into the brighter light or taking them out of it, by having them face the audience or turn their backs, by putting them in the center or near the side. It is all very much more delicate and allusive than simply getting them into common-sense positions to perform certain actions.

Finally, I should like to discuss what to me is the most interesting part of the job, the blending of intuition with technique. If I may elaborate those terms, by intuition I mean the expression of a creative idea that comes straight from the subconscious, that is not arrived at by a process of ratiocination at all. It is my experience that all the best ideas in art just arrive, and it is absolutely no good concentrating on them and hoping for the best. The great thing is to relax and just trust that the Holy Ghost will arrive and the idea will appear. The sought idea is nearly always, in my opinion, the beta plus idea. The alpha plus idea arrives from literally God knows where. Prayer and fasting can no doubt help, but concentration and ratiocination are, I think, only a hindrance. And yet I think no artist worth his salt will feel he can rely on inspiration. Inspiration must be backed up by a very cast-iron technique.

It is the case that as one gets older one's technique, if one is an industrious and intelligent person, tends to become better; but there is also the danger that it becomes a little slick. I think not only artists, but anybody engaged in any activity must feel the same thing. The record begins to get worn, and we slip too easily into old grooves, the same association of ideas comes back too readily and easily. I notice with my own work in the theater—and I have been at it now for nearly thirty years—that I have to check myself all the time from slipping into certain very obvious and, to me now, rather dull choreographic mannerisms. I instinctively think, "Oh, obviously the right place is so-and-so, and the right way to group this is such-and-such." Then I think, why do I think that? And usually the only reason is that one has done it that way a good many times before. That is obviously frightfully dangerous in any creative work. It is the negation of creation; it is just falling back onto habit.

Yet there are certain very valuable things about experience and about technique. It is now comparatively easy for me, in late middle age, to establish a good relation with actors. They think because I have been at it for a long time that I know something about it, and they are readier to take suggestions from me now than they were twenty-five years ago when I was a beginner, though I am inclined to think that most of the suggestions are duller ones. Twenty-five years ago, intuition functioned oftener and more readily. That is, I think, one of the very difficult paradoxes about production.

Clearly, for practical reasons, it is very difficult to put the highly intuitive, gifted youngster in charge of a responsible production. He will make too many mistakes. He will be too dependent on the things that experience and authority bring easily from the older people. Also, it is difficult for the senior actors. It requires enormous tact, both on the part of the young producer and the old actor, to be helpful to one another. Yet the young producer is precisely what the experienced actor with a cast-iron technique—and consequently a great many mannerisms, too many clichés and short cuts—needs. He needs a very bright, sharp, critical young person of twenty-five to say, "No, Sir X, don't do it that way. You have been doing it that way for twenty-five years and it has been fine for twenty-five years, but that is just the reason for not doing it that way now." Well, you can see that unless that is done with supreme tact it is all too easy for Sir X or Dame Y to cast down their script and summon their Rolls-Royce.

I should like to conclude by telling a little anecdote which was told to me by a distinguished producer now resident in this country, who began life in Czechoslovakia and early in his career went to Germany. He soon got quite a good position while still in his early twenties in one of the German provincial theaters. He was a fine-looking young fellow and very "castable" in hero parts, and the management of the theater sent him to see Reinhardt, then at the very apex of his celebrity and power in Berlin. My friend was still young enough to be madly thrilled, not only with the great opportunity of meeting this god and the possible advancement that it might produce, but with such childish and naïve, but extremely natural, things as the overnight journey in a first-class sleeper and all that kind of thing. All that was a terrific thrill, and he described very touchingly how he enjoyed it. He arrived in Berlin on a delicious crisp autumn morning, and went to the theater at which Reinhardt was working, the Grosses Schauspielhaus. He described the grand chandeliers, the polished floors, the gentlemen in livery who collected him at the door, how he swept up the marble staircase, along a passage with portraits of eminent people all down the side, through a less important door in the side of the passage, down some stairs with no polish and carpets at all, through a very squalid little passage, round various corners, and across a courtyard, until he came to a room really more like a kitchen. He said at first the only things he could see were the long windows all down one side with the sun streaming in. Then, as he began to get accustomed to that, he saw a group of rather drab-looking actors rehearsing at one end. Then he suddenly saw that one of these actors was somebody whose face had been familiar to him all his life, a great star of Germany, and I think he had that experience which anybody has who suddenly comes face-to-face with a very familiar face that he has seen illustrated, whether politician, film star, or anybody else. You suddenly think, "How small they are! I thought they were much bigger." He was busy taking all this in and thinking what a small person this gentleman was whom he had always thought so great when suddenly, at the end of the room, he saw a very unimportant-looking gentleman sitting on the kitchen table swinging his legs and looking at his hands. It was Reinhardt. He thought, "Now the great moment has come and I shall hear Socrates pour out words of wisdom and technical advice to these people. Eminent they may be, but they will not be above getting a little tip or two from Reinhardt." But nothing happened. Then he thought,

"Well, they must be so bad that he is going to give them a hell of a slating at any minute. There will be a few glorious minutes when high-powered abuse will pour from the golden lips and the boys down there will get very hot under the collar." Nothing happened, and nothing continued to happen for quite a long time until the actors came to the end of a scene. Then there was a short pause, not a rudely long pause at all, but *quite* a pause, and my friend was agog with excitement to know what would be said. Reinhardt just looked up and said, "Thanks very much. Now can we go back to the maid's entrance?" That, or something like it, went on through the whole morning, and he said that, far from it being a dull rehearsal, it was clearly—he was artist enough to perceive it—an immensely constructive rehearsal, and he began to think why it was, because nothing was being said, no instructions were given, no abuse poured forth and no praise. He analyzed it this way, and the more I think of it the more profoundly convinced I am that he is right, that Reinhardt was performing the one really creative function of the producer, which is to be at rehearsal a highly receptive, highly concentrated, highly critical sounding-board for the performance, an audience of one. He is not the drill sergeant, not the schoolmaster, and he does not sweep in with a lot of verbiage and "Stand here and do it this way, darling, and move the right hand not the left." He is simply receiving the thing, transmuting it, and giving it back. When you come down to analyzing what the creative part of acting is, it is the giving of impressions to the audience and then, on the part of the actor, the taking back of their impressions and doing something about them. The best simile that I can make is that the actor throws a thread, as it were, out into the house which, if the house is receptive, it will catch. Then it is the actor's business to hold that thread taut and to keep a varying and consequently interesting pressure on it, so that it is really pulled in moments of tension and allowed to go as slack as possible in moments of relaxation, but never so slack that it falls and cannot be pulled up again. The producer at rehearsals can be that audience. He can perform that function, and if he is a good producer he will perform it better than the average audience; he will be more intelligently critical and alive, and the rehearsals will not be dreary learning of routine; they will be a creative act that is ultimately going to be a performance.

That is why, in my opinion, the analogy between the producer and the conductor holds good. A *good* conductor is a man with a fine technique of the stick. He has a clear beat and an expressive beat, and is an interesting chap for the audience to watch. He can bring one section in with a fine gesture and blot another out. He knows his score, and so on, but it is all interesting showmanship. But the *great* conductor does not require any of those things. He can have a terrible beat and look like nothing on earth, but if he is a great conductor every man in the orchestra will give, under his baton, not only a better performance than he would under another conductor, but a better performance than he knew he could give. That is not got out of them by instruction; it is a process of psychic evocation. Precisely the same thing holds good for the producer of a play. His function at its best is one of psychic evocation, and it is performed almost entirely unconsciously. Certain conscious tricks can come in the way or aid the process, but this evocative thing comes from God knows where. It is completely unconscious. Nobody knows when it is working, and nobody knows why it is working. Some people, and only the very best, have it; others do not. I could not answer why or wherefore, but I am just convinced that that is so.

NIKOLAI OKHLOPKOV

(b. 1900)

Creative Interplay

Why have I been so concerned with the "mass spectacle"—where the playing area is carried into the thick of the audience? Because once having sampled this method of staging a production (I directed a "mass spectacle" in Irkutsk in 1921) I had to go on thinking about and searching for new playing areas and different forms through which the action would unfold, not only with the maximum proximity to the spectator, but also with an active involvement of the audience in the maelstrom of the action.

The second production of my life, Mayakovsky's *Mystery Bouffe*, I staged in an enclosed municipal theater in Irkutsk, with only a partial transfer of the action into the auditorium. The thought of locating the entire action in the middle of the audience would not let me rest: I wanted to make the action "his own" for the spectator, to propel the spectator into the action, and make the action itself more graphic, more vivid, more three-dimensional. I wanted to do everything I could to make the audience creatively share the characters' life, feelings, thoughts, and hopes.

... The "mass spectacle" was the beginning of my creative search. From that time on, I have been seeking the spiritual ardor born out of the creative interplay of actors and audience in the course of a performance. I have been looking for that atmosphere which cannot

Nikolai Okhlopkov: "Of Stage Platforms," *Teatr* (Moscow), Vol. XX, January 1959, 44-50 *passim*.

be found in the enclosed court theaters, but on streets and open platforms. From the first I turned to the tradition of the popular shows. Let "my theater" travel along this road!

For a long time, however, this road was undefined. I realized in the first place that one needed plays in which the people would recognize themselves and their lives. One needed popular ideas, popular subjects, popular images, and popular language. And finally one needed popular staging, marked by outspokenness, simplicity, artlessness, vividness, and clarity. I saw numerous companies and productions, but, alas, in all of them, with the most subtle playing of the actors, with the most profound and feeling play, within the frame of a proscenium theater there was almost something pre-set: some "show" —others, separated by footlights or the orchestra pit, "look on." . . .

I searched long and without success, walking into theaters, movie houses, art exhibitions, and concerts, until accidentally I walked into an outlying workers' club. Having seen their poster announcing for that evening a meeting of young people with Maxim Gorky, I entered a large auditorium and saw Gorky onstage. The hall was filled with youngsters listening eagerly to their beloved author. Gorky had recently returned from abroad, he was seeing the youth of the Soviet Union after a long separation. He spoke of life, of work, of creativity, of Man. He spoke simply, humanely and at the same time sternly, without a trace of sentimentality. But he was moved. He spoke and the treacherous tear would now and then roll down his cheek. As he spoke his listeners, and I among them, without realizing it climbed on the stage and sat on the bare floor, surrounding this remarkable man from all sides.

Gorky talked, then suddenly would interrupt his speech, and in the pause would stare at the faces of his eager young listeners encircling him in a tight ring. The young people answered him with the same thoughts, the same feelings. What was taking place here was not a speech, not a lecture, but a veritable "religious spectacle." I never knew before that human eyes could emit . . . ardor! Yes, it really was ardor from their burning eyes, their touched and shaken souls. And may I be forgiven, I thought immediately: How to get that in art! What high thoughts art must contain for that! What feelings must art "pour" from its inspired soul to the soul of the listeners! And it became quite clear to me that one must also seat the audience in a new way to help them to be not merely "observers" of what happens on the stage. . . .

Why does art so often insult itself by giving voice to plays with so little thought, so little experience of life? But when the theater has a play of profound thoughts and great heart, then, in considering the form of the production, one should also think of the architectural design—of new playing areas on which to mount the production. This architectural design must fully match the spirit of the play itself and be ready to add something to what the theatrical collective—the author, director, actors, and the scene designer—want to say.

In the Moscow Realistic Theater from 1930 to 1936 I staged productions of plays and dramatizations of great social significance, on great themes, of monumental character. But the theater had a small stage, the smallest of all the Moscow theaters. After I came to the theater all the new productions were put on with the box-stage dismantled, and with the placement, new each time, of playing platforms of various shapes and uses amid and around the spectators (and even above them). Fate seemed to be laughing at me: after my "spectacle" on a city square, after the scope of *Mystery Bouffe,* after directing in the movies where almost nothing limited me, I acquired, for the realization of my dreams, a tiny stage and a small auditorium with a capacity of 325 persons! . . .

I decided then to use the small theater for "directorial sketches"; like a painter who first makes small-scale drawings, then transfers the design to a large canvas. Thus I decided not to stage "productions" but only "directorial sketches" for future hoped-for productions. But first I needed plays which would have great themes that would deeply affect me personally, very great themes—not simply "pleasing" but stirring one relentlessly, giving one neither peace nor rest.

In recent times we have clearly begun to be contemptuous of the theme. Having grasped and tested in practice that the theme alone, no matter how good in itself, does not give us the right to think of the work written on it as high artistry, and knowing that the theme also always demands a full artistic treatment, many of us, for some reason, do not pause for long or very deeply on the theme itself, but pass quickly to its artistic interpretation. You cannot glide over the theme. It is of tremendous importance. Every composition begins with it. It is the beginning of beginnings.

Everyone started to demand high artistic values—and that's justified; everyone started to search for deep and refined psychological solutions of the theme in presentation—and that's also quite justified; everyone started looking more and more for the verisimilitude and liveliness of the play—and that is also indubitably very wise, talented, and important. But . . . behind all this one often forgets the theme itself, which frequently only seems to be great on the surface, and in reality does not step outside the framework of exhortation for beginners.

Very definitely the theme has to stir to the utmost the dramatist, the director, and the actor; the theme must provide the essential inner push which brings the artist to his full creative inspiration. In addition, the theme is not simply one play or one production; it is a whole stage of the artist's creativity. The theme can evolve as part of the process of the artist's growth; but if the artist simply betrays it, art will take its revenge. Thus, I have been and am today searching first of all for my basic theme.

Themes, ideas . . . they live in works of art inseparable from subject matter and plot, from the descriptions of people, their interrelationships and their behavior; but . . . these themes must be determined and defined long before one can fully grasp, to the last dot and comma, the entire content, the complete beauty of every breath, every step, every smallest detail of the artistic world of a play. . . .

Thus I deliberated on what I should direct which would express the heroic spirit of the nation, its will, its wisdom, its love of freedom, the breadth and depth of its soul. I think of the heroic without any "heroic" grandiloquence or stiltedness. I am for Shakespearization! How much it would help playwrights, directors and actors today!

Alas . . . as I was dreaming of this on Triumphal Square (its very name seemed ironic to me), there was not even a hint of success in finding such plays. If such plays existed at all (and they did), they were naturally earmarked for established theaters. What was I to do? Dramatizations of great novels, heroic tales, sharp political sketches on burning issues of the day—these helped the theater. I won't hide my pride in the repertory of those years: *Take-Off* based on a sketch by Stavsky, *Mother* based on Gorky's novel, *The Iron Stream* based on a novel by Serafimovich, Shakespeare's *Othello,* Romain Rolland's *Colas Breugnon,* and Pogodin's *Aristocrats.*

These large-scale plays demanded large-scale staging! These were not "intimate" works and they demanded new solutions, a new approach. As a result of our search, we moved the action to various parts of the orchestra. We surrounded the audience with action, we transferred the spectator to the place of action of the plays. The spectators of *The Take-Off* sat in the orchestra, but there was no box-stage in front of them; it had been dismantled. Seats were placed where the stage used to be. Here the audience sat in place of the former stage. A wide passage was made between the audience sitting in the old orchestra and the audience sitting on the old stage. On this wide aisle some of the central scenes of the play were staged. Around both parts of the audience stretched another, narrower aisle of great length. This aisle went around three fourths of the audience and in addition went upwards, over the heads of the spectators, forming an upper passageway. The action took place everywhere at once, or changed instantly from one spot to another. These changes were aided by switching lights from one spot to the next. I had difficulties in finding a designer immediately who would have the courage to take such risks with me. But a designer was found—the daring, talented Yakov Shtoffer. We knew that amateur guardians against theatrical sedition, and supporters of the academic, brought up from childhood on the "box-stage," not even aware of the existence of other stages in the history of the theater, would be down on us.

But now we have sufficient and thoroughly tested experience to give us good reason to say that our best friend is the spectator. And if again someone tries to "unmask" me as a formalist, I can only tell him that the problem of stages, or of theatrical convention as a feature of theatrical art, are problems of our art which are neither simple nor anywhere near complete solution in all their aspects. These problems are very serious; they demand, in addition to an honest and objective approach to the work of the theater, deep analysis and proper knowledge, not only from me, but also from professional critics.

The experiment of *The Take-Off,* as well as the experiments in staging *The Iron Stream, Mother,* and *Aristocrats,* logically and naturally flowing from the first, indicated that, with the maximum proximity of the stage action to the audience which creates an especially tense interplay and through it a unique atmosphere for the production as a whole, the basic and essential condition is the high ideological content of the play. Only a play of deep meaning can dare to "wish" for its action, its plot, its images to "come into contact" with such a sensitive, demanding, and responsive power as the audience. And since a play is not created for itself—it is, after all, not "a thing in itself"—but for the edification of the audience, you can judge for yourselves how important for each play is the manner and the stage on which it is presented.

The theater must do everything to make the spectator believe in what goes on in the play, let him laugh till he cries, let him hold back his tears only with great effort. One should not fear the burning grief, the deep suffering of the spectator in the theater, because these must be creative emotions, not naturalistic ones. . . . And they will be creative, these emotions, if there is no naturalism on stage, no naturalism in the playing of the actors, no naturalism in the directing or decoration. There should be neither theatricalism nor naturalism.

With modest means but, believe me, with burning sincerity, I aim at the same atmosphere which the Moscow Art Theater achieved with such great efforts and such great talents—indeed, what talents! Yes, I do. I aim at the same atmosphere in which, in the best productions of the Moscow Art Theater, the footlights dividing the audience from the stage disappear and the spectator stops feeling a spectator and becomes an invisible participant of the action on the stage. I also aim for this, but, I repeat, through different means, and, alas, without those special personal qualifications which determine immediately to whom the victory belongs. As Mayakovsky said: "Here I am shouting, but don't know how to prove a thing."

Translated by Gala Ebin

JEAN VILAR

(b. 1912)

Theater Without Pretensions

Q. Do you think there is anything one might call a new "school" of French direction?

A. No, and I'm glad of it, because the first thing we have to get rid of today is precisely this notion of the "art of direction," seen as an end in itself by such spokesmen as Gordon Craig.

Q. Do you feel you have anything in common with other directors, past or present, and if so, which?

A. I am chiefly indebted to the work of certain of my predecessors and contemporaries through some of their writings.

When Jouvet writes: "In point of fact, a play directs itself. One has only to be attentive and relatively detached, to see it come to life and work upon the actors. Acting upon them, in some mysterious way, it tests them, enlarges or diminishes them, embraces or rejects them . . ."; when Pitoëff, according to Lenormand, refuses to direct a play down to the beatific level of understanding of the public, in order to fill the theater at least a hundred times; then, as you see, I feel we have something in common.

I should also mention the writing of Stanislavsky, Baty, Dullin, and

Jean Vilar: *The Tradition of the Theater* (an unpublished translation by Christopher Kotschnig), 17-37 *passim*. Courtesy of Robert Corrigan. By permission of Jean Vilar.

These lines were written several years before Vilar's work at Avignon and his appointment to the Théâtre National Populaire (T.N.P.).

Copeau, of Talma, Clairon, etc. What I know of the work of Antoine and Gémier, on the other hand, leaves me cold. Hostile, I should say. It's not enough for a man to be a martyr or a prophet—you have to belong to his religion, too.

I don't think it's really surprising that I should be indebted to the writings and not to the stage practice of these men (in production, direction, set design, costuming, acting, etc.). Actually, though our points of view may be very nearly identical *intellectually* (in respect to insight and sincerity, at least), our subjective reactions (our approach or, if you like, *manner of attacking subject and object*) are necessarily different.

Q. Inversely, on what points do you disagree with past or present methods of direction?

A. I am against all methods of direction whose aim is, in the frightful expression current a few years ago, the "re-theatricalization" of the theater. I am against everything that is "theater for theater's sake"; hence, against "set-itis." Against the primer art of lighting, and against the Parisian claptrap of costumery. Against "symbolic" acting.

There is room, between the realism of Antoine and the "theatrical conventions" of those who followed and opposed him, *for a theater of simple effects, without pretensions, accessible to all.* This is not to say that settings should be slighted, that costumes should not be carefully designed and executed, or that the actor's gestures should be those of the man in the street. Quite the reverse!

It would perhaps surprise some of our past directors, who were poor, to be told that their productions nevertheless belonged to a highly refined art of spectacle. They often borrowed from some of the major or minor arts (architecture, sculpture, design, cinematography, music, *haute couture,* etc.) the most subtle and effective of their methods. This is the kind of theater on which we must resolutely turn our backs. Furthermore, it seems to me that a people whom war has brought, not only to a new awareness of what the basic needs of existence really are, but perhaps to a clearer understanding of life itself as well, that such a people will ask more of us than a glittering—let me repeat, *refined*—surface in the theater. The amateur actors of the *stalags,* for instance, will have their ideas about it.

It remains to be seen whether we shall have the clear-sightedness and stubbornness to impose on the public what it obscurely desires. That will be our struggle, and it goes beyond the role of the director.

Q. What foreign schools have influenced French direction in general? Yourself? How?

A. This question, like the rest, is so phrased that you're really asking for a course in the history of directing. Even if I had enough knowledge to answer it, several pages would still be inadequate to do so. Still, let's give it a try.

As far as my knowledge of the early greats goes, I believe two foreign schools have influenced the stage art (let's use "direction" as little as possible, if you don't mind): the German and the Russian— and to a lesser extent the Japanese as well. Let's not forget the *Commedia dell'Arte,* either. But what do we mean when we say "the Russian school," for example? Stanislavsky, the Kamerny Theater, the Russian ballet? In his preface to Stanislavsky's book, Copeau wrote: "If *My Life in Art* had appeared a few years earlier; if it had been given me to read before meeting the founder of the Moscow Art Theater, how much better I should have understood him! Equally, if he had taken us into his confidence and shared his experience with me in the talks we had in Paris, I should undoubtedly have approached the problems which then vexed me and isolated me among my companions in a more enlightened and intelligent way."

I rather think that these few lines of Copeau's sum up the relationships between French and foreign directors: often a history of missed *rendezvous.*

Before going any further, let me refer you to the books and prefaces of Jacques Copeau, to the *Conversations with Gémier* edited by Paul Gsell, and to the articles and works of Baty.

A French craftsman, I may say, exerted a considerable influence on the European theater: Antoine. On the other hand, in a letter written to Sarcey in 1888 (a year after the founding of the Théâtre-

Libre), Antoine described in admiring detail several productions he saw in Brussels of the Duke of Saxe-Meiningen's famous troupe—the same one that so profoundly impressed Stanislavsky. It seems to me, then, that what we have is not what you could accurately call "influence" of one foreign school on another, French school, but rather a sort of interaction between the various schools, often without the craftsmen's being aware of it. Again, if we consider historically the achievements separately realized by Antoine, Lugné-Poe, Copeau, Gémier and the Cartel, we will find it easier to isolate the original elements in their work than to trace the influence of foreign schools.

Personally—in answer to the last part of your question—I have watched and followed very attentively the direction and painstaking methods of Vladimir Sokoloff. From Charles Dullin, I learned that without emotional involvement, without profound and *greathearted* sincerity on the part of the interpreter, our craft is nothing, is a grimace. But by and large, I have worked alone. . . .

Q. When you direct a play, do you attempt to mold the various parts of the production into the concept of *ensemble* you have developed, or do you modify your conception according to the materials you have to work with?

A. The staging of a play is always the result of compromise. Compromise, at least, between the visual and aural imagination of the director and the living, anarchic reality of the actors. For my part, I never set anything definitely or precisely before the first rehearsals. I have no papers, no notes, no written plans. Nothing in my hands, nothing up my sleeve: *Everything in the minds and bodies of others.* Facing me, the actor.

To compel an actor to integrate voice and body into a predetermined harmony or plastic composition smacks of animal-training. An actor is more than an intelligent animal or robot. Slowly and patiently, I believe, a sort of *physical rapport* grows up between him and me, so that we understand each other without need of many words. It is essential for me to know him well, and to like him even if he isn't very likeable. It is impossible to produce successfully a work dependent on the good will of so many, to direct a play well, *with people one doesn't like.* To love the theater is nothing. To love those who practice it may be less "artistic," but it gets better results. Nevertheless, though I do not "attempt to mold the various parts," in your words, to a concept of *ensemble,* it is still true that after a (variable) number of rehearsals one sometimes has to guide some of the actors (without their being necessarily aware of it) toward an *ensemble* play, to bring them into a certain harmony of tone with the rest. Not that the director arbitrarily selects this tone; it is born of the polygamous interaction of the voices, bodies, and minds of the other actors and the script.

When this point is reached, it must be "set." It is the first, mysterious moment when the fate of the production is decided. The actor is sometimes unaware of it, and so much the better, for he would otherwise freeze what should remain spontaneous. Now, too, the director can see clearly what a particular actor can "give." Often, he will see many other things besides, such as, for example, the contrapuntal importance of a part hitherto seen as purely subsidiary.[1] The indefinite visions of the loving reader of a play are replaced by the physical view and orchestral audition of the work, through the intermediary of the Misses X and Y and Messrs Z and W. The drama has just been born. At least, for the director.

This is the moment when the very virtues of the gentle, patient autocrat who is the director are in danger of falsifying the meaning of the play. That is to say, are in danger of giving birth to a play the author never intended or wrote. The director must return to the author; listen to him; follow him. He must guard against those petty dictatorial faults which always lie as temptations in his path. On the other hand, he must implore the author not to be deaf to the complaints and suggestions (ill-expressed, usually) of the actors singly or severally. The opinion of an actor rehearsing a part is of fundamental importance. Apelles accepted the cobbler's criticism of the sandals he had painted. An author, no matter how great, must be

---

[1] To take a classic example, the part of Don Sancho in Corneille's *Cid.* (J. V.)

driven from the theater if he deliberately ignores the actors. . . .

Q. In directing a play, do you set any one element (script, set, acting) above the others?

A. Can anything be set above script and actors? I'm very much afraid, though, that those who have "set-itis," as others have tonsillitis, would give a different answer.

Q. Do you consider the development of stage machinery to be progress or an impediment?

A. Why progress?

And why an impediment?

There is no progress in art, is there?

And it admits of no impediment.

Q. Do you think productions possible whose aim is to revive past theatrical conventions: for example, Elizabethan, Greek, Roman, medieval, or Italian *commedia?* Under what conditions?

A. You ask me if I "think productions possible, etc." I don't quite understand. Do you want to know whether it is possible for such revivals to be faithful copies of the performances given in the playwright's lifetime? Or whether they would be of artistic interest? Or whether those conventions could attract today's audiences? I'll try a rough-and-ready answer.

Such a production, scrupulously mounted, would always be interesting, at least to theater workers. But I doubt whether we have the means to convey to contemporary audiences the explosive Italian comedy, for instance, with its *lazzi* and scenarios. It was a specialized actors' art, and died with them. It was a compound of traditions whose oral transmission (through apprenticeship, and handing down of experience and routines, etc.) seems to me to have been of prime importance—much more instructive than its written transmission (in the words of Gherardi, etc.). A popular tradition, if it is to survive, cannot suffer a break in its continuity without mortal damage.

As for the classics and Elizabethan theaters, they were above all playwrights' theaters. And what playwrights! Every age goes to them for its profit. The *Richard III* of Irving or Garrick, Dullin's *Volpone,* Copeau's production of *Twelfth Night,* all are as important in the

history of the theater and *of a society* as were the original performances given on the banks of the Thames around 1600. On the other
hand, while it is certainly delightful to see a production as faithful
as possible to the original, what actor or director could convince us
that Burbage played Hamlet in just this or the other way? Really,
theater and revival seem to me antagonistic brothers.

Q. Do you believe new forms of theatrical architecture are needed
for some kinds of plays?

A. I am tempted to reply in various ways to your question concerning theatrical architecture, which would seem to indicate either
ignorance or profound indifference on my part. Perhaps I should
recall Lope de Vega's aphorism here: "Three boards, two actors, and
a passion," which many invoke without ever acting on it. . . .

Q. Is directing creative or interpretive work?

A. The creator in theater is the playwright, insofar as he provides
the essential element, and to the extent that the dramatic and philosophical virtues of his play are such that they leave us no room for
personal creation, so that after each performance we still feel ourselves
to be his *debtors*. Which is not to say that his work must be perfect
(Voltaire's dramaturgy is *perfect*).

To give a scene of Shakespeare its full meaning, through the play
of the actor's minds and bodies, for example, is a task demanding the
use of all the director's artistic faculties, but it is never more than
a work of interpretation. The text is there, rich in stage directions
embodied in the lines themselves (locale, reactions, attitudes, setting,
costume, etc.); one need only have the sense to follow them. Whatever is *created,* beyond these directions, is "direction," and should
be despised and rejected. I take the example of Shakespeare because
each of his works affords the overimaginative director all the illusions
and temptations of "creation." It is not for the director, using his
imagination, to decide the interpretation of any of Shakespeare's
characters; that's intolerable. The character himself, stripped and
laid bare, must be left "open" to the imagination of the public. This
bareness, made easy by the very economy of Shakespeare's stage directions, naturally implies a smooth, disciplined style of acting, but

demands at the same time the most acute sensitivity on the part of the actor, who must remain in complete contact with the audience.

I might add that if any director rehearsing a masterpiece feels that he is a creator, then so is the actor. And the audience, too, why not? Remember the old actors' sally: "The author writes one play, the actor performs another, and the audience sees a third." Where, then, are the interpreters? If only to give a precise meaning to the words of the profession, it is indispensable that we make a reasonable distinction between the ideas of creation and interpretation.

There does remain a field in which the director starving to create can find fodder for his ravening genius: when the play is nil; when, through relentless attrition of rehearsal, it has become nothing more than a pretext, a sort of necessary *aide-mémoire*. There is also an authentically creative art among the actor's skills: that of Mime. "A back-cloth, and my body speaks."

HAROLD CLURMAN

(b. 1901)

In a Different Language

Being a director, it may be assumed that I am prejudiced against the playwright who proposes to direct his own play. If I cited examples of playwrights who had ruined their plays by directing them, I should find myself in the awkward position of also having to list the playwrights who have done very good jobs directing their own plays. The debate cannot be argued on an absolute basis. Obviously a good playwright may prove himself a good director, just as there is no law that says a good playwright may not also be a first-class tap dancer. The point is that one capacity does not necessarily imply the other.

There are people who maintain that all playwrights should direct their own plays. Shakespeare and Molière are there to give the contention historical precedent. It is considered a reasonable premise that since no one can know a play as well as the person who wrote it, the playwright must clearly be the best director for his own work. This is hollow logic. We all know playwrights who are rendered tongue-tied the moment they are asked to deal with a company of actors. Chekhov's answers to questions about his plays were so cryptic that it was practically impossible for his colleagues to act on his advice. His was not an isolated case.

The question is not one of personalities but of principles. How is it possible for a theater-wise playwright to be a bad director? Why

Harold Clurman: "In a Different Language," *Theatre Arts*, Vol. XXXIV, January 1950, 18-20. By permission of Harold Clurman.

are there directors, far less acute than the playwrights whose work they are interpreting, who nevertheless bring this work to life on the stage in a manner the playwrights will readily admit is beyond their ability?

To answer these questions one must go back to the theater's rudiments. The art of the theater does not consist in adding actors, scenery, movement and music to a dramatist's text, as one inserts a set of illustrations into a published book. What we call a play in the theater is something radically different from a play on the page. The dramatist expresses himself mainly through words, the director through *action* which involves people amid the paraphernalia of the stage.

The theater is a collective art not only in the sense that many people contribute to it, but in the subtler sense that each of the contributors to the final result actually collaborates in his partner's function. The playwright himself is a director when he writes his play: he does not simply set down what his characters have to say, he tries to visualize the effect of his scenes on the stage. The playwright may be described as a writer who has been to the theater and has a feeling for what will play, what will be interesting to see rather than exciting only to hear or to imagine.

What holds true for the playwright holds for the other theater craftsmen—the actor, the scene-designer, the director. Jokes are often cracked about the vanity and obtuseness of actors, but everyone knows of actors whose intuitive insights not only generate new qualities in a part or in a play but whose feelings—often clumsily expressed by a combination of inadequate words and incomplete gestures—serve the playwright with creative ideas which finally become incorporated into the actual text of the play. There are directors, too, whose sense of a play's meaning is so acute that they are able to bring elements in the dramatist's text to full fruition chiefly through their own inspiration. I know, moreover, of one very fine play now running in New York which might not have found its present form if a designer had not suggested a scenic method for handling simultaneous action on the stage.

There is nothing exceptional in these instances of cooperative creativity. They are of the theater's very essence; they have obtained at all times, and in the very greatest examples of theatrical art. What prevents us from being more aware of this constant give-and-take in theater is the intense specialization of the contemporary stage and the demonic commercial competitiveness that has set in—particularly in our country—during the past ten years.

Still, the functions of playwright, actor, designer, director are distinct from one another. The dramatist usually sets forth the general scheme and theme of the play. (I say "usually" because there have been instances of scenarios and material for plays having been suggested by the director or even a leading actor.) The dramatist's conception—his story-line and plan of action conveyed through descriptive words and dialogue—serves the other theater craftsmen as the *raw material* from which they make the thing we finally witness at performance.

Before asking why the playwright should not direct the performance of his text, we might ask ourselves why he should not act in it, or at least play the leading part. One might immediately remark that many playwrights, from Shakespeare and Molière to Sacha Guitry and Noel Coward, have been actors. But this would be an evasion of the basic problem. In his heart every playwright is an actor even more than he is a director, but still we rarely think of playwrights as actors because what makes an actor good does not arise from the kind of understanding of a part which is supposedly possessed by the man who first conceived it. The actor's body, his voice, appearance, temperament, imagination, his background and experience on and off the stage, are as crucial to the actor as that part of him which is the equivalent of the playwright's mind. There is no theater without the actor, and when an actor enters upon the stage an entirely new factor has to be taken into account: a human personality, with everything which that connotes in physical and emotional behavior. No longer is the dramatist's character something to be imagined: he becomes a specific person who does not "bring something" to the words he is given to speak, but in a very real sense *replaces* them. Shakespeare's Hamlet exists only in Shakespeare's text. The Hamlet we see is Barrymore's, Hampden's, Gielgud's, Evans', Olivier's. What has happened to Shakespeare's creation? He is still there on the page, or in your mind as you read, but on the stage he cannot be other than the actor you see—occasionally an inspiration, more often a duffer. If you deny this, you don't understand the theater and probably don't even like it.

You would not have a Hamlet without a personality, and the actor, if he is to be anything more than a sound and an image, must always be a personality of some sort: that means a human entity with its own individual color, rhythm, emotional tone and content. In this lies one of the main sources of the theater's glamor. In the face of it, that playwright is an idiot who cries out: "But all the actor has to do is to 'understand' my lines and repeat them as I wrote them." Any playwright of experience knows that if *that* is all the actor did, he (the playwright) would be induced to commit murder, probably followed by suicide.

Have we wandered far afield from our inquiry? Not at all. The handling of the diverse materials of the theater so that the parts—actors, stage space, properties, light, background, music, and even the text itself—become a coherent, meaningful whole is the director's job. It is true that the playwright has his scenes, characters and actions in mind, but on the stage all these things have dimensions and qualities which are not of the mind.

That action speaks louder than words is the first principle of the stage; the director, I repeat, is the "author" of the stage action. Gestures and movement, which are the visible manifestations of action, have a different specific gravity from the writer's disembodied ideas. Theatrical action is virtually a new medium, a different language from that which the playwright uses, although the playwright hopes that his words will suggest the kind of action that ought to be employed. The director must be a master of theatrical action, as the dramatist is master of the written concept of his play.

The playwright may know that he wants a scene to be light, airy, suggestive of a summer day in the country and so forth, but except in a very general way he rarely knows how this atmosphere may be created through the actor's feeling and movement, through the placement of properties or the use of colors and lights. He does not know, because these are not primarily his tools; they are not what he has been trained to deal with. On the stage the dramatist's language must be translated; his spirit must be made flesh.

Composers are not always the best interpreters of their own music. However, when a composer indicates what note he wants struck, he and his interpreters are pretty sure where that note is to be found on a given instrument. The playwright writes for an instrument where the location of the "notes" is infinitely variable. It is all very well for the playwright to indicate that a speech be said "angrily" or "with a sob" or in a "high querulous treble." He will frequently find that if his directions are followed literally, the results will be ludicrous. The actor and director generally take the playwright's instructions as a clue to something the playwright is seeking to express. They often find that to express most effectively what the playwright had in view they have to employ quite different means than those which the playwright has suggested.

It is rarely the director's intention to alter the playwright's meaning. (Of course this has often been done—consciously as well as unconsciously—and occasionally with very happy results.) But it is a mistake amounting to ignorance to believe that the playwright's meaning is necessarily conveyed by merely mouthing the playwright's dialogue and following his stated instructions. In a sense the playwright's text disappears the moment it reaches the stage, because on the stage it becomes part of an action, every element of which is as pertinent to its meaning as the text itself. A change in gesture, inflection, movement, rhythm or in the physical background of a speech may give it a new significance.

The playwright who says, "Just for once I'd like to see my characters as I imagined them," and therefore proceeds to direct his play himself, is more than a little naïve. What he usually means is: "The directors who have done my last two or three plays murdered them.

Now I'm going to take a chance on doing it myself." This sort of complaint is understandable and in many cases justified, but it is not craftsmanlike. The playwright can never get the characters he imagined: he gets actors who are always themselves transfigured into stage images which the playwright may feel correspond to a reality he was seeking. How often have we heard a playwright say, "I see the character as a tall, thin, freckle-faced, red-headed man," only to find either that the actor who answered to this description has destroyed what the playwright really felt about the character, or that a short, stocky, clear-faced, dark-haired man has given him more truly what he wanted. The playwright's description of a character is often only a momentary and almost accidental way of expressing a sentiment, the actual embodiment of which has very little to do with the color of a man's hair or the nature of his complexion and figure.

The difference between the dramatist's function and the director's is often revealed when a playwright declares that the director has carried out his—the playwright's—intention to the letter, while a knowledgeable audience discerns that the director, even if he be the playwright himself, has fallen below the play's promise or distorted it. So distinct is the ability to write a play from the ability to judge it in the theater *as theater*, that a playwright will frequently fail to realize that what is on the stage is a parody of what he has written.

I have refrained throughout this discussion from becoming personal, since particular instances applied to a theoretical problem usually prove misleading. Yet the reader's experience will bear me out when I say that the playwright-director who boasts that there really isn't much to direction, that "It's a cinch," is nine times out of ten a fairly pedestrian director about whose work as a director one can only say that it is "adequate." Such playwright-directors use their actors as puppets to say their words, and scenery merely to illustrate the place of action. In this way they fashion performances that are not only anti-theater, but in so doing limit what they might have to say as artists. For when all the elements of a theatrical production are treated as part of a unified but varied creative vision, a play takes on a rich extension of meaning that cannot be achieved when the stage is treated as a platform from which only the solitary voice of the "teacher" (playwright) may be heard.

As a director, critic and above all as a playgoer, I prefer by far the attitude of a Gorky to the productions of his plays to that expressed by the kind of playwright who is eminently satisfied when he has dumped the bare bones of his play on the stage. In 1935, Gorky's play *Yegor Bulichev* was done at two different theaters in Moscow. At one theater the play was interpreted as the drama of a dying man seeking the truth in a world of liars; at another the play became the drama of a man with the inability to understand a truth which was new and unfamiliar to him. When Gorky was asked which was the true interpretation he answered: "Both—and perhaps there are more."

Gorky knew that a really live play has within it the possibilities of almost as many meanings as there are creative people to find them. The playwright-director who is satisfied with the one little meaning he can register with a kind of sound-recording and demonstration-by-slides of his text is usually a playwright whose play has very little chance of ever being done in more than one production, or one who has belied and belittled his meaning even the first time. The written play is not the goal of the theater—only the beginning. If the play at the end is not something beyond what it was at the beginning, there is very little point in the process of transposing it from the book to the stage; very little point, that is, to the whole art of the theater.

3

The Director at Work

KONSTANTIN STANISLAVSKY

(1863-1938)

Production Plan for

The Lower Depths, *A scene from Act II*

Stanislavsky's Planirovka, *or plan of the action of* The Lower Depths, *consists of three acts: I, II, and IV. Only one page of Act III has been preserved. Each page of Gorky's text is accompanied by a page of Stanislavsky's directorial comments which parallel the entire text of the play. Each* mise en scène *is worked out with great care for detail and illustrated by a special chart. The first act alone has thirty-nine charts which indicate the location of sets and movement and interrelation of the actors on the stage. Judging by this painstaking work it would seem that a tremendous amount of time was spent on this prompt book. Actually, from the date written by Stanislavsky himself on the manuscript, it is known that he started to work on it on August 28, 1902, and completed it less than a month later on September 17. The opening of the play took place on December 18, 1902, after three months of rehearsals.*

In the selection from My Life in Art *which precedes the plan, Stanislavsky tells of his search for "creative material" before beginning his production notes. In later years Stanislavsky discarded the elaborate, detailed instructions for the actors found in this early example of his directing practice.*

Excursion to Khitrov Market

. . . We received the play from Gorky, which he called *The Lower Depths of Life,* but later changed to *The Lower Depths* on the advice of Nemirovich-Danchenko. Once again we faced a difficult problem— a new tone and manner of playing, and a new and peculiar romanticism and pathos that bordered both on theatricality, on the one hand, and on sermon, on the other.

"I can't bear to see Gorky come out on the pulpit like a clergyman and read his sermon to his congregation as he would in a church," Chekhov once said about Gorky. "Gorky is a destroyer, who must destroy all that deserves destruction. Therein lies his strength and his calling."

One must know how to pronounce Gorky's words so that the phrases live and resound. His instructive and propagandist speeches, those like the one about Man, must be pronounced simply, with sincere enthusiasm, without any false and highfalutin theatricality. If they are not, his serious plays become mere·melodramas. We had to have our own peculiar style of the tramp, and not to confuse it with the accepted type of theatrical vulgarity. The tramp must have a breadth, freedom and nobility all his own. Where were we to get them? It was necessary to enter into the spiritual springs of Gorky himself, just as we had done in the case of Chekhov, and find the current of the action in the soul of the writer. Then the colorful words of the tramp's aphorisms and flowery phrases of the sermon would imbibe of the spiritual content of the poet himself, and the actor would share his excitement.

As usual, Nemirovich-Danchenko and I approached the new play each in our individual manner. Vladimir Ivanovich gave a masterly analysis of the play. Being a writer, he knows all the approaches of literature which serve him as short cuts to creativeness. I, as usual at the beginning of all work, was in a helpless muddle, rushing from local color to feeling, from feeling to the image, from the image to

Konstantin Stanislavsky: *My Life in Art*. Moscow: Foreign Languages Publishing House (n.d.), 303-307.

the production. I bothered Gorky, looking for creative material. He told me how he wrote the play, where he found his types, how he wandered in his youth, how he met the originals of his characters and particularly Satin, the role I was to play. . . .

Gorky's stories excited us and we decided to see for ourselves how these "creatures that once were men" lived. We arranged an excursion, in which many of the actors in the play, Nemirovich-Danchenko, Simov, and I took part. Under the leadership of the writer Gilyarovsky, who studied the life of tramps, we went one night to the Khitrov Market. The tramps' religion was freedom, their sphere, danger, burglary, adventure, theft, murder. All this created around them an atmosphere of romanticism and peculiar savage beauty which we were seeking at that time.

We were out of luck that night. It was hard to get permission from the secret organizations of the Khitrov Market. A large theft had taken place that night and the entire Market was in a state of emergency. Everywhere we came across armed patrols. They stopped us continuously, demanding to see our passes. In one place we had to steal by unseen lest the patrols should stop us. After we had passed the first line of defense our progress became easier. We walked freely about the dormitories with numberless board cots on which lay tired men and women who resembled corpses more than anything else. In the very center of the underground labyrinth was the local university and the intelligentsia of the Market. They were people who could read and write, and who at that time were occupied in copying parts for actors. These copyists lived in a small room. . . .

These people received us like welcome guests. . . . We brought along vodka and sausage, and a feast began. When we told them that we intended to produce a play by Gorky about people like them, they were deeply touched.

"This is indeed an honor!" cried one of them.

"What is there so interesting in us that they want to show us on the stage?" another wondered naïvely.

They talked about what they would do when they stopped drinking, became decent people and left this place. . . .

One of them spoke about his past. His only reminder about it was a little picture cut out of some illustrated magazine in which an old man was showing a promissory note to his son, while the mother stood by weeping. The son, a handsome lad, stood ashamed, his head lowered. It was apparently a forgery. Simov did not like this picture. This was a signal for chaos to break out. The living vessels full of alcohol came to terrible life; they grabbed bottles and stools, and attacked Simov. Another moment, and he would have been killed, but Gilyarovsky thundered a quintuple oath, astounding not only us by the complexity of its construction, but even the denizens of the depths. The copyists turned to stone from the unexpectedness of the curse and the enthusiasm and aesthetic satisfaction it brought them. Their mood changed at once. There was mad laughter, applause, ovations, gratefulness, and congratulations for the inspired oath, which perhaps saved us from death or injury.

The excursion to the Khitrov Market, more than any discussion or analysis of the play, awoke my fantasy and inspiration. There was nature which one could mold to his desire; there was live material for the creation of images. Everything received a real basis and took its proper place. Making the sketches and the *mises en scène,* or showing the actors any of the scenes, I was guided by living memories, and not by invention or guesswork. But the chief result of the excursion was the fact that it revealed to me the inner meaning of the play.

"Freedom at any cost!" that was its meaning for me. That freedom for the sake of which men unknowingly descend into the depths of life and become slaves. . . .

After our memorable excursion to the lower depths, I did not find it difficult to make sketches and *mises en scène*—I felt like an inmate of the flop house. . . .

The Lower Depths, A SCENE FROM ACT II

Vassilisa steals into Pepel's room. Pepel is heard grumbling and getting up to his feet. He opens the door, slams it shut behind him and walks out.

Konstantin S. Stanislavsky: *"Na Dne: Rezhisserskii Ekzempliar"* ("The Lower Depths: Director's Copy") , in *Moscow Art Theatre Yearbook,* 1945, 198-209.

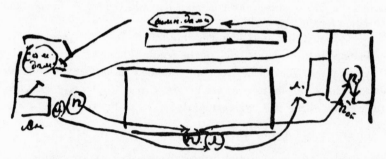

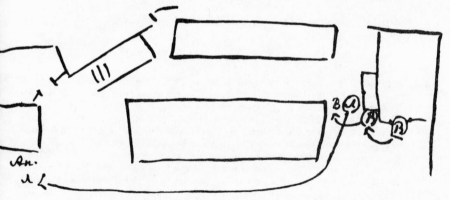

Pepel leaves. Goes out. Pepel sits. Vassilisa in the doorway.

Luka goes to the forestage. Vaska follows him. Both stop on the way. Vaska goes behind the partition and returns. Vaska stands in the doorway. Luka sits down to drink tea.

Vaska sits down. Vaska gets up and goes behind Luka. Luka goes over to Anna.

Drawings by Stanislavsky for the production plan of **The Lower Depths.**

Hands thrust in pockets he begins to pace between the bunks pretending not to pay any attention to Vassilisa.

VASSILISA *(calling from Pepel's room)*: Vaska, come here!

PEPEL: I won't come—I don't want to. . . .

VASSILISA: + Why? +[1]

Vassilisa appears at the door. Opens it a bit. Pepel continues to pace in a lumbering fashion. The fact that Pepel is drunk must not be forgotten. The love scene played with drunken accentuation will yield more interest and variation for the actor.

What are you angry about?

PEPEL: + I am sick, + sick of the whole thing. . . .

VASSILISA: + Sick of me, too? + (VASSILISA *draws her shawl about her, pressing her hands over her breast. Crosses to* ANNA, *looks carefully through the bed curtains, and returns to* PEPEL.) [2]

PEPEL: Yes! Of you, too!

Vassilisa is partly visible through the half-open door. Vaska continues to pace. Action as indicated by the author. Vassilisa looks angry. There are sounds of snoring, howling noise in the chimney, rattling in plumbing. A pause.

Pepel sits down with his back to Vassilisa. He stares at the floor. Leans his elbows on his knees.

Well—out with it!

---

[1] Pauses are indicated throughout by crosses (+). Nemirovich-Danchenko in his autobiography, *My Life in the Russian Theatre,* writes: "In the art of the Art Theater these pauses would have an important place: the nearer to life, the farther from the gliding, uninterrupted 'literary' flow so characteristic of the old theater. . . . A pause is not something that is dead, but is an active intensification of experience, sometimes marked by sounds stressing the mood: the whistle of a factory or steamer siren, the warbling of a bird, the melancholy hoot of an owl, the passage of a carriage, the sound of music coming from a distance. With the years the pauses entered to such an extent into the art of the Art Theater as to become a characteristic feature, often fatiguing and even irritating. At that time, however, they were alluringly new. They were attained with difficulty, and only through persistent and involved research, not merely external but also psychological; the quest was for harmony between the experiences of the characters of a play and the entire setting."

[2] The first part of Gorky's direction is underlined, but the words: "Crosses to Anna . . . etc." are deleted by Stanislavsky.

VASSILISA: What do you want me to say? I can't force you to be loving, and I'm not the sort to beg for kindness. Thank you for telling me the truth.

PEPEL: What truth?

VASSILISA: That you're sick of me—or isn't it the truth? (PEPEL *looks at her silently. She turns to him.*)

She is at the door running her fingers along its side. Pepel turns in her direction a bit, looks up at her. He is eyeing her.

What are you staring at? Don't you recognize me?

PEPEL: (*sighing*) : You're beautiful, Vassilisa! (*She puts her arm about his neck, but he shakes it off.*)

Vassilisa smiles a seductive and possessive smile. Pulls him by the sleeve toward his room. Pepel, his elbows still on his knees, shakes off her arm with a movement of his shoulders.

But I never gave my heart to you . . . I've lived with you and all that—but I never really liked you . . .

VASSILISA (*quietly*): + That so? + Well—?

PEPEL: What is there to talk about? Nothing. Go away from me!

He wants to move away from her, she holds him back.

VASSILISA: Taken a fancy to someone else?

PEPEL: None of your business! Suppose I have—I wouldn't ask you to be my match-maker!

VASSILISA (*significantly*): That's too bad . . . perhaps I might arrange a match . . .

She holds him, looks straight into his eyes.

PEPEL (*suspiciously*): Who with?

VASSILISA: You know—why do you pretend?

After a pause. She has made her decision.

Vassily—let me be frank (*with lower voice*).

Vassilisa is in Pepel's room, she takes a chair and sits down inside. She is afraid to come out for fear of being seen. Pepel also sits down. They are separated by a partition. Vassilisa's head sticks out through the door.

I won't deny it—you've offended me . . . it was like a bolt from the blue . . . you said you loved me—and then all of a sudden . . .

PEPEL: It wasn't sudden at all. It's been a long time since I . . . woman, you've no soul. A woman must have a soul . . . we men are beasts—we must be taught—and you, what have you taught me?

VASSILISA: Never mind the past! I know—no man owns his own heart—you don't love me any longer . . . well and good, it can't be helped!

There is an obvious rise in temper and tension in both of them. In Vassilisa, because she is anxious to go through to the end with what she has started to say. In Pepel, because he is unnerved and irritable.

PEPEL: So that's over. We part peaceably, without a row—as it should be!

Pepel gets up. Vassilisa quickly grasps his arm and does not let him go.

VASSILISA: Just a moment! All the same, when I lived with you, I hoped you'd help me out of this swamp—I thought you'd free me from my husband and my uncle—from all this life—and perhaps, Vasya, it wasn't you whom I loved—but my hope—do you understand? I waited for you to drag me out of this mire . . .

The whole scene is played in a quiet, confidential voice. Vassilisa is anxious to tell him all. Pepel stands trying carefully to free his arm of her grip.

PEPEL: You aren't a nail—and I'm not a pair of pincers! I thought you had brains—you are so clever—so crafty . . .

Pepel tries to free himself of her grasp.

VASSILISA (*leaning closely towards him*): Vasya—let's help each other!

PEPEL: How?

A pause. Vassilisa quickly looks out of the partition. Her eyes examine the stage to see if anyone is spying on them. Mysteriously she nods to Pepel and pulls him in behind the partition. She makes him sit down while she remains standing.

VASSILISA (*low and forcibly*): My sister—I know you've fallen for her . . .

PEPEL: And that's why you beat her up, like the beast you are! Look out, Vassilisa! Don't you touch her!

VASSILISA: Wait. Don't get excited. We can do everything quietly and pleasantly. You want to marry her. I'll give you money . . . three hundred rubles—even more than . . .

In the darkness of the partitioned-off corner, their figures are not visible, only the voices can be heard. It is essential to speak very distinctly and to give the voice a tinge of mystery.

PEPEL (*moving away from her*): Stop! What do you mean?

VASSILISA: Rid me of my husband! Take that noose from around my neck . . .

PEPEL (*whistling softly*): So that's the way the land lies! You certainly planned it cleverly . . . in other words, the grave for your husband, the gallows for the lover, and as for yourself . . .

VASSILISA: Vasya! Why the gallows? It doesn't have to be yourself —but one of your pals! And supposing it were yourself—who'd know?

Looks out quickly to make sure they are not being overheard.

Natalia—just think—and you'll have money—you go away somewhere . . . you free me forever—and it'll be very good for my sister to be away from me—the sight of her enrages me . . . I get furious with her on account of you, and I can't control myself. I tortured the girl—I beat her up—beat her up so that I myself cried with pity for her—but I'll beat her—and I'll go on beating her!

PEPEL: Beast! Bragging about your beastliness?

An exclamation of outrage and disgust from him. It is very likely that he is shaking a fist at her. Noises of furniture being pushed. He gets to his feet and begins to pace behind the partition.

VASSILISA: I'm not bragging—I speak the truth. Think now, Vasya. You've been to prison twice because of my husband—through his greed. He clings to me like a bed-bug—

The scene is played in darkness. Speech must be very clear and well enunciated. Pauses should be used to create a mood. Actor's faces are turned to the audience.

he's been sucking the life out of me for the last four years—and what sort of a husband is he to me? He's forever abusing Natasha—calls her a beggar—he's just poison, plain poison, to every one . . .

PEPEL: You spin your yarn cleverly . . .

VASSILISA: Everything I say is true. Only a fool could be as blind as you.

(*Kostilyoff enters quietly and stealthily moves forward.*)

The audience must not notice where Kostilyoff appears from. It seems as though he materialized out of thin air. The chart indicates how the actor comes on. When the audience first sees him he stealthily covers the distance separating him from Pepel's partition.

PEPEL (*to Vassilisa*): Oh—go away!

Pepel pushes her out. Vassilisa resists as she emerges from the partition.

VASSILISA: Think it over! (*Sees her husband.*)

Sees her husband and is taken aback but just for a fleeting moment. Kostilyoff is pale and shaking. An awkward pause. Kostilyoff attempts to say something but only emits shrieking noises. Pepel jumps out of the partition. He is boiling mad. An awkward pause. Vassilisa composes herself completely. She leans against the partition and casts meaningful glances at Pepel.

What? You? Following me?

(PEPEL *leaps up and stares at* KOSTILYOFF *savagely.*)

A pause. Kostilyoff still attempts to say something but succeeds only in making piercing noises. He moves stealthily to the proscenium, stands with his back to the audience and tries to look through the door inside the partition.

KOSTILYOFF: It's I, I! + So the two of you were here alone—you were—ah—conversing? (*Suddenly stamps his feet*[3] *and screams.*) Vassilisa—you bitch! You beggar! You damned hag! (*Frightened by his*

---

[3] Words "stamps his feet" crossed out by Stanislavsky and changed to "trembles."

*own screams which are met by silence and indifference on the part
of the others.*)

Suddenly and quite unexpectedly, still standing with his back to the audience, Kostilyoff shakes all over, screams and begins to advance on Vassilisa. She does not make a move, stands calmly, her arms folded. Pepel is holding on to the door, his fingers gripping it tensely. He can hardly control his temper. Pepel makes a move as though to pounce on Kostilyoff. Vassilisa's eyes are riveted on Pepel. They seem to goad him on to murder. An awkward pause. Kostilyoff tries to collect himself. He is frightened by his own screams and Pepel's look. Pepel's fingers tighten their grip on the door. Both men breathe in rapid, loud gusts. Kostilyoff attempting to calm himself and also out of fear of Pepel, begins to back away. Now he stands with his profile to the audience. Kostilyoff is carrying a dirty bottle with oil and a battered box which contains wicks and other utensils for lighting icon lamps. Kostilyoff was on his way to fix the lamps when he happened to discover the rendezvous.

> Forgive me, O Lord . . .

Breathing heavily, backs away, looking fearfully at Pepel. Trembles. Speaks in a tone of phony holiness.

> Vassilisa—again you've led me into the path of sin.

The last words are very syrupy.

> I've been looking for you everywhere.

Vassilisa, very calmly, makes a move to go. This self-sure attitude enrages Kostilyoff. He cannot control himself and starts after the woman, screaming at her. Vassilisa stops. Looks back. Taken aback, Kostilyoff stops, pulls himself together.

> It's time to go to bed. You forgot to fill the lamps—oh, you . . . beggar! Swine! (*Shakes his trembling fist at her, while* VASSILISA *slowly goes to the door, glancing at* PEPEL *over her shoulder.*) [4]

He hands her the bottle and the box. She takes them and goes to her room. A pause. Kostilyoff, not knowing what to do next, returns to Pepel, who seems stonelike, so great is his effort to control his temper. Before Vassilisa left, she gave him a meaningful look.

---

[4] Words "to the door, glancing at Pepel over her shoulder" crossed out by Stanislavsky.

PEPEL (*to* KOSTILYOFF): Go away—clear out of here—

KOSTILYOFF (*yelling*): What? I? The Boss? I get out? You thief!

They stand face to face at a short distance. Glare at each other like two beasts ready to pounce. Both are trembling. Both speak in low, muffled voices. Both are greatly unnerved. The atmosphere is pregnant with murder which may occur at any moment.

PEPEL (*sullenly*): Go away, Mishka!

KOSTILYOFF: Don't you dare—I—I'll show you. (PEPEL *seizes him by the collar and shakes him. From the stove come loud noises and yawns.* PEPEL *releases* KOSTILYOFF, *who runs into the hallway, screaming.* ANNA *is groaning.*)

Suddenly Kostilyoff screams and threateningly advances a few steps towards Pepel. Something has happened. You cannot quite grasp exactly what. Pepel, with a quick, almost perceptible movement, grabs Kostilyoff by the throat. Pulls him towards himself. Kostilyoff sprawls on his stomach on the floor at Pepel's feet. In the fall Kostilyoff's face bumps against the floor. Pepel stands on his knees over the man and seizes him by the throat from the back. Bearing down with the whole weight of his body he presses his face against the floor. Kostilyoff squirms, gags. Pepel's breathing is heavy. A pause.

They hold the same pose for about five seconds. Another groan from Anna. There come good-natured friendly sounds of Luka yawning and stretching. Pepel lets go of his victim. Frightened he backs away looking at the stove. He thus frees the path for Kostilyoff, who, still gagging and coughing, runs headlong to his own apartment. Luka stretches on the stove in a homey, good-natured manner. Unobserved by the audience he climbed on the stove from the kitchen.

PEPEL (*jumping on a bunk*): Who is it? Who's on the stove?

Pepel comes up to the stove and looks up.

LUKA (*raising his head, friendly, simply and calmly*): Eh?...

PEPEL (*embarrassed*): You?

LUKA (*calmly*): I—I myself—oh, dear Jesus!

Pepel makes a dash for the hallway door. Peers out to make sure no one saw the scene.

The streetwalker walks across to the kitchen and begins to wash there. She is dishevelled, unwashed and not dressed.

PEPEL (*Shuts hallway door, looks for the wooden closing bar, but can't find it.*):   The devil!

Looks behind the entrance door. Luka begins to get down.

Come down, old man!

LUKA: I'm climbing down—all right . . .

PEPEL (*roughly*):   + What did you climb + on that stove for?

LUKA (*stops climbing down, looks around*):   Where was I to go?

PEPEL: + Why + didn't you go out into the hall?

LUKA: The hall's too cold for an old fellow like myself, brother.

PEPEL: + You + overheard?

Pepel stands by the stove. Luka is climbing down, sometimes stopping and turning around.

The gay lodger who is always high, is awakened by the noise and begins to pick out the same old tune on his accordion. He falls asleep, wakes up, plays a little, falls asleep again. This is repeated with intervals.

LUKA: Yes—I did. How could I help it? Am I deaf? Well, my boy, happiness is coming your way. Real, good fortune I call it!

PEPEL (*suspiciously*):   What good fortune—?

LUKA: In so far as I was lying on the stove . . .

PEPEL: Why did you make all that noise?

LUKA: Because I was getting warm . . .

Luka very calmly makes his way across the proscenium to the table. Like a thief cornered, Pepel is confused and worried. He is unable to leave the old man alone, follows him, plies him with questions, anxious to find out if Luka saw anything. Pepel walks right behind Luka, constantly looking around, fearful that someone else may have awakened and seen what happened. He looks trapped.

It was your good luck . . .

Luka stops, turns to Pepel and speaks in a low, secretive voice.

I thought if only the boy wouldn't make a mistake

Speaks even quieter

and choke the old man . . .

PEPEL: Yes—

Pepel pulls at his beard nervously. He is ashamed.

> I might have done it . . . how terrible . . .

Luka calmly resumes to move on.

LUKA: Small wonder! It isn't difficult to make a mistake of that sort.

PEPEL (*smiling*): What's the matter? Did you make the same sort of mistake once upon a time?

The streetwalker returns. A pause. The streetwalker, now washed, walks through to her bunk to get dressed. Luka and Pepel watch and do not talk while she walks across.

LUKA: Boy, listen to me. Send that woman out of your life. Don't let her near you! Her husband—she'll get rid of him herself—and in a shrewder way than you could—yes! Don't you listen to that devil! Look at me! I am bald-headed—know why? Because of all these women. . . . Perhaps I knew more women than I had hair on the top of my head—but this Vassilisa—she's worse than the plague . . .

Luka sits down to finish his cold tea. Pepel, who during the interlude with the streetwalker stepped into his room for a cigarette, is now lighting it nervously. He stands smoking in his doorway, listening attentively to Luka.

Luka drinks his tea tranquilly. During pauses he takes little bites of sugar. Pepel smokes in a jerky, nervous way. He watches the old man with suspicion. He doesn't trust him: who knows, maybe he is a stool-pigeon?

PEPEL: I don't understand . . . I don't know whether to thank you —or—well . . .

Pepel's attention is fixed on the old man. He listens and watches as he sits down by Luka's side.

LUKA: Don't say a word! You won't improve on what I said. Listen: take the one you like by the arm, and march out of here—get out of here—clean out . . .

PEPEL (*sadly*): I can't understand people. Who is kind and who isn't? It's all a mystery to me . . .

LUKA: What's there to understand? There's all breeds of men . . . they all live as their hearts tell them . . . good today, bad tomorrow!

But if you really care for that girl . . . take her away from here and
that's all there is to it. Otherwise go away alone . . . you're young—
you're in no hurry for a wife . . .

PEPEL (*taking him by the shoulder*) : Tell me! Why do you say
all this?

It occurs to Pepel that Luka is not playing straight with him. He stands
up, with urgency and force he takes him by the shoulders and turns Luka
towards himself. Pepel is determined to get at the truth.

A pause, sound of terrible groaning. Anna's hoarse groans. It's the death
rattle this time. Luka is sly and he uses this as a pretext to get away.

LUKA: Wait. Let me go. I want to look at Anna . . . she was coughing so terribly . . . (*Goes to* ANNA'S *bed, pulls the curtains, looks,
touches her.* PEPEL, *thoughtfully and distraught, follows him with
his eyes.*) Merciful Jesus Christ! Take into Thy keeping the soul of
this woman Anna, newcomer amongst the blessed.

PEPEL (*softly*): Is she dead? (*Without approaching, he stretches
himself and looks at the bed.*)

Pepel stretches to see. He is tense. Speaks his line nervously. He is frightened. Murderers are afraid of corpses.

LUKA (*gently*): Her sufferings are over!

Luka is calm and composed as he crosses the dead woman's hands and pulls
the curtains closed. He makes his announcement in an ordinary voice—the
kind one might use to say: "she is asleep."

Translated by Zina Voynow

MAX REINHARDT

(1873-1943)

Regiebuch for

The Miracle, *Scene I*

The Reinhardt Regiebuch *has long been a legend in the theater. A staggering number of annotations makes it extremely difficult to transfer a typical Reinhardt* Regiebuch *to the normal printed page. We are fortunate, however, in having a relatively uncomplicated* Regiebuch *which was prepared by Reinhardt in close collaboration with the designer Norman Bel Geddes for* The Miracle, *a wordless play by Karl Vollmoeller, with score by Engelbert Humperdinck. The first time such a* Regiebuch *was made public was in* Max Reinhardt and His Theatre, *edited by Oliver M. Sayler, an elaborate commemorative volume published in 1924, during the run of* The Miracle *at the Century Theater in New York. It is from this source that the specimen scene which follows is drawn. The brief credo that introduces it—one of Reinhardt's rare statements about his work—originally appeared in the program for the New York production.*

It would be a theory as barbaric as it is incompatible with the principles of theatrical art, to measure with the same yardstick, to press into the same mold, the wonderful wealth of the world's literature. The mere suggestion of such an attempt is a typical example of pedantic scholasticism. There is no one form of theater which is the

Max Reinhardt: *"Regie* Book of *The Miracle," Max Reinhardt and His Theatre*, edited by Oliver M. Sayler. New York: Brentano's, 1924, 64-66, 251-262.

only true artistic form. Let good actors today play in a barn or in a theater, tomorrow at an inn or inside a church, or, in the Devil's name, even on an expressionistic stage: if the place corresponds with the play, something wonderful will be the outcome. All depends on realizing the specific atmosphere of a play, and on making the play live. And yet, do not banish from the temple merely the traders and moneymongers, but also the overzealous high priests who desire to rob the theater of all its brilliancy and sensuousness, who would like nothing better than to turn it into a preacher's pulpit, who swear by the written word, and who after having murdered the spirit of that word, would like to press it back again into its place in the book.

Just the contrary is the true mission of the theater. Its task is to lift the word out of the sepulcher of the book, to breathe life into it, to fill it with blood, with the blood of today, and thus to bring it into living contact with ourselves, so that we may receive it and let it bear fruit in us. Such is the only way; there is no other. All roads which do not lead into life, lead us astray, whatever their name may be. Life is the incomparable and most valuable possession of the theater. Dress it up in any manner you wish, the cloak will have to fall when the eternal human comes to the fore, when, in the height of ecstasy, we find and embrace each other. The noble dead of a hundred, of four hundred, of a thousand years ago, arise again on the boards. It is this eternal wonder of resurrection which sanctifies the stage.

Therefore, do not write out prescriptions, but give to the actor and his work the atmosphere in which they can breathe more freely and more deeply. Do not spare stage properties and machinery where they are needed, but do not impose them on a play that does not need them. Our standard must not be to act a play as it was acted in the days of its author. To establish such facts is the task of the learned historian, and is of value only for the museum. How to make a play live in our time, that is decisive for us. The Catholic Church which aims at the most spiritual, the most supernatural, does so by means which appeal directly to the senses. It overwhelms us with the pathos of its temples towering in the sky; it surrounds us with the mystical dimness of its cathedrals; it charms our eye with wonderful master-

*For **The Miracle** of Max Reinhardt in 1924 Norman Bel Geddes transformed the Century Theater in New York into a replica of a Gothic cathedral, left. Below left, the forest, and, right, a street for the Inquisition. (Drawings copyright, 1955, by Norman Bel Geddes. Reprinted by permission.)*

pieces of art, with the brilliancy of its colored windows, with the lustre of thousands of candles, which reflect their light in golden objects and vessels. It fills our ear with music and song and the sound of the thundering organ. It stupefies us by the odor of incense. Its priests stride in rich and precious robes. And in such a sphere of sensuousness, the highest and the most holy reveals itself to us. We reveal ourselves, and we find the way to our innermost being, the way to concentration, to exaltation, to spiritualization. . . .

SCENE I . . . CATHEDRAL

Characters

THE NUN	THE LAME PIPER
THE ABBESS	THE KNIGHT
THE OLD SACRISTAN	THE MADONNA

Nuns and Novices. Peasants, Townsfolk and Children. Bishops, Priests, Monks and Pilgrims. Cripples, Blind, Lame and Lepers. Patricians of the Town, Knights and Troops of Soldiers.

1. The interior of an early Gothic Church.
2. High, massive columns rise into mystic darkness.
3. Gothic arches, stone ornaments representing tendrils and lace work, a richly decorated iron grating, entangled scrolls and figures.
4. Narrow, high church windows in deep, rich coloring.
5. Aisles, corridors, doors, an unsymmetrical arrangement of mysterious openings, windows, stairways.
6. Votive statues on columns, small statues with candles and flowers before them, crucifixes, offerings brought by grateful people, wax flowers, embroideries, jewels, a child's doll, decoratively painted candles.

7. In the background a richly carved altar, with a golden shrine and candles seen through a grilled screen.

8. The eternal lamp burns before it.

9. A Cardinal's hat hangs above.

10. Altar, with table, to divide and open, with steps through it.

11. The floor is of large gray stones, some of which are tombstones. In the center of the floor the stones are to be glass with lamps below, so wired as to spread the light from the middle outwards.

12. Flickering light from behind columns as from invisible candles throws fantastic shadows.

13. Shafts of sunlight, coming through the high windows at the right, project patterns on the floor.

14. At left and right of auditorium [stage directions read "right" and "left" from the point of view of the audience], cloisters with vaulted ceilings and stone floors.

15. Chandeliers of various sizes in the auditorium to cast light downwards only, adding depth and mystery to the ceiling.

16. Several poles for flags and lanterns fastened to the seat ends in aisles of auditorium.

17. Panelling of balcony rail to show here and there between flags.

18. A clock above pulpit. This clock is to strike at various times during the dream parts, to suggest the existence of the church. Remember the sound before the clock strikes.

19. On top of the clock two figures to mark the hours, by striking a large bell between them. One of these figures symbolizes life; the other death.

20. Clerestory windows around upper part of auditorium. Choir stands and triforium openings below windows.

21. All doors have heavy bolts, locks and knockers to create business and noise.

22. Large keys on rings for various doors.

23. The doors immediately behind proscenium lead to sacristy.

24. The doors below the loges lead to exterior.

25. Small midnight Mass bell, near top of tower, to be rung from rope on stage floor.

26. Wind machines, thunder drums and voices also to be there.

27. When audience take their seats, everything is dark.

28. The sound of a storm far away.

29. Soft candlelight in the auditorium, only where it is absolutely necessary, and flickering behind the columns around the altar screen.

30. Clusters of candlelights in distant places in the auditorium and stage, high up in the tower to produce an effect of tremendous size and of incredible distance.

31. There are to be candles around the altar screen and on the altar itself. The candles should be of various lengths and the bulbs of very low voltage and of various pale colors.

32. In chapels tiny candles suggest side-altars against darkness. Prominent clusters of them unsymmetrically chosen. Flickering candles on the columns in the apse and cloisters throwing shadows.

33. Candles on altar, altar screen and in chapels to be wired individually and lighted or extinguished by nuns. Candle bulbs to be no larger than one-half inch in diameter. The bulb must not show.

34. Candle extinguishers and wax tapers.

35. The large altar is dark.

36. One recognizes gradually among the towering columns several dark figures huddled together absorbed in prayer.

37. From a distant tower a bell sounds.

38. Large bells are located in ventilating shaft over auditorium and controlled from orchestra gallery.

39. A praying voice from behind the triforium windows is indistinctly heard; now and then a Latin word is audible.

40. Chairs are pushed about, some one blows his nose, others cough. The echo resounds through the church.

41. After that, silence.

42. An old sexton appears carrying a lantern.

43. His stick taps the pavement, and his steps drag over the stone floor.

44. He pulls back the green curtain over the Madonna statue.

45. He goes to the tower. Up the winding staircase the lantern shows through little windows and finally at the top.

46. He crosses a bridge and disappears through a doorway in the wall.

47. The organ starts and bells ring high above the church.

48. Nuns in pairs march through the cloisters toward the altar in two long columns, to take part in the coming ceremony.

49. The windows of the church become more brilliant from sunlight without.

50. Outside a young bright spring morning has awakened.

51. Sixty nuns dressed in ivory-colored garments trimmed with black. They all wear ropes. The black nuns' costumes appear like shadows passing in the dark and must be cut in such a way that the white undergarments show conspicuously when the nuns flutter like white doves in their excitement at the loss of the Madonna.

52. The chin cloths must be drawn very tightly, so that they never look slovenly. In fact they are to be made so that they can not be worn otherwise.

53. One column is headed by the Abbess.

54. The Abbess may be dressed either in white or in black, wears a crown and carries a silver staff, like the Bishop's, but smaller.

55. In this column the aged feeble Sacristan of the convent is carried in on a chair by four nuns.

56. In the other column a young nun, still but a child, is led in. She takes a tearful farewell of her mother, father, and grandmother who are seated at the right.

57. In an impressive ceremony the young Nun is dressed in an overgarment similar to that of the old Sacristan and receives the keys and office.

58. The Abbess sits in a special chair during the ceremony. She sings while one nun holds a music book for her and another holds a lighted candle.

59. This is accompanied by responses without music from the choir gallery.

60. In front are the holy pictures and the statue of the Madonna which stands on a column. It is a stone statue, painted in blue tempera and gold-leaf and wearing a crown set with precious stones.

61. The statue is to look as stonelike as possible and heavy, even if clumsy.

62. She must wear the white muslin nun's garb, as an undergarment.

63. The white head-cloth always has to remain on and be drawn as tightly as possible.

64. The Madonna holds the child in her arms.

65. The pedestal is decorated with many flowers, and large and small candles.

66. Crutches stacked around the base.

67. This pedestal altar conceals steps, covered with soft rubber. There must be supports for the Madonna under her armpits, at her waist, a seat, and recesses cut in floor for her feet. Her shoes are rubber-soled.

68. There are five statues of saints at other positions.

69. Large bells in the distance begin to sound as the Convent Church is revealed in its full glow of light.

70. The Nun, for the first time as the new Sacristan, opens all the doors with her keys.

71. A great commotion and the hum of voices come from without.

72. The sound of music grows nearer, the organ starts with massive tones.

73. A great procession pours into the church through all the doors. Men and women who are making the pilgrimage to the celebrated miracle-working statue of the Madonna.

74. First come the visiting orders of nuns in white.

75. Then peasants with banners.

76. Women in vivid-colored clothes, some barefooted.

77. Townspeople following, carrying banners with coats of arms of towns.

78. Tradesmen carrying the various emblems of their trade on poles.
79. A group of peasants bring in an enormous cross.
80. A great crowd of children with a Maypole.
81. Priests carrying church banners.
82. Acolytes swinging incense.
83. Choirboys with their large books.
84. The Archbishop carries his staff and walks beneath a canopy carried by four men.
85. Under another canopy is carried the monstrance. Church dignitaries follow.
86. Then monks carrying wooden statues of saints on poles.
87. A great mass of cripples on primitive crutches and stretchers, wearing dirty ragged clothes.
88. Blind people, who are led.
89. Widows in mourning.
90. Mothers carrying sick children on their backs, in their arms, and with others clinging to their skirts.
91. Lepers with clappers.
92. Pilgrims with broad-brimmed hats, staves, bundles and flasks.
93. Finally the knights in vivid color.
94. Followed by heralds, squires, men-at-arms, in full dress.
95. No one comes empty-handed. All who have nothing else to carry bring full-leafed birch branches.
96. The procession fills the whole stage and all the aisles in the auditorium.
97. There is much singing and waving of the yellow green branches. It looks almost like a green forest, waving to and fro.
98. The voice of a priest, whom no one sees, is heard.
99. The music stops.
100. A bell rings at the altar.
101. A white vapor begins to rise from the vessels containing the incense.
102. The crowd falls on its knees.
103. The sick crowd up to the statue of the Madonna and pray without halt. The Archbishop leads the prayers from the pulpit.

104. The tension grows. A breathless silence.

105. Finally there arises in the audience a completely lamed man, who had been carried in on a stretcher. He gets heavily to his feet, with convulsive twitching, and raising his arms high in ecstasy strides to the figure of the Mother of God, where he dances with joy.

106. A cry, the organ, rejoicing of the crowd. A miracle has come to pass.

107. The pilgrims leave the church singing.

108. The candles are extinguished and the nuns slowly pass out.

109. The young Sacristan goes about her duties of locking the doors.

110. In the last doorway there stands the healed fellow blowing harmlessly upon a flute. This demoniac figure, who runs through the play and has an evil influence upon the fate of the young Nun, is the lure of sensual life. At this moment his appearance resembles that of the Pied Piper. He wears a broad-brimmed hat over his faunlike ears.

111. Children surround him in their curiosity and listen to his music.

112. The Nun stands still as if under a spell and hears his tunes with the same astonishment and naïve joy as the children.

113. The children, unable to resist longer, fall into the rhythm, crowd into the church and force the Nun, who resists, into their ranks.

114. An unconscious yearning for the spring without causes her momentarily to forget her new office.

115. In her childishness, the Nun lets herself be forced into the dance.

116. She lets her keys fall and dances joyfully.

117. In the meantime, the Piper's tune has attracted a young Knight, who quietly enters and is fascinated by the graceful dancing of the Nun.

118. Suddenly, on seeing him, she becomes frightened and rooted to the spot as they exchange glances.

119. The Nun hears nothing as the bell rings for vespers.

120. Nuns approach in a column, the Abbess at their head.

121. They become enraged on seeing this pair in the church.

122. The children and the Piper slyly escape through the open door.

123. The Abbess rebukes the young Sacristan who stares about her, dazed.

124. At a nod from the angry Abbess the keys are taken away from her and the heavy bolts locked behind the Knight who has slowly gone out.

125. She is sentenced to spend the night in prayer before the statue of the Madonna.

126. The nuns again depart and the church sinks gradually into night and silence.

127. The Nun prays fervently before the statue of the Holy Virgin.

128. In her confusion she scarcely knows what is happening to her.

129. Her thoughts, which she seeks vainly to discipline, escape through the stone walls and wander tirelessly into the night in the direction of the young Knight.

130. The poor child returns again and again to her prayers, seeking peace and comfort there.

131. Her youth, awakened for the first time, struggles against the cold discipline offered her.

132. She runs to the font and sprinkles herself madly with holy water.

133. Her heart beats wildly, she throws herself about on the steps leading to the miracle statue.

134. She wrings her hands and plunges desperately into passionate prayer.

135. At this moment something happens that can just as well be a raving dream of fever as a fantastic reality. With the rapid pace of dreams, one experience chases after another and drives the Nun back into the church after a moment of actual happiness through a martyrdom of indescribable suffering. Dream, or reality. It is intense, terrible, vital, as endlessly long as an intense dream, as horribly short as a full life.

136. Suddenly there is a light but insistent knocking at the gate. The Nun grows tense.

137. The knock is repeated. Is it her own heartbeat? She tries not to hear and prays aloud.

138. The knocking continues, always louder, and finally sounds from all sides and from all doors. Each door should have a heavy knocker.

139. She springs up involuntarily, takes several steps toward the door.

140. She stands still in fright. throws herself on her knees, wrings her hands, is torn back and forth.

141. Finally like an excited but caged bird, she flutters anxiously to and fro, beating her head against the cold walls.

142. The knocking grows wilder, her yearning more uncontrollable.

143. She shakes the locked doors with all her strength.

144. Throwing herself on her knees, she begs the Mother of God to set her free.

145. The moon shines through the windows.

146. As if mad, she dashes toward the Holy Virgin and points fiercely at the child in her arms. She is yearning for the child, for everything out there.

147. Completely out of her mind she finally takes the holy child from the arms of the Madonna and holds it high.

148. A warm glow radiates from it and then suddenly the child disappears in a flash of light.

149. Everything grows dark. A sound like thunder resounds through the high church.

150. When it is again light Mary has heard the passionate pleadings and has performed a miracle.

151. The high altar glittering with candles, slowly opens, forming a Gothic arch, with a knight in silver armor and a blue mantle, visible through the high candles on the altar tables.

152. The Knight and the Nun stand regarding each other.

153. The Nun shrinks back frightened and flees to the foot of the Madonna.

154. The Mother of God smiles as graciously as ever. Her will is plain.

155. The altar table, with the candles on it, opens slowly, exposing a flight of steps.

156. The Knight slowly approaches the Nun. She rises shyly.

157. He offers her his hand to lead her forth. She looks at her clothing and hesitates to go out in her holy costume.

158. She removes the black nun's veil, the white cape, the rosary with its large cross, the belt and finally her dark dress and lays them all tenderly on the steps of the miracle statue.

159. Rising, she shudders at the sight of her underdress, feeling that she is without clothes.

160. The Piper who was behind the Knight brings in the blue cloak of the Knight and covers the young Nun with the dress of life.

161. Again she kneels, and the Knight with her, at the foot of the Virgin.

162. Then he catches her in his arms and runs off with her into the world.

163. The church is deserted.

164. A sigh comes from somewhere within the walls.

165. The Madonna statue begins to glow with an unearthly light.

166. It seems as if she were opening her lips and smiling. The figure moves.

167. The light on her face changes from unearthly to the pink of life.

168. She opens her eyes.

169. She smiles.

170. She turns her head.

171. She drops her robe.

172. She descends.

173. She lifts her arm.

174. She removes her crown.

175. She holds it up high.

176. She lays it on the pedestal.

177. Then she gives a sign for the altar to close, and it becomes as before.

178. The Virgin bends low, and in sweet humility puts on the simple costume of the Nun.

179. She goes to the tower and rings the bell.

180. Voices of singing nuns. The Virgin kneels and prays in front of her pedestal.

181. The nuns come into the church for mass.

182. The Abbess glances at the supposed Nun, sunk in prayer, and chuckles fondly at the repentance of her favorite.

183. By accident her glance falls on the spot where the miracle statue has stood, but now where only her cloak and crown lie. She does not trust her eyes, stares, consults the sister.

184. A terrible fear seizes all the nuns.

185. They scream, run around enraged, cry out, weep, threaten their supposed sister, fetch the priest and ring the alarm bell.

186. With clenched fist and swinging cords, all rush at the poor Nun, who has obviously permitted the theft of the precious treasure in her impious sin.

187. The Nun's head remains humbly bowed.

188. Whenever the threatening sisters surround her in a wild rush, she gently floats a short distance into the air without changing her position. This is done on a trap on the right.

189. In silent awe they draw back from her; staring at this miracle speechlessly, they recognize that a higher power is obviously at work here, and that the young Nun is the chosen agent.

190. Returning to the earth, she goes about her duties like an ordinary nun, taking a jar of oil to fill the eternal lamp.

191. The nuns form open rows and follow their holy sister spreading their arms wide and singing in ecstasy.

192. The scene grows dark.

VSEVOLOD MEYERHOLD

(1874-1942)

Rehearsals of
The Inspector General

In the annals of the theater it is unusual to find a verbatim transcript of an actual rehearsal. Meyerhold, accustomed to doing the unusual, made this a possibility with his corps of assistant régisseurs who recorded the minute details of every aspect of a production. Even in the transcripts available to us of two rehearsals of The Inspector General, *Meyerhold's improvisatory methods of directing are clearly revealed. In order to preserve the continuity of a rehearsal, the editors have taken the liberty of integrating transcripts dated February 13 and March 4, 1926, into a single reconstruction of Meyerhold at work on the opening scenes. A difficulty posed by the reconstruction grows out of the fact that Meyerhold made numerous changes in Gogol's text. Not having the text of the play as it was being evolved, we have taken the liberty of interpolating Meyerhold's directions where they most logically seem to fall in Gogol's original text.*

ACT I . . . A ROOM IN THE MAYOR'S HOUSE

  (The Mayor, Charity Commissioner, School Superintendent, Judge, Police Superintendent, Doctor, and two Police Officers)

MAYOR: I have called you together, gentlemen, to give you a very unpleasant piece of news: there's an Inspector General coming.

"Na Repetitzia *Revizora*," *Teatr i Dramaturgia,* February 1934, 40-42.

The Mayor's entrance should be acted out to the hilt. Once we have agreed that the role should move along in a certain tempo, it is my duty, technically, to create an atmosphere in which the actor will feel at ease. The actor should be relieved of anything that makes for ponderousness.

JUDGE AND CHARITY COMMISSIONER: What, an Inspector?

When everybody says: "What, an Inspector." there should be no uniformity. There should be a variety of accents, and also a difference in enuncia-

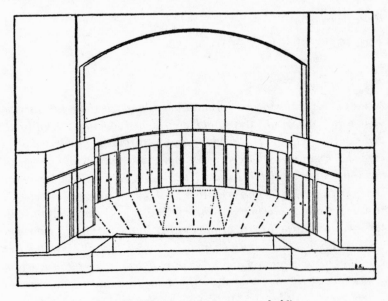

General plan of setting of Meyerhold's
The Inspector General** (1926). (From **New
***Theatres for Old**, by Mordecai Gorelik.)*

tions. Some break up the word: "In-spec-tor." Some speak rapidly, others with a drawl. Their reaction is an immediate one and they do not speak in character. Anyhow, the audience cannot make out who says what. They are all crowded into the sofa, nearly ten of them. [Meyerhold has added to the group.] Character quality should be toned down a little. Everybody speaks at once. Their remarks are in chorus.

MAYOR: Yes, an Inspector General from Petersburg, incognito. With secret instructions, too.

JUDGE: Well, I declare!

CHARITY COMMISSIONER: Now we're in for it!

SCHOOL SUPERINTENDENT: Good Lord! With secret instructions!

MAYOR: I had a sort of presentiment of it: all last night I dreamed about a pair of monstrous rats. I never saw the like of 'em—so black and enormous. They came and sniffed about—and vanished. . . . Here's a letter which I will read you from Khmikov. (*To the Charity Commissioner*) You know him, Artemy Filipovich. This is what he says: "My dear friend, my comrade and benefactor . . . (*He quickly mutters over the first few sentences*) . . . and to let you know"—Ah! that's it—"I hasten to let you know, among other things, that an offi-

The inn scene, Meyerhold's **The Inspector General.**
(*From* **New Theatres for Old,** *by Mordecai Gorelik.*)

cial has been sent with instructions to inspect the whole province, and your district especially. (*Lifts his finger significantly*) That he *is* coming I know from very reliable sources, but he pretends to be a private person. So, as you have your little faults, you know, like everybody else (you're a sensible man, and don't let what swims into your hand slip through your fingers) . . ." (*Stopping*) H'm, that's only a manner of speaking . . . "I advise you to take precautions, for he may come any moment—if he has not already done so, and is staying somewhere incognito. Yesterday . . ." Oh, then come family matters, "My cousin, Anna Kirilovna, paid us a visit, with her husband. Ivan Kirilovich has gotten very fat, and is always playing the fiddle . . ." Et cetera, et cetera. Now, here's a pretty business!

A groan. A groan helps to raise the tone of the voice and out of the groan you come directly to the words: "Now, here's a pretty business!"

The Mayor is in the chair. The two servants and Hubner, the Doctor, stand near him. This, by the way, imparts something of the generalissimo to him. He is like a Czar in this town.

It appears to me that in such an environment, in such a collection of idiots—and the Commissioner, the Superintendent, the Judge—are all idiots —that among all of these complete idiots, the Mayor does somehow stand out. He is shrewder, he does have some kind of polish. He has climbed to some position of prominence. He has lived in quite a few places. All his instructions show that he is head and shoulders above the others. His education is hard to pin down. Judging from what he says later of the teacher,

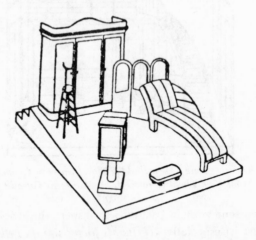

*The Mayor's home, Meyerhold's **The Inspector General**.*
*(From **New Theatres for Old**, by Mordecai Gorelik.)*

he does have some vague knowledge of history. He betrays some sort of a pseudo-culture. Of course, what sort of culture can there be in that God-forsaken hole? The Mayor shows a certain fluency in his speech. He builds his phrases, for instance, better than Bobchinsky and Dobchinsky. With them, we can almost hear their brains creaking. The Mayor quickly orients himself. He can say something to the point. He is an orator, he can deliver a whole monologue.

Don't play him as an old man. He needs to be rejuvenated. How did it happen that the Mayor was always enacted as an old man? Because in the past the Mayor was always played by old actors with many years of acting behind them. Maksheyev, for instance, Vladimir Davydov—they played it when they were quite old. And when young actors undertook this role, they copied the performances of old men with big names. That is how these devices and intonations entrenched themselves.

You are young, you are about fifteen or twenty years younger than I— forget this old man's diction. Shoot it out with a free, distinct diction. No doddering right now, that will come later—we will go into it then. Perhaps we will give you a chair during the rehearsals—you sit, think it out, everything is arranged and then you begin. Give him the chair we used in *The Forest*. He doesn't feel too good and is seated in the chair. And give him a glass of water.

JUDGE: Yes, extraordinary, simply extraordinary. There must be some reason for it.

SCHOOL INSPECTOR: But why, Anton Antonovich? Why should *we* have an Inspector?

MAYOR: (*Sighing*): Oh, it's fate, I suppose! (*Sighs again*) Till now, thank goodness, they've pried into other towns; but now our turn has come.

JUDGE: It's my opinion, Anton Antonovich, that it's a deep political move, and it means—let me see—that Russia . . . yes, that's it . . . Russia wants to make war, and the Government has surreptitiously sent an official to see if there's any disaffection anywhere.

"It's my opinion, Anton Antonovich . . ." should have more of an "into the ear" intonation. More of the confiding tone, of tale-bearing. He hasn't given a thought to it, but already he begins to elaborate. Then you can put it into the tempo.

MAYOR: Ah, *you've* got it. *You* know a thing or two! The idea of treason in an inland town. As if it lay on the frontier! Why, from here you may gallop for three years before you reach a foreign country.

JUDGE: No, I'll tell you how it is—you don't understand—the Government looks very closely into matters; it *may* be far away, yet it observes everything—

MAYOR (*Cutting him short*): It may or it may not—anyhow, gentlemen, I have warned you. I have made some arrangements on my own behalf, and I advise you to do the same. You especially, Artemy Filipovich! Without doubt, the Inspector will want first of all to look at your hospital; and so you had better see that everything is in order; that the nightcaps are clean, and that the patients don't go about as they usually do—looking like blacksmiths.

"You especially, Artemy Filipovich . . . and so on." This is blurted out in one breath.

CHARITY COMMISSIONER: Oh, that's all right. They shall have clean nightcaps, if you like.

Now, the first thing the Charity Commissioner says is remarkably sugar-coated—pure honey—real strawberry. [Gogol frequently gave his characters revealing surnames. The Charity Commissioner's name is Strawberry.] I don't know how we will develop this. It does not come out right because both the Commissioner and the Judge are too reasonable in their dialogue. Some other version should be found—it should not be played according to the script. We will work on it later.

MAYOR: And you might write up over each bed, in Latin or some other lingo—(*To the Doctor*) that's *your* business, Hubner—the name of each complaint, when the patient got ill, the day of the week and month . . . and I don't like your invalids smoking such strong tobacco; it makes you choke when you come in. It would be better too if there weren't so many of them; otherwise it will be ascribed to bad supervision or unskillful doctoring.

CHARITY COMMISSIONER: Oh, Hubner and I have settled all about the doctoring; the nearer we get to Nature the better; we don't go in for costly medicines. A man is a simple affair—if he dies, he dies; if he gets well, why, then he gets well. And it isn't easy for the patients to understand our Doctor—he doesn't know a word of Russian. (*The Doctor grunts unintelligibly*)

And this is the assignment for the Doctor. [A German-speaking Doctor who has no lines in Gogol's text. Meyerhold has asked for some props to be brought in including a glass of water to be used as medicine.] Is this water all right to drink? You stir it and from time to time you hand the Mayor a spoonful. You keep on stirring. And the Mayor must take it. At times he pushes it away, at times he drinks, takes the glass with his own hands, gulps down a little. The medicine is of a kind that can be taken by the glassful. And you must have something to say in German and say it so as to overlap the Mayor's speeches. This will help him to handle the scene. You will step up his tempo. Inasmuch as there is an obstacle, there is always the need of overcoming it. You keep on talking—*perpetuum mobile*. Do you speak German? You are of German descent, aren't you?

Has anyone got a handkerchief? A muffler? (The Mayor's head is wrapped up.) There you are. Let the Mayor say a few lines and then begin to administer the drink. You will walk around him, rap at his chest, apply a mustard plaster to his feet to draw off the blood from his head. Do you know some German words? Repeat some phrases.

Every time there is a flurry of feeling, it has its effect upon the Doctor. He soothes the Mayor, and then pounces upon the others when they talk. Agitation is harmful for his patient. I don't quite know what, but you keep on saying something like *Sein Sie ruhig*. That irritates the Mayor, and this irritation enables the Doctor to put his acting into the required tempo. The Doctor exhorts everyone in his own unintelligible manner and continues to treat the patient. It is a very intricate thing—special instruction is needed here. *Warum sprechen Sie so?*—something of this kind. The Doctor has a tremendously bigger role here than that of the Mayor.

MAYOR: Also I would recommend you, Ammos Fyodorovich (*the Judge*)—to turn your attention to the court-house buildings. There's the antechamber, where the petitioners usually wait; you've let the attendants breed geese there, and the goslings go poking their beaks among people's legs. Of course, raising geese is a most laudable pursuit, and there's no reason why the clerk should not do so; only, you see, the County Court is not exactly the place for it. . . . I intended to mention it before, but it somehow escaped my memory.

JUDGE: Well, I'll tell them to take 'em all into the kitchen today. Will you come to dinner?

(To the Mayor) The remark addressed to the Judge has an undertone of irritation. Then the tempo will be right. "Of course, raising geese is a most laudable pursuit" and so on. . . . You seem to take it in parenthesis and that is why there is that drop. The transition should be effected rapidly. Keep in mind the phrase "not exactly the place for it." The preceding words should not be spoken in a lowered tone, not in parenthesis. They are the springboard in the direction of "not exactly the place for it." The latter phrase should be kept in mind from the very beginning of the monologue and then the preceding words will be given the right expression. The basic function of the Mayor's role is that he carries the movement of the script forward.

MAYOR: Besides that, it doesn't do for the court chamber to get so full of rubbish of all sorts. Why, there was a whip lying among the papers on your own desk. I know you're fond of sports, but there is a proper time and place for everything. When the Inspector is gone you can put it back again. Then your assessor—he's certainly a learned man, but he reeks of vodka, as if he had just come out of a distillery; that also is undesirable. I meant to tell you of this some while ago, but something or other put it out of my head. There are ways of remedying it, if it is really, as he says, a natural failing. You can recommend him to eat onions or garlic, or something of the sort. Hubner can help him there with some of his nostrums. (*The Doctor grunts as before.*)

When the Doctor hears his name he begins to speak: *"Das habe ich schon gesagt."* He continues to stir the medicine.

JUDGE: No, it's quite impossible to get rid of it. He says his nurse knocked him down when he was a child, and ever since he has smelled of vodka.

MAYOR: Well, I just reminded you of it. As regards the local administration, and what Khmikov is pleased to call one's "little faults" in his letter, I don't understand what he means. Why, of course, there isn't a man living who has not *some* peccadilloes to account for. Heaven made him so—let *freethinkers* say what they like.

JUDGE: What do you mean by peccadilloes, Anton Antonovich? There are peccadilloes and peccadilloes. I tell everyone plainly that I take bribes, but what kind of bribes? Greyhound puppies! That's a totally different matter.

MAYOR: H'm, whether they're puppies or anything else, they're all bribes alike.

JUDGE: No, indeed, Anton Antonovich. But suppose, for example, one receives a *cloak* worth five hundred rubles, or your good lady receives a *shawl*. . . .

MAYOR: Yes, but what has that got to do with your being bribed with puppies? Besides, you're an atheist, you never go to church, while I, at least, am a firm believer, and go to church every Sunday. Whereas *you*—oh, I know *you,* when I hear you talking about the Creation my hair simply stands on end.

JUDGE: What of that? I have reasoned it all out with my own unaided intellect.

MAYOR: Anyhow, too much knowledge is worse than none at all. However, I only made a remark about the County Court, and I dare say nobody will ever look at it, there's an odor of sanctity about the place. But you, Luka Lukich, as School Superintendent, ought to keep an eye on the teachers. They're very clever people, no doubt, and are blessed with a college education, but they have very funny habits—inseparable from their profession, I suppose.

We'll do it this way. You—the Mayor—will be seated in a half-turned position so that when you cut loose from the Doctor you always turn toward someone. "But you, Luka Lukich . . . ought to keep an eye on the teachers." You rise, stand up in the chair on your knees. You rise and keep firing away. Nuances will come all by themselves. You rise, and Hubner removes the trousers, and, taking advantage of the change of position, applies a mustard plaster. I am suggesting all that in order to furnish the necessary crescendoes of the tempo.

MAYOR (*Continued*): One of them, for instance, the fat-faced man —I forget his name—can't get along without screwing up his phiz like this—(*imitates him*)—when he's got into his chair, and then he sets to work clawing his necktie and scratching his chin. It doesn't matter, of course, if he makes a face at a pupil—perhaps it's even necessary—I'm no judge of that, but you yourselves will admit that if he grimaces at a visitor, it may make a very bad impression. The honorable Inspector, or anyone else, might take it as meant for himself—and then the deuce knows what might come of it.

LUKA: What can I do with him, I ask? I have told him of it time after time. Only the other day, when our headmaster came into class, your friend made such a face at him as I had never seen before. I dare say it was with the best intentions, but people come complaining to me about radical notions being instilled into the juvenile mind.

Here, Luka Lukich, with this new treatment of the Mayor, you don't get it right. He advances upon the Mayor: "What can I do with him" . . . he must keep on pushing himself forward, advancing, like one who in repudiating what you say, reviles you and thrusts himself upon you.

MAYOR: And then you should look to the master of the history class. He has a learned head, that is evident, and has picked up any amount of knowledge, but he lectures with such ardor that he quite forgets himself. I once listened to him. As long as he was holding forth about the Assyrians and Babylonians, it was all right, but when he got on Alexander of Macedon, I can't describe his behavior. Good Heavens, I thought, there's a fire! He jumped out of his chair, and smashed a stool on the ground with all his might! Alexander of Macedon was a hero, we all know, but that's no reason for breaking the furniture—besides, the State has to pay for the damages.

LUKA: Yes, he is fiery! I have spoken to him about it several times. He only says: "Do as you please, but in the cause of learning I will even sacrifice my life!"

MAYOR: Yes, it's a mysterious law of fate, your clever man is either a drunkard, or makes faces that would scare the saints.

LUKA: Ah, Heaven save us from being schoolmasters! You're afraid of everything, everybody meddles with you, and wants to show you that he's as learned as you are.

"Ah, Heaven save us from being schoolmasters!" Here again is your leit motif. The Mayor has already dropped the subject while you still continue to advance upon him. Luka Lukich is beyond himself.

(Enter the Postmaster)

POSTMASTER: Tell me, gentlemen, who's coming? What sort of official?

MAYOR: What, haven't you heard?

POSTMASTER: I heard something from Bobchinsky. He was with me just now at the post office.

The Mayor not only beckons the Postmaster, but rises up, leaning upon both the Doctor and the Postmaster. He speaks in a confidential tone, but rather rapidly and loudly, so that everyone should hear. You understand, confidentially, but at a terribly accelerated speed. You grab the Postmaster and smother him, so he will find it hard to shake himself loose, while the Doctor keeps on grumbling, *"Dieser Postmeister, Gott!"*

MAYOR: Well, what do you think about it?

POSTMASTER: What do *I* think about it? Why, there'll be a war with the Turks.

JUDGE: Exactly. That's just what I thought!

MAYOR: Well, you're both wide of the mark.

POSTMASTER: It'll be with the Turks, I'm sure. It's all the Frenchmen's doing.

MAYOR: Pooh! War with the Turks, indeed! It's *we* who are going to get it in the neck, not the Turks. That's quite certain. I've a letter that says so.

"It's we who are going to get it in the neck, not the Turks. I've a letter . . ." The Mayor has to turn over the letter to the Postmaster and the latter glances at it with an experienced eye. He can read the letter rapidly, this is his specialty. Take a beat and a half. You are through with the reading. Then—"Oh, then we shan't go to war . . ." That is, if it's true what is written there. The phrase should be motivated, otherwise it will not be determined by anything. And this pause becomes significant by the Mayor's action—he approaches the Postmaster and lowers his tone to a confidential whisper.

POSTMASTER: Oh, then we shan't go to war with the Turks.

MAYOR: Well, how do *you* feel, Ivan Kuzmich?

POSTMASTER: How do *I* feel? How do *you* feel, Anton Antonovich?

MAYOR: I? Well, I'm no coward, but I *am* just a little uncomfortable. The shopkeepers and townspeople bother me. It seems I'm unpopular with them, but, the Lord knows, if I've blackmailed anybody, I've done it without a trace of ill-feeling. I even think (*Buttonholes the Postmaster, and takes him aside*)—I even think there will be some sort of complaint drawn up against me. . . . Why should we have an Inspector General at all? Look here, Ivan Kuzmich, don't you think you could just slightly open every letter which comes in and goes out of your office, and read it (for the public benefit, you know) to see if it contains any kind of information against me, or only ordinary correspondence? If it is all right, you can seal it up again, or simply deliver the letter opened.

That should be done in a different tone—more intimate and wheedling in character. To come right out and say a thing like "slightly open every letter" is rather hard for him to do. The Mayor speaks very quietly, rapidly and in a monotone. When you whisper into someone's ear, you do not embellish your speech with all kinds of melodic ornaments. Let it be done in a hardly audible tone so that the audience will be forced to strain itself to catch the meaning.

POSTMASTER: Oh, I know *that* game. Don't teach me *that!* I do it out of sheer curiosity, not as a precaution. I'm keen on knowing what's going on in the world. And they're highly interesting reading. I can tell you! Now and then you come across a love letter, with bits of beautiful language, and so edifying . . . much better than the *Moscow News!* Just wait, wait.

As to the Postmaster, his "highly interesting reading" makes him fall into the same tone. The Mayor eyes him foolishly. He is thinking of the Inspector General, while the Postmaster fumbles in his pockets. "Just wait, wait." The Postmaster has letters in all his pockets. He is a walking container. Why do you slow down on the tempo? Dash along, dash along. Give the Postmaster a lot of letters so that he can keep on taking them out, seeking, until he finds the right one.

MAYOR: Tell me, then, have you read anything about an official from Petersburg?

POSTMASTER: No, nothing about anyone from Petersburg, but plenty about the Kostroma and Saratov people. It's a pity you don't read the letters. There's some fine passages in them. For instance, not long ago a lieutenant writes to a friend, describing a ball in first-rate style—splendid! "Dear Friend," he says, "I live in Elysium, heaps of girls, music playing, flags flying" . . . quite a glowing description, quite! I've kept it by me, on purpose. Would you like to read it?

His hand should tremble in the handling of the letters, and many letters at that. Ordinary description should be avoided. The text of the play is no guide in this case. The description of the ball was always read realistically, while one should do it very lightly, almost in a whisper. And then "Would you like to read it?" "Let me have it"—and the Mayor snatches the letter away from the Postmaster. [Note the deviation from Gogol's text. Meyerhold evidently prefers to have the Mayor read the letter aloud.] The acting should be done with the object—the letter itself. (Question: And perhaps he puts on glasses while reading the letter? Answer: No, you shouldn't put it on too thick. He reads without glasses. A candle should be held before him.)

MAYOR: Thanks, there's no time now. But oblige me, Ivan Kuzmich—if ever you chance upon a complaint or a denouncement, keep it back, without the slightest compunction.

POSTMASTER: I will, with the greatest pleasure.

JUDGE (*Who has overheard a little*): You had better look out. You'll get into trouble over that sometime or other.

POSTMASTER: Eh! The saints forbid!

MAYOR: It was nothing—nothing. It would be different if it concerned you or the public—but it was a private affair, I assure you!

JUDGE: H'm, *some* mischief was brewing, *I* know! . . . but I was going to say, Anton Antonovich, that I had got a puppy to make you a present of—a sister to the hound you know. I daresay you've heard that Cheptovich and Varkhovinski have gone to court with one another; so now I live in clover—I hunt hares first on one's estate, and then on the other's.

The Judge has an air of self-consciousness about him. He forces himself into the group and shoves into the heap of letters, a young, slobbering, very small puppy. The Judge mumbles something, turns the puppy over and shows that it is a female: "A sister to the hound you know." A purely physiological scene, a pleasant scene, such as one sees in a surgical laboratory when a transplantation of glands is being performed. And so all the others look on, while the Judge turns the puppy over on her back, puts its feet wide apart—and everybody looks, everyone wants to see it for himself. A laboratory puppy—we'll work out this scene.

MAYOR: I don't care about your hares now, my good friend. I've got that cursed incognito on the brain! I expect the door to open any minute . . .

"I don't care about your hares now"—this should not be said, but should be rather conveyed in mimic movements. "I expect the door to open any minute . . ."—you say it by way of realization that nothing can be done with these people. The only thing to do is to leave, otherwise the Judge will insist on presenting you with a hound. I will make up those passages, the scene should be fully worked out. I will come back to the Mayor last.

(*Enter Bobchinsky and Dobchinsky, out of breath*)

BOBCHINSKY: What an extraordinary occurrence!

DOBCHINSKY: An unexpected piece of news!

ALL: What is it—what is it?

DOBCHINSKY: Something quite unforeseen. We go into the inn——

BOBCHINSKY (*Interrupting*): Yes, Pytor Ivanovich and I go into the inn—

DOBCHINSKY (*Takes him up*): All right, Peter Ivanovich, let *me* tell it!

BOBCHINSKY: No, no, allow me—allow me. You haven't got the knack——

DOBCHINSKY: Oh, but you'll get mixed up and forget it all.

BOBCHINSKY: Oh, no, I shan't—good Heavens, no! There, don't interrupt me—*do* let me tell the news—don't interrupt! Pray oblige me, gentlemen, and tell Dobchinsky not to interrupt.

MAYOR: Well, go on, for God's sake, what is it? My heart is in my mouth! Sit down, sirs, take seats! Pytor Ivanovich, here's a chair for you! (*They all sit round Bobchinsky and Dobchinsky*) Well, now, what is it, what is it?

"My heart is in my mouth"—there should be a light groan from the Mayor. A physiologically determined groan. "My heart is in my mouth." He has a heart murmur and he must show it at once. Now the groan sounds somewhat stylized. Of course, by varying it somewhat, you will neutralize it. And then what will happen will be that groans will be followed by some kind of fatigue. The groans determine the music of the words, or rather the timbre of the text. Your acting will consist in the succession of such moments. He clutches at his heart, his pulse is irregular. The audience should be given to understand that the groans are not stylized, that there is, indeed, something the matter with his heart. He groans, he clutches at his heart in a way that arouses in the audience the fear that he might have an apoplectic stroke.

The first part of the scene is very well done. Sharp gesture, marionette-like quality. It will not militate against the atmosphere of illness. It will be all right if you obtain the effect of ease. Now you have just one note in your groaning, but when variety appears then we'll have real illness. Then there will be new moments, new occasions for groaning, and they will break up some of the artificiality.

There are certain achievements to be recorded. Excellent. The Mayor's part is becoming sharp. The lines are charged with a kind of trenchancy. We begin to hear the coining of italics, peculiar turns of phrase are cropping up. This, in my opinion, is a big gain. It means that you have already reached the plane where it will be easier to carry on the work of further improvement. In the later work you will have to aim at greater lightness. Now it is still somewhat ponderous; but the first half is especially well worked out in the sense of poignancy, clear-cut chiselling. We even see the old man disappearing, there is no more of the senile cud-chewing.

You have gained a great deal by finding all the colors, but when the entire system of the role unfolds, we see that since the monologue of the fifth act dominates over the rest, the role should be built up to a certain crescendo, otherwise there may be a sudden drop, so that nothing will remain but the tone of the first act.

LEOPOLD JESSNER

(1878-1945)

Staging of
The Weavers, *Act IV, The Looting Scene*

From 1919 on, Leopold Jessner, director at the State Theater in Berlin, aroused audiences with his startling expressionist productions. On February 4, 1928, the premiere of his interpretation of the great naturalist drama The Weavers *took place, and once again a Jessner production provoked controversy. The famous Looting Scene which follows, a typical example of Jessner's ingenious embellishment of a text, was the high point of this production.*

On stage Mrs. Dreissiger and Mrs. Kittelhaus, the Pastor's wife. They are sitting on Chairs 5 and 7.

MRS. DREISSIGER (*In tears*): Is it my husband's fault if business is bad?

A loud commotion is heard below: laughter, jeering shouts, whistling. Dreissiger dashes in excitedly through the Main Door.

DREISSIGER: Rosa, put your things on and get into the carriage. I'll be right with you.

He rushes over to the window and shuts the blinds. Then he opens the strongbox (4) and hastily takes from it money and valuables.
Both women have sprung up in alarm. The Pastor's wife backs up toward the staircase and listens to the commotion.

Leopold Jessner: "*Weber* Inscenierung IV, Act Die Plunderung," *Die Scene,* March 1928, 92-94.

326

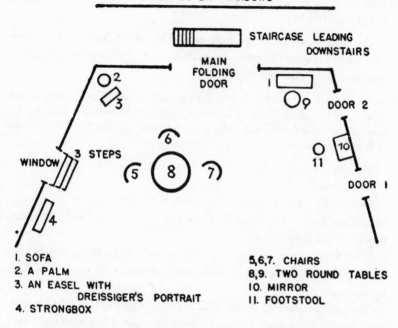

1. SOFA
2. A PALM
3. AN EASEL WITH
        DREISSIGER'S PORTRAIT
4. STRONGBOX

5,6,7. CHAIRS
8,9. TWO ROUND TABLES
10. MIRROR
11. FOOTSTOOL

John, the old family coachman, enters stage right through Door 1. He remains standing by the door.

JOHN: Everything's ready! But come quickly, before they break down the back gate!

Terrified, Mrs. Dreissiger rushes over to John and throws her arms around his neck. She sobs:

John, oh, my good old John! Save us, save us, John, my dear old John! Save my children, oh, oh!

Dreissiger stamps his foot impatiently. He continues meanwhile to hunt feverishly for his valuables:

Will you please come to your senses, and let go of John!

John has stood by helplessly while Mrs. Dreissiger embraced him. Now that he is again free, he says:

Madam, madam! Calm yourself, please. Our horses are in good condition. Nobody'll catch up with 'em. And if anyone does get in our way, we'll run 'em down.

He exits stage right—Door 1. Mrs. Dreissiger stands there helplessly, sobbing quietly. Mrs. Kittelhaus, having waited in vain near the stairs for her husband to come, walks agitatedly toward Dreissiger. She speaks in a voice of frightened despair:

But my husband! Where's my husband? Mr. Dreissiger, where's my husband?

DREISSIGER (*As he stuffs his pockets with money and valuables*): Mrs. Kittelhaus, Mrs. Kittelhaus, he's all right now. Don't be upset: he's quite all right.

MRS. KITTELHAUS (*Losing her self-control*): Something terrible has happened to him. I know it. You won't tell me; you're trying to keep it from me!

DREISSIGER: Please, please, pull yourself together. (*Pointing menacingly at the window*) They'll be sorry for this. They won't get away with their shameless, their outrageous behavior! A congregation laying hands on its own preacher! (*With an outcry, Mrs. Kittelhaus staggers back*) Mad dogs, that's what they are, raging brutes! And that's how they'll be treated.

He snatches up a few more valuables and quickly crosses to stage right, where Mrs. Dreissiger is standing as if stunned.

Go now, Rosa, please go! And quickly!

From below comes the sound of fists pounding at the front door. Then the noise of shattered windowpanes. Mrs. Dreissiger, weeping, slumps onto the sofa. Dreissiger, laughing nervously:

Can't you hear? The mob is running wild.

Shouts and cries are heard from below. Dreissiger, furious with rage:

That mob has gone crazy. There's nothing else we can do; we've got to get away from here.

The outcries grow ever louder and more ominous. Many voices shout in a chorus: "Pfeifer, Pfeifer, we want Pfeifer!"

Mrs. Dreissiger, prostrate on the sofa, moans:

Pfeifer . . . Pfeifer . . . they want Pfeifer.

Pfeifer lurches through the door stage right. He is pale, trembling, out of breath. He is so frightened he can hardly stand up.

PFEIFER: Mr. Dreissiger, Mr. Dreissiger, they're back at the back gate. (*He comes closer to Dreissiger*) The front door won't hold out much longer. The blacksmith's pounding at it with a heavy bucket.

Louder, more distinct shouts from below: "Send out Pfeifer! We want Pfeifer!"

Dreissiger picks his wife up from the sofa and pushes the two women through the door. Pfeifer, petrified with fear, follows him. He tries to stop Dreissiger, clinging to the latter's arms and hands:

Please, please, Mr. Dreissiger, I beg of you, don't leave me behind.

For a second the stage is empty. The loud noises continue from below, and off-stage right Pfeifer wails with terror. Dreissiger, off-stage, tears himself away from Pfeifer and then quickly crosses the stage to the strongbox. He has forgotten something. Pfeifer follows him:

I've always served you faithfully. And I've treated the workers good too. But I couldn't give them more pay than the fixed rate.

He flings himself to his knees before Dreissiger and clutches at him like a drowning man:

Don't leave me here, they'll kill me! If they catch me, they'll beat me to death! Oh God, God! My wife, my children! . . .

Dreissiger brutally tears himself loose:

It'll come out all right, I tell you, everything will turn out all right.

He exits right. Pfeifer follows him, pleading and sobbing. The stage remains empty.

A terrific din below. The house door is battered in; more windowpanes are shattered. Jubilant shouts of "Hooray!" Then utter silence. A few seconds pass, then the sound of many running feet is heard. Again silence.

In the midst of this silence a titter is heard: "Tee-hee-hee!" Then cautious, muffled outcries: "Go to the left." "Go on up!" "Shhh, take it easy!" People come up the stairs—slowly, hesitantly, timidly. The first to appear on stage is the figure of a haggard young weaver dressed in tatters. He goes carefully up the stairs and remains standing timidly at the Main Door.

Behind him are men and women weavers—all poor, thin, dressed in ragged or patched clothing. Many of them are sickly looking. They seem afraid to go in. "All right, go in there!" "No, *you* go first!"

Wittig the blacksmith, a stout bucket in his hand, pushes his way through the group: "Out of my way!" He rushes into the room with five young weavers and then exits right.

An old woman enters the room and sees a coffee set on the table stage right. "Oh, look at that!" She sits down on the sofa and pours herself some coffee. Slowly the room fills with weavers. The blinds are thrown open and the windows opened wide. Bright sunlight floods the room.

Silently, almost ghostlike, the looting now takes place. Not a word is spoken, not a question asked, not an order given. The weavers have overcome their timidity: hatred and the desire for revenge have the upper hand. Pictures are ripped from the walls and flung out of the window and through the door. A woman comes to the table, sees the richly brocaded tablecloth, takes it off, sits down on a chair and, panting softly, tears the tablecloth into shreds. Everything Dreissiger has left behind in the strongbox is thrown on the floor. Curtains are torn down. Pieces of furniture are smashed; upholstery cut to pieces. All this occurs almost in silence. Only a little weaver's boy runs around, tinkling a hand-bell he has found on the table. Old Baumert sits on the footstool stage right and drinks coffee.

In this silence Old Hieber comes downstage:

No, no, I don't like what's goin' on here. There's no sense to what you're doin'. I'm keepin' out of it; I'll have no part of such goings-on.

Shaking his head in disapproval, he exits right.

During the looting, "Red" Becker has taken Dreissiger's portrait down from the easel. Now he stands near the window and studies it mockingly: "So . . . here he is . . . here he is." He tosses the picture out the window.

Moritz Jaeger appears in the Main Door.

Where did he go?

BECKER (*Quietly, in a controlled voice*): Where's the slavedriver?

Wittig the blacksmith enters the door stage right:

He's gone! He got away!

BECKER: Pfeifer too?

All the weavers, not violently but with repressed emotion, quickly call out: "Get Peifer! Look for Pfeifer!"

Some of the weavers hastily exit right with Becker. On stage are Old Baumert, who is drinking coffee, Moritz Jaeger, Old Ansorge, who is gazing at the mirror in mute bewilderment, and several of the weavers' wives.

Baumert gets up from the footstool, lets the cup fall to the floor, and staggers stage left. He is half drunk:

Find Pfeifer! Tell him there's a weaver here for him to starve!

Moritz Jaeger holds a piece of broken easel in his hand:

If we can't lay hands on that dirty dog Dreissiger (*smashing the large chandelier with a club*) at least we'll make him poor. Ya, we'll see to that!

BAUMERT: As poor as a church mouse . . . that's what we'll make him!

Old Ansorge sits down on a footstool in front of the mirror and seems to be in a daze as he looks at everything going on around him.

"Red" Becker enters Door 2 stage right with the other weavers: "Stop!" They all gather around him. He speaks in a low voice but with intense energy and concentration:

That's enough here. We've only just begun. From here we'll go straight to Bielau, to Ditrich's, where the power-looms are. These factories . . . they're the cause of all our troubles.

He exits through the Main Door. They all follow him. When they get outside, they begin to sing the weaver's song. Old Ansorge remains on stage, sitting in front of the mirror. Women come out of the next room with bolts of cloth, which they roll across the floor. When Ansorge begins speaking, they stop what they are doing and gaze blankly at him.

ANSORGE: Who am I? Anton Ansorge, the weaver. Has he gone crazy—Old Ansorge? Sure enough, my head's spinnin' round and round like a top. Be off with you, you rebel upstarts! Off with your heads, off with your legs, off with your hands!

He gets up, looks into the mirror, then says menacingly:

   If you take my house, I'll take your house. (*He beats against the mirror with his fists*) Take this! And this!

He smashes the mirror to bits. Lights out.
(Curtain)

Translated by Joseph M. Bernstein

BERTOLT BRECHT

(1898-1956)

Model for

Mother Courage and Her Children *Scenes XI and XII*

These Notes were first published in German as a separate booklet, to go along with the text of the play and a book of photographs of the Berlin production, by Henschelverlag, East Berlin, 1958, under the general title of **Courage-Modell** *1949.*

They are chiefly notes on the production that opened at the Deutsches Theater, Berlin, January 11, 1949, with Helene Weigel, the playwright's wife, in the title role. Brecht later added some comments on the restaging of the play which opened at the Deutsches Theater September 11, 1951, with a partly changed company. In the autumn of 1950 Brecht staged his play at the Kammerspiele in Munich with Therese Giehse as Mother Courage, a production also referred to in the Notes.

Pertinent questions on the use of the Model put to Brecht by the Wuppertal stage director Winds follow the Notes.

ELEVENTH SCENE

Dumb Kattrin Saves the City of Halle

The city of Halle is to be taken by surprise. Soldiers force a young peasant to show them the way. A peasant and his wife ask Kattrin to

Bertolt Brecht: *Anmerkungen Mutter Courage und ihre Kinder.* East Berlin: Henschelverlag Kunst und Gesellschaft, 1961, pp. 47-57. By permission of Henschelverlag.

pray with them for the city of Halle. The dumb girl climbs onto the roof of the stable and beats the drum in order to awaken the city of Halle. Neither the offer to spare her mother in the city, nor the threat to smash the wagon keep Kattrin from going on drumming. Dumb Kattrin's death.

BASIC ARRANGEMENT

The city of Halle is to be taken by surprise. Soldiers force a young peasant to show them the way. A Lieutenant and two soldiers enter a farm during the night. They fetch the drowsy peasants, and Kattrin from her wagon. By threatening to cut down the only ox, they force the young peasant to guide them. (They lead him to the back, all exit to the right.)

Peasant and wife ask Kattrin to pray with them for the city of Halle. The peasant props a ladder against the stable (right), climbs up, and sees that the woods are teeming with soldiers. Climbing down, he and his wife say that they must not endanger themselves by an attempt to warn the city. The woman goes up to Kattrin (downstage right), asks her to beg God to help the city; and they and the peasant kneel down to pray.

The dumb girl climbs onto the roof of the stable and beats the drum in order to awaken the city of Halle. From the peasant woman's prayer Kattrin learns that the children of the city of Halle are in danger. Stealthily she fetches a drum from the wagon, the same one that she had brought back when she was disfigured, and climbs onto the stable roof with it. She starts drumming. In vain the peasants try to keep her quiet.

Neither the offer to spare her mother in the city, nor the threat to smash the wagon keeps Kattrin from going on drumming. Upon hearing the drum, the Lieutenant and the soldiers come running back with the young peasant; the soldiers post themselves in front of the wagon; and the Lieutenant threatens the peasants with his sword. One of the soldiers steps into the middle of the stage in order to make promises to the drumming girl; and after him the Lieutenant. The peasant runs up to a tree (downstage left) and hits it with an axe, in order to drown the noise of the drum. Kattrin emerges victorious from this competition in noise. The Lieutenant wants to enter the house to set it on fire; the peasant woman points to the wagon. One of the soldiers forces the young peasant to deal blows to the wagon by kicking him. The other soldier is sent to get a musket. He sets it up, and the Lieutenant orders him to fire.

Death of Dumb Kattrin. Kattrin falls forward, the drumsticks in her faltering hands strike one more blow and a weaker afterblow. For a moment the Lieutenant triumphs; then the guns of Halle answer, taking up the rhythm of the drum beats of Dumb Kattrin.

Bad comedians always laugh, bad tragedians always cry

In playing funny as well as sad scenes, everything depends on a blending of precision and casualness, on the assurance of a nimble wrist in handling the story within the arrangement. The actors take their places and form their groups very much in the manner in which marbles, scattered, fall into hollowed-out parts of wooden trays in some roulette-like toys. In such a game, it is not predetermined which marble will fall into which hole, whereas in theatrical arrangement it only *seems* not to be predetermined. The rigidity and heaviness which generally prevails during sad scenes in Germany stems from the fact that for no good reason *the human body is forgotten.* The actors seem to be seized with a muscle cramp. What nonsense!

The two fears of Dumb Kattrin

Her dumbness does not help Kattrin one bit—war holds out a drum to her. With the unsold drum, she has to climb to the stable roof to save the children of the city of Halle.

It is necessary to steer free of the heroic cliché. Two fears fill Dumb Kattrin: for the city of Halle, and for herself.

"The dramatic scene"

The drum scene excited the audience in a special manner. This was sometimes explained by the fact that this is the most dramatic scene of the play, and that the audience preferred the dramatic to the epic. Actually, Epic Theater is able to present much more than agitated events, clashes, complots, mental tortures, etc., but it is also able to represent these. Spectators may identify themselves with Dumb Kattrin in this scene; they may project their personality into this creature; and may happily feel that such forces are present in them, too. They will, however, not have been able to project in this manner throughout every bit of the play; hardly, e.g., in the first scenes.

Alienation

If one wants to keep the scene free from wild excitement on the stage—excitement that spells destruction to whatever is remarkable in the scene—one must carry out certain "alienations" especially carefully.

E.g., the conversation of the peasants about the surprise attack is in danger of being simply sympathized with, if it is part of a general turmoil. It would not show how they justify their doing nothing and assure each other of the necessity of doing nothing—so that the only "action" possible is prayer.

Therefore the actors were told, during rehearsals, to add after their lines "said the man," "said the woman." As follows:

" 'The watchman will give warning,' said the woman."
" 'They must have killed the watchman,' said the man."
" 'If only there were more of us,' said the woman."
" 'But being that we are alone with that cripple,' said the man."
" 'There is nothing we can do, is there?' said the woman."
" 'Nothing,' said the man." Etc.

Dumb Kattrin's drumming

The drumming is interrupted since Kattrin always keeps an eye on the events in the farm. The interruptions come in after:

"Heavens, what is she doing?"

"I'll cut you all to bits."
"Listen you! We have an idea—for your own good."
"No wonder with your face!"
"We must set fire to the farm."

DETAILS DURING STORMY SCENES

Scenes like the one in which the peasant tries to drown Kattrin's drumming by chopping wood must be acted out fully. While drumming, Kattrin must look down at the peasant and must take up the challenge. A certain persistency in directing is needed to make such pantomimes last long enough in stormy scenes.

A DETAIL

Hurwicz showed increasing exhaustion while drumming.

CEREMONIAL CHARACTER OF DESPAIR

The lamentations of the peasant woman whose son the soldiers take away and whose farm they threaten must sound somewhat hackneyed. They must be somewhat of a "generally accepted form of reaction" at the time when Dumb Kattrin begins her act of waking and drumming. The war has lasted a long time. Lamenting, begging and informing have become rigid forms: this is the way to behave when the soldiery appears.

It pays to forego the "immediate impression" of the apparently unique, actual horror in order to reach more subtle strata of horror where frequent, ever repeated misfortune has forced man to formalize his defensive gestures—though of course, he cannot substitute these gestures for real fear. Fear must show through the ceremony in this scene.

TO ACT OLD AGE

During a tour, a very young actress had the opportunity to play the peasant woman of the 11th scene—who is at least forty, but probably prematurely aged, as befits her class. In such cases one usually tries (wrongly) to produce from the start the image of old age by changing one's voice and gestures. Instead, one should assume that the lines and attitudes are those of a forty-year-old woman in the text and one should simply work out, from the text, one sound after the next and one gesture after the next, and should be assured that the image of a forty-year-old will eventually emerge by virtue of this inductive method. The "age" of the peasant woman was created through the disfigurings and rapes that she was exposed to, the miscarriages and processions behind the coffins of little children, hard labor during childhood, physical abuse from parents and husband, psychic abuse from clergy, the necessity of boot-licking and snivelling, etc. This way only, by being herself raped and informed on, could she turn into an informer and opportunist. On account of the actress's youth it was difficult for her during rehearsals to hit the mark in kneeling down to pray in that wretchedly routine fashion, or in kneeling down to whimper for mercy. To her, whining and kneeling down were one thing, but the peasant woman had first to kneel down, and then whine—the whole action being a deliberate production put on regularly. While praying, she had to strike a pose that was to her as comfortable as possible—putting one knee on the ground first (careful not to chafe it), then the other one, and then the hands folded over her belly. Besides, it must be an act of leading in prayer. The peasant woman is teaching the stranger how to pray. In doing this, the actress had a very good thought that made her "older" than an artificial change of voice could have made her. After the treacherous little dialogue in which the peasant and his wife assure each other that they could do nothing for the threatened city, she saw Dumb Kattrin standing there, motionless. She shuffled up to her, looking reproachfully at her: "Pray, poor wretch, pray!"—as if she accused the stranger of an unforgivable omission, of an unwillingness to do anything. The act of prayer consisted of the usual vapid bleating: the soothing sound of one's own voice, the cadence learned from clergymen, which express submission to all heavenly decrees . . . But, when describing the enemies moving toward the city, she made it clear that she well realized what was going on—thereby making her indifference all the more a crime—and toward the end of the prayer she almost prayed "genuinely": praying, so to speak, made her more pious. All this is usually not within the scope of young people, but the actress managed to age visibly and gradually by absorbing the reality of her lines and gestures. Or rather, she allowed herself *to be aged.* Of course, the director has to judge objectively and honestly the final result of such methods, and, in case the necessary age has not been reached, must recast the role without delay.

When Regine Lutz played the camp whore Yvette Pottier, who marries the colonel, it was also a matter of having the age of the colonel's widow emerge from the story, as a very special kind of age. She showed Yvette as a creature whom war has turned into a whore, and whom whoring has made a rich colonel's wife. She showed how much the rise cost. She has aged prematurely, way ahead of her years. Stuffing herself and giving orders are the only pleasures she has left. These pleasures have disfigured her completely. She waddles and carries her belly before her as a sight for sore eyes. Her contemptuously drawn mouth (corners pulled down) reveal the degree of her besottedness: she grasps for air like a codfish on dry land. With the urge for revenge that is typical of old unhappy people she barks at the Cook. But even now, this grotesquely deformed person lets us guess the bygone charm of the camp whore.

In the same fashion the young Käthe Reichel tried the role of the tradeswoman who, together with her son, tries to sell housewares to Courage in the 8th scene. Since this scene describes the reaction of several people to the news that peace has been concluded, she solved her problem within the short space of this scene by showing the somewhat slow reactions of an elderly person. When the call "Peace" sounded from far away, she pushed her kerchief from one ear with her hand. This gave the impression not so much of deafness as of a mental seclusion from the world around her, such as one finds with old people. Her head followed with jerky movements the words of the people around her, as if she were trying to form an opinion from their opinions.

She comprehends the fact that there is peace, and she faints with joy. But she hurries to regain her composure so as to be able to go home quickly. She leaves, short as she is, taking long strides, the way elderly people walk who have to economize on energy.

THE LIEUTENANT IN THE NEW PRODUCTION

was the kicking soldier of the 4th scene. Courage's lesson and several other lessons seem to have been effective: the great capitulation has turned this man into a void, cold, and brutal officer. He can be recognized (from his old role), if at all, through his words "I am an officer, I give you my word," which at one time had read "I've done something special, I want my reward."

Dumb Kattrin wears him out completely. In his desperation, he stops yelling at his men, and begs them for advice instead. When the cannons of the city that has been awakened by the drum start roaring he sits down and beats the ground with his fists like a child.

THE SOLDIERS IN THE NEW PRODUCTION

show complete apathy. They leave excitement over the escapade to the officer. The action of Dumb Kattrin makes an impression on them, too. They relish the defeat of their officer; they grin when he is not looking. The soldier who has to fetch the musket trots with the well-known kind of tardiness that cannot be proven. Nevertheless, he fires. These soldiers do not resemble the Chinese volunteers in Korea about whom the West German *Spiegel* wrote: "The Chinese dashed into the mine fields of the Americans. The soldiers of the first waves let themselves be torn to bits by the exploding mines so that those behind them could break through. Bunches of dead or dying Chinese hung on the American barbed wire. The flabbergasted GI's thought the attackers had been doped. (They were all sober, as examinations of prisoners revealed.)"

TWELFTH SCENE

Courage Moves On

The peasants have to convince Courage that Kattrin is dead. Kattrin's lullaby. Mother Courage pays for Kattrin's funeral and re-

ceives the expressions of sympathy of the peasants. Mother Courage harnesses herself to her empty covered wagon. Still hoping to get back into business, she follows the tattered army.

BASIC ARRANGEMENT

The wagon stands on the empty stage. Mother Courage holds dead Kattrin's head in her lap. The peasants stand at the foot of the dead girl, huddled together and hostile. Courage talks as if her daughter were only sleeping, and deliberately overhears the reproach of the peasants that she was to blame for Kattrin's death.

Kattrin's lullaby. The mother's face is bent low over the face of the daughter. The song does not conciliate those who listen.

Mother Courage pays for Kattrin's funeral and receives expressions of sympathy from the peasants. After she has realized that her last child is dead, Courage gets up laboriously and hobbles around the corpse (right), along the footlights, behind the wagon. She returns with a tent cloth, and answers over her shoulder the peasant's question whether she had no one to turn to: "Oh yes, one. Eilif." And places the cloth over the body, with her back toward the footlights. At the head of the corpse, she pulls the cloth all the way over the face, then again takes her place behind the corpse. The peasant and his son shake hands with her and bow ceremoniously before carrying the body out (to the right). The peasant woman, too, shakes hands with Courage, walks to the right and stops once more, undecided. The two women exchange a few words, then the peasant woman exits.

Mother Courage harnesses herself to her empty covered wagon. Still hoping to get back into business, she follows the tattered army. Slowly, the old woman walks to the wagon, rolls up the rope which Dumb Kattrin had been pulling to this point, takes a stick, looks at it, slips it through the sling of the second rope, tucks the stick under her arm, and starts pulling. The turntable begins to move, and Courage circles the stage once. The curtain closes when she is upstage right for the second time.

THE PEASANTS

The attitude of the peasants toward Courage is hostile. She got them into difficulties, and they will be saddled with her if she does not catch up with the regiments. Besides, she is to blame for the accident herself, in their opinion. And moreover the canteen woman is not part of the resident population, and now, in time of war, she belongs to the fleecers, cutthroats, and marauders in the wake of the armies. When they condole with her by shaking her hand, they merely follow custom.

THE BOW

During this entire scene, Weigel, as Courage, showed an almost animal indifference. All the more beautiful was the deep bow that she made when the body was carried away.

THE LULLABY

The lullaby must be sung without sentimentality and without the desire to arouse sentimentality. Otherwise, its significance does not get across. The thought that is the basis of this song is a murderous one: the child of this mother was supposed to be better off than other children of other mothers. Through a slight stress on the "you," Weigel revealed the treacherous hope of Courage to get her child, and perhaps only hers, through the war alive. The child to whom the most common things were denied was promised the uncommon.

PAYING FOR THE FUNERAL

Even when paying for the funeral, Weigel gave another hint at the character of Courage. She fished a few coins from her leather purse, put one back, and gave the rest to the peasant. The overpowering impression she gave of having been destroyed was not in the least diminished by this.

THE LAST VERSE

While Courage slowly harnessed herself to her wagon, the last verse of her song was sung from the box in which the band had been placed. It expresses one more time her undestroyed hope to get something out of war anyway. It becomes more impressive in that it does not aim at the illusion that the song is actually sung by army units moving past in the distance.

Giehse in the role of courage

When covering up the body, Giehse put her head under the cloth, looking at her daughter one more time, before finally dropping it over her face.

Before she began pulling away her covered wagon—another beautiful variant—she looked into the distance, to figure out where to go, and before she started pulling, she blew her nose with her index finger.

Take your time

At the end of the play it is necessary that one see the wagon roll away. Naturally, the audience gets the idea when the wagon starts. If the movement is extended, a moment of irritation arises ("that's long enough, now"). If it is prolonged even further, deeper understanding sets in.

Pulling the wagon in the last scene

For the 12th scene, farm house and stable with roof (of the 11th scene) were cleared away, and only the wagon and Dumb Kattrin's body were left. The act of dragging the wagon off—the large letters "Saxony" were pulled up (out of sight) when the music begins—took place on a completely empty stage: whereby one remembered the setting of the first scene. Courage and her wagon moved in a complete circle on the revolving stage. She passed the footlights once more. As usual, the stage was bathed in light.

Discoveries of the realists

Wherein lies the effectiveness of Weigel's gesture when she mechanically puts one coin back into her purse, after having fished her money out, as she hands the peasant the funeral money for dead Kattrin? She shows that this tradeswoman, in all her grief, does not completely forget to count, since money is so hard to come by. And she shows this as a discovery about human nature that is shaped by certain conditions. This little feature has the power and the suddenness of a discovery. The art of the realists consists of digging out the truth from under the rubble of the evident, of connecting the particular with the general, of pinning down the unique within the larger process.

A CHANGE OF TEXT

After "I'll manage, there isn't much in it now," Courage added, in the Munich and then also in the Berlin production: "I must start up again in business."

MOTHER COURAGE LEARNS NOTHING

In the last scene, Weigel's Courage appeared like an eighty-year-old woman. And she comprehends nothing. She reacts only to the statements that are connected with war, such as that one must not remain behind. She overhears the crude reproach of the peasants that Kattrin's death was her fault.

Courage's inability to learn from the unproductiveness of war was a prophecy in the year 1938 when the play was written. At the Berlin production in 1948 the desire was voiced that Courage should at least come to a realization in the play. To make it possible for the spectator to get something out of this realistic play, i.e., to make the spectator learn a lesson, theaters have to arrive at an acting style that does not seek an identification of the spectator with the protagonist.

Judging on the basis of reports of spectators and newspaper reviews, the Zurich world premiere—although artistically on a high level—presented only the image of war as a natural catastrophe and an inevitable fate, and thereby it underscored to the middle-class spectator in the orchestra his own indestructibility, his ability to survive. But even to the likewise middle-class Courage, the decision "Join in or don't join in" was always left open in the play. The production, it seems, must also have presented Courage's business dealings, profiteering, willingness to take risks, as quite natural, "eternally human" behavior, so that she had no other choice. Today, it is true, the man of the middle class can no longer stay out of war, as Courage could have. To him, a production of the play can probably teach nothing but a real hatred of war, and a certain insight into the fact that the big deals of which war consists are not made by the little people. In that sense, the play is more of a lesson than reality is, because here in the play the situation of war is more of an experimental situation, made for the sake of insights. I.e., the spectator attains the attitude of a student—as long as the acting style is correct. The part of the audience that belongs to the proletariat, i.e., the class that actually can struggle against and overcome war, should be given insight into the connection between business and war (again provided the acting style is correct): the proletariat as a class can do away with war by doing away with capitalism. Of course, as far as the proletarian part of the audience is concerned, one must also take into consideration the fact that this class is busy drawing its own conclusions—inside as well as outside the theater.

THE EPIC ELEMENT

The Epic element was certainly visible in the production at the *Deutsches Theater*—in the arrangement, in the presentation of the characters, in the minute execution of details, and in the pacing of the entire play. Also, contradictory elements were not eliminated but stressed, and the parts, visible as such, made a convincing whole. However, the goal of Epic Theater was not reached. Much became clear, but clarification was in the end absent. Only in a few recasting-rehearsals did it clearly emerge, for then the actors were only "pretending," i.e., they only showed to the newly-added colleague the positions and intonations, and then the whole thing received that preciously loose, unlabored, non-urgent element that incites the spectator to have his own independent thoughts and feelings.

That the production did not have an Epic foundation was never remarked, however: which was probably the reason the actors did not dare provide one.

CONCERNING THE NOTES THEMSELVES

We hope that the present notes, offering various explanations and inventions essential to the production of a play, will not have an air of spurious seriousness. It is admittedly hard to establish the lightness and casualness that are of the essence of theater. The arts, even when they are instructive, are forms of amusement.

Translated by Eric Bentley and Hugo Schmidt

The Use of the Epic Model

WINDS: You have made the entire Model of the Berlin production available for the local rehearsals of *Mother Courage*. Your representative Frau Berlau has given me and the stage manager, the stage designer, and the actors a thorough briefing on your wishes. They were further elucidated by a great number of stage photos with explanatory texts and your written instructions to the directors. Since, in general, it is not customary theater practice for an author to exert such a strong and detailed influence on the performance, and since we here in Wuppertal are trying this experiment for the first time in this distinct form, it would be of interest to know your reasons for bringing out a Model and establishing this as a standard for other rehearsals .

BRECHT: In and by itself *Mother Courage and Her Children* can also be performed in the old style. (The theater indeed can perform everything from *Oedipus* to Hauptmann's *Beaver Coat,* for instance, not in consequence of a powerful style of its own which melts down the products of so many cultures, but in consequence of the lack of any style of its own.) What indeed would be lost thereby would be the special effects of such a play, which would also fail in its social function. If one had left coach-drivers alone with an auto their first remark would probably have been: "And this is supposed to be something new?" Whereupon they would have harnessed eight horses

Theaterarbeit. Dresden: VVV Dresdner Verlag, 1952, 309-314 *passim.*

and taken off. There is no pure theoretical approach to the methods of the epic theater; at best it is a practical copying linked to the effort to find out the reasons for the groupings, movements, and gestures. Probably one must have made a copy before one can himself make a Model. . . .

WINDS: Isn't there a danger that through the Model, as you understand it, a certain artistic freedom will be lost in initiating creative scenic figuration?

BRECHT: The complaint of the loss of freedom of artistic expression is to be expected in an age of anarchistic production. Nevertheless even in our time there is a continuity in development. For example, the acceptance of advances, the standard, in technology and science. And if we look more closely into the matter, the "freely creating" artists of the theater are not especially free. Usually they are the last who are able to free themselves from centuries-old prejudices, contentions, complexes. Above all they stand in a relation of undignified dependence upon "their" public. They must unconditionally hold its attention, "put it in a state of suspense"; which means to set up the first scenes in such a way that the public "buys" the final ones, to apply psychic messages to it, to divine its taste and to accommodate oneself to it accordingly. In short, it is not they themselves whom their activity must amuse, instead they must build according to alien standards. At bottom, our theaters are still in the position of a purveyor vis-a-vis the public. How can there be any freedom that might be lost here? At best, perhaps, that of ferreting out the way in which the public may be served.

WINDS: And isn't there also the danger that the Model may lead to a certain routinization and stiffness so that the performance merely has the significance of a copy?

BRECHT: We must free ourselves from the present contempt for copying. It is not the "easier" thing. It is not a shame but an art. This means that it must be developed into an art, and indeed, so that no routinization sets in. Take my own experience with copying: as a playwright I have copied Japanese, Greek, and Elizabethan drama; as a stage manager I have copied the arrangements of the folk-comedian Karl Valentin and Caspar Neher's scene-sketches, and I have not felt unfree. Give me a reasonable Model of *King Lear* and I will take delight in building according to it. What difference does it make if in the text of the play you find that Courage has given the peasants money for Dumb Kattrin's burial before she goes away, or further that by a study of the model you learn that she has counted the money out in her hand and put a coin back in her leather bag? In fact, you find only the first in the text of the play, the second in the model with Weigel. Should you keep the first and forget the second? After all we give the theater only copies of human behavior. The groupings and the way in which the groups are moved are statements on human behavior. Hence our theater is already not realistic because it underestimates observation. Our actors look inside themselves instead of upon their environment. They take the goings-on between people, on which everything depends, as a vehicle for the display of temperament, etc. The directors utilize the play as an inspiration for their "vision," even the new ones which are not visions but accounts of reality. We should put an end to this today rather than tomorrow. Naturally artistic copying must first be learned, exactly like the construction of Models. In order to be able to be imitated the Models must be imitable. The inimitable must be disengaged from the exemplary. There is such a thing, after all, as a slavish and sovereign imitation. Whereby care must be taken that the latter does not contain, for instance, a "similarity." That is quantitatively less. Practically speaking it will suffice if the arrangement which tells the story in the Model is used as a point of departure for the work of rehearsal. Entirely apart from the fact that arrangements which tell the story are not common among our stage directors and that even the social function of these stories of the new plays are unknown to them and in part unappealing, it is high time that in the theater we arrive at a way of working that is in keeping with our epoch. In short, a way of working that is collective and collates all experiences. We must attain an ever closer description of reality, and, viewed aesthetically, this is always a more delicate and powerful description. This can happen only if we utilize achievements already made, but of course, do not stop there. The changes of Models which should ensue only in order to make the representation of reality more exact, more differentiated, artistically more fanciful and charming for the purpose of influencing reality, will be all the more expressive, thereby, since they present a negation of what exists—this for those who know dialectics.

WINDS: In your stage directions for *Mother Courage* you also make mention of the Epic Theater or the Epic style of presentation. May I ask you to enlighten me briefly on this? Doubtlessly not only stage artists but the whole public interested in the theater would like to learn more about this.

BRECHT: It's extremely difficult to give a brief description of the Epic style of play production. Where it is attempted it generally leads to erroneous vulgarization. (It appears to involve an eradication of emotional, individual, and dramatic elements, etc.) A somewhat more detailed explanation can be found in *Versuche*.[1] I should also like to point out that this acting style is still in a developmental state. To put it more exactly, it is in its beginning stage and still requires the cooperation of many others.

WINDS: Do you believe that the Epic style is to be considered only in connection with *Mother Courage* as a chronicle, or does it have a practical significance for our whole contemporary theater work? For example, can it also be applied to the classics and to plays of the turn of the century?

BRECHT: An Epic acting style is not to be considered in the same way for all classics. It seems to be most applicable, that is to say it promises results sooner, with works like that of Shakespeare and the first works of our classics (*Faust* included).

Translated by Salvator Attanasio

---

1 *Versuche*, Vols. I-VII, published by Gustav Kiepenheur, Berlin (out of print since 1933). Vol. VIII reached proof stage only. Vols. IX-XV published by Suhrkamp Verlag, Berlin. They contain poems and essays as well as plays.

JEAN-LOUIS BARRAULT

(b. 1910)

Mise en Scène of

Phaedra, *Act II, Scene V*

In Reflections on the Theatre, *Jean-Louis Barrault writes about* Phaedra: *"A classic is like a hidden treasure. Its core is buried under so many layers of varnish, so many polishings, that it can be reached only by patience and infiltration. But once it is reached—or once we think it is—there are dazzling riches to be discovered at every turn. Its resources are inexhaustible." With the "methods and tenacity of a speleologist" Barrault has explored the depths of Racine in his* Mise en scène *and Commentary for* Phaedra *(1944), one of the excellent volumes in the French series* Mises en scène. *There he discusses the stage history of the play, special rehearsal problems centering primarily on delivery and gesture, and his "symphonic" arrangement of the scenes, as the background to his elaborate commentary which accompanies the text.*

(HIPPOLYTUS, PHAEDRA, OENONE)

Third Part

Phaedra—Phaedra the widow, Phaedra the free—comes forward. Silence during which Hippolytus stands downstage left center like an attractive statue, like a young tiger with an inscrutable look.

Jean Racine: *Phèdre, mise en scène et commentaires de Jean-Louis Barrault.* Paris: Editions du Seuil, 1946, 118-129. By permission of Editions du Seuil, Paris. (Translation of *Phaedra* text by Robert Henderson from *Masterworks of World Literature,* Vol. II, 362-366, Dryden Press, New York, 1955.)

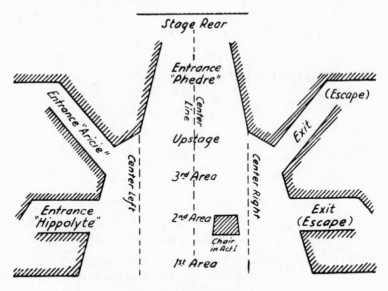

SETTING

PHAEDRA (*To Oenone*):   Look, I see him!

> My blood forgets to flow,—tongue will not speak
> What I have come to say!

First Movement

Phaedra almost stumbles. Without looking at Oenone, but clinging to her, she murmurs her lines. Oenone supports her, standing face to face with her but without looking at her either. Oenone utters her reply out of the corner of her mouth.

OENONE: Think of your son.

> And think that all his hopes depend on you.

A pause during which Hippolytus bows while Phaedra advances, then straightens up again, mustering all his energy. The first phase of the scene is completely symmetrical with the first phase of the preceding scene. It is characterized by the effort made by the characters to maintain an "official" tone and to discuss "affairs of state."

PHAEDRA: They tell me that you leave us, hastily.

> I come to add my own tears to your sorrow,
> And I would plead my fears for my young son.

Since Hippolytus had made use of his father, Phaedra now tried to plead
for her son. Breathing pause. Inner conflict.

> He has no father, now; 'twill not be long
> Until the day that he will see my death,
> And even now, his youth is much imperiled
> By a thousand foes.

Breathing pause. Inner conflict, change of timbre.

> You only can defend him.

Breathing pause. Inner conflict, artificiality in the official tone.

> And in my inmost heart, remorse is stirring,—
> Yes, and fear, too, lest I have shut your ears
> Against his cries; I fear that your just anger
> May, before long, visit on him that hatred
> His mother earned.

HIPPOLYTUS: Madam, you need not fear.
> Such malice is not mine.

Hippolytus, motionless, is polite but cold. His having spoken makes Phaedra draw closer to Oenone. She leans on the latter in order not to collapse.

PHAEDRA: I should not blame you
> If you should hate me; I have injured you.
> So much you know;—you could not read my heart.

Phaedra's words give the impression that she no longer knows where she is;
that she is torn by inner conflict and is trying to control herself.

> Yes, I have tried to be your enemy,
> For the same land could never hold us both.
> In private and abroad I have declared it;—
> I was your enemy! I found no peace
> Till seas had parted us; and I forbade
> Even your name to be pronounced to me.

She smiles bitterly, then suddenly she grows serious and moving. This whole scene must be played subtly. While exuding sensuality, the characters must lose nothing of their grandeur and nobility; and even when they give the impression of being "right next to each other," they are really from two to three feet apart. With this in mind, their explanations must come from within, yet they must not forget their sense of dignity.

> And yet, if punishment be meted out
> Justly, by the offense;—if only hatred
> Deserves a hate, then never was there woman
> Deserved more pity, and less enmity.

HIPPOLYTUS: A mother who is jealous for her children
> Will seldom love the children of a mother
> Who came before her. Torments of suspicion
> Will often follow on a second marriage.
> Another would have felt that jealousy
> No less than you; perhaps more violently.

Polite and cold, yet, in spite of himself, full of charm.

PHAEDRA: Ah, prince, but Heaven made me quite exempt
> From what is usual, and I can call
> That Heaven as my witness! 'Tis not this—
> No, quite another ill devours my heart!

During his reply, Hippolytus has been charming in his sincerity. Phaedra has turned around. She is lashed by her passion. Her voice is in her throat. All her blood literally races at the charm of Hippolytus' voice. The "Ah" she utters is a cry of suffering. She leans more and more on Oenone, who stands there stolidly like an executioner's stake.

HIPPOLYTUS: This is no time for self-reproaching, madam.

Seeing Phaedra's "drawn" features, which he misinterprets, Hippolytus takes a step toward her. In order to move out of his way, she turns lightly on herself . . . and faces forward.

> Perhaps your husband still beholds the light,
> Perhaps he may be granted safe return
> In answer to our prayers; his guarding god
> Is Neptune, whom he never called in vain.

*Jean Hugo's décor for the Barrault production of **Phaedra**.*

Hippolytus' candor and purity are more and more alluring. This power of attraction is Phaedra's undoing. The latter utters virtually a curse against Theseus. Hard-faced, she expresses her regret which sounds like a wish.

PHAEDRA: He who has seen the mansions of the dead
Returns not thence. Since Theseus has gone
Once to those gloomy shores, we need not hope,
For Heaven will not send him back again.
Prince,

Ten syllables for her to turn her head toward Hippolytus.

there is no release from Acheron;—

A short pause during which the entire theater—that is, reality, or better still, the present—reappears, tense and motionless. A change of timbre. Phaedra is drawn toward Hippolytus—where does she find the strength to tear herself away from Oenone and to advance slowly toward him? Their two faces are riveted to each other; their two breaths draw closer.

It is a greedy maw,—and yet I think
He lives and breathes in you,—and still I see him
Before me here; I seem to speak to him—
My heart—!

Their two breaths are almost one.

My heart—!

Her voice breaks off. Phaedra, terrified, flees wildly toward the imperturbable Oenone (who seems more and more like the statue of Fate). Clinging to her, Phaedra reminds one of a criminal who cannot, who dares not commit his crime.

Oh, I am mad! Do what I will,
I cannot hide my passion.

HIPPOLYTUS: Yes, I see
What strange things love will do, for Theseus, dead,
Seems present to your eyes, and in your soul
A constant flame is burning.

Hippolytus is now filled with compassion for this queen wracked with sorrow. He is all the more compassionate in that he himself is happy; he has not been happy for long, of course, but right now he feels a fresh access of happiness. Happiness makes people generous: hence Hippolytus comes up to Phaedra, leans over her, his face above her face. Misinterpreting the situation, he is attentive to Phaedra, exciting her passion all the more.

PHAEDRA: Ah, for Theseus
       I languish and I long,

Phaedra, still leaning on Oenone, has only to turn her head to have her mouth and eyes right beneath Hippolytus' mouth and eyes. She does this slowly, sensually, as she utters the line: "Ah, for Theseus I languish and I long." At the same time, her eyes and the timbre of her voice cause Hippolytus to draw back slightly.

                               but not, indeed,
       As the Shades have seen him,

For the second time Phaedra can no longer resist Hippolytus' power of attraction. She advances as if magnetically drawn toward him. This is a situation in which the actors' movements are of great plastic interest. Phaedra, during this soliloquy which is not a "recitative" but a "period," does not advance *voluntarily* toward Hippolytus (which would give a confusing and uncalled-for impression of a threat); she advances because Hippolytus *voluntarily* draws back and *involuntarily* draws her toward himself. Hippolytus draws back, *then* Phaedra advances in spite of herself toward him. So Hippolytus has withdrawn slightly. She straightens up.

                         as the fickle lover
       Of a thousand forms, the one who fain would ravish
       The bride of Pluto;—but one faithful, proud,

She advances.

       Even to slight disdain,—the charm of youth

Hippolytus retreats.

       That draws all hearts, even as the gods are painted,—

He stops retreating. From a distance she observes him.

       Or as yourself. He had your eyes, your manner,—
       He spoke like you, and he could blush like you,
       And when he came across the waves to Crete,

My childhood home, worthy to win the love
Of Minos' daughters—what were you doing then?
Why did my father gather all these men,
The flower of Greece, and leave Hippolytus?

Again irresistibly drawn, she advances. Oenone begins quietly to move
backstage right, from which position she will keep close watch.

Oh, why were you too young to have embarked
On board the ship that brought your father there?
The monster would have perished at your hands,
Despite the windings of his vast retreat.
My sister would have armed you with the clue
To guide your steps, doubtful within the maze.—
But no—

Phaedra is quite close to him, her face almost touching his; but their two
bodies are still slightly apart from each other.

for Phaedra would have come before her,
And love would first have given me the thought,

Again he retreats.

And I it would have been, whose timely aid
Had taught you all the labyrinthine ways!

(If Hippolytus had accompanied Theseus, he himself would have triumphed
over all the obstacles which Theseus had to overcome, for Phaedra would
have replaced her sister Ariadne at his side and would have helped him in
the episode of the labyrinth.)

The care

He stops retreating, she watches him.

that such a dear life would have cost me!
No thread could satisfy my lover's fears.
I would have wished to lead the way myself,
And share

She advances.

> the peril you were sure to face.
> Yes, Phaedra would have walked the maze with you,—
> With you come out in safety, or have perished!

She is coming right up to him. Now, realizing only too well what is going on, Hippolytus takes two quick steps back. She is silent and her face hardens instantly. Hippolytus has come close to the footlights about two-thirds of the way to the exit stage left. Phaedra stands there—downstage slightly left.

There is an atmosphere of extreme sensuality in this portion of the scene. Phaedra's femininity blossoms out to the outer limits of decency. By a clever and perfidious subterfuge, she leaves us in doubt as to whether she is speaking for herself when she puts herself in Ariadne's place; we do not know if she is playing with Hippolytus or if she is sincere. But we do know that she is displaying all her charm and trying to snare him sensually. Her extreme unrest infects everyone and everything. The air is charged with her images and thoughts; her walk is seductive and tantalizing; her voice is languorous and muffled. Her flesh glistens with passion; the palms of her hands are damp. The air is perfumed with her scent—one can almost perceive the "passion" that grips her. She has just "secreted" all her reserves of seduction.

HIPPOLYTUS: Gods! What is this I hear? Have you forgotten
> That Theseus is my father and your husband?

Hippolytus, the pure and "puritanical" Hippolytus, can no longer believe his eyes. After retreating two steps, "bowled over," he speaks these two lines with a maximum of prudence and caution, in order not to re-arouse her abject passion.

PHAEDRA: Why should you fancy I have lost remembrance
> And that I am regardless of my honor?

Second Movement

Pause. Everyone on stage motionless. The second phase of the scene begins.

It is hard to imagine without a shudder Phaedra's expression at this moment. As a woman, she is now humiliated, crushed. As a queen, she is dying of shame. Already half dead because of this passion which is tearing at her insides, she now stands there, her eyes glassy, her features dangerously hard and implacable. Rigid in her dignity, the unhappy daughter of the Sun is now a potential menace.

If a snapshot of Phaedra were taken at this moment, one would attach to it a sign reading: "Danger! Live Wire!"—like the warnings displayed on high-tension wires. Ashen pale, she proffers her vague and frightening threat.

> HIPPOLYTUS: Forgive me, madam! With a blush I own
> That I mistook your words, quite innocent.
> For very shame I cannot see you longer—

Hippolytus, the pure and candid Hippolytus, has been mistaken. Now it is his turn to feel a sense of shame bordering on utter confusion.

> Now I will go—

He turns around to leave (taking three quick steps upstage).

> PHAEDRA: Ah, prince, you understood me,—

A single cry stops Hippolytus dead in his tracks. It is Phaedra's "Ah." Then her voice grows hoarse, slightly choked up with suffering. But save her maximum of strength for Act IV. Do not force the word "prince"—let it be sufficient unto itself.

It is obvious that we are at the beginning of a recitative. The first three lines of this speech should be spoken with full *emotion*.

> Too well, indeed! For I had said enough.
> You could not well mistake. But do not think
> That in those moments when I love you most

The phrase "I love you most" must long reverberate. As if physically struck by this phrase, Hippolytus takes up his position at the very spot where Aricia had taken refuge a few minutes previously; downstage left, a dark warm corner in which he can conceal his disgust. He reminds one of a Saint Sebastian whom Phaedra is about to pierce with her arrows.

Now comes a leveling-off of emotion.

> I do not feel my guilt. No easy yielding
> Has helped the poison that infects my mind.
> The sorry object of divine revenge,

After bringing Hippolytus to a halt, Phaedra moves freely about and now finds herself in the center of the stage. Oenone is hidden against the set— far upstage right.

I am not half so hateful to your sight
As to myself. The gods will bear me witness,—

Recitative

Here the recitative really begins. Must be spoken in a full, vibrant voice—
a tragedienne's voice—but without false heroics. The grandeur must all
come from within.

They who have lit this fire within my veins,—
The gods who take their barbarous delight
In leading some poor mortal heart astray!
Nay, do you not remember, in the past,

She goes toward him; but if he were not there, and she only imagined him
present, she would speak no differently to him. Hippolytus can no longer
check her flow of words. She speaks to him as to the passive object of her
insane love. No one can stop Phaedra now. She is possessed. The fire is
sweeping the palace.

How I was not content to fly?—I drove you
Out of the land, so that I might appear
Most odious—and to resist you better
I tried to make you hate me—and in vain!
You hated more, and I loved not the less,

Hippolytus, his eyes shut, his features distorted in disgust, the palms of his
hands flattened behind him and resting against the wall, has turned his
face away (so that he now faces the audience).
   Quite close to him now but slightly upstage, Phaedra twists around and
now has her back three-quarters turned to the audience. She seeks out
Hippolytus' eyes.

While your misfortunes lent you newer charms.
I have been drowned in tears and scorched by fire!
Your own eyes might convince you of the truth
If you could look at me, but for a moment!

With an abrupt and savage twist of his neck, Hippolytus turns his head
(looking over her, toward the backdrop).

What do I say?

Now she speaks directly to Hippolytus' breast and heart—as if the latter will listen to her more readily than Hippolytus himself. Ah! If she could only speak as though the problem were solved! The few lines she utters (down through the line: ". . . and came to beg you not to hate him") will be all the more heart-rending if she really *speaks* them. At this moment Phaedra is a wretched woman groveling with desire. The pity she inspires is almost unbearable. This is the most painful moment of all, during which Hippolytus, dismayed, extends his arms as if trying to escape Phaeda vertically.

> You think this vile confession
> That I have made, is what I meant to say?
> I did not dare betray my son. For him
> I feared,—and came to beg you not to hate him.
> This was the purpose of a heart too full
> Of love for you to speak of aught besides.

She also extends her arms—but with longing; and she rears back. Then she straightens up and, about three feet away from him, her body wrenched like a twisted stalk, she says the lines "Take your revenge, and punish me my passion!" to "Does Theseus' widow dare to love his son?" We are at the high point of the recitative. Phaedra appears in all her splendor of a full-blown woman. Young, beautiful, ripe, she is altogether desirable.

> Take your revenge, and punish me my passion!
> Prove yourself worthy of your valiant father,
> And rid the world of an offensive monster!
> Does Theseus' widow dare to love his son?
> Monster indeed!

Finally she runs forward and plants herself right next to him. This time her stomach juts forward. The recitative now gradually declines.

> Nay, let her not escape you!
> Here is my heart!

The recitative has ended. Tragic reality reappears—like a hallucination. Feverish agitation returns. Extreme rapidity of speech. The orchestra plays furiously, the conductor finding it difficult to keep pace with the action.

Oenone slips out of her hiding place.

Phaedra is unchained. As she tears her garments, she uncovers a portion of her breast.

Hippolytus *must* remain absolutely motionless. He must show *absolutely no reaction. Perhaps his surprise accounts for his silence.*

Here is the place to strike!

It is most eager to absolve itself!

It leaps impatiently to meet your blow!—

Strike deep!

While the rest of her speech is given with sweeping gestures, in the last four lines Phaedra advances and turns slowly on herself, her right arm extending toward Hippolytus' left side. As she starts to say "Or if, indeed, you find it shameful . . ." she slowly unsheathes Hippolytus' sword, and suddenly brandishes it; then she takes two steps and cries *with all her might:* "Give it now!"

Or if, indeed, you find it shameful

To drench your hand in such polluted blood,—

If that be punishment too mild for you,—

Too easy for your hate,—if not your arm,

Then lend your sword to me.—Come! Give it now!—

"Give it now!" must resound like a deafening gong.

OENONE: What would you do, my lady? Oh, just gods!

But someone comes;—go quickly. Run from shame.

You cannot fly, if they should find you thus.

(Exeunt Phaedra and Oenone)

"Give it now!" is the cue for Oenone to move forward. She rushes toward Phaedra. At "Oh, just gods!!" she grasps Phaedra's arms. At "But someone comes" she whirls her around. At her physical contact with Oenone, Phaedra seems somehow to become aware of the situation again. Unable to endure it any longer, she almost faints and allows herself to be moved about like a puppet. At "Run from shame" Oenone fastens her grip. Then, as she speaks the last line, Oenone takes (or rather: drags) her away. At ". . . find you thus" the two women are well on their way out (diagonal exit upstage).

(End of Act II)

Translated by Joseph M. Bernstein

ELIA KAZAN

(b. 1909)

Notebook for
A Streetcar Named Desire

The vitality of the characterizations in both the stage and screen versions of A Streetcar Named Desire *derives in large part from a minute analysis of the life of each character before as well as during the actual events of the play. Elia Kazan, originally a versatile Group Theater actor and now one of America's most dynamic directors, applied the Stanislavskian principle of seeking the "spine" of each character. The following selection from the director's private notebook, dated August 1947, was kept before and during the rehearsals of the play. Never intended for public perusal, these unedited creative memoranda reveal a director's intimate search for the inner spirit of a play.*

A thought—directing finally consists of turning Psychology into Behavior.

Theme—this is a message from the dark interior. This little twisted, pathetic, confused bit of light and culture puts out a cry. It is snuffed out by the crude forces of violence, insensibility and vulgarity which exist in our South—and this cry is the play.

Style—one reason a "style," a stylized production is necessary is that a subjective factor—Blanche's memories, inner life, emotions, are a real factor. We cannot really understand her behavior unless we see the effect of her past on her present behavior.

This play is a poetic tragedy. We are shown the final dissolution of a person of worth, who once had great potential, and who, even as she goes down, has worth exceeding that of the "healthy," coarse-grained figures who kill her.

Blanche is a social type, an emblem of a dying civilization, making its last curlicued and romantic exit. All her behavior patterns are those of the dying civilization she represents. In other words her behavior is *social*. Therefore find social modes! This is the source of the play's stylization and the production's style and color. Like-wise Stanley's behavior is *social* too. It is the basic animal cynicism of today. "Get what's coming to you! Don't waste a day! Eat, drink, get yours!" This is the basis of his stylization, of the choice of his props. All props should be stylized: they should have a color, shape and weight that spell: style.

An effort to put poetic names on scenes to edge me into stylizations and physicalizations. Try to keep each scene in terms of Blanche.

1. Blanche comes to the last stop at the end of the line.
2. Blanche tries to make a place for herself.
3. Blanche breaks them apart, but when they come together, Blanche is more alone than ever!
4. Blanche, more desperate because more excluded, tries the direct attack and makes the enemy who will finish her.
5. Blanche finds that she is being tracked down for the kill. She must work fast.
6. Blanche suddenly finds, suddenly makes for herself, the only possible, perfect man for her.
7. Blanche comes out of the happy bathroom to find that her own doom has caught up with her.
8. Blanche fights her last fight. Breaks down. Even Stella deserts her.

9. Blanche's last desperate effort to save herself by telling the whole truth. The *truth dooms her.*
10. Blanche escapes out of this world. She is brought back by Stanley and destroyed.
11. Blanche is disposed of.

The style—the real deep style—consists of one thing only: to find behavior that's truly social, significantly typical, at each moment. It's not so much what Blanche has done—it's how she does it—with such style, grace, manners, old-world trappings and effects, props, tricks, swirls, etc., that they seem anything but vulgar.

And for the other characters, too, you face the same problem. To find the Don Quixote character for them. *This is a poetic tragedy, not a realistic or a naturalistic one. So you must find a Don Quixote scheme of things for each.*

Stylized acting and direction is to realistic acting and direction as poetry is to prose. The acting must be styled, not in the obvious sense. (Say nothing about it to the producer and actors.) But you will fail unless you find this kind of poetic realization for the behavior of these people.

BLANCHE

"Blanche is Desperate"

"This is the End of the Line of the Streetcar Named Desire"

Spine—find Protection: the tradition of the old South says that it must be through another person.

Her problem has to do with her tradition. Her notion of what a woman should be. She is stuck with this "ideal." It is her. It is her ego. Unless she lives by it, she cannot live; in fact her whole life has been for nothing. Even the Alan Gray incident as she now tells it and believes it to have been, is a necessary piece of romanticism. Essentially, in outline, she tells what happened, but it also serves the demands of her notion of herself, to make her *special* and different, out of the tradition of the romantic ladies of the past: Swinburne, Wm. Morris, Pre-Raphaelites, etc. This way it serves as an excuse for a great deal of her behavior.

Because this image of herself cannot be accomplished in reality, certainly not in the South of our day and time, it is her effort and practice to *accomplish it in fantasy*. Everything that she does in *reality* too is colored by this necessity, this compulsion to be *special*. So, in fact, *reality becomes fantasy too*. She makes it so!

The variety essential to the play, and to Blanche's playing and to Jessica Tandy's achieving the role demands that she be a "heavy" at the beginning. For instance: contemplate the inner character contradiction: bossy yet helpless, domineering yet shaky, etc. The audience at the beginning should see her bad effect on Stella, want Stanley to tell her off. He does. He exposes her and then gradually, as they see how genuinely in pain, how actually desperate she is, how warm, tender and loving she can be (the Mitch story), how freighted with need she is—then they begin to go with her. They begin to realize that they are sitting in at the death of something extraordinary . . . colorful, varied, passionate, lost, witty, imaginative, of her own integrity . . . and then they feel the tragedy. In the playing too there can be a growing sincerity and directness.

The thing about the "tradition" in the nineteenth century was that *it worked then*. It made a woman feel important, with her own secure positions and functions, her own special worth. It also made a woman at that time *one with her society*. But *today* the tradition is an anachronism which simply does not function. *It does not work*. So while Blanche must believe it because it makes her special, because it makes her sticking by Belle Reve an act of heroism, rather than an absurd romanticism, still *it does not work*. It makes Blanche feel *alone, outside of her society*. Left out, insecure, shaky. The airs the "tradition" demands isolate her further, and every once in a while, her resistance weakened by drink, she breaks down and seeks human warmth and contact where she can find it, not on her terms, on theirs; the merchant, the traveling salesman and the others . . . among whom the vulgar adolescent soldiers seem the most innocent. Since she cannot integrate these episodes, she rejects them, begins to forget them, begins to live in fantasy, begins to rationalize and explain them to herself thus: "I never was hard or self-sufficient enough . . . men don't see women unless they are in bed with them. They don't admit their existence except when they're love-making. You've got to have your existence admitted by someone if you are going to receive someone's protection," etc. As if you had to apologize for needing human contact! Also n.b. above—the word: protection. That is what she, as a woman in the tradition, so desperately needs. That's what she comes to Stella for, Stella and her husband. Not finding it from them she tries to get it from Mitch. *Protection.* A haven, a *harbor.* She is a refugee, punch drunk, and on the ropes, making her last stand, trying to keep up a gallant front, because she is a proud person. But really if Stella doesn't provide her haven, *where is she to go.* She's a misfit, a liar, her "airs" alienate people, she must act superior to them which alienates them further. She doesn't know how to work. So she can't make a living. She's really helpless. She needs someone to help her. Protection. She's a last dying relic of the last century now adrift in our unfriendly day. From time to time, for reasons of simple human loneliness and need she goes to pieces, smashes her tradition . . . then goes back to it. This conflict has developed into a terrible crisis. All she wants is a haven: "I want to rest! I want to breathe quietly again . . . just think! If it happens! I can leave here and have a home of my own. . . ."

If this is a romantic tragedy, what is its inevitability and what is the tragic flaw? In the Aristotelian sense, the flaw is the need to be superior, special (or *her* need for protection and what it means to her), the "tradition." This creates an apartness so intense, a loneliness so gnawing that only a complete breakdown, a refusal, as it were, to contemplate what she's doing, a *binge* as it were, a destruction of all her standards, a desperate violent ride on the Streetcar Named Desire can break through the walls of her tradition. The tragic flaw creates the circumstances, inevitably, that destroy her. More later.

Try to find an entirely different character, a self-dramatized and self-romanticized character for Blanche to play in each scene. She is playing 11 different people. This will give it a kind of changeable and shimmering surface it should have. And all these 11 self-dramatized and romantic characters should be out of the romantic tradition of the Pre-Bellum South, etc. Example: Sc. 2 Gay Miss Devil-may-care.

There is another, simpler and equally terrible contradiction in her own nature. She won't face her physical or sensual side. She calls it "brutal desire." She thinks she sins when she gives in to it . . . yet she does give in to it, out of loneliness . . . but by calling it "brutal desire," she is able to separate it from her "real self," her "cultured," refined self. Her tradition makes no allowance, allows no space for this very real part of herself. So she is constantly in conflict, not at ease, sinning. *She's still looking for something that doesn't exist today, a gentleman,* who will treat her like a virgin, marry her, protect her, defend and maintain her honor, etc. She wants an old-fashioned wedding dressed in white . . . and still she does things out of "brutal desire" that make this impossible. *All this too is tradition.*

She has worth too—she is better than Stella. She says: "There has been some kind of progress. . . . Such things as art—as poetry and music—such kinds of new light have come into the world . . . in some kinds of people some kinds of tenderer feelings have had some little beginning that we've got to make *grow!* And cling to, and hold as our flag! In this dark march toward whatever it is we're approaching . . . don't . . . don't hang back with the brutes!" And though the direct psychological motivation for this is jealousy and personal frustration, still she, alone and abandoned in the crude society of New Orleans back streets, is the *only voice of light.* It is flickering and, in the course of the play, goes out. But it is valuable because it is unique.

Blanche is a butterfly in a jungle looking for just a little momentary protection, doomed to a sudden, early violent death. The more I work on Blanche, incidentally, the less insane she seems. She is caught in a fatal inner contradiction, but in another society, she *would* work. In Stanley's society, no!

This is like a classic tragedy. Blanche is Medea or someone pursued by the Harpies, the Harpies being *her own nature*. Her inner sickness pursues her like *doom* and makes it impossible for her to attain the one thing she needs, the only thing she needs: a safe harbor.

An effort to phrase Blanche's spine: to find *protection,* to find something to hold onto, some strength in whose protection she can live, like a sucker shark or a parasite. The tradition of *woman* (or all women) can only live through the strength of someone else. Blanche is entirely dependent. Finally the doctor!

Blanche is an outdated creature, approaching extinction . . . like the dinosaur. She is about to be pushed off the edge of the earth. On the other hand she is a heightened version, an artistic intensification of all women. That is what makes the play universal. Blanche's special relation to all women is that she is at that critical point where *the one thing above all else that she is dependent on: her attraction for men, is beginning to go.* Blanche is like all women, dependent on a man, looking for one to hang onto: only *more so!*

So beyond being deeply desperate, Blanche is in a hurry. She'll be pushed off the earth soon. She carries her doom in her character. Also, her past is chasing her, catching up with her. Is it any wonder that she tries to attract each and every man she meets. She'll even take that protected feeling, that needed feeling, that superior feeling, for a moment. Because, at least for a moment, that anxiety, the hurt and the pain will be quenched. The sex act is the opposite of loneliness. Desire is the opposite of Death. For a moment the anxiety is still, for a moment the complete desire and concentration of a man is on her. He clings to you. He may say I love you. All else is anxiety, loneliness and being adrift.

Compelled by her nature (she must be special, superior) she makes it impossible with Stanley and Stella. She acts in a way that succeeds in being destructive. But the last bit of luck is with her. She finds the only man on earth whom she suits, a man who is looking for a dominant woman. For an instant she is happy. But her past catches up with her. Stanley, whom she's antagonized by her destructiveness aimed at his home, but especially by her need to be superior, uses her past, which he digs up, to destroy her. Finally she takes refuge in fantasy. She must have protection, closeness, love, safe harbor. The only place she can obtain them any longer is in her own mind. She "goes crazy."

Blanche is a stylized character, she should be played, should be dressed, should move like a stylized figure. What is the physicalization of an aristocratic woman pregnant with her own doom? . . . Behaving by a tradition that dooms her in this civilization, in this "culture"? All her behavior patterns are *old-fashioned, pure tradition*. All as if jellied in rote——

Why does the "Blues" music fit the play? The Blues is an expression of the loneliness and rejection, the exclusion and isolation of the Negro and their (opposite) longing for love and connection. Blanche too is "looking for a home," abandoned, friendless. "I don't know where I'm going, but I'm going." Thus the Blue piano catches the soul of Blanche, the miserable unusual human side of the girl which is beneath her frenetic duplicity, her trickery, lies, etc. It tells, it emotionally reminds you what all the fireworks are caused by.

Blanche—Physically. Must at all times give a single impression: her social mask is: *the High-Bred Genteel Lady in Distress.* Her past, her destiny, her falling from grace is just a surprise . . . then a tragic contradiction. But the mask never breaks down.

The only way to understand any character is through yourself. Everyone is much more alike than they willingly admit. Even as frantic and fantastic a creature as Blanche is created by things you have felt and known, *if you'll dig for them and be honest about what you see.*

STELLA

Spine—hold onto Stanley (Blanche the antagonist).

One reason Stella submits to Stanley's solution at the end, is perfectly ready to, is that she has an unconscious hostility toward Blanche. Blanche is so patronizing, demanding and superior toward her . . . makes her so useless, old-fashioned and helpless . . . everything that Stanley has got her out of. Stanley has made a woman out of her. Blanche immediately returns her to the subjugation of childhood, younger-sister-ness.

Stella would have been Blanche except for Stanley. She now knows what, how much Stanley means to her health. So . . . no matter what Stanley does . . . she must cling to him, as she does to life itself. To return to Blanche would be to return to the subjugation of the tradition.

The play is a triangle. Stella is the Apex. Unconsciously, Stella wants Blanche to go to Mitch because that will take Blanche off Stella.

And there is a Terrific Conflict between Blanche and Stella, especially in Stella's feelings. Blanche in effect in Sc. 1 *Resubjugates* Stella. Stella loves her, hates her, fears her, pities her, is really through with her. Finally rejects her for Stanley.

All this of course Stella is aware of only unconsciously. It becomes a matter of conscious choice only in Sc. 11 . . . the climax of the play as it is the climax of the triangle story.

Stella is a refined girl who has found a kind of salvation or realization, *but at a terrific price.* She keeps her eyes closed, even stays in bed as much as possible so that she won't realize, won't *feel* the pain of this terrific price. She walks around as if narcotized, as if sleepy, as if in a daze. She is waiting for night. She's waiting for the dark where Stanley makes her feel *only him* and she has no reminder of the price she is paying. She wants no intrusion from the other world. She is drugged, trapped. She's in a sensual stupor. She shuts out all challenge all day long. She loafs, does her hair, her nails. fixes a dress, doesn't eat much, but prepares Stanley's dinner and waits for Stanley. She hopes for no other meaning from life. Her pregnancy just makes it more so. Stanley is in her day and night. Her entire attention is to make herself pretty and attractive for Stanley, kill time till night. In a way she is actually narcotized all day. She is buried alive in her flesh. She's half asleep. She is glazed across her eyes. She doesn't seem to see much. She laughs incessantly like a child tickled and stops abruptly as the stimuli, the tickling, stops and returns to the same condition, a pleasantly drugged child. Give her all kinds of narcotized business.

She has a paradise—a serenely limited paradise when Blanche enters—but Blanche makes her consider Stanley, judge Stanley and find him wanting, for the first time. But it is too late. In the end she returns to Stanley.

Stella is doomed too. She has sold herself out for a temporary solution. She's given up all hope, everything, just to live for Stanley's pleasures. So she is dependent on Stanley's least whim. But this can last only as long as Stanley wants her. And *secondly* and *chiefly*— Stella herself cannot live narcotized forever. There is more to her. She begins to feel, even in the sex act, *taken*, unfulfilled—not recognized . . . and besides she's deeper, needs more variety. Her only hope is her children and, like so many women, she will begin to live more and more for her children.

She tries to conceal from herself her true needs through hiding and drugging herself in a sex relationship. But her real needs, for tenderness, for the several aspects of living, for realization in terms of herself—not only in terms of Stanley, *still live . . . she can't kill them* by ignoring them. Blanche, despite apparent failure, makes her realize certain things about Stanley. She hugs Stanley in Sc. 4 out of desperation, and out of a need to silence her doubts by the violence of sexual love (the "old reliable") . . . but Blanche has succeeded in calling Stella's attention to her own "sell-out" . . . she never sees Stanley the same again—or their relationship.

Stella, at the beginning of the play, won't face a *hostility* (concealed from herself and unrecognized) toward Stanley. She is *so* dependent on him, so compulsively compliant. She is giving up so much of herself, quieting so many voices of protest. She is Stanley's slave. She has sold out most of her life. Latent in Stella is rebellion. Blanche arouses it.

Stella is plain out of her head about Stanley. She has to keep herself from constantly touching him. She can hardly keep her hands off him. She is setting little traps all the time to conquer his act of indifference (he talks differently at night, in bed). She embarrasses him (though he is secretly proud) by following him places. They have a game where he tries to shake her all the time and she pursues him, etc. He makes her a panther in bed. He is her first man, really; he made her a woman. He fulfilled her more than she knew possible and she has to stop herself from *crawling* after him. She's utterly *blind* as to what's wrong with Stanley. She's blind to it and she doesn't care, *until* Blanche arrives. At the end of the play, her life is entirely different. It will never be the same with Stanley again.

Note from Tennessee Williams on the fourth day of rehearsal: "Gadge—I am a bit concerned over Stella in Scene One. It seems to me that she has too much vivacity, at times she is bouncing around in a way that suggests a co-ed on a benzedrine kick. I know it is impossible to be literal about the description 'narcotized tranquillity' but I do think there is an important value in suggesting it, in contrast to Blanche's rather feverish excitability. Blanche is the quick, light one. Stella is relatively slow and almost indolent. Blanche mentions her 'Chinese philosophy'—the way she sits with her little hands folded like a cherub in a choir, etc. I think her natural passivity is one of the things that makes her acceptance of Stanley acceptable. She naturally 'gives in,' accepts, lets things slide, she does not make much of an effort."

STANLEY

Spine—keep things his way (Blanche the antagonist).

The hedonist, objects, props, etc. Sucks on a cigar all day because he can't suck a teat. Fruit, food, etc. He's got it all figured out, what fits, what doesn't. The pleasure scheme. He has all the confidence of resurgent flesh.

Also with a kind of naïveté . . . even slowness . . . he means no harm. He wants to knock no one down. He only doesn't want to be taken advantage of. His code is simple and simple-minded. He is adjusted *now* . . . later, as his sexual powers die, so will he; the trouble will come later, the "problems."

But what is the chink in his armor now, the contradiction? Why does Blanche get so completely under his skin? Why does he want to bring Blanche and, before her, Stella *down to his level?* It's as if he said: "I know I haven't got much, but no one has more and no one's going to have more." It's the hoodlum aristocrat. He's deeply dissatisfied, deeply hopeless, deeply cynical . . . the physical immediate pleasures, if they come in a steady enough stream quiet this *as long as no one gets more* . . . then his bitterness comes forth and he tears down the pretender. But Blanche he can't seem to do anything with. She can't come down to his level so he levels her with his sex. He brings her right down to his level, beneath him.

One of the important things for Stanley is that Blanche *would wreck his home.* Blanche is dangerous. She is destructive. She would soon have him and Stella fighting. He's got things the way he wants them around there and he does *not* want them upset by a phony, corrupt, sick, destructive woman. *This makes Stanley right!* Are we going into the era of Stanley? He may be practical and right . . . but what the hell does it leave us? Make this a removed objective characterization for Marlon Brando.

Choose Marlon's objects . . . the things he loves and prizes: all sensuous and sensual—the shirt, the cigar, the beer (how it's poured and nursed, etc.).

The one thing that Stanley can't bear is someone who thinks that he or she is better than he. His only way of explaining himself—he

thinks he stinks—is that everyone else stinks. This is symbolic. True
of our National State of Cynicism. No values. There is nothing to
command his loyalty. Stanley rapes Blanche because he has tried and
tried to keep her down to his level. This way is the last. For a moment he succeeds. And then, in Scene 11, he has failed!

Stanley has got things his way. He fits into his environment. The
culture and the civilization, even the neighborhood, etc., etc., the
food, the drink, etc., are all his way. And he's got a great girl, with
just enough hidden neuroticism for him—yet not enough to even
threaten a real fight. Also their history is right: he conquered her.
Their relationship is right: she waits up for him. Finally God and
Nature gave him a fine sensory apparatus . . . he enjoys! The main
thing the actor has to do in the early scenes is make the physical environment of Stanley, the *props* come to life.

Stanley is deeply indifferent. When he first meets Blanche he
doesn't really seem to care if she stays or not. Stanley is interested in
his own pleasures. He is completely self-absorbed to the point of
fascination.

To physicalize this: he has a most annoying way of being preoccupied—or of busying himself with something else while people are talking with him, at him it becomes. Example, first couple of pages
Scene 2. Stanley thinks Stella is very badly brought up. She can't do
any of the ordinary things—he had a girl before this that could really
cook, but she drank an awful lot. Also she, Stella, has a lot of airs,
most of which he's knocked out of her by now, but which still crop up.
Emphasize Stanley's love for Stella. It is rough, embarrassed and he
rather truculently *won't show it.* But it is there. He's proud of her.
When he's not on guard and looking at her his eyes suddenly shine.
He is grateful too, proud, satisfied. But he'd never show it, demonstrate it.
Stanley is supremely indifferent to everything except his own pleasure and comfort. He is marvelously selfish, a miracle of sensuous self-

centeredness. He builds a hedonist life, and fights to the death to defend it—but finally it is *not* enough to hold Stella

and

this philosophy is not successful even for him—because every once in a while the silenced, frustrated part of Stanley breaks lose in unexpected and unpredictable ways and we suddenly see, as in a burst of lightning, his real frustrated self. Usually his frustration is worked off by eating a lot, drinking a lot, gambling a lot, fornicating a lot. He's going to get very fat later. He's desperately trying to squeeze out happiness by living by *ball and jowl* . . . and it really doesn't work . . . because it simply stores up violence and stores up violence, until every *bar in the nation is full of Stanleys ready to explode.* He's desperately trying to drug his senses . . . overwhelming them with a constant round of sensation so that he will feel nothing else.

In Stanley sex goes under a disguise. Nothing is more erotic and arousing to him than "airs" . . . she thinks she's better than me . . . I'll show her. . . . Sex equals domination . . . anything that challenges him—like calling him "common"—arouses him sexually.

In the case of Brando, the question of enjoyment is particularly important. Stanley feeds himself. His world is hedonist. But what does he enjoy. Sex equals sadism. It is his "equalizer." He conquers with his penis. But objects too—drunk. Conquest in poker, food . . . sweat. *Exercise.* But Enjoy! Not just cruel and *unpleasant* . . . but he never graduated from the baby who wants a constant nipple in his mouth. He yells when it's taken away.

As a character Stanley is most interesting in his "contradictions," his "soft" moments, his sudden pathetic little-tough-boy tenderness toward Stella. Scene 3 he cries like a baby. Somewhere in Scene 8 he almost makes it up with Blanche. In Scene 10 he *does* try to make it up with her—and except for her doing the one thing that most arouses him, both in anger and sex, he might have.

MITCH

Spine—get away from his mother (Blanche the lever).

He wants the perfection his mother gave him . . . everything is approving, protective, *perfect for him*. Naturally no girl, today, no sensible, decent girl will give him this. But the tradition will.

Like Stella, Mitch hides from his own problem through mother-love.

Mitch is the end product of a matriarchy . . . his mother has robbed him of all daring, initiative, self-reliance. He does not face his own needs.

Mitch is Blanche's ideal in a comic form, 150 years late. He is big, tough, burly, has a rough southern voice and a manner of homespun, coarse, awkward, overgrown boy, with a heart of mush. He's like that character (who cries easy) in *Sing Out Sweet Land*. He is a little embarrassed by his strength in front of women. He is straight out of Mack Sennett comedy—but Malden has to create the reality of it, the truth behind that corny image. Against his blundering strength there is shown off the fragility and fragrance of a girl. Her delicacy. "Lennie" in *Mice and Men*.

Mitch, too, is most interesting in his basic contradictions. He doesn't want to be Mother's Boy. Goddamn it he just can't help it. He does love his Mother, but is a little embarrassed at how much. Blanche makes a man out of him, makes him important and grown-up. His Mother—he dimly realizes—keeps him eternally adolescent, forever dependent.

Violence—he's full of sperm.

energy
strength

the reason he's so clumsy with women is that he's so damn full of violent desire for them.

Mitch's Mask: He-man mama's boy. This mask is a traditional, "corny" one in American dramatic literature. But it is true.

This play contains the crucial struggle of Mitch's life. For Mitch instinctively and even consciously, to a degree, knows what's wrong with him. He is jibed at often enough. And in his guts he knows they're right. Mitch, in his guts, hates his Mother. He loves her in a way—partially out of *early habit,* partially because she is clever—but much more fundamentally he *hates her.* It is a tragedy for him when he returns to her absolute sovereignty at the end. He will never meet another woman who will need him as much as Blanche and will need him to be a man as much as Blanche.

HAROLD CLURMAN

(b. 1901)

Some Preliminary Notes for

The Member of the Wedding

"To put it as simply as possible, the function of the stage director is to translate a play text into stage terms: that is, to make the play as written, clear, interesting, enjoyable, by means of living actors, sounds, colors, movement." With these words Harold Clurman defines the task of the director. From his earliest productions as a mentor of the Group Theater, interpretation has always been the creative keynote of this sensitive, articulate director. How he initiates and develops the process of interpreting the language of the script in theatrical terms is revealed in this specimen of the personal notes he prepares for himself during the formative period of production. To accompany their publication here, Mr. Clurman has written a retrospective postscript which indicates the manner in which he employs the notations he makes in his "little book."

(NOVEMBER-DECEMBER 1949)

What is the audience to enjoy?

The poetry of first impulses expressed naïvely, sweetly,. directly. The first "shoots" of life and emotion (adolescent longing) appreciated by grownups thinking back on the purity of their first contact with life.

By permission of Harold Clurman.

The production style.

Poetic—which means concentrated: every moment visually significant of the inner state.

The main action of the play: to get "connected."

It all happens in a hot summer atmosphere. The world is "dead"— the people suspended. Everything is slightly strange, not altogether real.

"Less us have a good time" says John Henry. He seeks "connection" but there's so little to connect with in this environment.

People who seek connection and aren't able to—ache. Frankie aches all the time. Her sobbing in the first act is the climax of an ache delicately indicated all through . . . part of the loneliness inherent in the main action.

(Frankie has no one to talk to about her resolve—so she talks to strangers: the Monkey Man or to a cat. . . . She wants connection with the whole wide world of experience.)

A stage direction reads: "Frankie scrapes her head against door." These strange gestures of children make one think that they are re-enacting man's past living through the ages—animal-like, weird, primitive. More of such "gestures" must be invented for Frankie. "Flying around the world together"—Frankie will "fly" through the kitchen.

A mighty loneliness emanates from this play. It is as if all the characters were separated from the world—as if the world were only a mirage in a vaporous space making wraiths of the people.

The Main Actions for the Leading Characters

Frankie

Her main action—*to get out of herself.*

Getting out of herself means *growth.* . . . She has "growing pains": she is both tortured and happy through them. . . . The juices of life are pouring through her. She is a fragile container of this strange elixir.

Growth twists and turns her—as it does us—gives us new shapes. Frankie twists and turns. The play is the lyric drama of Frankie's growth. At the end of the play, she runs or twirls out—"to go around the world." She has achieved her aim—imaginatively. She is ready "to get out of herself."

The Main Characteristics

1) Frankie is tomboyish. (She puts on no shows with kissing. Her father is a "widowman" with his nose to the grindstone. She has no mother, no "social" environment.)

2) Frankie is crazy with first love: literally head over heels: the love of the *wedding*.

3) She is intense. She's trying to see underneath everything, seize its essence, "cozen it in her mind"; she even tries to seize the atmosphere of heat as a unique experience. "The kitchen's the hottest place in the U. S." she says.
   Thus she is a "poetic" character. She is terribly aware of every little thing: Berenice's fur, Frankie says, has "a sad, foxwise face."

4) All the above produces an awkwardness that is weird and occasionally graceful.

5) Frankie is hostile. You hate what you can't connect with and want to hurt it. Or you want to hurt yourself for failing to make the connection.

6) She is given to self-examination. She is self-absorbed in relation to her desire for connection and wanting to "get out."

7) Her torture comes from a sense of a past vaguely remembered, troubled and painful—and the future—wondrous, void, unrealized and therefore frustrating. "I have this feeling," she moans.

8) She is imaginative. Her mind and spirit leap: they stretch, lift, dart, fly . . . to whatever place she wants to go. When the destination is too vague, she explodes or drifts in all directions.

(Remind Julie Harris: The main action makes her a very active character. She is straining to get out. When she fails, she has one sort of emotion; when she almost succeeds, another.)

Frankie is fascinated by Honey. He is romantic, exciting, lightfoot. He's been "out."

Berenice Sadie Brown

To do her deed (work) . . . "normally."
For her to live is to be connected.

A woman who is naturally and easily connected. Once she was connected with Ludie Maxwell Freeman. He died. "It leaves you lonesome afterward." After that, she sought connection with scraps and bits of what she loved—even to a madman. Now she's alone, relatively unconnected. But she manages somehow to connect with her community, with T.T., with Honey, with John Henry—but some people she doesn't desire connection with (Mrs. West, "them Germans and Japs," Mary Littlejohn). Of John Henry she says, "We enjoys him." It's as simple as that. Everything is approached without fuss, without sentimentality, without "eloquence."

She is plain—direct, earthy, quiet. Hers is the poetry of the "prosaic!" She's basic: "Two is company" she says.

Her life "We just talks and passes the time of the day"—that's enough.

"Stop commenting about it" she tells Frankie. She does not need to "comment" to make things real to herself.

"Sunday will come." Sufficient unto the day——

When people want to go away from her—John Henry or Frankie or Honey—she just lets them go.

Unnaturalness ("freaks") give her the creeps.

She rarely tries to prevent anything from happening that seems to have to happen: when Frankie wants to take a splinter out of her foot with a kitchen knife, when Frankie smokes, when Honey needs a stimulant, when Frankie rushes out to the town, she cautions, but does not fight. ("I'm just trying to head this thing off, but I see it's no use.")

This is her wisdom: the acceptance of the pain and sorrow of life. All this is, as she puts it, a "thing known and not spoken."

Her movement is quiet, solid, strong. Her eyes look deep with a slight slanting glance—so that she may see better out of her one good eye.

And suddenly——
She too feels the loneliness, the fear, the terror of life . . . and needs consolation from John Henry or anyone else. This pain of life is always sensed by her, but she lives on despite it. She knows the irony of life—John Henry's death—she didn't believe he was sick—a rebuke to her "practicality," to her too-sensible nature.

She ends alone—tragic, majestic, patient, waiting—while Frankie dashes out joyously to learn—some of the things Berenice knows.

This contrast in their destinies (that of Frankie and Berenice) must be clear in action at the end. They change "colors"—Frankie becomes more "extroverted" and "superficial" at the end. Berenice more quietly profound than ever.

John Henry

To learn to connect.

The pathos of the child is that it imitates the process of life as it beholds life being lived. There is mystery and comedy in this, too.

The child repeats a pattern of behavior without realizing its significance. The child has hardly any conscious tastes, appetites, or desires (they all seem automatic).

The child develops conscious appetites and ideas through imitation.

Hence it is likely to imitate bad things as well as good, it might kill or die almost as easily as live and love. The environment teaches the child through its tendency to imitate, its capacity to be formed unconsciously.

The child's imitation is a species of attachment: hence the child appears to be "loving." It loves to repeat what it sees and hears—and since most life is an effort to "connect"—the child is always learning to connect and so grows to be a man.

"Me too" is the keynote. But since this is just the sign of a desire to follow or imitate a pattern without any reason or justification beyond what appears to be merely an imitative impulse—it strikes us (grownups) as funny.

John Henry says "how pretty" about Frankie's dress, but repeats Berenice's less flattering description; that is, he imitates Berenice, attaching himself or reflecting her . . . so that Frankie calls him a "double-faced Judas."

The child reflects life: it reflects connection, attachment, but it has to learn to develop a conscious connection which it doesn't possess at first.

The child's lack of consciousness makes much of its behavior seem meaningless and mysterious. Hence there is something sad as well as funny, and, from a conscious point of view, oddly pathetic about the child.

The child is fragile: death is "natural" to it . . . it is always close to death. The "realest" thing John Henry does is to say he is sick, but because he says such things as a reflex he is not taken seriously.

A child is like the light of a flickering candle—bright, gay, pretty, sad, extremely sensitive to the atmosphere around it—easy to intensify or to extinguish.

Frankie wants to get out of herself so that she can connect, even more with the world. Berenice connects because she has learned to live and

John Henry is learning the process in the unconscious way of a child—but he stops (dies) before he has gone very far in the process. . . . In a word, he presents the image of the fragility of the whole process—hence our tender feeling toward him. How susceptible he is (the life process) to destruction—disappearance—"the ghost in the arbor with a little silver ring!"

The first step in connection after imitation is attachment and from the attachment, "love" develops which we observe in John Henry's consolation of Frankie and Berenice.

When the child's connection is sharply cut off, it becomes afraid—"scary." It has become used to the connection. The child isn't a bit lonesome (as John Henry says) but comes running to get together—connected—with what he has become used to.

The child "studies" to be a man. Observe the rapt look of a concentrated child. This "study" is the essence of the child's activity—the study and the action that follows—sometimes slow and hesitant, sometimes sudden as if inspired.

Addams (Frankie's father)

To keep in touch.

He can barely make it. . . . His connection is faltering, bleak. "Marriage is a sacred institution," he says, but it's a long time since he's been married. He keeps on going, but he has connection only with memories and the little mechanisms—watches—to which he has set, automatic responses.

Life is queer, a little strange or "funny" to him—he has a trace of humor—— Life is sad for him because its objects are dim, sweet because he realizes no evil, sour because he's pushed into a corner and his area of nourishment is limited.

He's widowed of life. "A good provider"—he works without aim. He pets life (Frankie) in passing, and wanders off into bleakness—and rest.

All that remains to him is his "white superiority." Even his porter doesn't show up to work for him. People don't pay attention to him—because he's not there for them. ("Answer me when I call.")

Handling people who are "alive" embarrass him. He's "evasive"—constantly clearing his throat in embarrassment.

A baffled man.

Jarvis

To make the simplest connection . . .
  with the first thing that's nice—a girl.

He's an ordinary boy—rather unimaginative—his father's son—proper, good-natured, conventional, cautious—pleasant and inconspicuous—except to Frankie and people who admire his looks.

He smiles a lot, friendly, even sentimental, normally affectionate, but without much expression. He is comparatively "mute"—awkward in expressing his feelings. Affectionate gibberish is the best he can manage in response to Frankie's adoration.

T.T.

To make as much connection as he can find.

Modest, resigned, soft, unhappy. He hasn't enough energy for his unhappiness to develop into resentment. He is acquiescent.

He is self-effacing, "understanding," honorable—"understanding" in a mediocre, practical way. Hence his deaconish fat. "Respected"—walking in a state of grace. He is almost "womanish" (or eunuch-like.)

He would take a blow, quietly, hurt, unangry. ("I'm not particular—whichever way is convenient.")

He's even afraid—or at least shy—of being unseemly in front of Frankie. . . .

Yet he is not obsequious—honorable in a way, dignified, understanding and kindly—slightly depressed.

Henry Brown

To force connection—(or die).

Rejected, humiliated, his only connection is through violence, hostility (defiance) or mad escape ("snow," liquor, the protection and romance of jazz).

He is depressed and crazed by his own violence.

He's always on the verge of breaking loose or getting into a stupor of sadness—followed by an outbreak toward escape. He's repentant about hurting John Henry—for a second—tries to make up for it by playing with him, giving him money.

He has a kind of hysterical lyricism about him—(his movements are dance-like in their nervousness).

A kind of terrified joy in being pursued. He takes a kind of mad pleasure in his violent connection through pistol or razor. . . .

(DECEMBER 1952)

Such notes set down for my own use when I have read a play at least a half-dozen times are never communicated to the actors in the form which they take in my "little book." They would be unintelligible to actors in this form as well as practically useless. They serve to make the thought and sentiments I experience in reading the script somewhat more specific than they might be if I allowed them to remain inchoate within myself. They are springboards and tracers for my own feelings. They lead me on and point to the objectives I hope to attain.

(What folly it would be to "explain" my notes on John Henry to a seven-year-old actor. But I found things for Brandon de Wilde to *do* which were a concrete embodiment of my "abstract ideas.")

With these notes as a basis, I am able to approach the actor. In rehearsal (by careful study and observation of my actors) I find the best way of directing—stimulating, leading—the actors—by allusion, suggestion, explanation, encouragement, demonstration, criticism. The method of reaching the actor varies with the gifts, character and total personality of each actor. There is no right way—except the way that brings results.

More decisive than any of these notes is my line by line "breakdown" of the script, which indicates the aim of each scene and what particular actions and adjustment (mood) moment by moment the actor must carry out and convey. These actions—what the character wants to do and why—together with any physical action (or "stage business") which might result from the character's purpose are duly noted by the director or, in most cases in my own work, they may be left to the actor's nature and imagination—under the director's guidance—to accomplish.

My working script is packed with notations for almost every moment of the play, but this does not delude me into believing that the entire direction of a play can be written down or that I, or anybody else, can direct from the written notes alone. The play on the stage is written with and through the actor's being. One works with flesh, blood and spirit much more than with the words one has written or spoken to the actor.

JOAN LITTLEWOOD

Working with Joan

Joan Littlewood has said: "If the theater is to fulfill its social purpose it is contemporary and vital material which must make up the dramaturgy, and its theme must be important to the audience. Theater must be in the present tense." This belief has determined her special approach to actors, playwrights, and staging from the origin of the Theatre Workshop in 1945 as a mobile troupe to its success with the plays of Shelagh Delaney and Brendan Behan at its own Theatre Royal in London's working-class East End. Influenced by Stanislavsky, Brecht, and Rudolf Laban, she has worked out productions rich in meaning but as direct in theatrical appeal as the English music hall. Here some of her colleagues tell how she achieves a theater which, in her words, is "grand, vulgar, simple, pathetic— but not genteel, not poetical."

At the start of rehearsals, Joan sets out to establish the very basis of the play's atmosphere—its super-objective. This is often done even before the scripts come into play:

For the first week of rehearsals of [Brendan Behan's] The Quare Fellow we had no scripts. None of us had even read the play. We knew it was about prison life in Dublin, and that was enough for Joan. None of us had ever been in prison, and although we could all

Clive Goodwin and Tom Milne: "Working with Joan," *Encore,* Vol. VII, July-August 1960, 9-20 (with the assistance of a number of Theatre Workshop artists). By permission of the Encore Publishing Company Limited, London.

half-imagine what it was like, Joan set out to tell us more—the narrow
world of steel, of stone, high windows and clanging doors, the love-
hate between warder and prisoner, the gossip, the jealousy, and the
tragedy—all the things that make up the fascination of dreariness. She
took us up onto the roof of the Theatre Royal. All the grimy slate
and stone made it easy to believe we were in a prison yard. We formed
up in a circle, and imagined we were prisoners out on exercise. Round
and round we trudged for what seemed like hours—breaking now and
then for a quick smoke and furtive conversation. Although it was
just a kind of game, the boredom and meanness of it all was brought
home. Next, the "game" was extended—the whole dreary routine of
washing out your cell, standing to attention, sucking up to the screws,
trading tobacco, was improvised and developed. It began to seem
less and less like a game, and more like real. By degrees the plot and
the script were introduced, although some of us never knew which
parts we were playing until halfway through the rehearsals. The in-
teresting thing was that when she gave us the scripts we found that
many of the situations we had improvised actually occurred in the
play. All we had to do was learn the author's words.

Once Joan has got the actors thinking creatively along the lines of
the play, she will introduce the script broken down into units. This
division is very much a part of Stanislavsky's approach—he compares
it to the carving up of a turkey into palatable mouthfuls. It is also,
of course, intelligent theater practice, although Joan uses the technique more positively than most. Every play is divided into short
scenes, each with a beginning, a middle, and an end; some of them
may only be a few lines long. In each scene, the actor, or actors, have
an objective—the thing they want most at that moment. In the second act of *The Quare Fellow,* for example, there is a big scene set in
the exercise yard, where the prisoners are marched on, then allowed
ten minutes' break. This scene was built up slowly during four weeks
of rehearsal. The different units—the condemned man's breakfast
tray, the note-passing, the quick scuffle—were all rehearsed separately
and built into a whole:

At one point the cook hurried across the stage with a tray of bacon

*and eggs—it was the Quare Fellow's tea. We all crowded round him,
sniffing the bacon, fighting to get a look, and improvising lines—you
know—like "Wish I was getting topped"* . . . *"Give us a bit"*. . . .
"It's worth getting topped for this" . . . *then a warder came out and
stopped us. The whole bit must have been over in about forty-five
seconds, but we rehearsed it over and over again.*

Joan Littlewood.

Improvisation is one of Joan's most constantly used rehearsal aids.
It is employed in all sorts of ways. For instance, in its simplest form,
if a particular unit gives trouble, she will give an analogous situation.
If you are in a classical play, and you have a situation which can be
reduced to the simple terms of a courtier begging a favor of a king,
this will be transposed to the modern context of an employee and his
boss, and the actors will improvise their own lines. They will thus be
brought slap up against the problem, not of phrasing a line, pitching
the voice, or finding a gesture, but of how you *act* a person who is
really trying to beg a favor. Or she will improvise an illustrative episode. In *Macbeth,* the actors improvised the scene which Shakespeare

never wrote, when Macbeth actually meets the murderers for the first time—in a pub; the murderers, two ex-R.A.F. types; Macbeth saying, "How would you boys like to do a job for me?" This kind of thing can enrich the background to a scene, and fill in the character for the actor so that he is not just acting on breath. In *A Taste of Honey*, the opening scene shows a mother and daughter arriving in new lodgings. They are worn out and quarrelsome. The rooms are drearily squalid. For an hour one morning the two actresses dragged heavily weighted suitcases around the stage, trying to get on buses, arguing with landladies, struggling through the rain. (Joan will often take the analogy a stage further, beyond the realistic. The two actresses mimed dragging their suitcases down long, dark, filthy tunnels.) If, in rehearsal, a scene is playing too slow, or too small, the actors will mime the situation to music. This will be done even with a serious play, and can have a magnificently releasing effect on the actor. Contrary to rumor, Joan will never alter an author's lines without his consent. Good phrases, however, often emerge from improvisations, and in a modern play she will often get the author to work alongside the actors, rewriting on the spot where early rehearsals showed weaknesses. This happened with Frank Norman's *Fings Ain't Wot They Used T'Be:*

Frank sat in at all our rehearsals. He improvised with us as an actor, and when new script was needed, the way it was produced was by Frank improvising it himself on the stage to find out if it was theatrically possible. Sometimes we played our own parts, sometimes he did the acting. And if he felt he could use the lines he wrote while he was improvising, they were in. What Joan was after was the relationship of a scene to some facet of the character playing it. Frank knew far more about criminals and the way they reacted than any of us—he would be able to improvise what he thought a criminal would do in a given situation. That would be taken as a lead. An actor would take it and build on it. Or if an actor did an improvisation, Frank would give his o.k. to it or not. This is a way of working for a unity between actor, author and producer. Authors sometimes fight for their texts:

In Make Me an Offer *one of the actors found he had difficulty saying a particular line—he just couldn't make it sound right. And Joan
turned round to Wolf Mankowitz and said, "This actor is having
difficulty." Wolf said, "Nonsense!" And Joan said, "Right, Wolf,
up on the stage and say it for him." He stumbled over the line as
well, so she turned round and said, "The boy's right, isn't he—rewrite
it tonight." And he had no option.*

Joan, of course, will not accept such quick solutions to textual problems when she is producing a work of genuine literary value: "Mind
you, she's a stickler if she's got a well-written play. She'll do all she
can to get out of you what the author demands." And anyone who
saw the extraordinary series of productions of Elizabethan plays
which she did between 1954 and 1956—*Volpone, Arden of Faversham,
Richard II, Edward II*—must have noted their remarkable textual
clarity. To twist a quote—it was like watching Shakespeare in one
continuous shaft of lightning. The stark simplicity of John Bury's
sets, and the perfectly disciplined group playing of the company,
combined to launch at the audience plays which were as fresh, exciting and meaningful as if they had only just been written. In plays
of this period, many lines have lost their immediate and obvious
relevance, but Joan rarely resorts to tricks like the one Tyrone Guthrie used to "help over" the long speech on justice in *The Thrie
Estaits,* where one of the soldiers intermittently and inescapably
scratched his bottom. Very funny, but this is an important speech,
and it became impossible to *listen* to it. When faced with a similar
difficult passage, Joan works to render the *effect* of the lines:

In The Dutch Courtesan *I had a practically impossible speech
about* Euphues and His England, *a book by John Lyly, and I was
supposed to get a laugh on it. Well, of course, no one had ever heard
of it. But we did get a laugh out of it, because of the way Joan explained she thought it ought to be done. The explanation was a
purely technical one. She said "If you* gather *the first half of the
speech, and* scatter *the second, the sense will come over." Well, I knew
what she meant. So I gathered like mad and scattered like hell, and
got a big laugh.*

With a classical play in verse, once the improvisations have enabled the actors to grasp the tenor of the play and their characters, she will spend hours on the verse and its rhythms. She will not allow decoration—as soon as you spout "poetry," you are stopped. The hard, driving rhythms which elucidate the meaning—and sometimes *are* the meaning—are all-important. Sometimes an actor is made to physically punch his way through a speech, beating out the meter with his fists like a shadow-boxer. This is making him physically move the verse—"Is this a dagger, which I see before me"—actually pacing it out. When you have the physical movement which underlies the verse its meaning is brought right out. The movement might eventually be used in a modified way in the production itself. "Is this a dagger" was helped by a four-pace forward movement; while not actually retained, it gave the grasping surge of movement behind the line ("Come, let me clutch thee").

Movement is thus a vital element in Joan's work—not only the moves the actor makes, but the unity between movement and character. For the actor new to Joan, this can be a most unsettling aspect of her methods. He will have come from a world where his moves are given to him literally: "On this line you move downstage, then you will not be masking, and you will be ready for your next cue." This kind of production is carefully planned in advance like a military campaign, even to the drawing of movement diagrams in the prompt-copy. The amount of give-and-take varies, of course, but it is a practice which is seriously defended, and used by the great majority of directors. It is sometimes said—and supported by actors who have worked with her for a short time—that Joan "never gives a move." In the sense outlined above, this is true. The contention is backed up by the fluidity and apparent chaos of modern plays she has done like *The Hostage* and *Fings Ain't Wot They Used T'Be*. The theory is a puzzling one, however, when one remembers the formal beauty and controlled simplicity of her Elizabethan productions: the extraordinary thing is the fact that her rehearsal approach is very much the same with both kinds of play.

It isn't strictly true, you know, that Joan never gives you a move.

She might say to you, "In this scene you're coming out of a cellar, and fighting your way down a long, dark passage. You can't see, but you just know you have got to get out and through the door at the end." Well, that's not saying to someone, "Here you move from right to left," which isn't giving a move at all—it's just sort of placing someone in a particular position. No, Joan really gives you a move—she explains the particular effort required to get into a particular position. I would say that she gives people movement, she gives actors an objective, and a motive to get there. It's a difference of words, but she does give you movement as an actor, rather than a move as a pawn. And it's a very strong pattern of movement, because it grows out of what the play means and what the character is after. Some people have remarked on the beautiful grouping in her classical productions, but she never arranges us on the stage: somehow the grouping just grows out of the action. If the characters are right, the feelings are right, and the motivations are right, the grouping must be right.

Joan's productions always strive toward a style best suited to illuminate the playwright's intentions. The casual gusto of *The Hostage* was because *The Hostage* was essentially that kind of play—inchoate and rumbustious. Elsewhere her styles are very different; the classically austere *Edward II* (Marlowe); the hot, dusty, violent *Fuente Ovejuna* (Lope de Vega); the speeded-up Keystone Cops cartoon *Good Soldier Schweik* (Hasek); the dark, brooding, malevolent *Duchess of Malfi* (Webster); the soft, romantic, lithograph *A Christmas Carol.*

Obviously to create these styles the actor must be able to integrate actively into the movement of the production. In other words, he is a unit of vital importance in himself but ultimately only important in so far as he can be welded into the ensemble. Paradoxically, the secret of ensemble production is concentration on the individual actor. However small or unimportant the actor's role may be, if he is not "with" the production, it will be flawed.

The tremendous compliment she will pay to an actor is that she will give him complete and utter concentration. You know for the next few minutes, or an hour, or however long it takes, she is going to grapple with your problem. And everybody gets this—even if you are playing a big scene with a lot of people on the stage—everybody will get this terrific individual criticism. Some people who aren't used to such a close personal analysis of their work may find it harsh. After all, she's quite capable of saying to somebody: "You can't do that—it's beyond your capabilities." She's a great psychologist—if she thinks an actor needs putting down, she'll put him down. But she won't come the Boss-Director on you. If an actor has an idea and she has an idea, you have full time and opportunity to debate, try it out, and quite often a compromise is found. She is very willing to chuck out her idea if yours is better. She is always saying, "Don't let yourself be 'produced.'" In fact I once heard her say, "The theater will only triumph when all the producers are dead!" She's right against the usual conception of a producer—you know, the great genius, someone who comes into the theater with a preconceived idea of what he wants and will bash at the actor until he gets it. She never says to you: "You have got to do it like this." She will let you experiment with complete freedom. And she will be experimenting herself. If you astonish her, she is sensible enough to know that you will astonish an audience in the same way.

Very often, of course, she knows exactly what she wants from an actor, and will do everything in her power to get it. Sometimes her methods can be startling:—

There was a scene in The Quare Fellow *when a young prisoner had to say goodbye to another prisoner who was being released. Joan wanted him to look embarrassed about it. The actor worked and worked, but couldn't manage it. Joan tried everything without success, and finally, in despair, she said: "Come on, I'll make you look embarrassed." and she whispered something in his ear. He went red immediately and we played the scene. He got it and never had any difficulty with the scene again. He never would tell us what she said to him.*

Once a show is in performance, a director's work has not finished, it has merely entered a new phase. Joan does not believe a production can be perfected in three or four weeks and placed upon the stage as a glossy-finished product. It is a living, breathing thing, subject to change, and needs continual testing and checking. Here is the opening to four foolscap pages of roneoed notes given the cast after a production had been running some time:—

Dear Company,

As a young "actress" I was told "stick your behind out, dear, it's always good for a laugh." Well, this show of ours, at the moment, is one big behind.

We may as well go the whole hog and start throwing whitewash at the audience and custard pies at the obtruding behinds, only that would need better timing.

Can we stop regarding the audience as morons, cut out the rubbish, get back a bit of tension, pace and atmosphere in Act II. Can we stop wriggling our anatomies all over the script, over-acting, bullying laughs out of the audience and playing alone, for approbation. This latter, which looks like selfishness, is mere insecurity and lack of trust in yourselves and each other. You cannot play alone, stop wanting the audience to adore you and you only, they do anyway. People love actors and actresses, so relax and let them have a look at a play for a change.

All Joan's work with actors has in mind that elusive thing, the permanent company—the Group. From the Greeks to Bert Brecht it has been shown that a pre-condition for the emergence of theater art has been the existence of permanent companies. The company must of course be in step with society (the Elizabethans) and/or have a genuine creative personality at its head. (The existence of a permanent company in itself can mean nothing—*vide* The Old Vic.) Otherwise theater art can only exist accidentally by some lucky fusion of talents, or in the body of one great actor. . . .

The hours of work and practice put in by a dancer or musician would astonish the average actor. Very few in this country work at their art. This attitude has always been quite incomprehensible to Joan. The group and the training of that group—these are the things most important to her. To train a company to the pitch of perfection expected from a ballet company or a great orchestra.

*When we had a long period together as a group we used to impro-
vise and take classes. And it wasn't just singing scales—we made definite, quite surprising vocal experiments. We had fascinating classes
in voice and movement, the combining of efforts, moving sticks and
shifting weights—and you surprise yourself—you find a lot out about
your own personality. . . .*

. . . Her auditions alone were enough to put some people off. Others
found them a fascinating lesson:

*When I went along for my audition she gave me a script and she
said "Read all the parts—play all the characters." I said "I can't do
this"—and she said "Go ahead and do it. You are either an actor, or
you can't!" Well, I did it. Women, children, old men, young men;
I was terrible—you know—I felt such an idiot. She said "Well, at least
you don't mind making a fool of yourself—and any man who has courage on the stage and is willing to make a fool of himself can, in fact,
become a good actor." I stayed with Joan, and although I'm not sure
whether I'm a good actor yet, now I'm playing a lead in the West End
for her.*

Joan demands that her actors give themselves completely to the
audience. As long ago as 1951, although Ewan MacColl's *Uranium
235* was not considered an unqualified success as a play, the Edin-
burgh critics remarked on the way the actors knocked themselves out
for the play, gave themselves completely to it. This was a far cry
from the polite restraint usually seen on the stage. The actors both
looked and sounded different. Gone were the hallmarks of main-
stream English acting—the dignified poise, well-cut profiles, modu-
lated tones. They didn't look like actors. They looked like people.

*This thing about releasing the actor. Sometimes you have to do
things on the stage which you find personally embarrassing, and you
don't want to do them, but when you try them out, they work. I
think her greatest asset is her ability to draw people out, to give them
confidence and build them up. The thing an actor needs most is
courage—the courage to get down to the footlights and do something
silly, something which will make him look ridiculous. If an actor has*

enough guts and confidence to do this, then he's capable of doing wonderful things. She can even take a man off the street and get him to give a good performance. There was one bloke in The Quare Fellow, *I remember—an American director said to me "Either this man is the most marvelous bloody actor I've ever seen, or a rank amateur."* But you see, you couldn't tell.

Obviously, the more latent talent an actor has the more use Joan can make of him. What she really detests is solidified technique—the mannerisms and routine gestures which are the stock-in-trade of the established actor. Like many great directors in the past Joan has found that to get what she wants often means starting from the ground up. To solve the problems posed by a particular play, she doesn't expect the actor to draw pat on immediate skill. She will ask him to call upon aspects of himself he may never have been aware of. To find the style a play demands is, in fact, a voyage of exploration for both director and actors (and sometimes even for the playwright):

A lot of actors have found that the first two or three shows they have done with her, they haven't understood what she's getting at. But then something dawns. I didn't know much before I joined her but I think you have to be prepared to chuck out an awful lot you have learned when you work for her. Some actors claim that their confidence is undermined because she won't let them use the tricks which have kept them in work before. But that's ungenerous. I think it's a result of not trusting her. What you have to be prepared to do, completely, is to take her word for it. You learn to understand that her ideas are good—that she is right—for an actor I would say she is right all the time. Her greatest capacity is to know the limitations of each individual actor—to know what he can do—and even more important, to know what he can't do. She has a tremendous love of actors, and a genuine curiosity—to other directors, we are just people they employ. She doesn't come to the first rehearsal knowing all the answers. She's obviously done a lot of work on the script, of course, but I think she's genuinely curious how far the group can go in any particular direction. If it takes them to a point that is satisfactory, she'll use it, but she will be surprised herself by what you do on the stage. I mean, she won't come out and say "How delightful, I didn't know you could do that," but you can see the surprise there. You suddenly find something and she's astonished.

And so is the audience—because the freshness of the actor's discovery is communicated. The kind of acting Joan is reacting against is the suave, polished, slick personality that repeats itself unchanged from play to play. The original sin of weekly repertory keeps this smooth tradition well supplied. It was precisely the same kind of cheapening that made Stanislavsky work out for himself, and set down in print, the basic principles of truthful acting. And Stanislavsky provides the basis for much of Joan's work. Her application of his theory is no slavish adherence to a set of iron principles. And certainly no one could accuse her productions of being "Method." It is merely an assimilation of all that is good and useful. The other great influence on her work is Rudolf Laban. He is sometimes called "The Father of Modern Dance." A Hungarian aristocrat, he studied ballet in Paris at the turn of the century, and became fascinated by the undeveloped potential for movement and dance in the human body. He led the revolution against the fixed and formal routine of classical ballet, and fought for a more natural and free-flowing mode of expression. His work laid the basis for most modern choreographers from Jooss to Jerome Robbins. This combination of Stanislavsky and Laban is what gives Joan's work much of its unique flavor.

4

Staging Shakespeare: A Survey of Current Problems and Opinions

The following survey reports the opinions of practicing directors of Shakespeare on a wide variety of problems: preserving the integrity of Shakespeare's text, modern sensibility and the classics, musical quality in the verse and dramatic construction, interpreting characters larger than life yet rich in human qualities, realistic "Method" acting and poetic drama, learning to speak the speeches, the ideal stage, economics of Shakespearean production, up-dating costumes and sets, using the resources of modern theater for plays of the past, releasing the imagination of the spectators, and reaching new audiences. Each director discusses one or more of these and other aspects of the subject. Their brief statements are not offered as final answers to the problems of staging Shakespeare. Rather, they constitute a first step toward a fuller exploration of one of the director's basic tasks, making the drama of the past live for his contemporaries. In pondering the problems of staging Shakespeare these directors question the conventions, resources, and potentialities of modern theater. Their quest for a style for Shakespeare is an important part of the director's continuing quest for a living stage.

JOHN GIELGUD

The classics, it seems to me, have to be rediscovered every ten years or so. The traditional elements must be appreciated and handed on; at the same time the actor must somehow contribute a contemporary approach from within. One must not stand still. The world goes so fast that at each decade there is a sort of different note in the air. One must find it. When he has found it, he reinterprets the text. This is not a matter of complete reinterpretation but one of approaching the play with real spontaneity and joy so that it has an absolutely topical effect. Otherwise the performance becomes what we call ham and old-fashioned and declamatory and all the things that one dreads in a bad Shakespearean performance.

Great plays do not date except through the occasional obscurity of archaic jokes and unfamiliar wording. The construction, of course, often seems old-fashioned to us, but this should be emphasized rather than altered or ignored in a revival. When I played in Otway's *Venice Preserved,* for instance, under Peter Brook's direction, it was the old-fashioned crudity of the construction that made the revival so curious and fascinating. We had only to cut occasionally where the dialogue was ridiculous. But cutting must be studied and considered with enormous care. Restoration plays especially need a lot of pruning for a modern audience; the ribaldry must be left intact, coarse though it often is, but the speeches and scenes are nearly always over-long. Shakespeare, however, is to be tampered with only when he is

John Gielgud: "A Shakespearean Speaks His Mind," *Theatre Arts,* Vol. XLIII, January 1959, 69-71. By permission of John Gielgud.

John Gielgud, the world-renowned Shakespearean actor, has also made notable contributions as a director.

obscure and long-winded. The order of his scenes is always masterly, and nothing betrays his intention so completely as changing them arbitrarily for the sake of pictorial effect.

It is dangerous, too, and confusing, to play Shakespeare in costumes of a period later than his own, for the practice complicates the problem for an audience and gives the actor an extra responsibility. The humor of *Much Ado About Nothing* and the passionate Renaissance poetry of *Hamlet* belong to the Elizabethan age, and the text cannot make its full effect if the actors are speaking Shakespeare's lines while trying to look and behave like Carolean or Victorian ladies and gentlemen whose manners, furniture and households would have been completely foreign to Shakespeare. The modern-dress offerings were of considerable value in their time, by stripping productions of operatic falseness, but now there is a trend toward an elaboration of fancy both in costumes and scenery, allied to a tendency to ignore the music of the verse and speak it like modern colloquial dialogue. This can damage the text almost as badly as did the productions of the Victorian and Edwardian periods with their ruthless cutting, many intermissions and phony declamatory style of speaking and gesticulation. The natural simplicity that abounds in Shakespeare must continually alternate with the rich rhetorical loftiness of the text, and the actor must somehow capture the two simultaneously in his performance.

Here in the United States and in Canada you now appear determined to follow our English example and train your players in the classics. But you have a difficult task before you. For it seems that no small theaters are being built any more, and many have already been demolished, both here and in England. Therefore, there is bound to be a swing toward productions in which restless movement, striking innovations in costuming, sensational crowd work and a general liveliness of invention are calculated to divert an audience in a very large house, even though the text itself may be distorted or garbled and the characterization reduced to a contemporary slovenliness that robs the poetry of all flow and melody. There are other unfortunate results. The grand sweep of Shakespeare's selective imagery is broken by a jerky and uncomfortable compromise. Young players try to dissect their roles, realistically and psychologically, instead of acting them with boldness and imagination. They need first to learn how to stand still and speak beautifully, without fidgeting and byplay. It is impossible to perform Shakespeare with authority and conviction unless one trusts to the pattern of the language to sustain the lines, building up to and down from the climax of speech and scene.

Many directors are too concerned with the choreography and the liveliness of a performance, and not enough with the actual texture and quality of the words. But if the words are delivered under proper orchestral harmony and control, they can have more effect than anything else. I have always wanted to direct actors in magnificent costume and with no scenery and very little movement because the moment you have too much movement you cannot do justice to the dialogue. There are many passages in Shakespeare that really are arias. If the necessary intensity, subtlety, character and truth are to be given them, the audience must not be distracted by too much movement on the stage. Shaw once said, very aptly, "Shakespeare must be acted with the lines and on the lines, never in between the lines."

I do not think *Troilus and Cressida* is made easier for actors to interpret (or for the audience to follow) by directing it as a 1913 German operetta, nor do I approve of the most beautiful invention in *The Winter's Tale,* that of the statue coming down from the pedestal in the final scene, being arbitrarily changed by the director to a reclining figure on a tomb. Shakespeare, after all, had used that device most successfully in *Romeo and Juliet,* and it is hardly likely that he wished to repeat it in a later play. Besides, the text is directly opposed to such an alteration.

Perhaps I have no right to make such violent strictures. Only three years ago I played in an abstract production of *King Lear* with scenery and costume by Isamu Noguchi, a designer for whom I have the greatest admiration and respect. The result (at least as regards the costumes) was little short of disastrous, though we conceived the idea of the production not as a stunt but with the intention of suggesting the cosmic timelessness of Shakespeare's greatest tragedy. Our efforts were greeted with horrified expressions of dismay. But I am also bound to admit that the play survived, though for me it was a somewhat scarifying experience. . . .

TYRONE GUTHRIE

The proscenium stage is certainly not out of date. It probably never will go out of date. But it cannot any longer be regarded as the only kind of stage upon which a professional production can be satisfactorily presented. For certain kinds of play—almost all those written since about 1640—it is suitable, because it is the sort of stage which their authors had in mind when they were writing. But quite a number of plays, and indeed quite a number of interesting and important plays, were written before 1640; and it by no means follows that, either in theory or in practice, the proscenium-arch theater is the best mechanism for their production.

Let us take a particular instance, a familiar comedy of Shakespeare, *Twelfth Night*. In the first six or seven minutes the scene changes five times: Orsino's house or near it, the seacoast of Illyria, Olivia's house, then back to Orsino's house and back again to Olivia's house. It is theoretically possible by the use of elaborate machinery—and I doubt not but that in Germany it has been tried—to create the necessary three "realistic" sets and to shift them about at incredible speed.

Tyrone Guthrie: *A Life in the Theatre,* New York: McGraw-Hill Book Co., 1959, pp. 202-206. By permission of McGraw-Hill Book Co., Inc. Copyright 1959 by Tyrone Guthrie.

Tyrone Guthrie has staged Shakespeare all over the world, but is principally identified with the great period of the Old Vic and the founding of the Stratford, Ontario (Canada) Shakespeare Festival.

But, however fast the changes (if only three seconds), the mere fact of change is an interruption of the audience's concentration; and paradoxically, the faster, the more magical the change, the greater is the interruption—its very magic causes comment irrelevant to the matter of the play.

In fact, the usual solution of the problem is by compromise: either a composite, permanent set does duty for all localities, suggesting all of them vaguely and none of them literally, aiming rather to interpret the mood, atmosphere, or feeling of the play. Or else there are one or two elaborate full-stage pictures—outside Olivia's house is the obvious choice in *Twelfth Night,* since the greater part of the play's action can be plausibly arranged to take place there; the other scenes are played on the front of the stage before a series of drop-curtains painted to represent various other localities—Orsino's house, seacoast, street, cellar, and so on. While these front scenes are going on, the next full-stage set can be prepared and the actors out on the front must holler good and loud to drown the thuds and rumbles and blasphemy which accompany scene changes.

This latter was the method in vogue in the nineteenth century. In principle, this is how Irving's great productions were staged at the Lyceum in London. The main scenes, perhaps two or three or four, were very elaborate and magnificent. Irving lighted them by gaslight with great skill, and they evidently made a tremendous impression upon audiences which most certainly were not simple unsophisticated hayseeds. The front scenes were necessarily skimpy and sketchy; but the text was hacked and rearranged (Bernard Shaw says "butchered") with great ingenuity to squeeze the plays into the scenic formula which Irving's presentation demanded.

Then came William Poel and after him Granville-Barker, who between them revolutionized British, and thence American, ideas of Shakespearean production. The text must be inviolate. If realistic scenery cannot—and it cannot—be suitably adapted to the constant changes of environment and atmosphere indicated in the text, then realistic scenery must go.

Poel's productions were given on a bare stage; Barker, less austere, used very simple "stylized" indications. Like most other directors who during the last thirty or forty years have seriously grappled with Shakespeare, I agreed with Poel and Barker that the first considera- tion must be the text, that Irving and his contemporaries were wrong to subordinate this to scenic convenience, and that Shakespeare must not be tied to a literal realism.

Yet, that Shakespeare is to some considerable degree a realist can- not be denied. I assume that in dramatic art it is always essential that some recognizable correspondence be established between the imita- tion and the thing imitated; between the character which the actor is playing and the situation of that character and a recognizably simi- lar character and situation in real life. If an audience is to be inter- ested in his assumption of Hamlet, Lady Teazle or Harpagon, then the actor must embody to a considerable extent the audience's notion of a prince of Denmark, a squire's young wife or a miser. To do this it is not necessary to present a stereotype. A good actor will not dream of doing so. The merit of his acting will lie in the fact that his charac- terization is recognizably valid without respect to stereotype. But this cannot be achieved without resort to realistic imitation of observed phenomena.

In writing, as in acting, the same principle holds. We recognize the greatness of Shakespeare not only because of the music of his verse, the sweep of his philosophy, his artifice in theatrical construc- tion; he is also great in the minute observation and precise record of individual character and mannerism. Justice Shallow is a great crea- tion and, though created of a different species in a different manner, bears no less surely than Othello the stamp of genius. But Shallow is a piece of realistic art and must be realistically interpreted.

However, Shakespeare is only intermittently concerned with real- ism. In the main, he is not writing realistic dialogue or dealing with realistic characters or situations. Most of his characters have great reality but this effect is not, as a rule, achieved by a literal imitation of life. Intermittently he uses a realistic method to establish a cor- respondence between his figments and recognizable fact; but not as an end, only as a means. He uses a realistic method to contrast life-sized personages—Justice Shallow, for instance, Pompey, Froth and Elbow in *Measure for Measure* or the gravediggers in *Hamlet*—with heroic characters, larger than life-size. But for the most part Shakespeare, in the highly artificial form of blank verse, is creating characters who are larger than life.

Further, his dramatic construction, conditioned by the sort of building in which his plays were first performed, does not demand—does not permit—realistic scenery. When it is important to indicate where the characters in the play are supposed to be, such indication is given in the text. . . .

Therefore, Shakespeare should not be produced as though he were a realistic dramatist. The intermittent realism of this or that scene or character must be faithfully interpreted. But actual indications of time, place, atmosphere and so on, must be avoided; as must a reduction of great tragic conceptions to life-size; or no less damaging, a reduction of romances—*The Winter's Tale,* for instance, or *As You Like It*—to make them plausible. One of the charms of a tall tale is its very tallness.

LAURENCE OLIVIER

Personally I loathe all abstract discussions about the theater. They bore me. I assure you I shall never write a book about my theories of dramatic art. [Olivier has been as good as his word and has been unwilling to discuss his methods as actor and as director. But from interviews such as this one it is possible to infer his approach to directing, which has brought Shakespeare to vast, popular movie audiences.]

The actor must be disciplined. He must be so trained that he automatically carries out the director's orders. I expect my actors to do exactly what I tell them to do and to do it quickly, so I can see my own mistakes immediately if I have gone wrong. I believe the director must know the play so well that he grasps every important moment of every scene. He knows—and he alone—when the action should rise and where it should fall. He knows where to place the accents. An individual actor may not see the logic of an action. I require him to do so, and he must do it, for if the director really knows the play there is a sound reason for that action. . . .

I'd rather have run the scene eight times than have wasted that time in chattering away about abstractions. An actor gets the right thing by doing it over and over. Arguing about motivations and so forth is a lot of rot. American directors encourage that sort of thing

Laurence Olivier: "The Olivier Method," Interview, New York *Times*, Sunday, February 7, 1960, X, 1-3. By permission of the New York *Times*.

Laurence Olivier, responsible for so many challenging interpretations of Shakespeare as an actor, has vastly extended the audience for Shakespeare by his film versions of several of the plays. His activities as actor, director, and producer have earned him the honor of becoming the first director of England's National Theater.

too much. . . . Instead of doing a scene over again that's giving trouble, they want to discuss . . . discuss . . . discuss. . . .

The chief business of the director is to provide a point of view on the shape, meaning, and rhythm of the play and the rhythm is most important. When to slow the tempo, when to speed it. When to use a pause. Pauses are as important in a play as rests are in music. When I study a script, I always seek out the pauses hidden in it. . . .

[Olivier feels that his own quasi-military type of rehearsing is universal in the English theater. He explains that in England everyone is schooled in the Elizabethan plays and Restoration comedy. Therefore they learn to work within highly conventionalized forms and train themselves to be disciplined and accept outward rules of order. Olivier says that one cannot play poetic drama with its conventions of syllables, accents, and caesuras or artificial comedy, by means of intuition or spontaneity.]

I am not against spontaneity. But these emotional improvisations have to be worked out within a framework, within boundaries set by the director, and the director sets the boundaries in terms of the play. After all, actors and directors are the servants of the play, aren't they?

JOHN HOUSEMAN

Today, in the absence of any consistent pattern of acting upon our American stages, the director of a Shakespearean production tends to assume greater responsibility and is credited with a more directly creative influence than in the days when a long-accreted pseudo-classic tradition, for better or worse, restricted the variety of successive revivals to the personal taste and physical idiosyncrasies of the presiding star. As a result, the director generally shares with his cast the approval or the condemnation of the critics and audiences alike; where the star and director are one, he is likely to find himself judged, separately, for each of his dual functions.

Indeed, the present fashion is rather to overestimate the scope and power of the director. Today, more than anyone else in our theater, the director is inevitably affected by the changing conditions of our disturbed world. No matter how personal and clear his original conception or how firm the imaginative structure upon which he had hoped to form the play of his choice, by the time it reaches the public it is likely to have been appreciably reshaped and colored by the cultural and economic circumstances under which he finds himself producing it.

How widely these conditions may vary, even within the major the-

John Houseman: "On Directing Shakespeare," *Theatre Arts,* Vol. XXXV, April 1951, 52-54. By permission of John Houseman.

John Houseman has staged Shakespeare at the Mercury Theatre with Orson Welles and on Broadway. He provided the initial artistic direction for the American Shakespeare Festival, Stratford, Connecticut, where he was assisted by the young director Jack Landau, and produced the film version of *Julius Caesar.*

atrical areas of the English-speaking world, may be seen by making a few quick comparisons between the material circumstances surrounding the preparation and performance of two . . . productions of the same play; Shakespeare's *King Lear* as presented at Stratford-on-Avon and in New York City.

John Gielgud's Lear (at Stratford) was played thirty-two times over a period of about three months; it usually had three performances a week, in a repertory of five Shakespearean plays of widely varying mood produced in diverse styles by the same company under several different directors. In New York, at the National Theater on 41st Street, Louis Calhern played Lear fifty-three times, under the standard conditions of a Broadway run, at the appalling rate of eight times a week. The Stratford version, priding itself on the integrity of its text, ran three and a half hours; on Forty-first Street, conforming to current theater-going habit, the audience was out within two hours and forty-three minutes of the curtain's rise.

One thing both Lears had in common: a nominal rehearsal period of five weeks. Yet even this similarity is deceiving when one examines the actual circumstances of these rehearsals. Of the Stratford company . . . about half had been with the theater the previous year; in fact, two of their productions were repeats from an earlier season. Its leading actors, almost without exception, had previously and frequently played together—in Shakespeare. Of the New York company . . . no three members had ever acted together before; less than one third had ever appeared, professionally, in any of the plays of Shakespeare; five had, at one time or another, worked with their present director. Finally, of the two actors playing the part of Lear, the one was playing the King for the third time . . . the other had not appeared in a Shakespearean part since boyhood.

As to the technical conditions of rehearsal: the members of the Stratford company rehearsed during the day, while currently appearing, in repertory *on their own stage* and *on the platforms* which subsequently became part of their scenery. The members of the New York company found themselves working, at one time or another, on five different stages; it was not until the evening of their first dress rehearsal that they finally set foot upon the step-units and platforms which formed the basis of their production.

There is one further comparison to be made of a predominantly economic nature. The Shakespeare Memorial Theatre at Stratford is an established and highly successful concern backed by solid financial guarantees. Broadway's *King Lear* was a straight commercial venture; its producers suffered a loss of over a hundred thousand dollars.

Do these strike you as sordid facts, quite unrelated to the art of the theater? It is the purpose of this piece to prove that they are, on the other hand, very closely related indeed. Without attempting, in any way, to pass judgment upon the social or theatrical merits of the two systems—Endowed Classical Repertory or the One-Shot Commercial—I am trying to make it clear how widely they vary in their working conditions and how different are the functions of their respective directors.

The one is working with a company of actors accustomed to each other's style, preparing and developing a number of well-known plays in the comparative security of a familiar stage, with an assured audience, under the economic guarantee of a seasonal engagement. His function, with each production, is to galvanize these established elements into fresh life.

The other, at his first rehearsal, faces a troupe of actors especially selected and gathered for the occasion from every corner of U.S. show business. Their experience, their training, their habits, even their personal attitudes toward the art and business of acting are different, and frequently in conflict. And all these diversities, which the director has a scant month to understand, assimilate and absorb into the body of his production, are aggravated by the economic anxiety inherent in the current Broadway production system.

You start bravely enough—vigorous and enthusiastic—stirred by the play's unfolding greatness and the newly discovered wealth of its parts. Then, as the days pass all too swiftly, the normal, healthy tensions, the groping and the self-doubting, all the inevitable hazards of rehearsal become distorted and magnified under the pressures of what Broadway's leading critic has aptly called its "neurotic ordeal."

It could be shown, I believe, that the erratic violence of playing that characterizes some of the contemporary American theater's most vital direction is a direct reflection of this particular anxiety, the obsessive preoccupation with the Smash Hit. Whether it is proper for Shakespeare to be subjected to such tensions is not a matter for argument. Under present conditions in the Commercial theater, he has no choice. And, by and large, it appears that the Bard can take it.

(SUMMER 1962)

Since this was written, there have been changes in our theatrical landscape—many of them for the worse. Under Broadway's current catastrophic economic set-up, commercial production of Shakespeare's plays have been entirely suspended. A number of Shakespeare festivals have been created in other places which function successfully on a limited, seasonal basis but offer no immediate hope for creative continuity. So, basically, the actor's and director's situation remains unchanged.

MARGARET WEBSTER

"The only grace and setting of a tragedy," wrote one of Shakespeare's contemporary playwrights, "is a full and understanding auditory." It is as true today as it was three hundred years ago. His plays,
the greatest in the English language, can only be kept alive, in the
fullest and most vivid sense, through the living theater.

. . . I have tried honestly to interpret the author's intention, as
nearly as I could divine it, to the audiences for whom the productions
were intended. I have never supposed that I was providing any definitive answer to the problems of the plays, specially those of the inexhaustible *Hamlet*. . . . I found that actors were plainly frightened of
Shakespeare, particularly of the verse, and were initially disinclined
to regard his characters as real people. Audiences were frightened,
too; but they also proved, I found, eager and swift, very ready to
respond, the kind of audience Shakespeare himself might have wished
for. . . .

One of the most vital tasks which confront the Shakespearean producer in America is the breaking-down of this unwholesome reverence for the Bard. There is at present no tradition as to the production or playing of Shakespeare, and this freedom is, in itself, an
opportunity. The repertory companies which used to tour the country
have been forced out of business by economic conditions and the
competition of new forms of entertainment. There have been indi-

Margaret Webster: "Producing Shakespeare," *Theatre Arts Magazine,* Vol. XXVI,
January 1942, 43-48. By permission of Margaret Webster.
    Margaret Webster has directed numerous Shakespeare productions in England
and America and has described her life's work in staging the classics in *Shakespeare
Without Tears*.

vidual, and blazing, performances by stars who have had the vision
and the ability to avail themselves of Shakespeare—John Barrymore,
Jane Cowl, Katharine Cornell, and others. But there has been no
standard against which succeeding actors and directors could measure
the truth of interpretation newly divined, little informed knowledge
of the plays and of their author. Tradition is sometimes a yardstick.
It need not be merely a collection of fusty and outworn shreds from
the theatrical wardrobe of an earlier time. The modern theater, confused and uncertain upon this as almost every other topic, vacillates
between excessive respectfulness and a determination to be novel at
any cost. . . .

The principles on which a director must base his approach to a
Shakespearean play are, after all, no different from those which govern his approach to any other play; his method will vary, since the
technique of directing is itself subject to every degree of personal
idiosyncrasy. I believe that he should determine first the mood of the
play, its material and spiritual atmosphere, its structural pattern, the
wholeness of its effect. What kind of a world is this of Arden or Elsi-
nore, Illyria or Verona? what forces are at work in it? what values
or what standards hold good within its confines? Shakespeare will
have employed certain dramatic devices whose origin and purpose
we must learn to recognize through a knowledge of the material,
human or inanimate, which he employed. But what was the intention behind these theater devices? Knowing his method, we may
guess at his mind; perceiving the familiar, we may divine the tran-
scendental. With the former, we must sometimes take liberties of
adaptation; the latter we may not violate except at our own peril.

The bridge over which we shall travel to Shakespeare's country,
like the bridge we ourselves shall build from stage to auditorium, is
built of human beings. Who are these people? From King Lear to
the Third Citizen, we must know them. It is always a sense of closeness at which we should aim, rather than an emphasis of separation.

We shall not have to dress Hotspur in the uniform of the R.A.F. in
order to invest him with life; we underrate both our author and our
audience in supposing that they can only be dragged into accord by

distorting Coriolanus to the image of General Franco; slyly insinu-
ating that there have been abdications of the English throne more
recent than that of Richard II; on claiming with gleeful shouts that
Enobarbus is an anticipatory Rudolf Hess. The truth of the plays is
a timeless truth, and similarity of external circumstances no more
than a fortuitous, though sometimes poignant, reminder that the
returning paths of history have been trodden by many feet. In these
days those who love the theater and are jealous for its power and
prerogative are rightly eager that it should prove itself as a contemporary force. But Shakespeare is not an escapist; he aims straight for
the heart. There is singularly little hatred in the plays, and infinite
understanding. It would be a barren world which ever felt that it
had gone beyond his wisdom and compassion.

PETER BROOK

Isolation is a very discredited ambition and complete detachment
has almost ceased to be a possibility: it is rare for an historian or a
philosopher to escape from the influences of his time, and for the
worker in the theater, whose livelihood depends upon his contact
with his audiences, this is impossible. Consequently, however hard
a producer or a designer may strive to mount a classic with complete
objectivity, he can never avoid reflecting a second period—the one in
which he works and lives. . . .

One of the greatest possible errors that a producer can make is to
believe that a script can speak for itself. No play can speak for itself.

Peter Brook: "Style in Shakespearean Production," *Orpheus*, Vol. I, 1948, 139-
146. By permission of Peter Brook.
Peter Brook, who began his career at the Shakespeare Festival, Stratford, England, has staged plays, classic and modern, in many countries.

If an actor delivers his lines clearly but monotonously, no one will think that he is doing his job well. However, it is still widely believed in this country that the flat and static production is good, whilst the one that uses all the resources of theater to illuminate the text is said to obscure the play. Indeed, in England, far too large a proportion of intelligent playgoers know their Shakespeare too well. They are no longer capable of going to the theater with that willingness to suspend disbelief which any naïve spectator can bring. They go coldly, as specialists, to listen to the over-familiar lines, and to watch the actor's treatment of them. It is their influence on the theater that has led to the type of Shakespeare production that is not uncommon nowadays, cold, correct, literary, untheatrical, winning great praise, but making no emotional impact on the average spectator.

The school of Poel and Granville-Barker rendered a great service to the theater by its reaction from the excessive elaboration of the His Majesty's style of presentation. However, it went to the other extreme and sought simplicity in retrogression. . . . It is a grotesque oversimplification to believe that anything can be achieved by going back on the developments of the theater in the course of the last few hundred years. . . . Realizing this, a number of producers attempt a compromise. Within the pictorial conventions of the present-day proscenium, they build a structure that fulfills the necessary geographical qualifications of the Elizabethan stage, and yet can be used and lit as though part of a modern production.

This method falls dangerously between two stools. It aims at freeing the text by turning the set into a formal platform, but it fails to recognize that simply by being inside a proscenium it ceases to be a platform and becomes a picture. . . . The error is very similar in modern-dress productions of Shakespeare. They emanate from the theory that modern clothes, like the contemporary clothes which the Elizabethan actors wore, are completely functional, and thus the least distracting form of costume for a tragedy. However, the Elizabethan actor was playing in his modern clothes on his formal platform stage; actors inside a picture frame are always actors in a period costume, even when the period happened to be the present day. One can not escape from their incongruity, and in the last resort they are less functional and more distracting than the most ornate of dresses.

When an audience enters a theater, its imagination is completely open. If, as in *Our Town,* it finds the curtain up, the stage bare, then the initial antipictorial gesture of the production makes it clear that no picture is going to be presented. . . . However, if the curtain is lowered, if, when the lights fade and the curtain rises, one sees a structure with period decoration, if the lighting suggests even as elementary an atmosphere as day or night, already the audience has accepted a pictorial convention, and at once surrenders its imagination into the hands of the producer. This imposes a heavy obligation on him not to betray his trust, and if he tried to compromise by allowing the play to be semiformalized, instead of going all the way pictorially, the audience will feel cheated. It will neither have the satisfaction of exercising its own imagination, nor will it have the thrill of yielding to a continually imaginative and convincing stage illusion. . . .

To communicate any one of Shakespeare's plays to a present-day audience, the producer must be prepared to set every resource of modern theater at the disposal of his text. . . . In *Romeo and Juliet* the problem was above all to find a modern stagecraft which would give freedom and space to the sweep of the poem. The time for the assumption that *Romeo and Juliet* is a sentimental story to be played against a series of backdrops giving picture-postcard views of Italy must surely be gone. It is a play of youth, of freshness, of open air, in which the sky—the great tent of the Mediterranean blue—hangs over every moment of it, from the first brawl in the dusty market to the calm and peaceful cadence in the grave. It is a play of wide spaces, in which all scenery and decoration easily become an irrelevance, in which one tree on a bare stage can suggest the loneliness of a place of exile, one wall, as in Giotto, an entire house. Its atmosphere is described in a single line, "these hot days is the mad blood stirring," and its treatment must be to capture the violent passion of two children lost amongst the Southern fury of the warring houses. Any approach to the play that takes as its starting point its essentially virile and very Elizabethan spirit soon finds that there is no place for sweetness and sentimentality in the characterization, in the speaking, in the settings or in the music. . . .

The producer is working with three elements: his text, his audience, and his medium, and of these only the first is constant. It is his primary duty to discover every intention of the author and to transmit these with every possible means at his disposal. As the theater develops, as its shape and geography, its machinery and its conventions change, so production style must change with it. There is no perfect production of any play, nor is there any final one: like a musician's interpretation, its existence is inseparable from its performance. . . .

PETER HALL

Speaking has lagged behind other aspects of present-day production. Shakespearean actors need a great deal of practice. They do not get it. Those who can act Shakespeare have been doing so on and off for twenty years. More often than not the director is in the position of a choreographer asked to stage a ballet with people who haven't had a lesson. A girl may have acted successfully in television and realistic drama. How can she trip gaily into a Shakespearean part and bring it off? It is as if you were to call on a singer with a natural aptitude for folk song to undertake Isolde. Given a month

Peter Hall: "Mr. Peter Hall on Speaking Shakespeare," The London *Times*, December 22, 1958, 5. Reprinted by permission from the *Times* (London) and *Mid-Century Drama*, by Laurence Kitchin, Faber and Faber, 1962.

Peter Hall is currently the director of the Shakespeare Festival at Stratford, England, under whose leadership the activities of the Festival are being substantially extended into London itself.

to stage a Shakespeare play you cannot also teach your cast to speak him.

Consider the case history of a young actor. He is singled out at drama school and does a term in repertory during which he will play one or two Shakespearean parts if he is lucky. This leads to some success in London, usually in a realistic modern play. Then, quite rightly on the strength of his talent, he is invited to the Old Vic or to Stratford, where he is faced with playing a part for which all his past training is largely superfluous.

Now Shakespeare is not a dramatist of understatement. What he says, what he literally means, is fully expressed in his writing as if it were a piece of music. A Shakespeare play like an operatic score gives one the end product, a complex image. You must work from that back to the actor and from that the actor finds the realistic human motives which made him able to sing or say the poetic impression. In a realistic prose play the dialogue is a raw material tending to become a realistic or poetic product which the actor has a greater hand in. He can phrase a line in an infinite variety of ways and still create the same effect. He may be forgiven for saying: "I can't speak this line. I don't feel it." But a Shakespearean actor who did that would be like a violinist in an orchestra who got up and said: "I can't play A. I don't feel it."

And so the critics often say of a newcomer that he is a good actor but cannot play Shakespeare, that his voice is too modern and his personality too; that he cannot play heroic drama. It was said of Sir Laurence Olivier and of Dame Edith Evans and of Mr. Richard Burton and recently of Miss Dorothy Tutin. So the actor leaves Shakespeare sore. But he may sooner or later come back and if he's got guts and keeps on shooting he'll get it in the end. By and large, training consists in doing it. The verse imposes itself on them at last, and after struggling to turn Shakespeare into modern prose, and suffering agonies, the actor sooner or later finds it plays itself.

[After lack of practice, Mr. Hall cites two other reasons for unsatisfactory diction.] Both the Old Vic and the Stratford Memorial Theater are unsuitable for speaking Shakespeare. You have to have more spectacle than the words can allow, because these are still picture-frame stages. Moreover, ours is a visual society in which, other than to music, people are not trained to listen. You've got to parade a bit. There is the lady who said: "It's so beautiful. The dresses are so pretty. It's charming. I'd never have known it was a Shakespeare play."

The ideal solution is a corps of actors based on Shakespeare, a permanent company. In reality as soon as you say: "We'll do that" in drama, compromise begins. The rhythm of *Waiting for Godot* is organized to such a point that you can't take a line out without altering the balance. But Beckett kept saying to me: "Play it slower!" and if you slow down beyond a certain point you cannot hold attention. As director you've got to come down on one side or the other. Inevitably in the theater you're going to be right for some and not for others. The greatest art, even Olivier's *Macbeth,* is always controversial. I am resentful of criticism that is uninformed or dismissive. After all, it is the only record of our work.

MICHAEL LANGHAM

In my view the most rewarding approach, in appraising what these works are about, is that of the humanist. But I think it needs to be at once both detached and compassionate—neither prejudiced, nor sentimental—and always seeking for those illuminating human truths which, coupled with the poetry, represent the heart of the work. There is, of course, a danger that such an approach will lead to the realistic human values gaining more attention than the poetic—which is folly, for the poetic values have in the theater the power to create an experience of sublime human ecstasy, and are unquestionably more important. But, conversely, emphasizing them to the point of excluding human values seems equally misguided. Ideally, I think, there should be a delicate blending of the two—and this will prove a highly precarious operation.

In searching for the essential style, or character, or essence of a Shakespeare play we are best advised to examine carefully the form of its writing. The Elizabethan age was passionately musical; indeed, musical virtuosity at that time was probably a more valuable social asset than literacy, and it is folly not to regard the texts primarily as musical scores. The Elizabethans, with no dramatic heritage to guide them, but in the spirit of adventure and discovery that distinguished their time, seem to have experimented vigorously with all possible forms of dialogue—rhyming verse, blank verse, the longer line, the

Michael Langham: "An Approach to Staging Shakespeare's Works," drawn from a lecture delivered at the Universities of Canada Seminar at the Stratford Shakespearean Festival, Stratford, Ontario, August 16, 1961. By permission of Michael Langham.

Michael Langham is the director of the Shakespearean Festival, Stratford, Ontario (Canada).

shorter line, prose—like a painter choosing and mixing his colors, until they found the exact answer to suit their various dramatic needs.

Dramatic verse should be no more awkward to speak than should vocal music be awkward to sing. If the latter is the case, we write the composer down as incompetent. So we should the dramatist. But there is nothing to stop the composer or dramatist trying his performer's skill to the utmost—as Marlowe tried the skill of his leading player, Edward Alleyn. Alleyn must have possessed not only incredible breath control but also an amazingly resourceful and powerful vocal organ, for it is most unlikely that Marlowe would have continued to make demands in his scripts that could not be met on the stage. (I know of no contemporary actor who can master these big vocal extravagances.) Shakespeare himself threw out similar challenges to the voice—especially to his highly trained boy actors: there are passages of Juliet, for instance, which are as deliberately bravura as an aria of Mozart's.

The modern actor, and director, for that matter, inhibited by an overabundance of naturalism, tends on the whole either to shirk these highly colored musical/emotional climaxes (sometimes by destroying their true quality through shapeless underplaying, sometimes by cutting them) or to present them with a loud, empty rhetorical flourish. It is perhaps a reflection of this age that our actors and we in the audience seem to have lost the appetite for the big dramatic aria where a "larger than life" hero or heroine faces a "larger than life" conflict. We have not lost this appetite in the opera house: indeed, we should be grossly affronted if an opera singer *hummed* his great aria. But such avoidance of the task set is—to our great loss—what we regularly tolerate in the "straight" theater. In my view it has grown too straight, flat, "natural," and musically unstimulating. The contemporary player, and especially the conscientious seeker after the "truth" of a part, is so preoccupied with this truth in his own small domestic terms that he continually overlooks and belittles his author's vaster intentions. He resists at all costs the "unnatural," while important theater, almost invariably, can only hope to convey its widest implications by eschewing naturalness—as in the Moscow Art

Theater's current productions of Chekhov. Many of our modern actors prefer to drop down on all fours, to scratch and grunt inarticulately, than to reach out and up and beyond to the world of the gods.

Our society, which we may call a society of disillusion, is no doubt responsible for this. In the past, man has always been ready to respond to a deep-rooted impulse to glory in his creation and his destiny. Indeed, out of this impulse he has often aspired to a kind of divinity. In our society today, moral values and faith being in short supply, he is generally cynical about such things. The astronomer/scientist almost alone finds a glory in his destiny: he has faith that all will be revealed. He keeps his head lifted to the stars, and finds a concrete meaning in Heaven. But western man, not truly understanding the mysteries of science (the interpreters—the poets, novelists and playwrights—have not yet enlightened him), and having lost much of his faith not only in a loving Heavenly Father but also—and perhaps more importantly—in Man himself, generally sees no point in dwelling on the glory of anything.

One manifestation of this is the "beatnik"; another may often be found in the theater, when an actor, made cynical and grasping by an overmaterialistic, disillusioned society, falls back upon his diminished view of himself to measure the great roles of Macbeth or Lear or Othello. Naturally enough, he finds himself "o'erparted," and so trims and hacks away at the role until he can fit it to his own puny stature. Insignificant, domestic themes are then made to take the place of the play's major timeless issues.

What is to be done? We cannot put the clock back. But we can, in the theater as in the other performing arts, struggle to retain our values and cling to a strength and a truth in our interpretation of the classics. We can surely use our gifts to enhance these works rather than to diminish them. We may fail ever so little or ever so much, but I think if we are deeply aware of the significance to us of their timeless universality before their immediate, contemporary implications, we can hope to maintain their true stature.

WILLIAM BALL

So strongly are we subject to the direct and indirect influence of advertising and commercialism that in our theater we frequently see artistic scripts misshaped, misrepresented, and even destroyed by imaginative directors who feel compelled to package their work with sensationalism, an allegedly unique approach, or a personalized, clever interpretation. A new production of a Shakespearean master-piece is often treated like oleomargarine: it is proclaimed to be better than the real thing; it is packaged in excessively ornate, easily recog-nized designs (derived, in the main, from homespun American cul-ture or repressed sexual drives); it is brought into focus by clichés and snappy slogans aimed at the coddled average American mentality; and the final coup—the gimmick—is calculated, if all else fails, to rescue the supposedly inferior product, and bludgeon the naïve con-sumer into a dazed conviction that the pretty girl on the package does, in fact, make the contents more palatable.

Bright-idea productions indicate that the director admits that (1) he considers the play, as written, dull or incomprehensible, and that it desperately needs his help, or (2) he assumes his audience to be so dull in the wits that they require graphic illustrations, a directorial browbeating in order to understand and enjoy the work, or (3) he is personally bored with the basic theme of the work and probably con-siders his boredom universal; to stimulate his own tired palate and

William Ball: "Give the Audience a Chance," *Theatre Arts,* Vol. XLV, August 1961, 61. By permission of William Ball.

William Ball, the young American director, is associated with the San Diego Shakespeare Festival and responsible for several productions of modern off-Broad-way plays.

the palates of those whom he believes to be his audience, he hunts among the sauces and spices for a new recipe.

We so often hear those supposedly creative expressions: "We're taking it out of the museum and brushing away the cobwebs," "We're rescuing it from the library and the classroom and all the stuffy old-fashioned productions," "We're going to give it *new life*." When "it" refers to a fine play, this kind of palaver suggests no more than bravado that may ruin a masterpiece. Instilling "new life" is obviously one of the reasons for reviving a classic. New life in depth and in breadth of values is, I hope, always our purpose; but playing games with the surface values of a great play is simple dilettantism, and any director who does so in the name of art is neither honorable nor trustworthy.

Recently, two phrases from Shakespeare—"Lend me your ears!" and "On your imaginary forces *work!*"—have most strongly influenced my work at the San Diego Shakespeare Festival. An audience's perception of Shakespeare is frequently muddied by an overloading of visual effects.

Since the decline of radio, very little has been done in drama to utilize the willingness of the audience to extend its vision *beyond* what it is looking at, and to help it to see with a larger vision—that is, to see with its imagination. The despair of many designers seems to be that they have neither sufficient money nor sufficient space to put an entire town or three entire towns or twelve rooms on stage either simultaneously or in rapid succession. Contrary to what most of those highly paid persons feel, I believe the less spectacle an audience sees with its eyes, the more it will see with its imagination. Very few scenic, costume and lighting designers in this country know anything about the power of *suggestion*. All fine artists respond to the notion that a single well-chosen detail or motif, well placed, well proportioned, will reveal worlds of reality. (Why is this such a rare concept in American film and stage art?) The audience's *imagined* spectacle can be counted on as more vital and real because it arises from the creative participation of each individual. It is more vivid because it springs from the total wealth of his past experience. Especially in Shakespeare I feel an audience should be subtly but thoroughly challenged to give that wealth to the playwright. I'm convinced that this challenge always evinces real, though often subconscious, excitement in the theater.

JOSEPH PAPP

If we are to accept the idea that directing is an art, then we must recognize the fact that any description of the director's approach is limited to enumerating a set of principles. Beyond that, we enter a world of throbbing intangibles which are extremely personal and have little meaning for anybody but the director—and sometimes not even for him.

To begin with, let me warn you that the rules that guide our work at the New York Shakespeare Festival are not startlingly original. Most of them have been expressed before, and with greater eloquence. Yet, while we resemble the other professional festivals in this country and elsewhere, we have a few special features that affect our work on the stage.

At first glance the fact that our productions are free to the public may seem to have little bearing on the directorial point of view. But a closer look at this unusual mode of operation may reveal that it is

Joseph Papp: "Modernity and the American Actor," *Theatre Arts,* Vol. XLV, August 1961, 63. By permission of Joseph Papp.

Joseph Papp has devoted his energies to the creation of the New York Shakespeare Festival, which presents Shakespeare in Central Park free of charge to the people of New York City.

one of the most significant influences. Because we want to attract a wide audience for Shakespeare, we don't charge admission. Our audience is therefore made up largely of people who have never seen professional theater. But they have been to the movies and they watch television. Both mediums have conditioned them to a style of acting that (without passing judgment on the quality) we may call generally natural and unaffected. It has a sense of reality about it, even though it may sometimes be superficial. Be that as it may, have an audience composed of persons who insist that we serve them a style of Shakespeare they can relate to their contemporary experiences—which means that it must be free of bombast and conventional stage artifices. They demand a Shakespeare that is believable, and will settle only for characters with whom they can identify.

The challenge for the director therefore is to achieve this modernity without sacrificing the form and poetry of Shakespeare, and without vulgarizing the period.

It is immediately apparent that our actors cannot be "natural" in the sense that Gregory Peck is natural. The language and costumes of our productions will not permit that. Then how are we to present classical plays in a natural way?

We look for the answer in our casting. In the choice of the actor, we determine the style of our productions. Putting it another way, to imbue our plays with the kind of reality understood by our modern audience, we select the actor who best communicates it.

We seek blood-and-guts actors, those who bring spice and vitality to the production—actors who have the stamp of truth on everything they say or do. Their roles always have a psychological base, which means they experience deep emotions on the stage.

We are lucky that our special economics do not force us to adopt a star system. We are free of the need to be satisfied only with a box-office success. We have the luxury of concentrating on the more significant concerns of the theater—the play and the production.

The discipline of Shakespeare is a challenge to the professional American actor. Since the only tradition he has to work with is that of realistic acting, he is approaching the problem of playing Shakespeare not merely by learning to scan lines and speak with well-rounded tones, but through the subtle and fascinating exploration into the deep emotional veins of Shakespeare's poetry. This is not a matter of arguing the merits of "working from within" and "working from without." Shaw understood the basic principle that works so well for modern American actors. It is founded on the creation of a feeling so deep and so full that one can only resort to poetry to express oneself adequately. Given a sustained experience in the classics, the good American actor will be able to achieve the greatest heights in poetic drama. He has the basic stuff. What he needs is consistent work.

STUART VAUGHAN

The real task we have—those of us who try to produce Shakespeare for modern audiences—is to reach those audiences with the essence of Shakespeare's human meaning. Shakespeare's plays had great significance for his own audiences. We must try to find what he intended his audience to receive and transmit the same effect and intention to our own. This is frequently very difficult to do.

For example, the young Isabella, about to become a nun in *Measure for Measure,* places such importance on her chastity that it seems more honorable to her that her brother should suffer death than that she should save him by surrendering to Angelo. Clearly it is difficult to show her situation today in a sympathetic light, for many people in our audience would say she suffers from a mistaken sense of values. Equally, Shakespeare obviously intended us to admire Isabella, not to think her a little prude or a silly mistaken child. The director's task, then, in casting and rehearsal, is to adjust his company and their motives so clearly that the audience can understand and sympathize with Isabella. His job is to transport the modern audience into a specific world of the past so completely that even a different set of moral values seems probable. Anyone who saw Peter Brook's production knows it is not necessary to evade or ridicule the tenets of Shakespeare's play for today's audience. This is not to say all *Hamlets* must be alike, but that the play should not be distorted or re-oriented because the director lacks faith in Shakespeare's longevity. We

Stuart Vaughan: "Some Thoughts on Shakespearean Production," *Playbill,* January 27, 1958, 33-35. By permission of Stuart Vaughan.

Stuart Vaughan, associated with the New York Shakespeare Festival when this essay was written, has also staged Shakespeare at the Phoenix Theater in New York City.

should have the courage to play the plays Shakespeare wrote if we bother to go to the expense and trouble of mounting them at all.

The Shakespeare I have directed has always been done in period costume, either the costume of Shakespeare's own period, the period he depicts in the play, or some satisfactory compromise between the two. I have made it an axiom never to present the plays in costume and period setting at a time significantly later than the period of their writing. In the theater, one achieves "universality" only by being really specific and detailed. We recognize Hamlet as a great characterization, not because Shakespeare wrote him "to speak for all of us;" but because in him Shakespeare wrote so truthfully, in such intimate examination, that he stands before us breathing. So with all Shakespeare's "universal" plays. They are very much of their time. We can illuminate that time so the audience understands it. Violate that time and one destroys the frame of reference in which the play has meaning.

Indeed, in reference to certain comedies, I feel that changing or modernizing the period is a camouflage (which deceives only a few members of the public and certain drama critics) for failing to understand the humor of the play. The "new" costumes and settings become a means of not running the race. Laughs are raised, but not the laughs of the script. The script is buried under piles of hokum with bicycles or six-shooters or bustles. Or some poor actor is made to look terribly silly spouting Elizabethan verse while dressed in a very decent dinner jacket. . . .

. . . I think my concept of what "style" and "poetry" are differs somewhat from the accepted "traditional" pattern. What passes on many stages for the poetic and the subtle sounds to me very much like meaningless song and self-indulgent speechifying. What passes frequently for "period movement" looks so often to me like posturing. Productions filled with this mouthing and posing tend to be set and lit with all the elegance and beauty of a Lord and Taylor Christmas window. Indeed, in such productions, the pearshaped tones have so little in common with the purpose of speech in life that the clever salesmanship of visual beauty is essential to persuade the audience that the product is worth having. The only visual beauty worth its cost must derive from a truly human approach to the play itself.

If we remember that almost all Shakespeare's characters are very intelligent, and that even his stupid clowns have an innate love of language and word-play, then it follows that in these crisp, clean, and sometimes harsh and primitive plays, the sense of the poetic is conveyed by an amazingly spontaneous speaking of just the right thing. The character himself chooses that word and delights in having found it. He does not sing it, or roll it in his mouth, because he is busy with his next thought, which probably comes along rapidly.

He does not speak in a Shakespeare play any differently than he does in life, because, as he is a character in a play, this *is* life to him. The actor must know not to break up the verse with incorrect pauses. He must learn how the lines scan and then how to "forget" that terrible and insistent iambic rhythm which can strangle variety. The actor must remember most of all that he must be inwardly and outwardly and impudently real. If the audience ever stops believing him in order to admire him, then Shakespeare has been replaced by something else, and the point of the evening has been lost. . . .

It seems to me that "period movement" simply means behaving naturally in clothes that are not your own. If you fence a lot, ride horseback, and wear tights with no pockets, this will condition the way you walk and stand. If you wear a skirt with a huge farthingale day after day, you will manage it with a certain aplomb and dispatch, and the way you sit on chairs will be conditioned, unquestionably, by the practical considerations of the farthingale. These are not matters of art, but of common sense. . . .

In the search for this simplicity of truly poetic speech and the straightforward elegance of honest and human behavior, American actors and directors of Shakespeare may tend for a time to do work which seems a bit "rough and ready." As we continue to apply that which is rewarding from the Stanislavsky Method to Shakespeare, and continue to accept the influence of Brecht as a means of sharpening our clarity and point of view, these temporary crudities will probably disappear.

We must not forget, too, that continued discipline of voice and body are necessary for our thinking actors, to enable them to realize theatrically those emotional and intellectual values which they so burn to convey. I strongly feel we must constantly remind ourselves that the theater consists only of what the audience can see and hear. If they can't see the concept, or hear the concept, it does not exist for them. Only if we examine the inner truth of every moment of a play, and then securely select and control that moment's outer form, vocal and physical, can we achieve a realization of total concept which will bring Shakespeare's meaning home to our supporters, the audience.

FRANCO ZEFFIRELLI

When the Old Vic invited me to produce *Romeo and Juliet,* my first reaction was to refuse because it is so difficult for a foreigner to believe that any but British or American people would be able to touch their own cultural heritage, especially with Shakespearean tradition.

Recollecting my reasons for accepting, I believe the decision was not dictated entirely by professional considerations but also for idealistic reasons beyond the limits of the theater. I had worked in England presenting Italian works and the real satisfaction I took back to Italy was simply that I had helped a little towards the better understanding of its culture by the English.

Now I have an even more interesting task—a combination of Italian feeling applied to a masterpiece of the classical English theater which

Franco Zeffirelli: Note written before London premiere of *Romeo and Juliet,* Oct. 4, 1960. Reprinted in *Playbill,* Feb. 12, 1962, 19-20. By permission of Franco Zeffirelli.

Franco Zeffirelli, young Italian director, staged and designed his first English production of Shakespeare, *Romeo and Juliet,* for the Old Vic.

might prove, if successful, that times have changed in Europe and people of different backgrounds can easily work together for creating a new European conscience.

This is to me far more important than any diplomatic or political maneuvers.

I know that it may sound presumptuous, but actually I have felt so elated because of the wonderful atmosphere created during the preparation of this *Romeo and Juliet*.

The Company the Old Vic management has called together for this production is far better than I could ever have imagined. They offer all the professional enthusiasm typical of young people still finding themselves, their "perfectionism" is astonishing, and they are not only remarkable actors, but are proving to be indeed the kind of "new Europeans" I was mentioning before. In our mutual understanding lie all the hopes for the success of this production.

.   .   .   .

At first the actors were a bit suspicious—it was like fitting them into a new suit.[1] But then came too much enthusiasm and participation. I had to control a flood. . . . [Zeffirelli likes to work freely, empirically, and improvisationally with his actors in an atmosphere of collaboration and love. He hates directors who use actors as puppets to carry out their own theories and ideas. He finds German directors from Reinhardt to Brecht most guilty of a lack of trust in their actors. In his view the Berliner Ensemble shows "great thought, great art, but not enough love."]

You can't force an actor. He doesn't play with his technique, he plays with his own human qualities. My job is to offer many different solutions to him, and then to choose the right one. It may be comic or tragic, but it must be the right one *for him*. It must become part of his own blood and flesh. . . .

I once saw a production of *La Forza del Destino* with tanks and

[1] These observations are culled from two interviews: "Reviving the Dead World of the Classics," Kenneth Tynan Interviews Zeffirelli, London: *The Observer*, Sept. 18, 1960, 13; "The Zeffirelli Way," The London *Times*, Sept. 19, 1960, 4. Reprinted by permission from the *Times* (London) and *Mid-Century Drama*, by Laurence Kitchin, Faber & Faber, 1962.

gas masks. That kind of thing is betraying the nature of a former creation. Direction is not pure creation. You take somebody else's conception and have to respect it. Your work is going to pass, their work is remaining. You can't take the Fifth Symphony and play it as jazz. . . .

You don't need many ideas [in directing a play], you need one. On that you work and the idea carries you if it's right. . . . [Each of his interpretations he reports is based on a controlling image, a core.] In *Cavalleria* [*Rusticana*] I have always seen the core as a wide white street going uphill in a Sicilian village, that and the sky. At night the wind blows, and a tiny figure with a black shawl comes down running, closing under her shawl her pain and sorrow. It is the destiny of some Sicilian women. I built the set that way. The stage hands at Covent Garden can tell how fussy I was about the platform. The curtain goes up on the prelude. After that it's easy. You are on your path and you follow the consequence. What happens at dawn in Sicily? All the old women come to church. And so on. . . . For *Lucia* [*di Lammermoor*], mine was the image of a woman shouting in a tremendous room, a castle hall, with her wedding veil covered with blood, crying and chasing her cries. How would that woman arrive at that point? How? I couldn't bear a kind of mechanical bird performance in the mad scene. It's a great tragic scene. . . .

[In justification of his "earthy, informal portrait" of Verona in *Romeo and Juliet,* Zeffirelli said he thought of Shakespeare as a "frustrated traveler" who wanted to take his audience on a trip to Italy. The director has to fill in the details of the scene Shakespeare never really saw.] Take the Montagues, for instance. They are a noble, military family who have gone to seed. They are in decline. They produce only students—Romeo learns verses and Benvolio carried books. The Capulets are a rich merchant family, full of social climbers, men of wealth as well as men of action. There is only one aristocrat, and that is Escalus. But anyway, in the English theater you don't need to emphasize upper-classness. In fact you need to underplay it. In Italy or America it would be different. You would have to build up the formal dignity. . . .

Squeeze Shakespeare's characters to the utmost and you still find poetry. [But it is the "poetry of human relationships" rather than the verbal music Zeffirelli stresses in his production.] What matters is modernity of feeling, modernity inside. The verse must always have an intimate rhythm, the rhythm of reality. It must never become music. . . . [He approached "the text on the assumption that it could have been spoken by real people in a real human context; and that many sacrifices were worth making in order to get it spoken that way."] The *verismo* of Verga and Zola, the use of real ingredients for imaginative purposes in surrealism . . . and Goldoni's middle-class plays, full of the small facts of life, but always with a touch of madness about them [are works whose devotion to the little details of life itself he takes as his model.]

[Zeffirelli would like to do *Hamlet*. He talks about the Prince with gossipy familiarity.] Hamlet, you see, is not healthy. He has very little time to spend on this earth and he must express himself very quickly. He has great gifts of intuition and fantasy, but he has not developed enough to know about affection and love. He is a boy taken just in the moment when his affections would move away from his mother, but he dies too soon. He is all ideas and broken feelings, jumping like a monkey from one thought to the next, but he cannot go beyond the dreams and fantasies of adolescence. His destiny is to die soon. The whole arc of his life is different from other people's. Also he is a coward, his palms are wet.

On the visual side, I see him living in a hard world—with no elasticity about it—a closed world, with high walls, no windows, lots of storms. Like a prisoner in a tower. But all that comes later. The first thing is to get the core of the character. Just the core. Then everything follows.

Bibliography

The following selected bibliography centering on the figures represented in this volume contains (I) books by and about individual directors, (II) pertinent general volumes and periodicals, and (III) historical studies of special value in the preparation of the introduction, "The Emergence of the Director."

I

Antoine, André: "Causerie sur la mise en scène." *La Revue de Paris,* X, April 1, 1903, 596-612.

Antoine, André: *Mes Souvenirs sur le Théâtre Antoine et sur L'Odéon.* Paris: Bernard Grosset, 1928.

Antoine, André: *Mes Souvenirs sur le Théâtre Libre.* Paris: Artheme Fayard, 1921.

Antoine, André: *Le Théâtre.* 2 vols. Paris: Les Editions de France, 1932.

Antoine, André: *Le Théâtre Libre.* Paris: May 1890.

Roussou, Matei: *André Antoine.* Paris: L'Arche, 1954.

Thalasso, A.: *Le Théâtre Libre.* Paris: Mercure de France, 1909.

Waxman, Samuel M.: *Antoine and the Théâtre Libre.* Harvard University Press, 1926.

Appia, Adolphe: *Art vivant ou nature morte?* Milan: Bottega di Poesia, 1923. (This essay is available in English translation in the *Theatre Annual,* 1943.)

Appia, Adolphe: "Comment reformer notre mise en scene." *La Revue (Revue des Revues),* L, June 1, 1904, 342-349.

Appia, Adolphe: *Goethes Faust: Erster Teil als Dichtung Dargestellt.* Bonn: Fritz Klopp Verlag, 1929.

Appia, Adolphe: *La mise en scène du drame Wagnérien.* Paris: L. Chailley, 1895. (An unpublished English translation by Robert Sencer of the above titled *Staging Wagnerian Drama* was made available to the editors.)

Appia, Adolphe: *Die Musik und die Inscenierung.* Munich: F. Bruckmann, 1899. (The above work, originally written in French, is available in that language in manuscript at the Main Reference Branch of the New York Public Library.)

Appia, Adolphe: "The Staging of Tristan and Isolde." Translated by Lee Simonson. *Theatre Workshop,* I, April-July 1937, 61-72.

Appia, Adolphe: *The Work of Living Art.* Translated by H. D. Albright. Florida: University of Miami Press, 1960.

"Adolphe Appia: A Memorial." *Theatre Arts Monthly,* XVI, August 1932.

Albright, H. Darkes: "Appia Fifty Years After," *Quarterly Journal of Speech,* XXXV, April 1949.

Artaud, Antonin: *The Theatre and its Double.* Translated by Mary Caroline Richard. New York: Grove Press, 1958.

Ball, William: "Give the Audience a Chance." *Theatre Arts,* XLV, August 1961, 61.

Barrault, Jean Louis: *Je suis homme de théâtre.* Paris: Editions du Conquistador, 1955.

Barrault, Jean-Louis: *Phèdre de Jean Racine, mise en scène et commentaires de Jean-Louis Barrault.* Paris: Editions du Seuil, 1946.

Barrault, Jean-Louis: *Reflections on the Theatre.* Translated by Barbara Wall. London: Rockliff, 1951.

Barrault, Jean Louis: *The Theatre of Jean Louis Barrault.* New York: Hill and Wang, 1962.

Barrault, Jean-Louis: *Une Troupe et ses auteurs; extraits et commentaires à propos de; Shakespeare, Molière, Marivaux, Claudel, Gide, Kafka, Feydeau, Achard et J. P. Sartre.* Paris: Compagnie M. Renaud—J. L. Barrault, et J. Vautrain, 1950.

Bentley, Eric: "Two Evenings *chez* Barrault," in *In Search of Theater.* New York: Knopf, 1953, 196-214.

Baty, Gaston: *Le Masque et l'encensoir; introduction à une esthétique du théâtre.* Paris: Bloud & Gay, 1926.

Baty, Gaston: *Théâtre nouveau; notes et documents.* Paris: A la Société des Spectacles, 1927.

Blanchart, Paul: *Gaston Baty.* Paris: Editions de la Nouvelle Revue Critique, 1939.

Belasco, David: *The Theatre Through Its Stage Door.* Edited by Louis V. Defoe. New York: Harper and Brothers, 1919.

Huneker, James Gibbons: "David Belasco," American Producers, III. *Theatre Arts Magazine,* V, October 1921, 259-267.

Timberlake, Craig: *The Bishop of Broadway: David Belasco.* New York: Library Publishers, 1954.

Winter, William: *The Life of David Belasco.* 2 vols. New York: Moffat, Yard and Co., 1918.

Bentley, Eric: "The Poet in Dublin" Directing Lorca at the Abbey Theatre, in *In Search of Theater.* New York: Alfred A. Knopf, 1953.

Brahm, Otto: *Kritische Schriften über Drama und Theater.* Berlin: S. Fischer, 1913.

Henze, Herbert: *Otto Brahm und das Deutsche Theater in Berlin.* Berlin: E. S. Mittler und Sohn, 1930. (An abridged adaptation of this work in English by Frank Freudenthal under the title "Otto Brahm and Naturalist Directing" appears in the *Theatre Workshop*, I, April-July 1937, 13-28.)

Newmark, Maxim: *Otto Brahm: The Man and the Critic.* New York: G. E. Stechert & Co., 1938.

Brecht, Bertolt: *Antigonemodell.* Berlin: Gebrueder Weiss, 1949.

Brecht, Bertolt: "Chinese Acting." Translated by Eric Bentley. *Furioso* (Carleton College, Northfield, Minnesota), Autumn 1949, 68-77.

Brecht, Bertolt: "A Little Organum for the Theatre," translated by John Willett, in *Playwrights on Playwriting,* edited by Toby Cole. New York: Hill and Wang, 1960.

Brecht, Bertolt: "A Model for Epic Theater." Translated by Eric Bentley. *The Sewanee Review,* LVII, Summer 1949, 425-436.

Brecht, Bertolt: *Mutter Courage Modell.* Berlin: Henschelverlag, 1958.

Brecht, Bertolt: "A New Technique of Acting." Translated by Eric Bentley. *Theatre Arts,* XXXIII, January 1949, 38-40.

Brecht, Bertolt: "Notes for *The Threepenny Opera*" in *From the Modern Repertoire,* Series One, edited by Eric Bentley. University of Denver Press, 1949, 391-400.

Brecht, Bertolt: *Schriften zum Theater; über eine nicht-Aristotelische Dramatik.* Berlin: Suhrkamp Verlag, 1957.

Brecht, Bertolt: *Theaterarbeit.* Dresden: VVV Dresdner Verlag, 1952.

Bentley, Eric: "The Stagecraft of Brecht," in *In Search of Theater.* New York: Knopf, 1953, 144-160.

Esslin, Martin: *Brecht: The Man and his Work.* New York: Doubleday, 1960.

Gorelik, Mordecai: "Epic Realism: Brecht's Notes on the *Threepenny Opera.*" *Theatre Workshop,* I, April-July 1937, 29-41.

"The Theatre of Bertolt Brecht." *Tulane Drama Review,* VI, September 1961.

Willett, John: *The Theatre of Bertolt Brecht.* New York: New Directions, 1959.

Brook, Peter: "Directing *The Visit*," in *Drama on Stage* by Randolph Goodman. New York: Holt, Rinehart and Winston, 1961, 401-404.

Brook, Peter: "Style in Shakespearean Production." London: *Orpheus,* I, 1948, 139-146.

Browne, Maurice: "The New Rhythmic Drama." *Drama,* IV, November 1914, 616-630, V, February 1915, 146-160.

Roeder, Ralph: "Maurice Browne," American Producers, I. *Theatre Arts Magazine,* V, April 1921, 113-124.

Clurman, Harold: "The Director's Job." *New Republic,* Vol. 121, August 8, 1949, 20-22, August 15, 20-21.

Clurman, Harold: *The Fervent Years: The Story of the Group Theater and the Thirties.* New York: Alfred A. Knopf, 1950.

Clurman, Harold: "In A Different Language." *Theatre Arts,* XXXIV, January 1950, 18-20.

Clurman, Harold: "Interpretation and Characterization." *New Theatre,* III, January 1936, 1, 44.

Clurman, Harold: *Lies Like Truth.* New York: Grove Press, 1958.

Clurman, Harold: "Mysterious Rites of the Rehearsal." *New York Times Magazine,* March 5, 1961, 54, 65, 67.

Clurman, Harold: "Notes for a Production of *Heartbreak House.*" *Tulane Drama Review,* V, March 1961, 58-67.

Clurman, Harold: "The Principles of Interpretation," in *Producing the Play,* by John Gassner. New York: Dryden Press, 1948, 280-302.

Cocteau, Jean
    Oxenhandler, Neal: *Scandal and Parade: The Theatre of Jean Cocteau.* New Jersey: Rutgers University Press, 1957.

Copeau, Jacques: "L'École du Vieux Colombier," *Les Cahiers du Vieux Colombier,* November 2, 1921. Paris: Editions de la Nouvelle Revue Française.

Copeau, Jacques: *Etudes d'art dramatique, critiques d'un autre temps.* Paris: Editions de la Nouvelle Revue Française, 1923.

Copeau, Jacques: *Les Fourberies de Scapin de Molière, mise en scène et commentaires.* Preface de Louis Jouvet. Paris: Editions du Seuil, 1951.

Copeau, Jacques: "La mise en scène." *Encyclopédie Française,* December 1935.

Copeau, Jacques: *Notes sur le métier de comedien.* Paris: Michel Brient, 1955.

Copeau, Jacques: *Souvenirs du Vieux-Colombier.* Paris: Nouvelles Editions Latines, 1931.

Anders, France: *Jacques Copeau et le Cartel des Quatre.* Paris: A. G. Nizet, 1959.

Bentley, Eric: "Copeau and the Chimera," in *In Search of Theater.* New York: Knopf, 1953, 256-265.

Doisy, Marchel: *Jacques Copeau, ou l'absolu dans l'art.* Paris: Le Cercle du Livre, 1954.

Frank, Waldo: *The Art of the Vieux Colombier.* Paris: Editions de la Nouvelle Revue Française, 1918.

Kurtz, Maurice: *Jacques Copeau.* Paris: Nagel, 1950.

Lermimier, Georges: *Jacques Copeau.* Collection "Les Metteurs en scène." Les Presses Littéraires de France, 1953.

Roeder, Ralph: "Copeau 1921." *Theatre Arts Magazine,* V, October 1921, 279-292.

Craig, Edward Gordon: *The Art of the Theatre.* London: T. N. Foulis, 1905.

Craig, Edward Gordon: *Index to the Story of My Days.* New York: The Viking Press, 1957.

Craig, Edward Gordon: *On the Art of the Theatre.* New York: Theatre Arts Books, 1961.

Craig, Edward Gordon: *A Production—Being Thirty-Two Collotype Plates of Designs Projected or Realized for The Pretenders of Henrik Ibsen.* London: Oxford University Press, 1930.

Craig, Edward Gordon: *Scene.* London: H. Milford, 1923.

Craig, Edward Gordon: *The Theatre—Advancing.* Boston: Little, Brown & Co., 1919.

Craig, Edward Gordon: *Towards a New Theatre: Forty Designs with Critical Notes.* London: J. M. Dent and Sons, Ltd., 1913.

Leeper, Janet: *Edward Gordon Craig: Designs for the Theatre.* London: Penguin Books, 1948.

Rose, Enid: *Gordon Craig and the Theatre.* London: S. Low, Marston & Co., Ltd., 1931.

Valogne, Catherine: *Gordon Craig.* Collection "Les Metteurs en scène." Les Presses Littéraires de France, 1953.

Dullin, Charles: *L'Avare de Molière, mise en scène et commentaires de Charles Dullin.* Paris: Editions du Seuil, 1946.

Dullin, Charles: *Cinna de Pierre Corneille, mise en scène et commentaires de Charles Dullin.* Paris: Editions du Seuil, 1948.

Dullin, Charles: *Souvenirs et notes de travail d'un acteur.* Paris: O. Lieutier, 1946.

Crozier, Eric: "Charles Dullin and the Atelier." *Theatre Arts Monthly,* XX, March 1936, 197-200.

Fuchs, Georg: *Revolution in the Theatre*. Condensed and adapted by Constance Connor Kuhn. Ithaca: Cornell University Press, 1959.

Gémier, Firmin: *Le Théâtre*, Entretiens réunis par Paul Gsell. Paris: B. Grasset, 1925.

   Blanchart, Paul: *Firmin Gémier*. Paris: L'Arche, 1954.

Gielgud, John: *Early Stages*. New York: Macmillan, 1939.

Gielgud, John: "A Shakespearean Speaks his Mind." *Theatre Arts*, XLIII, January 1959, 69-71.

Gielgud, John: "Staging *Love for Love*." *Theatre Arts*, XXVII, November 1943, 632, 662-668.

Gielgud, John: "Two Scenes from Promptbook for *The Lady's Not for Burning* by Christopher Fry," in *A Theatre in Your Head*, by Kenneth Thorpe Rowe. New York: Funk & Wagnalls, 1960, 32-44.

   Gilder, Rosamond: *John Gielgud's Hamlet: A Record of Performance, With Notes on Costume, Scenery and Stage Business by John Gielgud*. New York: Oxford University Press, 1937.

   Stevens, Virginia: "Gielgud Rehearses *Medea*." *Theatre Arts*, XXXI, November 1947, 31-34.

Granville-Barker, Harley: *The Exemplary Theatre*. London: Chatto and Windus, 1922.

Granville-Barker, Harley: "Rehearsing a Play." *Theatre*, XXX, September 1919, 142, 204, October, 236.

Granville-Barker, Harley: *Shakespeare's Comedy of Twelfth Night; An Acting Edition with a Producer's Preface*. London: 1912.

Granville-Barker, Harley: *The Winter's Tale . . . an Acting Edition Prepared with a Preface*. London: 1912.

   Purdom, C. B.: *Harley Granville-Barker, Man of the Theatre, Dramatist, and Scholar*. Cambridge: Harvard University Press, 1956.

Guthrie, Tyrone: *A Life in the Theatre*. New York: McGraw-Hill, 1959.

Guthrie, Tyrone: "The Producer's Job." *Listener*, March 20, 1941, 419-420.

Guthrie, Tyrone: "Some Notes on Direction." *Theatre Arts*, XXVIII, November 1944, 649-653.

Guthrie, Tyrone: *Theatre Prospect*. London: Wishart & Co., 1932.

Guthrie, Tyrone, and Tanya Moisewitsch: "The Production of *King Oedipus*," in *Thrice the Brinded Cat Hath Mew'd: A Record of the Stratford Festival in Canada*, edited by Robertson Davies, Tyrone Guthrie and Boyd Neil. Toronto: Clarke, Irwin and Co., Ltd. 1955.

Hall, Peter: "Mr. Peter Hall on Speaking Shakespeare." The London *Times*, December 22, 1958, 5.

Hopkins, Arthur: *How's Your Second Act?* New York: Philip Goodman Company, 1918.

Hopkins, Arthur: *Reference Point*. New York: Samuel French, 1948.

Eaton, Walter Prichard: "Arthur Hopkins," American Producers, II. *Theatre Arts Magazine*, V, July 1921, 230-236.

Houseman, John: "On Directing Shakespeare." *Theatre Arts*, XXXIII, April 1951, 52-54.

Houseman, John, and Jack Landau: *The American Shakespeare Festival*. New York: Simon and Schuster, 1959.

Jessner, Leopold: "*Weber* Inscenierung IV, Act Die Plunderung," *Die Scene*, March 1928, 92-94. (This is a special issue of *Die Scene* devoted entirely to the work of Jessner.)

Bluth, K. T.: *Leopold Jessner*. Berlin: Oesterheld & Co., 1928.

Grabbe, C. D.: *Hannibal: Bühneneinrichtung von Leopold Jessner*. Berlin: Oesterheld Verlag, 1926.

Ziege, Felix: *Leopold Jessner und das Zeit-Theater*. Berlin: Eigenbroedler Verlag, 1928.

Jouvet, Louis: "Problems de la mise en scène des chefs-d'oeuvre classiques; le point de vue du metteur en scène." *Revue d'Histoire du Theatre*, No. 4, 1951, 378-387.

Jouvet, Louis: "The Profession of the Producer." *Theatre Arts Monthly*, XX, December 1936, 942-949, XXI, January 1937, 57-64.

Jouvet, Louis: *Reflexions du comédien*. Paris: Editions de la Nouvelle Revue Critique, 1938.

Jouvet, Louis: *Témoignages sur le théâtre*. Paris: Flammarion, 1952.

Cezan, Claude: *Louis Jouvet et le théâtre d'aujourd'hui*. Paris: Editions Emile-Paul Frères, 1938.

Knapp, Bettina Liebowitz: *Louis Jouvet, Man of the Theatre*. New York: Columbia University Press, 1958.

"Louis Jouvet, 1887-1951 Notes et Documents." *Revue d'Histoire du Théâtre*, No. 1, 1952.

Kazan, Elia: "Excerpts from the Notebook made in Preparation for Directing Arthur Miller's *Death of a Salesman* and Annotated Playscript," in *A Theatre in Your Head*, by Kenneth Thorpe Rowe. New York: Funk & Wagnalls, 1960, 44-59.

Kazan, Elia, and Archibald MacLeish: "The Staging of a Play: The Notebooks and Letters behind Elia Kazan's staging of Archibald MacLeish's *J.B.*" *Esquire*, May 1959, 144-158.

Isaacs, H. R.: "First Rehearsals: Elia Kazan directs a modern legend: *Jacobowsky and the Colonel* by F. Werfel." *Theatre Arts*, XXVIII, March 1944, 143-5, 147-50.

Kommisarjevsky, Theodore: *Myself and the Theatre*. New York: E. P. Dutton & Co., Inc., 1930.

Kommisarjevsky, Theodore: "The Producer in the Theatre." *Drama*, XIII, November 1934, 19-21, December, 35-37.

Langham, Michael: "An Approach to Staging Shakespeare's Works." A lecture delivered at the Universities of Canada Seminar at the Stratford Shakespearean Festival, Stratford, Ontario, August 16, 1961.

Lewis, Robert: "Emotional Memory." *Tulane Drama Review*, VI, June 1962, 54-60.

Lewis, Robert: "Form in Production," in *Producing the Play*, by John Gassner. New York: Dryden Press, 1948, 303-309.

Lewis, Robert: *Method or Madness*. New York: Samuel French, 1958.

Littlewood, Joan: "Plays for the People." *World Theatre*, VIII, Winter 1959-60, 283-290.

    Goodwin, Clive, and Tom Milne: "Working with Joan." *Encore*, VII, July-August 1960, 9-20.

    Taylor, Charles: "Workshop with a Lust for Life." *Theatre Arts*, XLIII, May 1959, 16-17, 64-65.

Lugné-Poë, Aurélien: *Sous les étoiles, souvenirs de théâtre, 1902-1912.* Paris: Gallimard, 1933.

    Jasper, Gertrude R.: *Adventure in the Theatre: Lugné-Poë and the Théâtre de l'Oeuvre to 1899.* New Brunswick: Rutgers University Press, 1947.

    Robichez, Jacques: *Lugné-Poë.* Paris: L'Arche, 1955.

Meyerhold, Vsevolod: "The Booth." Translated by A. Bakshy. *Drama*, No. 26, May 1917, 203-216, No. 27, August 1917, 425-447.

Meyerhold, Vsevolod: "Farce." Translated by Nora Beeson. *Tulane Drama Review*, IV, September, 1959, 139-149.

Meyerhold, Vsevolod: "From *On the Theatre*." Translated by Nora Beeson. *Tulane Drama Review*, IV, May 1960, 134-147.

Meyerhold, Vsevolod: *Meyerhold on Theatre: Collected Essays and Speeches.* Selected, translated, and edited by Nora Beeson (unpublished).

Meyerhold, Vsevolod: "Na repetitzia *Revizora*." *Teatr i Dramaturgia*, February 1934, 40-42.

Meyerhold, Vsevolod: *O Teatr.* Petrograd: 1913.

    Alpers, B.: *The Theater of the Social Mask.* Translated by Mark Schmidt. New York: The Group Theater, 1934.

    Bely, A. and Others: *Gogol i Meyerkhold.* Moscow: 1927.

    Fagin, Bryllian: "Meyerhold Rehearses a Scene." *Theatre Arts Monthly*, XVI, October 1932, 833-836.

    Lozowick, Louis: "V. E. Meyerhold and his Theatre." *Hound and Horn*, IV, October-December 1930, 95-105.

Strasberg, Lee: "The Magic of Meyerhold." *New Theatre,* I, September 1934, 14-15, 30.

Volkov, Nikolai: *Meyerkhold.* 2 vols. Moscow: Academia, 1929.

Nemirovich-Danchenko, Vladimir: "Danchenko Directs: Notes on *The Three Sisters.*" *Theatre Arts,* XXVII, October 1943, 603-606.

Nemirovich-Danchenko, Vladimir: *Julius Caesar: Publikatsiia Rezhisserskoi Partituri (Publication of the Director's Promptbook of Julius Caesar)* in *Moscow Art Theatre Yearbook,* 1944, 551-670. Moscow: Museum of the Moscow Art Theatre, 1947.

Nemirovich-Danchenko, Vladimir: *My Life in the Russian Theatre.* Translated by John Cournos. Boston: Little, Brown & Co., 1936.

Okhlopkov, Nikolai: See *Moscow Rehearsals* by Norris Houghton and *Theatre in Soviet Russia* by Andre Van Gyseghem.

Okhlopkov, Nikolai: See *Teatr* (Moscow) issues: January 1959, 36-58; November 1959, 58-77; December 1959, 52-73.

Olivier, Laurence: "The Olivier Method." Interview. New York Sunday *Times,* February 7, 1960, X, 1-3.

Papp, Joseph: *"King Henry the Fifth* for the Modern Audience," in *Henry V* by William Shakespeare. New York: Dell (The Laurel Shakespeare), 1962.

Papp, Joseph: "Modernity and the American Actor." *Theatre Arts,* XLV, August 1961, 62.

Piscator, Erwin: "'Objective Acting," in *Actors on Acting.* Edited by Toby Cole and Helen Krich Chinoy. New York: Crown Publishers, 1949, 285-291.

Piscator, Erwin: *Das Politische Theater.* Berlin: Adalbert Schultz, 1929.

Pitoëff, Georges: *Notre Théâtre.* Paris: Messages, 1949.

Reinhardt, Max

Carter, Huntly: *The Theatre of Max Reinhardt.* London: F. & C. Palmer, 1914.

Fleischmann, Benno: *Max Reinhardt; Die Wierdererweckung des Barocktheaters.* Vienna: P. Neff, 1948.

Herald, Heinz: *Max Reinhardt; Ein Versuch über das Wesen der Modernen Regie.* Berlin: F. Lehmann, 1915.

Jacobsohn, Siegfried: *Max Reinhardt.* Berlin: Erich Reiss, 1910.

Rothe, Hans: *Max Reinhardt, 25 Jahre Deutsches Theater.* Munich: R. Piper & Co., 1930.

Sayler, Oliver M., editor: *Max Reinhardt and his Theatre.* New York: Brentano's, 1924.

Saint-Denis, Michel: *Theatre: The Rediscovery of Style.* New York: Theatre Arts Books, 1960.

Sakhnovski, V.: *Rezhissura i Metodika ee Prepodavanie (Directing and Methods of Teaching It)*. Moscow: Iskusstvo, 1939.

Saxe-Meiningen, George II, Duke of
Grube, Max: *Geschichte der Meininger*. Stuttgart: Deutsche Verlags-Anstalt, 1926.
(See also *The Stage is Set*, by Lee Simonson, and *New Theatres for Old*, by Mordecai Gorelik.)

Shaw, George Bernard: *The Art of Rehearsal*. New York: Samuel French, 1928.

Shaw, George Bernard: *Bernard Shaw's Letters to Granville-Barker*. Edited by C. B. Purdom. New York: Theatre Arts Books, 1957.

Shaw, George Bernard: *Dramatic Opinions and Essays*. 2 vols. New York: Brentano's, 1928.

Shaw, George Bernard: *Our Theatres in the Nineties*. 3 vols. London: Constable & Co., 1932.

D'Angelo, Evelyn: "Shaw's Theory of Stage Representation." *Quarterly Journal of Speech*, XV, June 1929, 330-349.

Stanislavsky, Konstantin S.: *An Actor Prepares*. Translated by Elizabeth Reynolds Hapgood. New York: Theatre Arts, 1936.

Stanislavsky, Konstantin S.: *Building a Character*. Translated by Elizabeth Reynolds Hapgood. New York: Theatre Arts Books, 1949.

Stanislavsky, Konstantin S.: *Creating a Role*. Translated by Elizabeth Reynolds Hapgood. New York: Theatre Arts Books, 1961.

Stanislavsky, Konstantin S.: *My Life in Art*. Translated by J. J. Robbins. New York: Theatre Arts Books, 1948.

Stanislavsky, Konstantin S.: *Na Dne: Rezhisserskii Ekzempliar (The Lower Depths: Director's Copy)* in *Moscow Art Theatre Yearbook*, 1945, 4-279. Moscow: Museum of the Moscow Art Theatre, 1948.

Stanislavsky, Konstantin S.: *The Seagull Produced by Stanislavsky*. Translated by David Magarshack. New York: Theatre Arts Books, 1952.

Stanislavsky, Konstantin S.: *Stanislavsky on the Art of the Stage*. Introduced and translated by David Magarshack. New York: Hill and Wang, 1961.

Stanislavsky, Konstantin S.: *Stanislavsky Produces Othello*. Translated by Dr. Helen Nowak. London: Geoffrey Bless, 1948.

Stanislavsky, Konstantin S.: *Stanislavski's Legacy: A Collection of Comments on a Variety of Aspects of an Actor's Art and Life*. Edited and translated by Elizabeth Reynolds Hapgood. New York: Theatre Arts Books, 1958.

Stanislavsky, Konstantin: *Stati, Rechi, Besedi, Pisma* (Articles, Speeches, Talks, Letters). Moscow: Iskusstvo, 1953.

Clurman, Harold: "Conversation with Two Masters." *Theatre Arts Monthly*, XIX, November 1935, 871-876.

Cole, Toby, editor: *Acting: A Handbook of the Stanislavsky Method.* New York: Crown Publishers, 1947.

Gorchakov, Nikolai M.: *Stanislavsky Directs.* Translated by Miriam Goldina. New York: Funk & Wagnalls, 1954.

Magarshack, David: *Stanislavsky: A Life.* New York: Chanticleer Press, 1951.

Toporkov, V.: *K. S. Stanislavskii na Repetitzii* (Stanislavsky at Rehearsal). Moscow: Iskusstvo, 1950.

Strasberg, Lee: "The Director," in *The Theatre Handbook,* edited by Bernard Sobel. New York: Crown Publishers, 1948, 219-220.

Tairov, Alexander: *Zapiski Rezhissera (Notes of a Régisseur).* Moscow: 1921. (More widely available in the German edition *Das Entfesseltes Theater,* Potsdam, G. Kiepenheuer, 1923.)

Vakhtangov, Eugene: *Materiali i stati (Materials and Articles).* Moscow, 1959.

Vakhtangov, Eugene: *Zapiski, Pisma, Stati* (Notes, Letters, Articles). Moscow: Iskusstvo, 1939.

Gorchakov, Nikolai: *The Vakhtangov School of Stage Art.* Moscow: Foreign Languages Publishing House, n.d.

Vaughan, Stuart: "A Director's Comments on Staging *Richard III,*" in *Richard III* by William Shakespeare. New York: Dell (The Laurel Shakespeare), 1958.

Vaughan, Stuart: "Some Thoughts on Shakespearean Production." *Playbill,* January 27, 1958, 33-35.

Vilar, Jean: "The Director and the Play." *Yale French Studies,* III, No. 1, 1949.

Vilar, Jean: "Le metteur-en-scène et l'oeuvre dramatique." *Revue Théâtrale,* III, October-November 1946, 297-320.

Vilar, Jean: "Murder of the Director." Translated by Christopher Kotschnig. *Tulane Drama Review,* III, December 1958, 3-7.

Vilar, Jean: "Secrets." Translated by Christopher Kotschnig. *Tulane Drama Review,* III, March 1959, 24-30.

Vilar, Jean: *The Tradition of the Theatre.* Translated by Christopher Kotschnig (unpublished).

Bermel, Albert: "Jean Vilar: Unadorned Theatre for the Greatest Number." *Tulane Drama Review,* V, December 1960, 24-43.

Gilder, Rosamond: "Vive Vilar & Co!" *Theatre Arts,* XLIII, January 1959, 62, 73, 77.

Webster, Margaret: "Credo of a Director." *Theatre Arts Monthly,* XXII, May 1938, 343-348.

Webster, Margaret: "A Director's Comments on Staging *The Taming of the Shrew*," in *The Taming of the Shrew*, by William Shakespeare. New York: Dell (The Laurel Shakespeare), 1958.

Webster, Margaret: "Producing Mr. Shakespeare." *Theatre Arts*, XXVI, January 1942, 43-48.

Webster, Margaret: *Shakespeare Without Tears*. New York: McGraw-Hill Book Co., 1942.

Zakhava, B. E.: *Igor Bulichov i Drugie, Rezhisserskii Kommentarii (Yegor Bulichev and Others, Director's Comments)*. Moscow: 1937.

Zakhava, B. E.: "Principles of Directing." *Theatre Workshop*, I, April-July 1937, 43-58, September-October 1937, 14-33.

Zavadsky, Yuri: "Conversation with a Young Régisseur." *Theatre Arts Monthly*, XX, September 1936, 726-730.

Zeffirelli, Franco: "Reviving the Dead World of the Classics." Kenneth Tynan Interviews Zeffirelli. *The Observer*, September 18, 1960, 13.

Zeffirelli, Franco: "Some Notes on *Romeo and Juliet*." *Playbill*, February 12, 1962, 19-20.

Zeffirelli, Franco: "The Zeffirelli Way." Interview. The London *Times*, September 19, 1960, 4.

II

Art of Directing Issue, *Theatre Workshop*, I, April-July 1937.

Bab, Julius: *Das Theater der Gegenwart*. Leipzig: Weber, 1928.

Ben-Ari, R.: "Four Directors and the Actor." *Theatre Workshop*, I, January-March 1937, 65-74.

Bentley, Eric: *The Playwright as Thinker*. New York: Reynal & Hitchcock, 1946.

Blanchart, Paul: *Histoire de la mise en scène*. Paris: Presses Universitaires de France, 1948.

Blanck, Karl, and Heinz Haufe: *Unbekanntes Theater; Ein Buch der Regie*. Stuttgart: J. G. Gotta'sche Buchhandlung Nachfolger, 1940.

Brassilach, Robert: *Animateurs de théâtre*. Paris: Corrêa, 1936.

Bricker, H. L., editor: *Our Theatre Today*. New York: Samuel French, 1936.

Carter, Huntly: *The New Spirit in the European Theatre, 1914-1924*. London: E. Benn, Ltd., 1925.

Carter, Huntly: *The New Spirit in the Russian Theatre, 1917-1928*. New York: Brentano's, 1929.

Cheney, Sheldon: *The Art Theatre*. New York: Alfred A. Knopf, 1925.

Cheney, Sheldon: "The Most Important Thing in the Theatre." *Theatre Arts Magazine*, I, August 1917.

Cheney, Sheldon: *The New Movement in the Theatre.* New York: M. Kennerly, 1914.

Chiari, Joseph: *The Contemporary French Theatre.* New York: Macmillan, 1959.

Clark, Barrett H., and George Freedley: *A History of the Modern Drama.* New York: D. Appleton-Century, 1947.

Cole, Toby, editor: *Playwrights on Playwrighting.* New York: Hill and Wang, 1960.

Cole, Toby, and Helen Krich Chinoy, editors: *Actors on Acting.* New York: Crown Publishers, 1949.

D'Amico, Silvio: *La Regia Teatrale.* Rome: Angelo Belardetti Editore, 1947.

Dickinson, Thomas H.: *The Theater in a Changing Europe.* New York: Henry Holt and Company, 1937.

Eustis, Morton: "The Director Takes Command." *Theatre Arts Monthly,* XX, February, March, April 1936. (A series of interviews with George Abbott, Guthrie McClintic, Max Reinhardt, Robert Sinclair, John Murray Anderson, and Harold Clurman.)

Fergusson, Francis: *The Idea of a Theater.* Princeton University Press, 1949.

Fuerst, Walter Rene, and Samuel J. Hume: *Twentieth Century Stage Decoration.* 2 vols. London: Knopf, 1928.

Gassner, John: *Form and Idea in Modern Theatre.* New York: Dryden Press, 1956.

Gassner, John: *Producing the Play.* New York: Dryden Press, 1952.

Gassner, John: *Theatre at the Crossroads.* New York: Holt, Rinehart and Winston, 1960.

Gervais, A. C.: *Propos sur la mise en scène.* Paris: Editions Françaises Nouvelles, 1943.

Gorchakov, N.: *Besedi o Rezhissure* (Discussions on Directing). Moscow: Iskusstvo, 1941.

Gorelik, Mordecai: *New Theatres for Old.* New York: E. P. Dutton, 1962.

Guicharnaud, Jacques, with June Beckelman: *Modern French Theatre from Giraudoux to Beckett.* New Haven: Yale University Press, 1961.

Gyseghem, Andre Van: *Theatre in Soviet Russia.* London: Faber and Faber, Ltd., 1943.

Hagemann, Carl: *Die Kunst der Bühne.* Vol. I: *Regie.* Berlin: Deutsche Verlags-Anstalt, 1922.

Helburn, Theresa: *A Wayward Quest.* Boston: Little, Brown, 1960.

Hewes, Henry: "How to Use Shakespeare." A Symposium. *Saturday Review,* July 13, 1957, 10-13.

Houghton, Norris: *Moscow Rehearsals: An Account of Methods of Production in the Soviet Theatre.* New York: Grove Press, 1962.

454   *Bibliography*

Houghton, Norris: *Return Engagement*. New York: Holt, Rinehart and Winston, 1962.

Ihering, Herbert: *Reinhardt, Jessner, Piscator oder Klassikertod*. Berlin: Ernst Rowohlt Verlag, 1929.

Isaacs, Edith J. R., editor: *Theatre: Essays on the Arts of the Theatre*. Boston: Little, Brown & Co., 1927.

Jelagin, Juri: *Taming of the Arts*. Translated by Nicholas Wredin. New York: Dutton, 1951.

Kutscher, Artur: *Grundriss der Theater-Wissenschaft*. Munich: Verlag Kurt Desch, 1936.

Langner, Lawrence: *The Magic Curtain*. New York: Dutton, 1951.

Langner, Lawrence: *The Play's the Thing*. New York: G. P. Putnam's Sons, 1960.

Legband, Paul: *Der Regisseur*. Hamburg: J. P. Toth Verlag, 1947.

Macgowan, Kenneth: *The Theatre of Tomorrow*. New York: Boni and Liveright, 1921.

Macgowan, Kenneth, and Robert Edmond Jones: *Continental Stagecraft*. New York: Harcourt, Brace & Co., 1922.

Marshall, Norman: *The Producer and the Play*. London: MacDonald, 1957.

Moderwell, Hiram Kelly: *The Theatre of To-day*. New York: J. Lane & Co., 1914.

Moscow Art Theater Yearbooks, 1943, 1944, 1945, 1946, 1947-48, 1949-50, 1951-52, 1953-58. Moscow: Museum of the Moscow Art Theatre.

Oppenheimer, George: *A Passionate Playgoer*. New York: Viking Press, 1958.

Owen, Alice C.: *The Art of Play Directing: A Tentative Bibliography*. Boston: Simmons College, 1943.

Rouché, Jacques: *L'Art théâtral moderne*. Paris: É. Cornély & Cie., 1910.

Sayler, Oliver M.: *Inside the Russian Theatre*. New York: Brentano's, 1925.

Sayler, Oliver M.: *The Russian Theatre*. New York: Brentano's, 1922.

Simonson, Lee: *The Stage is Set*. New York: Harcourt, Brace & Co., 1932.

Slonim, Marc: *Russian Theater*. New York: World Publishing Co., 1961.

Tolmacheva, Galina: *Creadores del teatro moderno—los grandes directores de los siglos XIX y XX*. Buenos Aires, 1946.

Vardac, A. Nicholas: *Stage to Screen*, Harvard University Press, 1949.

Winds, Adolf: *Geschichte der Regie*. Berlin: Deutsche Verlags-Anstalt, 1925.

Young, Stark: *Theatre Practice*. New York: Charles Scribner's Sons, 1926.

Periodicals

Cahiers de la Compagnie Madeleine Renaud—Jean-Louis Barrault (Paris)
Educational Theatre Journal (Organ of the American Educational Theatre Association)

Encore (London)
Gesellschaft für Theater Geschichte (Berlin)
International Theatre Annual (London)
Mask (Florence, Italy)
Moscow Art Theatre Yearbook (Moscow)
Revue d'Histoire du Théâtre (Paris)
Die Scene (Berlin)
Teatr (Moscow)
Theatre Annual (New York)
Theatre Arts Monthly (New York)
Theatre Workshop (New York)
Tulane Drama Review (New Orleans)
World Theatre (Brussels)

III

Adams, John Cranford: *The Globe Playhouse.* Harvard University Press, 1942.

Bruford, W. H.: *Theatre, Drama, and Audience in Goethe's Germany.* London: Routledge and Kegan Paul, Ltd., 1950.

Burnim, Kalman A.: *David Garrick, Director.* University of Pittsburgh Press, 1961.

Campbell, L. B.: *Scenes and Machines on the English Stage During the Renaissance.* Cambridge University Press, 1923.

Clark, Barrett H.: *European Theories of the Drama.* New York: Crown Publishers, 1947.

Cohen, Gustave: *Histoire de la mise en scène dans le théâtre religieux français du moyen age.* Paris: H. Champion, 1926.

Cohen, Gustave: *Le Livre de conduite du régisseur et le compte des depenses pour le mystère de la Passion joué à Mons en 1501.* Paris: Société d'Edition, 1925.

Dhomme, Sylvain: *La mise en scène contemporaine, d'Andre Antoine à Bertolt Brecht.* Paris: Fernand Nathan, 1959.

Downer, Alan: "Macready's Production of Macbeth." *Quarterly Journal of Speech,* XXXIII, April 1947, 172-181.

Goethe on the Theater. Edited by John Oxenford. Dramatic Museum of Columbia University, 1919.

Haigh, A. E.: *The Attic Theatre.* Oxford: Clarendon Press (3rd ed.), 1907.

Isaacs, J.: "Shakespeare as a Man of the Theatre," in *Shakespeare Criticism,* edited by Anne Bradby. Oxford University Press, 1936.

Mantzius, Karl: *A History of Theatrical Art in Ancient and Modern Times.* 6 vols. New York: Peter Smith, 1937.

Morley, Henry: *The Journal of a London Playgoer*. London: George Routledge, 1891.

Moses, Montrose, and John Mason Brown: *The American Theatre as Seen by its Critics*. New York: W. W. Norton, 1934.

Nagler, A. M.: *Sources of Theatrical History*. New York: Theatre Annual, 1952.

Nicoll, Allardyce: *The Development of the Theatre*. New York: Harcourt, Brace & Co. (4th ed., rev.), 1958.

Nicoll, Allardyce: *World Drama*. London: George G. Harrap, Ltd., 1949.

Petit de Julleville, Louis: *Les Mystères*. 2 vols. Paris: Librairie Hachette, 1880.

Wagner, Richard: *Essays*. Translated by William Ashton Ellis. New York: The German Publication Society, 1914.

Watson, Ernest Bradlee: *Sheridan to Robertson*. Harvard University Press, 1926.

Zola, Emile: *The Experimental Novel and Other Essays*. New York: Cassell Publishing Company, 1893.

Index

457